THE CAMBRIDGE
COMPANION TO
SHAKESPEARE'S
POETRY

EDITED BY

PATRICK CHENEY
Pennsylvania State University

CAMBRIDGE UNIVERSITY PRESS
Cambridge, New York, Melbourne, Madrid, Cape Town, Singapore, São Paulo

Cambridge University Press
The Edinburgh Building, Cambridge CB2 2RU, UK

Published in the United States of America by Cambridge University Press, New York

www.cambridge.org
Information on this title: www.cambridge.org/9780521608640

First published 2007

Printed in the United Kingdom at the University Press, Cambridge

A catalogue record for this publication is available from the British Library

ISBN-13 978-0-521-84627-1 hardback
ISBN-13 978-0-521-60864-0 paperback

For Richard Helgerson

CONTENTS

CONTRIBUTORS

JAMES P. BEDNARZ, Long Island University, USA
CATHERINE BELSEY, Cardiff University, Wales
PATRICK CHENEY, Pennsylvania State University, USA
DANIELLE CLARKE, University College Dublin, Ireland
LUKAS ERNE, University of Geneva, Switzerland
ANDREW HADFIELD, Sussex University, UK
HEATHER JAMES, University of Southern California, USA
COPPÉLIA KAHN, Brown University, USA
WILLIAM J. KENNEDY, Cornell University, USA
SASHA ROBERTS, University of Kent, UK
JOHN ROE, University of York, UK
KATHERINE ROWE, Bryn Mawr College, USA
DAVID SCHALKWYK, University of Cape Town, South Africa
MICHAEL SCHOENFELDT, University of Michigan, USA

PREFACE

The Cambridge Companion to Shakespeare's Poetry is the first volume in print to study the achievement of Shakespeare's poetry both in his poems and in his plays. As such, the companion aims to complement other volumes in the Shakespeare companion series. These volumes, all published by Cambridge University Press, concentrate on the plays and Shakespeare's role as a man of the theatre: *Shakespeare on Film*, edited by Russell Jackson (2000); *Shakespeare on Stage*, edited by Stanley Wells and Sarah Stanton (2002); *Shakespearean Comedy*, edited by Alexander Leggatt (2002); *Shakespeare's History Plays*, edited by Michael Hattaway (2002); *Shakespearean Tragedy*, edited by Claire McEachern (2002); and *Shakespeare*, edited by Margreta de Grazia and Stanley Wells (2001). This last volume includes only a single chapter on the poems (by John Kerrigan), and nothing on the topic of poetry in the plays, although it does include a few chapters relevant to the present volume: those on Shakespeare's texts by Barbara A. Mowat, on his reading by Leonard Barkan, and, most importantly, on his language by de Grazia. Only incidentally, however, do these chapters mention the poems, so that the texts, the reading, and the language discussed are overwhelmingly for and of the plays. Accordingly, this new companion assembles a distinguished group of scholars from the United Kingdom, the United States, the Republic of Ireland, Switzerland, and South Africa to present a series of chapters on the individual poems, on the topic of poetry in the plays, on the special contexts important for viewing 'Shakespeare's poetry', and on the afterlife of this topic.

The companion consists of fourteen chapters, each dealing with a literary, historical, or cultural feature of Shakespeare's poetry, and each concluding with a select 'Reading list' of recommended works. The volume also includes a chronology geared to the individual chapters and a concluding note on the reference works available on Shakespeare's poetry. The 'Introduction' draws a frame for viewing Shakespeare's poetry in the twenty-first century, while the structure of the subsequent chapters conforms to the tripartite format of the companion series.

The first part divides into three chapters, and establishes the critical foundation for viewing the volume topic, examining Shakespeare's role in 'the development of English poetry', his use of 'rhetoric, style, and poetic form', and the media of 'print and manuscript' that allowed his poetry to take its distinctive shape. These chapters suggest a range of cultural venues and contexts for witnessing how Shakespeare's poetry derives from, and responds to, the primary energies of the Renaissance, in Europe as in England.

The second part of the companion consists of five chapters on individual poems and ancillary volumes of published poetry, with one chapter each on *Venus and Adonis*, *The Rape of Lucrece*, the Sonnets, and *A Lover's Complaint*, and a combined chapter on the two works taught less often: *The Passionate Pilgrim* and 'The Phoenix and Turtle'. These chapters aim to orient readers to the poems and to the critical conversation about them, and (where relevant) to apply the material from the first part of the companion.

Finally, the third part consists of six chapters that seek to widen the topic of 'Shakespeare's poetry'. The first three chapters introduce important topics, contexts, and methodologies, attending to 'politics and religion', to 'love, beauty, and sexuality', and to the recurrent 'classicism' in Shakespeare's poems (especially Virgil and Ovid). The next two chapters each produce a different critical model for relating the poems to the plays, the poetical to the theatrical: the first on Shakespeare's use of 'poetry in the plays'; the second on the connection between 'poetry and performance'. A concluding chapter treats the afterlife of Shakespeare's poems – their 'reception and influence'.

The word 'poetry' in the volume title is deliberately open-ended, evoking Shakespeare's poems and simultaneously calling attention to the poetical as a major tool and concept in the Shakespearean craft, in plays as in poems, for the stage as for the page. Thus individual chapters focus on the poems but layer in commentary on the plays when relevant or possible.

ACKNOWLEDGEMENTS

The idea for a *Cambridge Companion to Shakespeare's Poetry* emerged through discussions with Sarah Stanton at the Press. I am grateful to her for support and advice throughout the project.

Also at the Press, I wish to thank Jackie Warren for guiding the volume through production with courtesy and efficiency, and Penny Wheeler for expertly copy-editing the manuscript.

The Press produced four readers' reports on the volume proposal, and each of them helped shape the final outcome. So did Lukas Erne and Colin Burrow, who read the Introduction and the note on reference works, and who offered scrupulous commentary. As always, at Penn State I wish to thank Robert R. Edwards, Garrett A. Sullivan, Jr., and Laura Lunger Knoppers for their continued conversation and collegial friendship. My department heads, Robert Caserio in English and Caroline D. Eckhardt in Comparative Literature, make my work possible through their generous support.

Three research assistants also made contributions. Alexis Hait, an undergraduate intern, helped assemble some of the upfront material; Eric Brune, also an undergraduate intern, compiled the Index; and Giuseppina Iacono, a Ph.D. student, prepared both the Chronology and the note on 'Reference works on Shakespeare's poetry'. My thanks to all three for doing excellent work.

Finally, let me thank the contributors themselves. Through their care, discipline, and scholarship, they have ensured that this volume appears in a timely fashion. The field is lucky to depend on so much expertise, assembled in a single volume, and devoted to Shakespeare's poetry.

NOTE ON TEXTS

All quotations from the poems and plays of Shakespeare come from Cambridge University Press editions, unless otherwise noted.

In particular, for *Venus and Adonis, The Rape of Lucrece*, 'The Phoenix and Turtle', and *A Lover's Complaint*, quotations come from *The Poems*, ed. John Roe (Cambridge University Press, 1992); and for the Sonnets, from *The Sonnets*, ed. G. Blakemore Evans (Cambridge University Press, 1996).

CHRONOLOGY

1533	Birth of Queen Elizabeth I.
c.1552?	Spenser born in London.
1553	Death of Edward VI and accession of Mary I. Virgil's *Aeneid* translated by Gavin Douglas.
1555	*Mirror for Magistrates* first published.
1557	Richard Tottel edits *Songes and Sonnettes* (i.e. *Tottel's Miscellany*); Surrey (tr.), *Certain Books of Virgil's Aeneis*.
1558	Death of Mary I and accession of Elizabeth I.
1563	John Foxe's *Acts and Monuments* ('Book of Martyrs') published.
1564	*26 Feb.* Christopher Marlowe baptized at St George the Martyr, Canterbury.
	26 Apr. Shakespeare baptized at Holy Trinity Church, Stratford-upon-Avon.
1565	Golding (tr.), *The First Four Books of P. Ovidius Naso's Work Entitled Metamorphosis*. Henry Parker (tr.), *The Triumphs of F. Petrarch*.
1566	Birth of James I. George Gascoigne, *Supposes* (tr. of Ariosto's *I Suppositi*). Adlington (tr. of Apuleius), *The XI Books of the Golden Ass, with the Marriage of Cupido and Psyches*. Painter (tr. of Boccaccio, Bandello, Belleforest), *The Palace of Pleasure*.
1567	The Red Lion playhouse opens. The complete edition of Golding's translation of Ovid's *Metamorphoses* appears.
1572	Ben Jonson born in Westminster, London.
1573	Gascoigne's *A Hundreth Sundrie Flowres* published (revised as *The Poesies* in 1575).
1576	Richard Edward's *The Paradise of Dainty Devyces* published. The Theatre playhouse opens.
1577	Curtain playhouse opens; Blackfriars Theatre opens.
1579	Spenser's *The Shepheardes Calender* published (entered into the Stationers' Register 5 Dec.).

1580	Mention of *The Faerie Queene* for the first time. Sir Philip Sidney, *Astrophil and Stella* (published 1591) and *Apology for Poetry* in MS circulation (*Defense of Poesie*; published 1595).
1581	Spenser's *The Shepheardes Calender*, second edition. Arthur Hall (tr.), *Ten Books of Homer's Illiads*.
1582	Shakespeare marries Anne Hathaway; the license is issued on 27 November and the first child (Susanna) is born six months later. Sir Walter Ralegh's poetry circulates at court. Thomas Watson's *Hekatompathia* published.
1585	Shakespeare's twin son and daughter, Hamnet and Judith, born. Marlowe probably composes *Ovid's Elegies*. *Dido, Queen of Carthage* probably first written by Marlowe while at Cambridge.
c.1586	Shakespeare leaves Stratford; nothing is known for certain of his life between this date and 1592, by which time he is in London.
1586	*17 Oct.* Death of Sir Philip Sidney in Zutphen, Netherlands. Babington Plot to assassinate Queen Elizabeth exposed. William Webbe, *A Discourse of English Poetry*. Third edition of Spenser's *Shepheardes Calender*.
1587–8	Marlowe possibly composes 'The Passionate Shepherd to His Love'.
1587	*8 Feb.* Execution of Mary, Queen of Scots. Rose playhouse opens.
1588	*28 July.* Spanish Armada defeated.
1589	Thomas Lodge's *Glaucus and Scilla* published.
1590	Publication of Spenser's *The Faerie Queene*, Books 1–3, and of Sidney's *Arcadia*.
1591	Publication of Spenser's *Complaints, Daphnaïda*, and fourth edition of *The Shepheardes Calender*. Sidney, *Astrophil and Stella* published. Sir John Harington publishes his translation of Ariosto's *Orlando Furioso*.
1592–3	Plague breaks out in London, closing the theatres.
1592	Samuel Daniel's *Delia* and *The Complaint of Rosamond* published. Henry Chettle publishes *Greene's Groats-worth of Wit bought with a Million of Repentance*, attacking Shakespeare.
1593	Lodge's *Phillis* and Watson's *The Teares of fancie* published. *18 Apr.* *Venus and Adonis* entered in the Stationers' Register. *30 May.* Christopher Marlowe killed by Ingram Frizer in Deptford. *28 Sept.* Marlowe's *Lucan's First Book* and *Hero and Leander* entered together in the Stationers' Register.

1594	9 May. 'A booke intituled *the Ravyshement of Lucrece*' entered in the Stationers' Register.
	The Rape of Lucrece published; Shakespeare becomes a sharer in the Chamberlain's Men. Marlowe's *Ovid's Elegies* and Sir John Davies' *Epigrams* published together. Richard Barnfield's *Cynthia* also published. Swan Theatre built.
1595	Publication of Spenser's *Amoretti* and *Epithalamion*, as well as *Colin Clouts Come Home Againe* and *Astrophel*. Sidney's *Defence of Poesie*, and Michel de Montaigne's *Essais*, also published.
1596	Publication of second instalment of Spenser's *The Faerie Queene*, Books 1–6. Spenser's *Fowre Hymnes* and *Prothalamion* also published.
1597	Fear of second Spanish Armada.
1598	Marlowe's *Hero and Leander* published, first as 818-line poem and later as a Homeric and Virgilian epic, completed by George Chapman. Homer's *Iliad* translated by Chapman (Books 1–7).
1599	Globe Theatre opens. *The Passionate Pilgrim* published with Shakespeare's name on the title page, and including versions of Marlowe's 'The Passionate Shepherd' and Ralegh's 'The Nymph's Reply'.
	13 Jan. Spenser dies in Westminster, London.
1600	*Lucrece* reaches its fourth edition, *Venus and Adonis*, its sixth. Marlowe's *Lucan's First Book* published with Marlowe's name on the title page. *England's Helicon* published, including versions of Marlowe's 'The Passionate Shepherd' and Ralegh's 'The Nymph's Reply'. Fortune Theatre built.
1601	'The Phoenix and Turtle' appears in Robert Chester's *Love's Martyr, or Rosalin's Complaint*. Jonson's *Poetaster*.
1603	Queen Elizabeth dies and is succeeded by James I.
1609	*Shake-speares Sonnets* published by Thomas Thorpe. First folio edition of Spenser's *The Faerie Queene*, Books 1–6, with 'Two Cantos of Mutabilitie'.
1611	First folio of Spenser's collected works published.
1616	Shakespeare dies in Stratford.
	Jonson's *Works* published in a folio edition, containing poems, masques, and plays.
1623	Publication of the First Folio, the first collected edition of Shakespeare's plays.
1625	James I dies. Accession of Charles I.
1637	*6 Aug.* Jonson dies in Westminster, London.

1638   Posthumously published book of poetic tributes to Jonson entitled *Jonsonus Virbius*.

1640   A second folio edition of Jonson's *Works* published, including the collection of poems *The Underwood*, assembled by his literary executor Sir Kenelm Digby. John Benson's edition of Shakespeare's *Poems* published.

PATRICK CHENEY

Introduction: Shakespeare's poetry in the twenty-first century

... we already know what poetry is. No problem there. It's <u>poesis</u> – a making,
a made thing. If we accept Aristotle's definition, it's specifically a thing made out of
speech and rhythm. We might press the matter further and agree with the Russian
formalists that it's a thing made out of speech and rhythm that calls attention to its
making and its made-ness.
Bruce R. Smith, 'Introduction', *PMLA*, 'Special Topic: On Poetry'[1]

Shakespeare ... wrote the best poetry ... in English, or perhaps in any
Western language.
Harold Bloom, *Shakespeare: The Invention of the Human*[2]

Poetry in the Shakespeare canon

The 'poetry' of William Shakespeare (1564–1616) constitutes one of the
supreme achievements of world art. Readers may know this poetry most
intimately from his drama, where it is on display across a dramatic canon of
nearly forty plays, in the genres of comedy, history, tragedy, and romance,
from early in his professional career (around 1590) to late (around 1614).
Indeed, poetry makes up the large percentage of Shakespeare's theatrical
writing (75 per cent), most of it in the blank verse (66 per cent) that he and
his contemporary Christopher Marlowe helped turn into the gold standard
of English verse.[3] But the plays also include a good deal of rhymed verse
(about 9 per cent), such as the sonnet prologue to *Romeo and Juliet*, as well
as a large body of in-set lyrics (both songs and poems) in a wide range of
metres and forms (over 130 pieces, with over 100 original compositions).[4]
Among the lyrics in the plays, we find some stunning poetry, from the
concluding songs of 'Spring' and 'Winter' in *Love's Labour's Lost*
(*Riverside*, 5.2.891) through the songs of Ariel in *The Tempest*: 'Those are
pearls that were his eyes' (1.2.399). These lyrics include professional singer
Amiens' 'Under the greenwood tree' in *As You Like It* (2.5.1), the clown
Feste's 'When that I was and a little tine boy' (5.1.389) concluding *Twelfth
Night*, and the lost princes of Britain's 'Fear no more the heat o'th' sun' in
Cymbeline (4.2.258). Not simply does William Shakespeare make his plays
fundamentally out of poetry, but he manages to use poetry to give birth to

I

'the most important body of imaginative literature of the last thousand years'.[5] We might say that Shakespeare's absolute mastery of poetry's idiom and form during the English Renaissance allowed this mysterious genius to create the most enduring body of dramatic works not simply in English but 'in any Western language'. For the next 400 years, his dramatic poetry would set the benchmark for achievement in artistic expression.

In addition to writing much of his drama in poetry, Shakespeare wrote five freestanding poems of major significance to the development of English verse. Early in his professional career, in 1593, he published *Venus and Adonis*, a 1,194-line poem of sixain stanzas (rhyming *ababcc*) in the popular erotic genre of the Ovidian epyllion or minor epic. Prefaced with a dedicatory epistle to Henry Wriothesley, the young earl of Southampton, and signed 'William Shakespeare', this 'first heir of [his] ... invention' promises a work of 'graver labour'. Then, in 1594, Shakespeare fulfils this promise by publishing *The Rape of Lucrece*, a 1,855-line poem in rhyme-royal stanzas (*ababbcc*), in the genre of tragic minor epic, again prefaced by a dedication to Southampton, and once more signed 'William Shakespeare'. While *Venus* became his most popular work during his lifetime, going through nine editions by 1616, *Lucrece* was popular as well, going through five editions. Together, the two epyllia make Shakespeare one of the most well-known print-poets during the reigns of Queen Elizabeth I and King James I. So much so that in 1599 the printer William Jaggard published a volume of verse titled *The Passionate Pilgrim*, which included versions of the poems we now know as Sonnets 138 and 144, along with three of the inset-lyrics from the love-sick courtiers in *Love's Labour's Lost* and fifteen other poems, by such poets as Marlowe, Richard Barnfield, and Bartholomew Griffin. This volume, too, was popular, going through three editions, the last in 1612. In 1601, Robert Chester published a curious volume titled *Love's Martyr*, which included the great 67-line philosophical lyric known today as 'The Phoenix and Turtle', which employs thirteen stanzas of four lines each in the unusual metre of a seven-syllable line with four accents (rhyming *abba*), and five stanzas of three lines each in trochaic metre (rhyming *aaa*). In 1611, this volume was re-issued with a different name, *Britain's Annals*.

If during the early stage of his career Shakespeare published his own poetry, and during the middle stage others published his poetry for him, late in his career we encounter a mysterious publication that blurs this distinction of authorial agency: the 1609 quarto titled *Shake-speares Sonnets*, which includes the 154 sonnets themselves and *A Lover's Complaint*, a 329-line poem in the rhyme-royal stanza of *Lucrece*, written in the popular Elizabethan genre of pastoral complaint. For complex reasons, we do not know whether Shakespeare authorized this publication or not.[6] Nonetheless, while scholars believe that Shakespeare worked on his sonnet sequence throughout his career, they think that he penned *A Lover's Complaint* between 1602 and 1605.

As such, Shakespeare wrote freestanding poems from early in his career till late, and succeeded in integrating their composition into his work in the theatre. Equally to the point, the many subsequent editions of his poems during his lifetime joined the burgeoning publication of his plays in quarto editions, keeping this 'Shakespeare' before the public eye (see Table 1). As we

Table 1   *Shakespeare's poems and plays in print 1593–1623*

Year	Plays	Poems
1593		Q1 *V & A*
1594	Q1 *Tit.*, Q1 *2H6*	Q1 *Luc.*
		Q2 *V & A*
1595	O1 *3H6*	O1 *V & A* (?)
1596	Q1 *E3*	O2 *V & A*
1597	Q1 *LLL*, Q1 *R2*, Q1 *R3*, Q1 *Rom.*	
1598	Q1, Q2 *1H4*, Q2 *LLL*, Q2, Q3 *R2*, Q2 *R3*	O1 *Luc.*
1599	Q2 *Rom.*, Q3 *1H4*, Q2 *E3*	O1, O2 *PP*, O3, O4 *V & A*,
1600	Q1 *H5*, Q *2H4*, Q1 *Ado*, Q1 *MND* Q2 *2H6*, Q1 *3H6*, Q2 *Tit.*, Q1 *MV*	O2, O3 *Luc.*
1601		Q1 *Love's Martyr*
1602	Q1 *Wiv.*, Q3 *R3*, Q2 *H5*	O5 *V & A* (?)
1603	Q1 *Ham.*	
1604	Q2 *Ham.*, Q4 *1H4*	
1605	Q4 *R3*	
1606		
1607		O6 *V & A (?)*, O4 *Luc.*
1608	Q1 *Lr.*, Q4 *R2*, Q5 *1H4*	O7 *V & A (?)*
1609	Q1 *Tro.*, Q1, Q2 *Per.*, Q3 *Rom.*	Q *Son.*
1610		O8 *V & A (?)*
1611	Q3 *Tit.*, Q3 *Ham.*, Q3 *Per.*	Q1 *Love's Martyr* reissued as *Britain's Annals*
1612	Q3 *Tit.*, Q3 *Ham.*, Q3 *Per.*, Q5 *R3*	O3 *PP*
1613	Q6 *1H4*	
1614		
1615	Q5 *R2*	
1616		O5 *Luc.*
1617		O9 *V & A*
1618		

Table 1   (*cont.*)

Year	Plays	Poems
1619	Q3 *2H6*, Q2 *3H6*, Q4 *Per.*, Q2 *Wiv.*, Q2 *MV*, Q2 *Lr.*, Q3 *H5*, Q2 *MND*	
1620		O10 *V & A*
1621		
1622	Q1 *Oth.*, Q6 *R3*, Q7 *1H4*, Q1 *Rom. (?)*, Q4 *Ham. (?)*	
1623	*F1*	

Note: All editions that advertise Shakespeare's authorship are underlined. When the title page contains Shakespeare's initials, dotted lines are used. Dotted lines also indicate works where there are two title pages (one of which contains Shakespeare's name) or an entire edition is lost. F = folio; Q = quarto; O = octavo

shall see, just as commentators since the seventeenth century emphasize the 'poetic' character of Shakespeare's plays, recent critics emphasize the 'dramatic' character of his poems. Perhaps only by recalling this historic integration of *theatrical poems* with *poetical plays* can we accurately measure Shakespeare's achievement as an English author.

A cultural context

To view Shakespeare's achievement in the art of poetry, both in his plays and in his poems, we may wish to recall the cultural environment in which he produced his metrical art. While the first three chapters chart important contours of this environment, we might here draw attention to a particular frame for viewing the historic conjunction of two institutions supporting the sixteenth-century invention of modern English poetry: the printing press and the theatre.

While the printing press had been invented in the fifteenth century, only toward the end of the sixteenth did it become a major institution for secular literature in England.[7] Usually, literary historians credit Edmund Spenser with being the first canonical English poet to use the printing press to present himself as a national poet. In 1579, Spenser published his Virgilian pastoral poem, *The Shepheardes Calender*, and in 1590 he followed with his Virgilian epic, *The Faerie Queene* (Books 1–3), with a second instalment appearing in 1596 (Books 4–6). Spenser's achievement was to invent the modern notion of the print-poet, the author who uses the publication of poetic books to present his cultural authority to the nation. In our English literary histories, Ben

Jonson succeeds Spenser as national or 'laureate' poet, and does so monumentally the year of Shakespeare's death (1616) by publishing a folio edition of *Works* that includes not just poems but also court masques and commercial plays.[8]

In 1567, John Brayne built the Red Lion playhouse, the first commercial theatre in England.[9] Then, in 1576, just a few years before Spenser published his pastoral poem, Brayne's brother-in-law, James Burbage (father of Richard Burbage, lead actor in Shakespeare's playing company) built a playhouse called the Theatre. During the next twenty-five years, England witnessed the building of several other commercial theatres, including the Curtain (1577), the Rose (1587), the Swan (1594), and, in 1599, the Globe. From the start, the playwrights who wrote plays for the new London theatre used poetry as their principal medium of dramatic speech.[10] Early on, they selected blank verse as most fit for dramatic performance, beginning with Thomas Sackville and Thomas Norton in *Gorboduc*, Thomas Kyd in *The Spanish Tragedy*, Marlowe in *Tamburlaine*, and Shakespeare in the *Henry VI* plays. While Spenser, along with Sir Philip Sidney, Samuel Daniel, Michael Drayton, and George Chapman, perfected the medium of non-dramatic verse – with all of them except Sidney relying on the printing press to do so – Kyd, Marlowe, Shakespeare, and after them Jonson perfected the medium of dramatic verse in the new theatre.

Until very recently, scholars of the English Renaissance tended to see the printing house and the playhouse as independent institutions. Yet, as the cases of Marlowe and then Chapman especially make clear, authors during the 1590s began to produce work important to both institutions. Shakespeare's accomplishment lies in following Marlowe down this professional path, rather than Spenser, who eschewed the commercial theatre. Yet in the end Shakespeare's dual relation with the printing house and the playhouse emerges as historically unique; for instance, he alone absorbed himself in the life of the theatre *and* produced a Petrarchan sonnet sequence.[11]

As recently as 2000, Julie Stone Peters' revisionary monograph, *The Theatre of the Book, 1480–1880: Print, Text, and Performance in Europe*, argued for a symbiosis between the theatre and the printing house:

> The printing press had an essential role to play in the birth of the modern theatre at the turn of the fifteenth century. As institutions they grew up together... [N]early a century before Shakespeare was born, there began, in fact, to develop a relationship that would help create the theatre for which he wrote. Printing, far from being marginal to the Renaissance theatre, was crucial at the outset... Drama was understood to play itself out in two arenas – on the stage and on the page.[12]

Thus, Peters situates the drama of Shakespeare in her revisionary model: 'In the English-speaking world, Shakespeare's career has helped to produce one of those enduring lies so convenient to the history of progress: that Renaissance dramatists were unconcerned with the circulation of their work on the page; that the press kept aloof from the stage and the early stage kept aloof from the press' (pp. 4–5). Following up on Peters in 2003, Lukas Erne argued that Shakespeare wrote his plays for both the page and the stage: 'printed playbooks became respectable reading matter earlier than we have hitherto supposed, early enough for Shakespeare to have lived through and to have been affected by this process of legitimation ... [T]he assumption of Shakespeare's indifference to the publication of his plays is a myth.'[13]

Although neither Erne nor Peters is concerned principally with the dramatic medium of poetry or with Shakespeare's poems, they revolutionize our understanding of the historical context for viewing one of the field's most pressing conundrums: that a man of the theatre writing a nonpareil drama could produce some of the most important freestanding poems in English, and even publish some of them under the signature of his own name.

A professional context

To a remarkable extent, the history of Shakespeare criticism depends on how individual commentators come to understand this author's 'poetry'.[14] Importantly, the earliest commentators showed a critical sensibility that gets lost during the ensuing centuries; they see William Shakespeare as a *poetic* author who writes *both poems and plays*. Thus, during the period, the term 'poet' meant both *author of poems* and *author of plays*. Today, in a culture that privileges Shakespeare's plays over his poems, and an academy whose critical theory has spent the past thirty years neglecting the 'literary' and the 'poetic' in favour of the 'historical' and the 'political', we might be surprised to discover that during Shakespeare's own lifetime only a few commentators mention a 'writer ... for the stage'.[15] Rather, the majority of Shakespeare's contemporaries mention a writer for the page, singling out his poems, as Richard Barnfield does in 1598 when he sees *Venus* and *Lucrece* as 'immortall Book[s]' that keep company with Spenser's *Faerie Queene*, Daniel's 'sweet-chast Verse', and Drayton's 'Tragedies' (*Shakspere Allusion-Book*, 1: 51).

Yet a significant number of contemporaries measure Shakespeare's poetic achievement in terms of both his poems and his plays. The most famous emerges in the 1598 *Palladis Thamia* when Francis Meres writes,

As the soule of Euphorbus was thought to live in Pythagorus: so the sweete wittie soule of Ovid lives in mellifluous & hony-tongued Shakespeare, witnes his *Venus and Adonis*, his *Lucrece*, his sugred Sonnets among his private friends, &c.

As Plautus and Seneca are accounted the best for Comedy and Tragedy among the Latines: so Shakespeare among the English is the most excellent in both kinds for the stage; for Comedy, witnes his *Gentlemen of Verona*, his *Errors*, his *Loves labors lost*, his *Loves labours wonne*, his *Midsummers night dreame* & his *Merchant of Venice*: for Tragedy his *Richard the 2. Richard the 3. Henry the 4. King John, Titus Andronicus* and his *Romeo and Juliet*.

(*Riverside*, p. 1, 970)

Meres identifies Shakespeare by the measure of his verse: he is an Ovidian author of poems and plays writing in a 'mellifluous & hony-tongued' style that expresses the contents of a 'sweete wittie soule'.

Yet the 1623 First Folio, the primary edition to print Shakespeare's plays for posterity, did not print any of his poems.[16] The effect of this editorial decision on the history of Shakespeare scholarship cannot be overestimated. In 1640, the printer John Benson tried to mend the lapse, and published a slender, octavo edition titled *Poems: Written By Wil. Shake-speare. Gent.* Modelled on the scheme of the First Folio, Benson aimed to give the poems 'the due accommodation of proportionable glory, with the rest of his ever-living Works'.[17] Yet Benson's noble enterprise largely failed: he did not include *Venus* or *Lucrece*; he reorganized the Sonnets; and he included poems by other poets. As a result, the ensuing centuries carried forward a 'dramatic' Shakespeare.

Indeed, between the late seventeenth century and the early part of the twentieth, commentators largely forgot the poems and fixed instead on what John Dryden called in 1668 the playwright's 'Dramatick Poesy'.[18] That is, they turned Shakespeare's theatre into poems, and admired the dramatic author as a poet. In *L'Allegro*, John Milton set the pace for the ensuing conversation when he spoke of 'sweetest Shakespeare, fancy's child', 'Warbl[ing] ... his native Wood-notes wild'.[19] During the Augustan, Romantic, and Victorian eras, a fancifully poetic Shakespeare of dramatic plays became the classificatory norm.[20]

During the later part of the twentieth century, two major developments occurred. First, most dominantly, scholars recovered the theatrical and performative dynamics of Shakespeare's plays from a literary or poetic dynamic. In the 1986 words of Harry Levin, 'Our century ... has restored our perception of him to his genre, the drama, enhanced by increasing historical knowledge alongside the live tradition of the performing arts'.[21] For many in the field today, the centrepiece has become the 1986 *Oxford*

Shakespeare, which presents Shakespeare as 'supremely, a man of the theatre', and edits his texts as they might have been originally performed: 'It is in performance that the plays lived and had their being. Performance is the end to which they were created'.[22] In 1997, the *Norton Shakespeare: Based on the Oxford Edition* institutionalized this theatrical 'Shakespeare' for the American academy: he is a 'working dramatist'.[23]

Second, during the closing years of the twentieth century and the opening years of the twenty-first, scholars began a backlash movement that aims to recover Shakespeare's considerable achievement in the art of poetry. During the past few years, Shakespeare studies has indeed entered a new phase of criticism, producing a large number of monographs, editions, collections of essays, and even international conferences devoted to the poems. The centrepiece here has become Colin Burrow's *Complete Sonnets and Poems* from Oxford World's Classics (2002) – surprisingly, the first edition since the late nineteenth century to print the full corpus of Shakespeare's poems in a single volume: 'Shakespeare's career as a poet is likely to have jolted along in fits and starts during periods of enforced idleness . . .; but the periods of idleness enabled the emergence of something which looks like an oeuvre, with a distinctive set of preoccupations' (p. 5).[24]

Among this body of work are too many essays to mention here (see the Reading list at the end of this Introduction for a selection, and the note on reference works on pages 281–6), but one essay deserves special mention: Burrow's 1998 Chatterton Lecture on Poetry, 'Life and Work in Shakespeare's Poems'. Burrow's essay supports his edition by solidifying a new 'non-dramatic' phase of Shakespeare criticism, which aims to 'give strong grounds for putting the poems at the front of our thinking about Shakespeare, and perhaps even at the front of collected editions of his works ... [We] also should ... ask why we do not think of Shakespeare as primarily a non-dramatic poet' (p. 17). The corpus of five major Shakespeare poems may be limited in number by comparison with the plays, but the recent surge of scholarship and criticism on this compelling corpus urges students of Shakespeare to see this author's poetic achievement as monumental in its own right, and then to set the poems alongside the plays. Indeed, only by conjoining Shakespeare's poems with his plays can we accurately gauge his full achievement. While other companions emphasize the plays, this companion foregrounds the poems in conjunction with the plays, even as it allows the historical accomplishment of the poems to emerge.

Hence, during the past few years scholars have drawn attention to the excellence and widespread importance of the non-dramatic part of Shakespeare's corpus. G. Blakemore Evans reminds us that the Sonnets have become Shakespeare's all-time best-seller (*Sonnets*, p. 1), and not surprisingly more books have been written on the Sonnets than on any of the plays, except perhaps *Hamlet*. Northrop Frye helps us understand why: 'Shakespeare's sonnets are the definitive summing up of the Western tradition of love poetry from Plato and Ovid, to Dante and Petrarch, to Chaucer and Spenser.'[25] Similarly, Jonathan Crewe calls *Lucrece* 'one of the most exhaustively discussed poems in the English language',[26] while those familiar with the voluminous criticism on *Venus* might speculate that the first heir of Shakespeare's invention couldn't be too far behind. Early in the last century, John Middleton Murray voiced a longstanding sentiment on 'The Phoenix and Turtle', shared by commentators from Ralph Waldo Emerson to Barbara Everett: this philosophical lyric is 'the most perfect short poem in any language'.[27] I. A. Richards was more circumspect: 'The Phoenix and Turtle' is 'the most mysterious poem in English'.[28] The recent work of John Kerrigan and Katherine Duncan-Jones on *A Lover's Complaint* confirms an anonymous yet shrewd nineteenth-century judgement: it is 'one of the most successful pastorals in the English language'.[29] Kerrigan calls *A Lover's Complaint* simply Shakespeare's 'most intricate long poem' (Kerrigan, p. 65), while Duncan-Jones adds that 'this short poem offers dizzyingly complex layers of reported speech'.[30] Finally, recent work on copyright and intellectual property has brought the 'pirating' problem of Jaggard's *The Passionate Pilgrim* back into the critical conversation.[31] Thus, Margreta de Grazia supplies a rationale for taking seriously Jaggard's enterprise in *The Passionate Pilgrim*: 'With the 1623 First Folio and the 1599 and 1612 editions of *The Passionate Pilgrim*, William Jaggard had printed the first collections of both Shakespeare's plays and his poems'.[32]

In addition to writing authentic dramatic verse for his plays and composing freestanding poems, Shakespeare probably produced a small body of occasional verse. Recently, scholars have attributed some new poems to the Shakespeare corpus. These include 'Shall I die', a ninety-line manuscript song argued by Gary Taylor to be an authentic Shakespeare composition, yet not fully accredited by the Shakespeare community; and *A Funeral Elegy*, a 578-line poem published in 1612 as a funeral celebration of William Peter, but no longer believed to be by Shakespeare. For these reasons, the present companion will not include discussion of either poem.[33]

We cannot even be certain that all of the other occasional poems sometimes assigned to Shakespeare are authentic. These short poems range in length from two lines to eight and appear in various poetic metres, some of them in the form of the funeral elegy: 'Upon a pair of gloves that master sent to his mistress'; two 'Verses upon the Stanley Tomb at Tong'; 'On Ben Jonson'; 'An Epitaph on Elias James', a London brewer whom Shakespeare knew; two epitaphs on the wealthy Stratford bachelor and usurer John Combe; and 'Upon the King' (James I).[34]

Yet Shakespeare likely did pen an 'Epitaph on Himself' (*Complete Sonnets and Poems*, p. 147), inscribed on his gravestone at Holy Trinity Church, Stratford-upon-Avon. This primitive-sounding apotropaic warning compels visitors even today to view 'William Shakespeare' through a wry 'everliving' lens, the poetic form of the epitaph itself:

> Good friend, for Jesus' sake forbear
> To dig the dust enclosed here.
> Blessed be the man that spares these stones,
> And cursed be he that moves my bones.
>
> (rpt *Complete Sonnets and Poems*, p. 728)

NOTES

1 Smith, 'Introduction: Some Presuppositions', *PMLA* 120 (2005), 9–15: p. 9. Cf. George T. Wright, *Shakespeare's Metrical Art* (Berkeley: University of California Press, 1988): 'Poetry is language composed in verse, that is, language of which an essential feature is its appearance in measured units, either as written text or in oral performance' (p. ix). All quotations from Shakespeare's poems and plays come from Cambridge editions, unless otherwise noted, when they will come from either the *Riverside Shakespeare*, ed. G. Blakemore Evans, et al. (Boston: Houghton, 1997), cited as *Riverside*, or *The Complete Sonnets and Poems*, ed. Colin Burrow, Oxford World's Classics (Oxford University Press, 2002).

2 Bloom, *Shakespeare: The Invention of the Human* (New York: Riverhead-Penguin Putnam, 1998), p. xviii. Bloom also singles out Shakespeare's prose as a historic invention.

3 These statistics come from Russ McDonald, *The Bedford Companion to Shakespeare: An Introduction with Documents*, 2nd edn (New York: St Martin's Press, 2001), pp. 77–8.

4 Conveniently collected in *Shakespeare's Songs and Poems*, ed. Edward Hubler (New York: McGraw Hill, 1959).

5 Stephen Greenblatt, *Will in the World: How Shakespeare Became Shakespeare* (New York: Norton, 2004), p. 12.

6 Katherine Duncan-Jones, 'Was the 1609 *Shake-speares Sonnets* Really Unauthorized?', *Review of English Studies* 34 (1983), 151–71. See also Chapters 7 and 8 in this volume.

7 On print culture, see Chapter 3 in this volume; Arthur F. Marotti, *Manuscript, Print, and the English Renaissance Lyric* (Ithaca: Cornell University Press, 1995); and Wendy Wall, *The Imprint of Gender: Authorship and Publication in the English Renaissance* (Ithaca: Cornell University Press, 1993).

8 On Spenser as England's 'first laureate poet', see Richard Helgerson, *Self-Crowned Laureates: Spenser, Jonson, Milton, and the Literary System* (Berkeley: University of California Press, 1983), esp. p. 100.

9 See Andrew Gurr, *Playgoing in Shakespeare's London*, 2nd edn (Cambridge University Press, 1996), pp. 10–16.

10 As Wright recalls, 'Throughout the fifteenth century and most of the sixteenth, English drama . . . was mainly written in rhyming forms' (*Shakespeare's Metrical Art*, p. 95). See also Chapters 1 and 2 in this volume.

11 Cheney, *Shakespeare, National Poet-Playwright* (Cambridge University Press, 2004), p. 207.

12 Peters, *The Theatre of the Book, 1480–1880: Print, Text, and Performance in Europe* (Oxford University Press, 2000), pp. 1–8.

13 Erne, *Shakespeare as Literary Dramatist* (Cambridge University Press, 2003), pp. 25–6.

14 For a complementary history, see Chapter 14 in this volume.

15 Smith, 'Introduction', esp. pp. 9–12; Edmund Bolton, in *The Shakspere Allusion-Book: A Collection of Allusions to Shakspere from 1591 to 1700*, ed. C. M. Ingleby, L. Toulmin Smith, and F. J. Furnivall; rev. edn John Munro; preface Edmund Chambers, 2 vols. (1909; Freeport, NY: Books for Libraries P, 1970), I: 213.

16 We do not know why, but Burrow speculates that it was due to copyright problems with *Venus* and *Lucrece*, still popular in 1623 (*Complete Sonnets and Poems*, p. 8). For scepticism about this view, see Cheney, *Shakespeare, National Poet-Playwright*, pp. 67–9.

17 Benson, *Poems* (London, 1640), sig. *2ʳ. See Chapter 6 in this volume.

18 Dryden, rpt in *Shakespeare: The Critical Heritage*, ed. Brian Vickers, 6 vols. (London: Routledge & Kegal Paul, 1974–81), I: 136.

19 Milton, *L'Allegro* 134–5, in *John Milton: Complete Poems and Major Prose*, ed. Merritt Y. Hughes (Indianapolis: Odyssey, 1957).

20 Harry Levin, 'Critical Approaches to Shakespeare from 1660–1904', in *The Cambridge Companion to Shakespeare Studies*, ed. Stanley Wells (Cambridge University Press, 1986), pp. 213–29.

21 Levin, 'Critical Approaches', p. 228.

22 *Oxford Shakespeare*, ed. Stanley Wells, Gary Taylor, John Jowett, and William Montgomery (Oxford University Press, 1986), pp. xxxvi and xxxviii.

23 *Norton Shakespeare*, ed. Stephen Greenblatt, et al. (New York: Norton, 1997), p. 1.

24 The Arden, Cambridge, Penguin, Pelican, and Folger editions all print the Sonnets in a volume separate from the other poems.

25 Frye, 'How True a Twain', in *Fables of Identity: Studies in Poetic Mythology* (New York: Harcourt-Harbinger, 1963), pp. 88–106: p. 106.

26 Crewe (ed.), *Narrative Poems* (New York: Penguin, 1999), p. xli.

27 Rpt in *A New Variorum Shakespeare: The Poems*, ed. Hyder E. Rollins (Philadelphia: J. B. Lippincott, 1938), p. 565. For a review of commentary from Emerson to Everett, see Cheney, *Shakespeare, National Poet-Playwright*, pp. 173–83.

28 Richards, *Poetries: Their Media and Ends*, ed. Trevor Eaton (The Hague: Mouton, 1974), p. 50.

29 Rpt in *A New Variorum Shakespeare*, ed. Rollins, p. 586.

30 Katherine Duncan-Jones (ed.), *The Sonnets and 'A Lover's Complaint'*, Arden 3rd series (London: Thomas Nelson, 1999), p. 92.

31 See Max W. Thomas, 'Eschewing Credit: Heywood, Shakespeare, and Plagiarism before Copyright', *New Literary History* 31 (2000), 277–93.

32 de Grazia, *Shakespeare Verbatim: The Reproduction of Authenticity and the 1790 Apparatus* (Oxford: Clarendon, 1991), p. 167. Since Jaggard published the 1612 edition first with Shakespeare's name on the title page and then without it, we need to be careful when assigning to his publishing venture an interest specifically in Shakespeare.

33 For commentary and scholarship, see *Complete Sonnets and Poems*, ed. Burrow, pp. 148–58. On *A Funeral Elegy* in particular, see Brian Vickers, *'Counterfeiting' Shakespeare: Evidence, Authorship, and John Ford's 'Funerall Elegye'* (Cambridge University Press, 2002).

34 For commentary, see Walter Cohen, Introduction to 'Various Poems' in the *Norton Shakespeare*, pp. 1,991–5; and Kay, 'William Shakespeare', in *Sixteenth-century British Non-dramatic Writers*, ed. David A. Richardson, *Dictionary of Literary Biography* 172 (Detroit: Gale Research, 1996), pp. 229–30. For scepticism about authenticity, see *Poems*, ed. John Roe (Cambridge University Press, 1992), pp. 2–3; and esp. *Complete Sonnets and Poems*, ed. Burrow, pp. 146–52.

READING LIST

Burrow, Colin. 'Life and Work in Shakespeare's Poems'. Chatterton Lecture on Poetry. *Proceedings of the British Academy* 97 (1998), 15–50.

Cannan, Paul. D. 'Early Shakespeare Criticism, Charles Gildon, and the Making of Shakespeare the Playwright–Poet'. *Modern Philology* 102 (2004), 35–55.

Cheney, Patrick. 'Shakespeare's Literary Career and Narrative Poetry'. In *Early Modern English Poetry: A Critical Companion*. Ed. Patrick Cheney, Andrew Hadfield, and Garrett Sullivan. New York: Oxford University Press, 2007, pp. 161–71.

Ellrodt, Robert. 'Shakespeare the Non-Dramatic Poet'. In *The Cambridge Companion to Shakespeare Studies*. Ed. Stanley Wells. Cambridge University Press, 1986, pp. 35–47.

Enterline, Lynn. ' "The Phoenix and Turtle", Renaissance Elegies, and the Language of Grief'. In *Early Modern English Poetry: A Critical Companion*. Ed. Patrick Cheney, Andrew Hadfield, and Garrett Sullivan. New York: Oxford University Press, 2007, pp. 147–59.

Ewbank, Inga-Stina. 'Shakespeare's Poetry'. In *A New Companion to Shakespeare Studies*. Ed. Kenneth Muir and S. Schoenbaum. Cambridge University Press, 1971, pp. 99–115.

Empson, William. 'The Narrative Poems'. In *Essays in Shakespeare*. Ed. David B. Pirie. Cambridge University Press, 1986, pp. 1–28.

Kay, Dennis. 'William Shakespeare'. *Sixteenth-century British Non-dramatic Writers*. Ed. David A. Richardson. *Dictionary of Literary Biography*. 172. Detroit: Gale Research, 1996, pp. 217–37.

Kerrigan, John. 'Shakespeare's Poems'. In *The Cambridge Companion to Shakespeare*. Ed. Margreta De Grazia and Stanley Wells. Cambridge University Press, 2001, pp. 65–81.

Lever, J. W. 'Shakespeare's Narrative Poems'. In *A New Companion to Shakespeare Studies*. Ed. Kenneth Muir and S. Schoenbaum. Cambridge University Press, 1971, pp. 116–26.

Magnusson, Lynne. 'Non-Dramatic Poetry'. In *Shakespeare: An Oxford Guide*. Ed. Stanley Wells and Lena Cowan Orlin. Oxford University Press, 2003, pp. 286–99.

Roberts, Sasha. 'Shakespeare's Sonnets and English Sonnet Sequences'. In *Early Modern English Poetry: A Critical Companion*. Ed. Patrick Cheney, Andrew Hadfield, and Garrett Sullivan. New York: Oxford University Press, 2007, pp. 172–83.

1

WILLIAM J. KENNEDY

Shakespeare and the development of English poetry

Shakespeare's relationship to the earlier development of English poetry is complex and multiform. Certainly in his time, perspectives about this development were changing as a new generation of poets and writers re-evaluated the past. Shakespeare himself shifted his perspective on poetry, alternately engaging his attention with older popular forms, currently fashionable elite forms, and newly conceived experimental forms. When he began writing poems for his earliest plays, lyric poetry appeared in popular broadside printings of traditional ballads, anonymous verse, and occasionally signed poems; in prestige, often reprinted anthologies such as Richard Tottel's *Songes and Sonnettes* (1557) and Richard Edwards's *The Paradise of Dainty Devyces* (1576); and in a few volumes of seriously crafted verse by signed authors such as George Gascoigne in *A Hundreth Sundrie Flowres* (1573, revised as *The Posies*, 1575). When in the early 1590s Shakespeare wrote *Venus and Adonis*, *The Rape of Lucrece*, and his early Sonnets, the literary current in London was marked by the dominance of Edmund Spenser (after the publication of the first three books of *The Faerie Queene* in 1590 and of *Complaints* in 1591) and Philip Sidney (after the pirated publication of his *Astrophil and Stella* with Samuel Daniel's *Delia* in 1591). When by 1609 Shakespeare revised his Sonnets for their publication, the development of English poetry was undergoing a sea-change at the hands of Ben Jonson, who had rejected the older fashions of native and Petrarchan forms and had promoted instead those of the classical epigram, ode, satire, and epistle. Shakespeare, as we will see, responded to each of these currents in his own poetic production, dipping into them, floating upon them, and swimming against them in various tides of native, continental, and classical convention.

Shakespeare had already begun his theatrical career in London by 1589, the year in which Thomas Nashe, a poor minister's son recently down from Cambridge, sought to ingratiate himself with London's University Wits by volunteering a preface for Robert Greene's pastoral romance *Menaphon*. Dedicated to 'the Gentlemen Students of Both Universities', this preface bristles at the work of 'vainglorious tragedians' skilled with inkhorn terms (Thomas Kyd?), 'idiot art-masters' swollen with blank verse (Marlowe?), and 'deeply-red grammarians [= grammar school graduates] . . . that feed on nought but the crumbs that fall from the translator's trencher [the early Shakespeare?]'.[1] Nashe disparages 'our English Italians' who prefer Petrarch, Ariosto, Tasso, and even the minor Livio Celiano to native poets. Among the latter, he commends Gascoigne, who 'first beat the path to that perfection which our best poets have aspired to since his departure'; the 'divine' Spenser, a 'miracle of wit'; and 'many most able men to revive poetry' such as Matthew Roydon, Thomas Atchelow, and George Peele, who would publish little and fade from view. This list gives us a pretty good idea of England's poetic canon just before Shakespeare began to sharpen his poetic quill in earnest.

If Nashe had insulted Shakespeare by referring to him as one who fed upon translators' crumbs, Henry Chettle added to Nashe's insult when he in 1592 published Greene's penitential *Groats-worth of wit bought with a million of repentance*, allegedly penned on the latter's deathbed with a caustic rebuke aimed at Shakespeare. Here Greene advises his fellow University Wits Marlowe, Nashe, and Peele to renounce atheism, write satires against vanity, and mistrust theatrical 'Puppets' and 'Apes' who debase their work. Chief among them is Shakespeare, thinly disguised as 'an upstart Crow' who 'supposes he is as well able to bombast out a blanke verse as the best of you'.[2] The attack could only edge Shakespeare toward proving that he might measure up to the most admired Elizabethan writers, including the University Wits themselves. A characteristic they all shared was the display of at least some (and in some cases, too much) erudition – familiarity with classical Latin authors, especially Ovid and Virgil, and with modern continental poets, especially Petrarch and those indebted to him such as Ariosto, Ronsard, Tasso, and Desportes. Shakespeare could compete with them by returning to Latin texts that he'd studied at Stratford grammar school, and by acquiring at least some rudiments of Italian, French, and other European languages.

This task was fairly easy to accomplish. London of the late 1580s embraced a population of some 500 Italian immigrants, most of them merchants, but many of them musicians, artists, and makers of luxury goods for the city's elite population.[3] In *Taming of the Shrew* Shakespeare had already incorporated casual Italian locutions into that play's dialogue. By the time he wrote *Love's Labour's Lost* with Holofernes's citation (4.2.89–90) of a proverb from John Florio's Italian grammar, *First Fruits* (1578), he had dipped yet deeper into the language of Petrarch and Ariosto. French speakers and French books were even easier to come by. After the

St Bartholomew Day's Massacre in 1572, some 5,000 Huguenots fled to London, and in 1604 and possibly earlier Shakespeare lodged at the home of one of them, Christophe Montjoy, a purveyor of quality headdresses to the city's elite and possibly to its South Bank theatres. By the late 1590s, he had already brought enough French into his plays to attest to his competence in that tongue – notably in the locutions of Dr Caius in *Merry Wives of Windsor* and in the language lesson scenes of *Henry V*.

Venus and Adonis

Shakespeare's familiarity with French and Italian texts proves difficult to estimate, but his experience with classical Latin texts, especially with Ovid's poetry, is evident. We do not know whether *Venus and Adonis* or Marlowe's *Hero and Leander* came first in composition, but it seems clear that one poem alludes to the other and that both share a playful, cheeky, tone-shifting attitude to the mode.[4] Marlowe, elaborating upon his Greek source by Musaeus, toys with Epicurean naturalism (Leander's fall into love, 167–91), jaded sensualism (his sacrilegious rhetoric, 209–90), social criticism (the narrator's digression on scholarly poverty, 461–82), and homoerotic titillation (Neptune's attraction to Leander, 639–76). Shakespeare magnifies his brief Latin source in Ovid's *Metamorphoses* 10.519–59 and 705–39 with strategic references to Adonis's genealogy as the incestuous offspring of Cinyras and Myrrha (168–74, 199–216, 1183–8), who are in turn the grand- and great-grand-offspring of Pygmalion and an ivory statue brought to life by Venus. From this derives the odd naturalism of Adonis' 'ivory' hand (363) and his stony silence (200, 427–38), of Venus's maternalistic – and vaguely incestuous – solicitude toward him (611–78), and perhaps of the sheer mismatch between the goddess's physical strength and the young man's diminutive stature (31–42, 589–612), playing on the etymology of Pygmalion's name (= Greek *pygmaios* 'pigmy, measuring a cubit or eighteen inches in length, the size of a well-endowed phallus').[5] In depicting these sexual pratfalls, Shakespeare deploys at least as much humour as Marlowe, and in investing his heroine's sexual rhetoric with economic figurations of loss and gain (*Venus and Adonis* 511–51), the author flirts with social criticism as did his rival in the digression on poor scholars (*Hero and Leander* 465–84). Such was the verse that had tickled the elite at court, at university, among the wealthy gentry of London, and among the legal-training societies populated by 'Gentlemen of the Innes of Court and Chauncerie'.

To the latter, Greene's friend Thomas Lodge had dedicated his Ovidian poem *Scillaes Metamorphosis* (1589) in England's first major example of this epyllionic genre.[6] Lodge knew his Latin sources for the legend of Glaucus and Scylla, especially Ovid's *Metamorphoses* 13.898–14.74, and he knew his French Petrarchists, especially Ronsard and Desportes, whose sonnets and poems he had translated in dozens and scattered through his own sonnet sequence *Phillis* (1593) and his prose romance *Rosalynde* (1590). In Petrarchan terms, but notably inverting the gendered parallels between himself and female speakers, Lodge's Glaucus compares his unrequited love for Scylla to Venus's for Adonis (stanzas 21–3, 23.3–4) and, improbably evoking Ariosto's *Orlando Furioso*, to Angelica's for Medoro (stanzas 24–6, 24.2–3). As lurid as any overwrought Petrarchist, he blazons Scilla from head to crotch (stanzas 48–53) and he sings of his despair ('Dead alas still I live', 59.2). At length, Cupid heals him and punishes Scilla so that when the poem closes, Glaucus enjoys his sexual vindication at her expense. So no doubt did those worldly connoisseurs of Ovidian erotica and Petrarchan amours who had constituted Lodge's readership.

Shakespeare knew he could do better. If Lodge had tapped Ronsard's poetry for some Petrarchan figurations, Shakespeare would tap the work of England's own Edmund Spenser for more powerful ones. The latter's *Complaints* (Stationers' Register, 29 December 1590) showed that Petrarchism held a greater potential for serious verse than any contemporary English sonneteer had yet imagined. Surrounding his Ovidian (and pseudo-Virgilian) mythic fables (*Virgil's Gnat*, *Mother Hubbards Tale*, and *Muiopotmos*) with poetic laments (*The Ruines of Time*, *Teares of the Muses*), Spenser offers three dream visions translated from Italian and French: *Visions of Petrarch* from the latter's apocalyptic canzone 323; *The Visions of Bellay* from Du Bellay's fifteen apocalyptic sonnets entitled *Songe*; and the *Ruines of Rome: by Bellay* from the latter's thirty-two sonnets on the fall of Rome, *Les Antiquitez de Rome*.[7] Although both *Visions* constitute juvenilia, while *Ruines* seems only a belated minor effort, they nonetheless gave English readers a glimpse of continental poets whose meditations on past, present, and future history drew upon scriptural texts from Psalms and classical texts from Virgil, Horace, and Ovid. Approaching *Venus and Adonis* from this Spenserian perspective, we find that Venus's address to Death, ' "Imperious supreme of all mortal things" ' (996), her discovery of Adonis 'Where, lo, two lamps burnt out in darkness lies' (1128), and her account of how Love's contrarieties ' "Pluck down the rich, enrich the poor with treasures" ' (1150) resonate deeply with figurations of mortality in *Complaints*.[8]

Book 3 of *The Faerie Queene* (Stationers' Register, 1 December 1589) proves yet more relevant. Midway through the Legend of Chastity, the Garden of Adonis (3.6.29–53) provides a place where Venus's sexuality and sensuality – previously represented as sheer carnality on Malecasta's Adonis tapestry (3.1.34–8) – become reconciled with married love and procreation. Before our eyes, Spenser is reversing and correcting earlier valuations attached to the goddess's passionate inclinations. Spenser plays upon the etymology of Adonis's name as related to *eden* (Hebrew 'garden') as well as to *hedone* (Greek 'pleasure'). The young man now presides over a locale where he dwells 'eterne in mutabilitie' and will forever be called 'father of all formes' (47). Judeo-Christian and Greco-Roman language, myth, and literary allusion conspire to edit, revise, supplement, and magnify Spenser's initial representation of Venus.[9] This kinetic approach, learned from Spenser, allows Shakespeare to modulate from an initially comic impression of Venus to one that grants her a deeply earned pathos at the end. Upon the goddess's apprehension of Adonis's untimely death, a sharp tonal change unearths 'variable passions' (967) in the contrarious Petrarchan manner. Fear, confidence, guilt, denial, hope, despair, compromise, self-assertion – each by turns overtakes Venus until her eyes shirk their duty and multiply her grief (1037–64). Her account of how contrariety originates in erotic turmoil (1135–64) extends the Petrarchan antagonisms of her complaint. Her retreat to Paphos consequently ends the poem on a note of suspension and dissolution, emulating the resistance to closure in Book 3 of *The Faerie Queene*. Shakespeare learned more from Spenser than versification or poetic technique: he learned principles of figurative repetition and thematic revision as well.

The Rape of Lucrece

Shakespeare's next poem, *The Rape of Lucrece*, likewise ends on a note of suspension, and it is one that portends a defining moment in Roman history when the aristocracy supplanted a tyrannical monarchy with limited republican rule. The poem's ancient sources derive chiefly from Ovid's poetic account of Lucrece in *Fasti* 2.685–852 and from Livy's prose account in *History of the Republic* 1.57–60, and its possible medieval sources include accounts in Chaucer's *Legend of Good Women* 1680–1885 and Gower's *Confessio Amantis* 7.4763–5130.[10] What appears fascinating about *Lucrece*, however, is that Shakespeare draws his chief stylistic and rhetorical models from Renaissance humanist writing, with references to Greene, Nashe, Spenser, and Marlowe and the ambitious projects that they spoke for.

Greene and Nashe had implied that Shakespeare possessed only a tyro's grasp of classical rhetoric. The formal declamations of *Lucrece* allow him to display his control over *suasoriae* and *sententiae* and to criticize stylistic assumptions subtending their development in English literary history. For example, the poem's seven-line rhyme royal stanza form hearkens back to that of Chaucer's *Troilus*, of the multiple-authored *Mirror for Magistrates* (1555–87), and of Samuel Daniel's *Complaint of Rosemond* (1592). Each of these predecessors undercuts celebratory versions of the past with a tragic or at least ironic view of human self-deception. So too does Shakespeare, but with a richness of texture and allusion that ranges over the entire canon of Tudor and Elizabethan literature. The moral sophistry of John Lyly's witty hero in *Euphues* (1578) subtends the rapist's decision to proceed with his act ('All orators are dumb when beauty pleadeth', 280), just as the Petrarchan blazon of the victim's body (386–420) suppositiously strengthens his resolve.

Shakespeare goes out of his way to fashion a distinctly performative rhetoric for Lucrece as well, enabling her to plan for action but also requiring her to confront its socially and politically gendered consequences. Her plea for Tarquin to live up to his monarchical dignity (575–644: ' "Thou seem'st not what thou art, a god, a king; / For kings like gods should govern every-thing" ', 601–2) draws upon advice to princes as represented in such treatises as More's *Utopia* (1516) and Sir Thomas Elyot's *Boke named the Governour* (1531) and in such plays as Sackville and Norton's *Gorboduc* (1562) and Gascoigne's translation of Lodovico Dolce's *Jocasta* (1566). But like the advice proffered by More's spokesperson and by the royal counsellors in both plays, it fails to deter the aggressor's wilful behaviour. Nor does she trust the power of rhetoric to defend her chastity in the eyes of others. Lucrece convinces herself that only suicide can prove her innocence and perhaps motivate a change in social values (' "To see sad sights moves more than hear them told" ', 1324). The poem's outcome provides a staging ground to test the power of argument itself and the self-deluding, self-dividing bases on which it stands.

In this respect, *Lucrece* builds upon Greene's blank-verse play, the grimly comic *The Scottish Historie of James the Fourth* (1591?), in which the King of Scotland plots to murder his wife, the daughter of England's monarch, so that he might marry the daughter of the countess of Arran. To no avail his advisors warn him of dangers to the state that will result from 'His lawless and unbridled vein in love'; happily, the queen foils his attempt and restores order to the kingdom in the end.[11] It builds too upon Nashe's prose fiction, *The Unfortunate Traveller*, dedicated to the earl of Southampton on 27 June 1593, ten months before Shakespeare's poem entered the Stationers' Register (9 May 1594). Nashe's narrative recounts a brutal rape whose victim fails to deter the deed with her classical rhetoric ('How thinkest thou, is there a power above thy power?').[12] Shakespeare consequently appears to be rewrit-ing the cynical rhetoric of his predecessors in darker, more self-conscious, more culturally loaded tones than they had imagined.

Here, too, *Lucrece* bears traces of Spenser's and Marlowe's influence.[13] Some emerge in the ecphrastic painting of Troy's siege, echoing Spenser's account of the event in *The Faerie Queene* 3.9.33–43 as well as Marlowe's paraphrase of Virgil's account in *Dido, Queen of Carthage* 2.1.121–288 (with the collaboration of Nashe, posthumously published in 1594). Others derive from Paridell's carnal attraction to chaste Britomart in *The Faerie Queene* 3.9.21–4 and his lusty seduction of Hellenore in 3.9.27–32 and 3.10.4–16. Still others recall Marlowe's effort around 1592 to translate into blank verse Lucan's late Roman epic, *De bello civili* (also known as the *Pharsalia*), about conflicts that followed upon the assassination of Julius Caesar. The result, *LUCANS firste booke of the famous Civill warr translated line for line by Christopher Marlowe*, depicts 'outrage strangling law and people strong' (2) amid rhetorical representations of duplicitous motives.[14] Marking a stunning improvement upon such fall-of-princes poems as *A Mirror for Magistrates*, it gave Shakespeare an important precedent for depicting a similar moment in Roman history when outrage provoked a new form of strength. *Lucrece* ends as the tyrant's kinsman Junius Brutus (Latin *brutus* 'dullard') casts off his formerly doltish demeanour 'Wherein deep policy did him disguise' (1815) and issues an unexpected plea for public action. This bravura display of cunning is not unlike that of Marlowe's dramatic Tamburlane and Barabas and is pregnant with anticipations of later cunning in Shakespeare's own dramatic Hamlet, Hal, Duke Vincentio, and Edgar. In *Lucrece*, Shakespeare moves beyond his earlier representation of Roman history in *Titus Andronicus* toward the later effects of his mature tragedies.

Poetry in Shakespeare's plays

The success of *Venus and Adonis* (sixteen editions before 1640) and *Lucrece* (eight editions before 1640) gave Shakespeare the assurance of being a published author, and empowered him toward further poetry in the plays of his middle period after the theatres reopened in June 1594. Here we find him experimenting with the sonnet form in *Love's Labour's Lost* and *Romeo and Juliet*, where it is applied to comic, dramatic, and romantic situations. Earlier in *Two Gentlemen of Verona* (3.1.140–9) and later in *Much Ado about Nothing* (3.1.107–16), the love-sick Valentine and the scorner of marriage Beatrice offer examples of truncated sonnets. In the much later *All's Well That Ends Well*, Helena casts her letter to the Countess about her marriage to Bertram in the form of a sonnet, 'I am Saint Jaques' pilgrim, thither gone' (3.4.3–17).

The plays of Shakespeare's extended middle period make distinct and explicit allusions to lyrics from an earlier generation. After the Nurse discovers Juliet's inert body, the minstrels assembled for her wedding perform a lament, 'When dripping grief the heart doth wound' (*RJ* 4.4.148–63), based on Richard Edwards's poem 'In Commendation of Music' published in *The Paradyse of Daynte Devises* (1576).[15] In *Much Ado about Nothing* 1.1.213, Don Pedro taunts Benedick with 'In time the savage bull doth bear the yoke', a line drawn from Sonnet 47 of Thomas Watson's *Hekatompathia* (1582), previously echoed in Kyd's *Spanish Tragedy* 2.1.13. When Benedick attempts to sing, he begins a popular ballad 'The god of love', whose simple rhyme eludes him (*Much Ado* 5.2.22–25). In *Merry Wives of Windsor*, the Welsh parson Sir Hugh Evans twists lines from Marlowe's 'Come live with me and be my love' and further contaminates them with metrical verses from Psalm 137 (3.1.13–25). Two scenes later Falstaff tries to seduce Mistress Ford by singing from the Second Song of Sidney's *Astrophil and Stella*, 'Have I caught my heav'nly jewell' (3.3.35). In *Twelfth Night*, Feste sings two traditional love ballads (2.3.36–48 and 2.4.50–65), and ends the play with a song that evokes a young man's passage from innocence to experience (5.1.376–95); he also torments the incarcerated Malvolio with a song (4.2.65–72) based on 'Ah Robin/Jolly Robin' composed by another expectant overreacher, Sir Thomas Wyatt, and drawn from Tottel's *Songes and Sonnettes*. From the same anthology, the Gravedigger in *Hamlet* sings 'In youth when I did love' (5.1.57–69), a poem by Lord Vaux that its editor captioned 'The Aged Lover Renounceth Love'.

This creative melding of echoes from Watson, Marlowe, Sidney, and various anthologies displaying their roots in Wyatt and Lord Vaux, reminds us of Shakespeare's role as an active reader who absorbed the major poetic currents of his time. This anthologizing spirit reaches its height in *As You Like It*, which offers a wide range of amatory and other modes, from Amiens's pastoral (2.5.1–8 and 32–9, mocked by Jaques in 2.5.44–51) to the trochaic tetrameter love letters of Orlando and Oliver (3.2.76–84 and 113–42, mocked by Touchstone in 3.2.90–101), and from Amiens's 'Blow, blow, thou winter wind' (2.7.174–93) and the exiled lords' hunting song (4.2.10–19) to the Page's wedding tribute to Touchstone and Audrey (5.3.14–37) and Hymen's epithalamium for the ensemble (5.4.97–104 and 114–35). As the shepherdess Phebe falls madly in love with Rosalind, her quotation of line 176 from *Hero and Leander*, 'Who ever lov'd that lov'd not at first sight' (*As You Like It* 3.5.82), brings to a climax Shakespeare's earlier competition with Marlowe. Referring to the latter in reverent terms as 'dead shepherd' (3.5.81), the impressionable young woman registers Marlowe's enormous popularity amongst ordinary readers, her own folly in having succumbed to unexamined impulses as she did, and the supercession of the author's envy toward his long deceased predecessor. By now, Shakespeare had earned the confidence and security of having mastered his own poetic styles, and even of surpassing Marlowe's.

'The Phoenix and Turtle'

The anthologizing tenor of these plays corresponds to two publishing ventures that involved Shakespeare just before and after the turn of the century. The first is *The Passionate Pilgrim*, printed by T. Judson for William Jaggard probably in 1599, an anthology of twenty poems that opens with two of the poet-playwright's yet unpublished Sonnets (numbers 138 and 144), along with versions of three sonnets from *Love's Labour's Lost*. The second is Robert Chester's *Love's Martyr* (Stationers' Register 1601), a long poem about Nature's plea for the phoenix to reproduce by mating with a turtledove in Wales, to which was appended Shakespeare's 'The Phoenix and Turtle' along with shorter poems on the same theme by John Marston, George Chapman, Ben Jonson, and anonymous others. Dedicated to the Welsh-born John Salusbury, the volume presumably celebrates the latter's recent elevation to knighthood. But Shakespeare's contribution, framed in a deflationary trochaic tetrameter to express the willingness of the phoenix and turtledove to immolate themselves, and then in a jangling monorhyme to express Reason's lament, seems an implausible attempt at commemoration.

Shakespeare's motivation may well have been commercial and even self-promotional. Just as Shakespeare might have enjoyed sharing the company of young, rising poets at the turn of the new century, so might they have hoped to gain from sharing his company. Chapman's 'Peristeros, or the Male Turtle' seemingly echoes Shakespearean topoi when it emblematizes the bird as a figure of 'truth eterniz'd'.[16] Marston's 'Perfectioni Hymnus' builds to a deferential conclusion that acknowledges Shakespeare's priority in stature and ability: 'Now feebler *Genius* end thy slighter riming' (p. 187). More complicated is Shakespeare's relationship with Ben Jonson, for whom the year 1600–1 marked a turning point.[17] After the success of *Every Man Out of His Humour* in autumn 1599, Jonson renounced his earlier theatrical hackwork and devoted himself to an intensive programme of classical study, the better to fortify printed editions of his work with learned annotations and scholarly glosses.[18] The play's publication in April 1600, dedicated to gentlemen at the Inns of Court, exemplifies his new format. And Jonson's next play, *Poetaster* (1601), dramatizes his new literary preferences by depicting the banishment from Augustus's Rome of Ovid, the exemplar of an old-fashioned courtly style in his amatory elegies, here a stand-in for Petrarchan verse, and by exalting the success of Horace, the master of a renovated plain style in his satires, epistles, and commendatory epigrams.

Jonson's Horatian contributions to *Love's Martyr* ('Praeludium', 'Epos', 'Ode ενθυσιαστικη') affirm this commitment.

Shakespeare would find Jonson's posture pallid and parched when measured against the development of English poetry. It is perhaps no accident that his figure of the phoenix evokes Matthew Royden's nostalgic lament for Philip Sidney, 'An Elegie', first printed in the anthology *The Phoenix Nest* (1593), and then re-printed along with Spenser's lament for Sidney, *Astrophel*, in the volume that features *Colin Clouts Come Home Again* (1595). Royden's poem expresses a wish that Sidney's spirit might rise from the phoenix's ashes, 'an offspring neere that kinde, / But hardly a peere to that, I doubt' (212–13).[19] Shakespeare's poem makes a bid to achieve this feat as its tetrameter verse and avian imagery replicate Sidney's in the Eighth Song of *Astrophil and Stella*, 'In a grove most rich of shade, / Where birds wanton musicke made' (1–2). It is possible too that Shakespeare's figuration of the phoenix owes something in a countervalent way to Sidney's deflated version of '*phenix Stellas* state' in Sonnet 92 of *Astrophil and Stella*, as well as to other representations of the phoenix in Petrarchan sonnets by Lodge, William Smith, Giles Fletcher the Elder, and Michael Drayton.[20] From Shakespeare's perspective, such late-Elizabethan lyrics afford warmer delight than the cold comfort inscribed in his rival's Horatian verse. Unlike the playwright of *Poetaster*, Shakespeare would never banish Ovid or Petrarch from his poetic pantheon.

Shakespeare in fact defiantly reprises the tetrameter and Elizabethan ballad forms of his early-middle plays and imbues them with self-parody in his later plays. The Fool's gnomic songs in *King Lear* deploy the trochaic tetrameter couplet form used for fairy spells, charms, incantations, and adjurations in *Midsummer Night's Dream*, as do Autolycus's sales-pitches in *Winter's Tale* (4.4.214–25, 301–10) and Ariel's various interventions and Prospero's epilogue in *The Tempest*. In *King Lear* (3.2.73–6), the Fool gives a dark turn to the refrain of Feste's exit song from *Twelfth Night*. A similar desolation pervades Desdemona's 'Willow Song' in *Othello* 4.3. Guiderius and Arviragus's 'Fear no more the heat o'th' sun' functions as a requiem for Innogen in *Cymbeline* 4.2.259–70. And when in *Winter's Tale* Shakespeare finally makes his peace with Greene by using the latter's romance novel *Pandosto* for his plot, he assigns Autolycus an old-fashioned ballad, 'When daffodils begin to peer' (4.3.1–22), to convey the character's free-wheeling roguery. In these final stages of his career, the poet-playwright continues to inhabit a literary world that Jonson and others had repudiated. It is no anomaly that he agreed at least tacitly, and perhaps with real enthusiasm, to the publication in 1609 of sonnets that he had drafted a decade and a half earlier.

The Sonnets and *A Lover's Complaint*

The Sonnets might seem a belated response to Jonson and his advocacy of classicized verse. Certainly they illustrate Shakespeare's abiding interest in and allegiance to the motifs, forms, and modes of the early 1590s. He had likely drafted the majority of his Sonnets in 1591–5, revising and augmenting them during the intervening period, and circulating them in manuscript among readers who transcribed and expressed their delight in them.[21] The decision to publish them – whether his or the printer's or yet someone else's – at a time when the form was no longer popular brings their author and us back to that pivotal moment in 1592 when Nashe's taunt and Greene's insult spurred him to test his competence against the canonical poetry of that time. In 1591 Thomas Newman's piratical edition of Sidney's *Astrophil and Stella* (with an introduction by the self-promoting Nashe), ignited a sonnet-craze that burned for three years.[22] Sidney's sequence abounds in knowing allusions to Petrarch and continental Petrarchism, echoed conspicuously in Sonnet 47, 'What, have I thus betrayed my libertie?', which replays the renunciation motif of Petrarch's Sonnet 169; Sonnet 71, 'Who will in fairest booke of Nature know', which duplicates the argument of Petrarch's Sonnet 248; and Sonnet 99, 'When far spent night perswades each mortall eye', which appropriates the topoi of Petrarch Sonnet 164, and of Ronsard's imitation, *Amours* 174.[23] *Astrophil and Stella* further refers to Pléiade poetic theories in Sonnets 3, 6, 15, 28, and 74. Daniel's *Delia*, published piratically with *Astrophil and Stella* and then revised in 1592 and in subsequent editions, refers to poems by Petrarch, Tasso, Desportes, and others.[24] Watson's *The Teares of Fancie* (1593) incorporates echoes from Petrarch and Gascoigne. Lodge's *Phyllis* (1593) offers direct translations from Petrarch, Ronsard, Desportes, and others. Twenty homoerotic sonnets addressed to a young man in Richard Barnfield's *Cynthia* (1594) gesture toward Ronsard's anacreontic verse. Shakespeare also had the precedent of Watson's above mentioned *Hekatompathia* (1582), a volume of translations from Petrarch, Serafino, Ariosto, Ronsard, and others, which includes snatches from the original Italian and French texts as well as commentaries on their sources, analogues, and moral import. And if he could keep his sides from splitting while reading it, he had the lumbering, unintentionally funny precedent of John Swoothern's *Pandora* (1584) with its hendecasyllabic translations of poems from Ronsard, Du Bellay, and Desportes.

Daniel, Watson, Lodge, Barnfield, and Swoothern serve their Petrarchism straight up with results that elicit curiosity, admiration, and occasional laughter. *Astrophil and Stella* and the Petrarchan poems distributed throughout Gascoigne's novella *The Adventures of Master FJ* (1573, offering eight sonnets) and Nashe's novella *Unfortunate Traveller* (1594, sustaining a fictionalized characterization of Henry Howard, earl of Surrey, two sonnets, and a ballad) more knowingly transmit their Petrarchism through witty, ironic, self-deprecating speakers overpowered by their passions to anguished, often hilarious defeat.[25] The lesson of these poets was to canonize the form through self-conscious references to the continental Petrarchism upon which it was based. So what did Shakespeare do? Each had mined Petrarch and Ronsard, and Daniel, Lodge, and Swoothern had drawn from Desportes as well. Shakespeare largely avoided these models. But he might have gone to a younger, lesser known, often irreverent member of the French Pléiade who had fashioned his own dark lady in a clever send-up of his elders' Petrarchan sonneteering. Etienne Jodelle in his aptly and provocatively titled *Contr'amours* (published 1574), a mini-sequence of seven poems ripe enough for quick and greedy plucking, offered just such a palinodic representation of adulterous love gone awry, one capable of winning the approval of London's savvy readership.[26] Shakespeare's analogous dark lady sonnets 127–52 appear to be his earliest efforts in the genre. But a parallel and more ambitious series seems to have followed closely upon it. The year 1591 marked the publication not only of Sidney's and Daniel's sequences, but also of Spenser's *Complaints*, which, as we have seen, offered English readers a view of Petrarch and Du Bellay as poets with more than amatory interests, and as poets whose meditations on past, present, and future history drew as well upon classical texts from Virgil, Horace, and Ovid. Even Daniel had incorporated Horatian and Ovidian 'eternizing' motifs into his sonnets about Delia. And so would Shakespeare in his eternizing sonnets in the procreation group (1–17) and in Sonnets 63–77. Behind them looms the Spenserian precedent in *Complaints* and possibly some encounter with the Italian and French poets who showed Spenser how to cross-pollinate Petrarchan forms with the matter of classical elegy.

Such poems as Sonnets 65 and 74 display Shakespeare's skills in using Ovidian materials, but they also display his skills in appropriating continental Petrarchism. In *Romeo and Juliet*, Mercutio jabs at 'the numbers that Petrarch flowed in' (2.3.35), and these numbers must have attracted the poet's attention. We've already noted one of Petrarch's most famous poems, Sonnet 248, as the model for Sidney's Sonnet 71, which dispenses with the Italian poet's *memento mori* warning and poetic boast. Shakespeare's Sonnets 65 and 74 echo this theme while reinstating Petrarch's admonition (65: 'How with this rage shall beauty hold a plea') and poetic challenge (74: 'My life hath in this line some interest'). But these sonnets go beyond any simple debt to Petrarch. Ronsard, too, had used the

Italian poem as a model for the first sonnet of *Les amours*, 'Qui voudra voyr comme un Dieu me surmonte'.

Praised by his compatriots as 'the prince of poets' and 'the poet of princes', Ronsard attracted celebrity in England, if not widespread imitation there.[27] Sidney, Spenser, Daniel, Watson, and Lodge all acknowledged him, and John Eliot's *Ortho-epia Gallica* (1593) commended him. What if Shakespeare, like his worldly, university-educated contemporaries, had dipped into Ronsard's poetry, not as a scholar hunting for sources, but as a gifted wordsmith or as an ambitious and cosmopolitan author curious about literary production beyond the Channel? No convincing evidence exists that Shakespeare directly imitated an entire poem in any foreign tongue. But tantalizing hints suggest that Shakespeare conducts a dialogue with continental authors and with English counterparts who professed to borrow from them.[28] For example, Ronsard's *Sonnets pour Hélène*, the last great sonnet sequence of his *Oeuvres*, represents the poet's career-threatening rivalry with Desportes, whom Lodge admired enough to translate. Such contestation evokes Shakespeare's own rival-poet Sonnets 79–86, in whose aftermath the speaker retreats from his young man in a gesture ('Farewell, thou art too dear for my possessing', 87) which resonates with Ronsard's 'Adieu, cruelle, adieu, je te suis ennuyeux' (*Hélène* 2.53). Elusive echoes, strategically placed, remind us that Greene's 'upstart Crow' might just have sought out more bounty in alien tongues than even his contemporaries credited him with.

When at the turn of the century Shakespeare revisited his Sonnets, elite literary taste was changing. 'The Phoenix and Turtle' summons the state of poetry at this pivotal moment, and the Sonnets that Shakespeare likely wrote at this time address the situation. Sonnet 110, 'Alas 'tis true, I have gone here and there', concurs with a sort of newly fashioned *flâneur* verse that positions the speaker as a witty observer of his own and others' misconduct. Sonnet 114 records his perceptions of fawning behaviour in high places, typifying the sycophancy and factionalism of James I's nascent court. Sonnets 124 and 125 contrast such 'policy' and 'outward honouring' with the speaker's avowal of his own constancy. These poems slyly undercut Jonson's famous proclamation to 'dwell as in my Centre, as I can', a boast made even as the latter's compass gravitated more and more toward the preferences of his patrons.[29] Shakespeare's speaker proclaims his own compass a flawed one, but one grounded in an honest attachment: 'If I have ranged, / Like him that travels I return again' (Sonnet 109). One sign of its steadiness is his use of the sonnet form itself, varied yet unvarying, and endorsed by him even and especially when it had fallen out of favour.

Viewed from this perspective, the final revised form of the first sixty Sonnets concurs with the aesthetic trajectory traced above. If Sonnets

65 and 74 filter Ovidian mutability through a distant recall of Petrarch's Sonnet 248, then Sonnet 17 – the last of the procreation Sonnets as published – now evokes the Italian model more boldly: 'Who will believe my verse in time to come.' Sonnet 22, 'My glass shall not persuade me I am old', recalls Ronsard's 'Quand vous serez bien vieille, au soir à la chandelle' (*Hélène* 2.24), and Sonnet 32 replicates the fantasy of this same poem as its speaker imagines the young man's regret, 'Had my friend's Muse grown with this growing age' (cf. Hélène's regretful 'Ronsard me celebroit du temps que j'estois belle', 2.24). And if Shakespeare had earlier acknowledged the pre-eminence of Sidney and Spenser in conferring such continental sophistication upon English poetry, he now affirms their pre-eminence by sharpening his echoes of their sonnets.

In Sonnet 4, for example, the rhyme words 'spend/lend' and the figure of unacceptable 'audit' recall those in Sonnet 18 of *Astrophil and Stella*; in Sonnet 21, the contrast of an artificial 'muse' with one who inspires genuine 'love' and 'beauty' recalls Sidney's Sonnet 3; in Sonnets 27 and 28, the contrast of 'night/day' and 'sight/light' draws upon the constricted rhymes of these same words in Sidney's Sonnets 89 and 99; and in Sonnets 50 and 51, the figurations of horsemanship and desire draw upon those in Sidney's Sonnets 49 and 84. References to Spenser's mature sonnets prove equally compelling. Shakespeare's effort to fashion a natural analogue in Sonnet 18, 'Shall I compare thee to a summer's day', replicates Spenser's *Amoretti* 9, 'Long-while I sought to what I might compare'; his effort to sustain a figuration of the young man as a rose in Sonnet 54, 'The rose looks fair, but fairer we it deem', recalls *Amoretti* 26, 'Sweet is the rose, but growes upon a brere'; and his effort to eternize the young man's worth amid the mutable tides of Sonnet 60, 'Like as the waves make towards the pebbled shore', addresses *Amoretti* 75, 'One day I wrote her name upon the strand.'

The concentration of these echoes among the first sixty Sonnets should give us pause. Spenser's *Amoretti* did not appear in print until 1595, two years after the poet-playwright had likely drafted the first hundred or so of his own Sonnets. Even if by 1593 Shakespeare had access to some of Spenser's early sonnets in manuscript, he still took materials from later poems in *Amoretti* which celebrate the poet's marriage in June 1594. These materials re-appear in sonnets that Shakespeare likely composed after the turn of the century, and they also influence his revisions of Sonnets 1–60 at that time or later. For example, Sonnet 106, 'When in the chronicle of wasted time', echoes Sonnet 69 in the *Amoretti*, 'The famous warriors of the anticke world.'[30] The speakers of both poems describe their competition with ancient poets to immortalize the objects of their praise. But the distinctive quality of *Amoretti*, followed by *Epithalamion*, is that it celebrates connubial love and married chastity. Shakespeare in his Sonnets faces the challenge of confronting this Spenserian precedent and adapting it to his sequence about love between men marred by the younger man's self-absorption and by their mutually sordid relationship with a dark lady. Shakespeare redeems this experience with poetry that expresses the profoundest longing and desire, self-loathing and self-doubt, and persistent moral contradiction amid all the exaltation or aversion that the situation might evoke. It makes dramatic turmoil the very stuff of his Sonnets.

With yet one more addition: just as Spenser's *Amoretti* had ended with his *Epithalamion* (and before that, Daniel's *Delia* with *The Complaint of Rosemond* and Lodge's *Phyllis* with *The Complaint of Eldstred*), so Shakespeare's Sonnets conclude with *A Lover's Complaint*. Cast in the stanzaic form of *Lucrece*, the poem abounds in archaisms that evoke Spenser's diction, if not exactly his lyric style.[31] Its narrative, however, is far too astringent and its figurative syntax too complicated to be compared with Spenser's. It tells of a young woman seduced by an appealing but curiously androgenous young man. Undermining her own best efforts to teach by moral example (' "But ah, whoever shunned by precedent / The destined ill she must herself assay" ', 155–6), she recounts his speech of seduction which demolished her resistance. In this way, the poem links a female complaint of ruin and abandonment to a male complaint of frustration and unrequited love. For his part, the young man remains coolly detached as he describes how he thwarted the longing of women whose 'deep-brained sonnets' (209) fell on his deaf ears, even as he heats up the urgency of his own plea to the woman who is rejecting him now. The poem ends in stasis with the latter's iteration that if she had it all to do over, ' "all that borrowed motion, seeming owed, / Would yet again betray the fore-betrayed" ' (327–8). Its conclusion can be thought of as both a homage to and a resistance against Spenser, an anti-epithalamion that expresses the frank and unrepentant acceptance of an intolerable, transgressive love experienced at great expense, a triumph of the flesh reined in by the acknowledgement of the pain and vexation that accompany it.

Conclusion

Shakespeare's poetic achievement, then, mirrors the development of English poetry in his time. The sonnet form so prevalent in his plays both early and late, whether in full structure (in *Love's Labour's Lost*, *Romeo and Juliet*, and *All's Well That Ends Well*) or in truncated mode (as in *Two Gentlemen of Verona* and *Much Ado About Nothing*), mirrors the Tudor fascination with that form from the days of Wyatt and Surrey through the rise of lyric anthologies to the emergence in the 1570s and 1580s of distinct authorial personalities such as Gascoigne, Spenser, Sidney, Daniel, and the poets of sequences published in the early 1590s. Yet side by side with this fashionable form, the lyrics of his major plays from *Taming of the Shrew* and *Midsummer Night's Dream* to *King Lear, The Winter's Tale* and *The Tempest* abound in trochaic tetrameter, the meter of popular old-style ballads as well as of Sidney's experiments in the songs of *Astrophil and Stella*. Early in his poetic career, Shakespeare established his credentials with *Venus and Adonis* by appropriating the Ovidian narrative form pioneered by Lodge and by developing it with stylistic features culled from Spenser and Marlowe. In *The Rape of Lucrece*, he reinforced these credentials by wedding the rhyme royal of the complaint mode from Chaucer to Daniel to rhetorical topoi drawn from Tudor treatises and political drama as well as from a range of texts by Greene, Nashe, Spenser, and Marlowe. In 'The Phoenix and Turtle', Shakespeare entered into the company of – and competition with – a generation of rising poets that included Jonson, Marston, and Chapman. When finally in 1609 he acquiesced to the publication of his Sonnets, he did so with the confidence of a body of work composed over a long period and brought to a finish in an era of divergent literary values. The Sonnets' deliberate echoes of Sidney, Spenser, other Elizabethan forerunners, and possibly of some continental poets as well, proclaim Shakespeare's deepest literary values and his recurrent aesthetic convictions.

NOTES

1 Robert Greene, *Menaphon* (London, 1589), A2^{r-v}. For Shakespeare's contacts with Nashe and Greene, see Eric Sams, *The Real Shakespeare: Retrieving the Lost Years* (New Haven: Yale University Press, 1995), pp. 49–59; Ernst Honigman, *Shakespeare's Lost Years*, 2nd edn (Manchester University Press, 1998), pp. 59–76; Katherine Duncan-Jones, *Ungentle Shakespeare*, Arden Shakespeare (London: Thomson Learning, 2001), pp. 54–81; and Stephen Greenblatt, *Will in the World* (New York: Norton, 2004), pp. 149–74. For London's literary culture at the time, see Dennis Kay, *William Shakespeare: Sonnets and Poems* (London: Prentice Hall, 1998), pp. 1–23.

2 *Greene's Groats-worth of wit, bought with a million of repentance* (London, 1592), F1^v.

3 See Laura Hunt Yungblut, *Strangers Here Amongst Us: Policies, Perceptions, and the Presence of Aliens in Elizabethan England* (London: Routledge, 1996), pp. 29–35 and 51–60. For Shakespeare's contact with them, see William J. Kennedy, '*Les Langues des hommes sont pleines de tromperies*: Shakespeare, French Poetry, and Alien Tongues' in *Textual Conversations in the Renaissance*, ed. Zachary Lesser and Benedict Robinson (Aldershot: Ashgate, 2006), pp. 77–97.

4 Specific echoes between *Venus and Adonis* and *Hero and Leander* include their shared Narcissus references (*VA* 161–2 > *HL* 74–5), procreation arguments (*VA* 163–74 > *HL* 223–54), horse metaphors (*VA* 263–70 > *HL* 625–9), and depictions of contrarieties (*VA* 1135–64 > *HL* 386–482).

5 See Frederick Ahl, *Metaformations: Soundplay and Wordplay in Ovid and Other Classical Poets* (Ithaca: Cornell University Press, 1985), pp. 254–62.

6 Quotations from *Elizabethan Minor Epics*, ed. Elizabeth Story Donno (New York: Columbia University Press, 1963). For Ovidianism in Renaissance poetry, see C. S. Lewis, *English Literature in the Sixteenth Century Excluding Drama* (Oxford: Clarendon Press, 1954).

7 For Spenser's approach to Petrarch, see A. Kent Hieatt, 'The Genesis of Shakespeare's *Sonnets*', *PMLA* 98 (1983), 800–14; William J. Kennedy, *Authorizing Petrarch* (Ithaca: Cornell University Press, 1994), pp. 195–280.

8 Among the lines just quoted, the first evokes 'They pray to Time, which all things doth devowre' (*Ruines of Rome* 3), the second 'And darkned was the welkin all about' (*Visions of Petrarch* 3), the third 'Lo, all is nought but flying vanitee' (*Visions of Bellay*, 1). Quotations from Spenser refer to *Poetical Works*, ed. J. Smith and E. de Selincourt (Oxford University Press, 1912).

9 For antecedents of such procedures in scriptural exegesis, see Carol V. Kaske, *Spenser and Biblical Poetics* (Ithaca: Cornell University Press, 1999), pp. 65–97.

10 For Shakespeare's use of Ovid's *Fasti* and its medieval progeny, see Jonathan Bate, *Shakespeare and Ovid* (Oxford: Clarendon Press, 1993), pp. 65–82.

11 Robert Greene, *Plays*, ed. Thomas H. Dickinson (New York: Scribner's, 1909), 2.2, p. 341.

12 Nashe, *Selected Writings*, ed. Stanley Wells (Cambridge, MA: Harvard University Press, 1965), p. 250. The parallels continue. Upon sating his lust, Nashe's rapist sinks into depravity, echoing the rape of Lavinia in *Titus Andronicus* ('Her husband's dead body he made a pillow to his abomination', 252). Cf. *Titus Andronicus* 2.3.129–30.

13 See Patrick Cheney, *Shakespeare, National Poet–Playwright* (Cambridge University Press, 2004), pp. 108–40.

14 Qtd from *The Complete Works of Christopher Marlowe*, ed. Fredson Bowers, 2 vols. (Cambridge University Press, 1973), II: 275–306. See David Riggs, *The World of Christopher Marlowe* (New York: Henry Holt, 2004), pp. 306–8.

15 See *Paradise of Dainty Devices* (Menston: Scolar Press, 1972). The quotations that follow refer to Watson, *The Hekatompathia, or Passionate Centurie of Love*, facsimile of 1582 edition, introd. S. K. Heninger, Jr (Gainesville: Scholars' Facsimiles & Reprints, 1964); Sidney, *The Poems*, ed. William Ringler (Oxford: Clarendon Press, 1962); and *Tottel's Miscellany (1557–1587)*, ed. Hyder Edward Rollins, 2 vols., 2nd edn (Cambridge, MA: Harvard University Press, 1965). For books that Shakespeare might have encountered, see Robert Miola, *Shakespeare's Reading* (Oxford University Press, 2000).

16 Quotations refer to *Robert Chester's 'Loves Martyr'*, ed. Alexander B. Grosart (London, 1878), here cited from p. 188.

17 For the 'poets' war' that recruited Marston and Dekker against Jonson, see James P. Bednarz, *Shakespeare and the Poets' War* (New York: Columbia University Press, 2001), especially pp. 105–33 on Shakespeare's response; and James

Shapiro, *Rival Playwrights: Marlowe, Jonson, Shakespeare* (New York: Columbia University Press, 1991), pp. 133–90.

18 David Riggs, *Ben Jonson: A Life* (Cambridge, MA: Harvard University Press, 1989), pp. 63–8.

19 *The Phoenix Nest*, ed. Hyder Edward Rollins (Cambridge, MA: Harvard University Press, 1931).

20 See Richard Allen Underwood, *'The Phoenix and the Turtle': A Survey of Scholarship* (Salzburg: Institut für englische Sprache und Literatur, 1974), pp. 190–239. Further comparisons with the paradoxes of two-in-one in such poems by John Donne as 'The Canonization' and 'The Dreame' seem too inexact to claim the latter's influence, though as Bednarz speculates in this volume, it may be possible that Donne echoes Shakespeare.

21 See A. Kent Hieatt, Charles Hieatt, and Anne Lake Prescott, 'When did Shakespeare Write Sonnets 1609?' *Studies in Philology* 88 (1991), 69–109; *Shakespeare's Sonnets*, ed. Katherine Duncan-Jones, Arden 3rd series (London: Thomas Nelson, 1997), pp. 1–28, 45–69, and 85–102; and *Complete Sonnets and Poems*, ed. Colin Burrow (Oxford University Press, 2002), pp. 91–138.

22 See Thomas P. Roche, Jr, *Petrarch and the English Sonnet Sequences* (New York: AMS Press, 1989); Heather Dubrow, *Echoes of Desire: English Petrarschism and its Counterdiscourses* (Ithaca: Cornell University Press, 1995).

23 See William J. Kennedy, *The Site of Petrarchism* (Baltimore: Johns Hopkins University Press, 2003), pp. 163–232.

24 For Italian and French models mentioned in this paragraph, see Janet G. Scott (Espiner), *Les Sonnets Elizabéthains: Les Sources et l'apport personnel* (Paris: Champion, 1929); Anne Lake Prescott, *French Poets and the English Renaissance* (New Haven: Yale University Press, 1978).

25 See Gascoigne, *A Hundreth Sundrie Flowres*, ed. George W. Pigman III (Oxford: Clarendon Press, 2000). Among the varied poems in Gascoigne's volume are twenty-three other sonnets, including one in praise of a 'brown beautie' whose less-than-perfect 'nutbrowne face' deters him from 'the tickle track of craftie *Cupides* maze' (Poem 13).

26 Shakespeare's Sonnet 140 parallels Jodelle's Sonnet 7, 'Combien de fois mes vers ont ils doré', and Sonnet 144 carries echoes of Jodelle's Sonnet 6, 'O traistres vers, trop traistres contre moy'. Quotations from Albert-Marie Schmidt, *Poètes du XVIe siècle*, Bibliothèque de la Pléiade (Paris: Gallimard, 1953). Francis Meres had compared Jodelle to Marlowe, 'As *Iodelle*, a French tragical poet, beeing an Epicure and an Atheist, made a pitifull end: so our tragical poet *Marlowe* for his Epicureanisme and Atheisme had a tragicall death', in *Palladis Tamia* (London, 1598), 286ᵛ.

27 See Prescott, *French Poets*, pp. 76–131. Quotations from Ronsard refer to his *Œuvres complètes*, ed Jean Céard, Daniel Ménager, and Michel Simonin, Bibliothèque de la Pléiade, 2 vols. (Paris: Gallimard, 1994).

28 See parallels and analogues listed throughout in Fernand Baldensperger, *Les Sonnets de Shakespeare traduits en vers français et accompagnés d'un commentaire continu* (Berkeley: University of California Press, 1943); and in the commentaries on Sonnets 116 and 122 in Shakespeare, *The Sonnets and 'A Lover's Complaint'*, ed. John Kerrigan (Harmondsworth: Penguin, 1986); on Sonnets 22, 23, 27, 46, 47, 53, 55, 99, and 104 in Shakespeare, *The Sonnets*, ed.

G. Blakemore Evans (Cambridge University Press, 1996); and on Sonnets 7, 109, and 125 in Helen Vendler, *The Art of Shakespeare's Sonnets* (Cambridge, MA: Harvard University Press, 1997).

29 See Jonson's 'An Epistle Answering to One That Asked to be Sealed of the Tribe of Ben', line 60.

30 Cf. Cheney, *Shakespeare, Poet–Playwright*, pp. 207–38.

31 Cheney, *Shakespeare, Poet–Playwright*, pp. 239–66. For the poem's relationship to themes of seduction and betrayal in the Sonnets, see *Poems*, ed. John Roe (Cambridge University Press, 1992), pp. 61–91.

READING LIST

Bate, Jonathan. *Shakespeare and Ovid*. Oxford: Clarendon Press, 1993.

Bednarz, James P. *Shakespeare and the Poets' War*. New York: Columbia University Press, 2001.

Dubrow, Heather. *Echoes of Desire: English Petrarchism and its Counterdiscourses*. Ithaca: Cornell University Press, 1995.

Hieatt, A. Kent. 'The Genesis of Shakespeare's *Sonnets*: Spenser's *Ruines of Rome: by Bellay*'. PMLA 98 (1983), 800–14.

Kay, Dennis. *William Shakespeare: Sonnets and Poems*. London: Prentice Hall, 1998.

Kennedy, William J. '*Les Langues des hommes sont pleines de tromperies*: Shakespeare, French Poetry, and Alien Tongues'. In *Textual Conversations in the Renaissance: Ethics, Authors, and Technologies*. Ed. Zachary Lesser and Benedict Robinson. Aldershot: Ashgate, 2006, pp. 77–97.

Miola, Robert. *Shakespeare's Reading*. Oxford University Press, 2000.

Prescott, Anne Lake. *French Poets and the English Renaissance*. New Haven: Yale University Press, 1978.

Roche, Thomas P., Jr. *Petrarch and the English Sonnet Sequences*. New York: AMS Press, 1989.

2

JOHN ROE

Rhetoric, style, and poetic form

Rhetoric matters in Shakespeare's poems not least because it is the principal means of creating variety. For instance, his two narrative poems are best distinguished from each other in terms of pace; *Venus and Adonis* being swift-footed throughout, whereas *The Rape of Lucrece*, despite Tarquin's initial eagerness to encounter the woman whose description has enthralled him, moves with deliberate inevitability, like God's grinding mills. Within themselves the two poems observe a larger number of differences of stylistic effect, so that the pleasure each affords consists of any number of local peculiarities. Differences within similarity, similarity within difference, all based on the primary and underlying principle of antithesis, constitute their main appeal to the reader's imagination. Sonnet rhetoric conforms to this process in terms both of overall structural antithesis and incidental pleasure or colouring. Otherwise a sonnet sequence lacks a consistent narrative, and instead makes use of a fractured or interrupted narrative development. In Shakespeare's case this creates endless problems of interpretation and evaluation. In this chapter, I shall focus on the narrative poems, but will refer to the Sonnets under the general topic of rhetoric.

We need to use the word 'pleasure' advisedly, since from the time of the narrative poems' first composition the question of the ethical purpose, or indeed ethical justification, of such literature has contributed in large measure to the kinds of debate they engender. In some respects, *Venus and Adonis* is the easier of the two poems to discuss in terms of pleasure for the simple reason that it aims throughout to delight readers with its mischievous presentation of the predicament of love. Yet the history of its reception, particularly in recent times, makes it by no means straightforward. Despite the poem's lightness of touch, it seems to have raised any number of issues that readers have felt require serious deliberation. By contrast, *The Rape of Lucrece* insists on its seriousness from the outset; the antithesis, which unites the two poems by opposition, is anticipated in

Venus and Adonis by the dedicatory letter's reference to 'some graver labour'. *The Rape of Lucrece* in its turn worries away at the old philosophical problem: what sort of delight can be taken in a work that depicts the infliction of suffering as a result of the loss of human control. We can say that both poems in their different ways afford pleasure; but is that all that we can observe about the lighter poem, and is it an adequate thing to say of its darker counterpart? The subject of ethics is never far away from such questions. As Brian Vickers points out in his informative essay 'Rhetoric and Poetics', a concern with ethics is what brought poetics and rhetoric together, the justification for both being 'their ability to convey the teachings of moral philosophy with more powerful effect'.[1] Notwithstanding, the problem of ethics may prove to be a good deal easier for such poetry to solve than might at first appear. At the very least, examining the rhetorical nature of each poem ought to give us some interesting insights into such matters.

Venus and Adonis

This 'first heir of [Shakespeare's] invention' brings out superbly the relation of rhetoric to form. Its great principle is energy or energetic movement.[2] In *Rhetoric* 3.10–11, Aristotle brings together three elements that constitute proper or authentic poetic style: metaphor, antithesis, and liveliness (energy).[3] This last, '*energia*', Sir Philip Sidney renders as 'forcibleness' in a famous passage in the *Apology for Poetry*:

> 'those passions, which easily ... may be betrayed by that same forcibleness or *energia* (as the Greeks call it) of the writer'.[4]

Sidney is referring to the ability of a true poet to convey what a passion such as love really feels like, as opposed to what it might seem to be from external observation or academic discussion. Since we mention *energia*, we might bear in mind its counterpart, often confused with it, *enargia*. Sidney's contemporary George Puttenham usefully distinguishes between the two in his discussion of 'ornament', where he says:

> This ornament then is of two sortes, one to satisfie & delight th'eare onely by a goodly outward shew set upon the matter with wordes and speaches smothly and tunably running, another by certaine intendments or sence of such wordes & speaches inwardly working a stirre to the mynde. That first qualitie the Greekes called *Enargia*, of this word *argos*, because it geveth a glorious lustre and light. This latter they called *Energia*, of *ergon*, because it wrought with a strong and vertuous operation.[5]

When Francis Meres paid his handsome tribute to Shakespeare's poetic genius he spoke in terms that correspond most nearly with *enargia*:

> the English tongue is mightily enriched in and gorgeously invested in rare ornaments and resplendent abiliments by *Sir Philip Sidney, Spencer, Daniel, Drayton, Warner, Shakespeare, Marlow* and *Chapman*.

Focusing on Shakespeare, Meres says:

> As the soule of Euphorbus was thought to live in *Pythagoras*: so the sweete wittie soule of Ovid lives in mellifluous & honytongued *Shakespeare*, witnes his *Venus and Adonis*, his sugred Sonnets.[6]

It is important to try and get a sense of how contemporaries received the poem, especially since, in an evolving culture, subsequent generations have inevitably brought to the poem readings that speak more about their own time than Shakespeare's. Which is not to say that such readings (indeed all readings) are wrong or irrelevant. When it comes to the substance of *Venus and Adonis* any number of interpretations have been advanced, and the least we can say is that we should be wary of all of them. The most reliable are those which try to derive their understanding of the poem from its form, or at least make it consistent with its form, in the manner that Aristotle, the prime champion of form, always insisted we must.

Catherine Belsey's fine essay on *trompe l'oeil* in *Venus and Adonis* works perfectly in its Lacanian application because the key definition of desire – absence/deferral – fits exactly the antithetical style of the poem while providing a psychological interpretation appropriate to the predicament of Venus, who, despite its even-handed title, is the protagonist of the poem and the character who most gives it its bearings and definition.[7] Whether or not we would accompany Belsey in her Foucauldian claim that the poem 'marks a moment in the cultural history of desire' (Belsey, p. 271), there is no denying that her argumentative expression tones in perfectly with that of the poetic narrative. For her part, Heather Dubrow makes an important distinction between form and behaviour (or substance) when, on the Aristotelian topic of mimesis she reminds us that in pulling Adonis from his horse (l. 30), Venus is not performing an action we would expect to find in the real world but that she – or the poem – is 'mimetic in the broader sense of the word'.[8] That is, in assisting the process of mimesis, rhetoric deals in universal categories; local peculiarities of detail and significance must all contribute to the main idea.

The stanza form of *Venus and Adonis* is the sixain, i.e. six lines arranged as a quatrain followed by a couplet, rhymed as follows: *ababcc*. The lines of the stanza are set off against each other antithetically, creating an overall effect of alternating tension and balance. This last effect is most important because it enables the poem eventually to achieve closure in a purely structural manner while allowing any thematic questions that it generates to remain open or unresolved. That too reflects the antithetical nature of the poetic enterprise. When Aristotle brings together his three components, metaphor, antithesis, and *energia*, he makes the point that the first two reflect each other: metaphor works antithetically. They form part of the same process rather than co-existing separately. In the sixain everything is balanced in an interdependent way; the principle of equation means that opposition can be replaced with similarity yet the effect of antithesis maintains itself. The four lines of the quatrain and the two of the couplet stand in a ratio of 2:1 to each other. The couplet summarizes and resolves the antithesis that marks the quatrain but can also produce an antithesis of its own. We can demonstrate these characteristics from the opening stanza, distinguished like so many of the narrative units of the poem by its energetic pace:

> Even as the sun with purple-coloured face
> Had tane his last leave of the weeping morn,
> Rose-cheeked Adonis hied him to the chase;
> Hunting he loved, but love he laughed to scorn.
> Sick-thoughted Venus makes amain unto him,
> And like a bold-faced suitor gins to woo him.　　　(1–6)

We might take first the compound epithets, for which Shakespeare may have found a source of inspiration in Marlowe, who himself furnished the combination 'Rose-cheeked Adonis',[9] but he may have just as easily got such compounds as 'purple-coloured' (1), made conventional by Homer, from the *Iliad* or from a Homer-derived text. There are four such compounds (see also 'sick-thoughted', 'bold-faced'), which occur across the face of the stanza, in lines 1, 3, 5, and 6, establishing a pattern of contrast and balance in conformity with its other operations. But – most importantly – the stanza has movement: as the sun takes its leave, Adonis sets off on his mission. The stasis of contrast is beautifully offset by contrast as motion, so that the pace never threatens to flag. When it does slow down, as happens at critical moments, the mood develops appropriately, with the result that changes of speed signal transitions from one state of mind or expectation to another. The opening stanza also effectively establishes the themes that are going to dominate the poem, and that will produce the conflict between the two 'lovers' (unlike his counterpart in Ovid's *Metamorphoses*, Shakespeare's Adonis never reciprocates Venus's feelings, and so the term 'lovers' can only be applied ironically). Take the compound epithets first: 'purple-coloured' referring to the sun as red and blushing, both in the literal sense of the sun's redness and in the more figurative one of blushing guiltily, as he abandons the 'weeping morn'. Nature thus enacts the trials that human lovers undergo, love being such a perilous occupation. Venus as both goddess and woman (as the poem portrays her) serves as a link between the natural world (rendered by classical tradition as continuously manifesting divine intention) and the human world, subject to divine will and powerless to affect it. The poetic narrative casts Venus appropriately as both an agency of power (her divine status) and yet helpless to control her situation (her human side). 'Sick-thoughted' and 'bold-faced' furthermore summarize her alternating suffering and determination. 'Rose-cheeked Adonis' brings out the soft feminine in a boy who immediately and contrastingly shows a vigorous, masculine scorn of the effeminate occupation of love-making: 'Hunting he loved, but love he laughed to scorn.' It is most important, when we try to account for the terms of opposition between the two principal figures, that we remember all these contrasts, which assert themselves repeatedly in terms of the controlling antithesis that is the poem's style. It is impossible to reduce either the goddess or the youth to a single interpretation, particularly a psychologically verifiable one, though an extraordinary amount of criticism has attempted to do precisely that. Overall they are distinguished by two main and opposing characteristics, her eagerness for love and his unwillingness; everything else is a sub-category of this conflict between them.

In his *Directions for Speech and Style*, the Elizabethan critic of rhetoric John Hoskins insisted on an important point of decorum that none of his contemporaries would have disputed: that a character should always behave *in* character. An heroic man is always heroic, a fool is always foolish, a wife exposed by her waywardness should be distraught with guilt, and so on. Hoskins takes most of his examples from the *Arcadia* of Sidney, and applying his observations we may see how at their trial the princes show an overpowering nobility, despite all the charges levelled against them, how the foolish Dametas displays throughout an appropriate cowardice, and how the would-be adulterous Gynecia expresses a remorseful anguish.[10] Similarly Shakespeare's characters, as they come to a crisis, express themselves fundamentally as the persona by which we have best known them. Accordingly, in *Romeo and Juliet* the devil-may-care jocular Mercutio dies making an off-hand jest: 'Ask for me tomorrow, and you shall find me a grave man' (3.1.89–90). When Othello makes his final declaration of love for the wife he has killed, and takes his own life in remorse, it is again

according to the stylistic laws of decorum that he should speak in a
soldierly, heroic fashion:

> And say besides that in Aleppo once,
> Where a malignant and a turban'd Turk
> Beat a Venetian and traduced the state,
> I took by th' throat the circumcised dog,
> And smote him – thus. (5.2.348–52)

Any number of critics, since the days of T. S. Eliot and F. R. Leavis, have
disapproved of Othello's state of mind on various grounds. Generally,
Othello is found to be suffering from a delusion of one kind or another, the
usual analytical practice being to observe a subtle Jamesian distinction
between author and speaker, so that whatever the critic feels about such
vehement outbursts can safely be ascribed to Shakespeare's purpose. Eliot,
for examples, observes: 'I do not believe that any writer has ever exposed this
bovarysme, the human will to see things as they are not, more clearly than
Shakespeare.'[11] But Shakespeare is in fact applying a style that underpins
Othello rather than undermining him. What the tragedy requires for it to
work is both a release (in the Aristotelian understanding of that term) and an
affirmation – that he truly loved Desdemona. Anything less than that, and
the whole ending (to say nothing of all that has gone before) falls flat.
Othello cannot crawl about the stage whimpering like a cur; even less so
can the audience harbour doubts as to his true motives. Besides, he has
acquired enough humility moments earlier when confronting the fact that
he has deprived himself of his wife. If affirmation is to be achieved, it must
occur plausibly, and the heroic, manly way is what comes most naturally to
this particular hero, whatever reservations we may now, outside *our* character as audience, entertain about both the military and the masculine
disposition.

If Othello is essentially bravery, then Venus is all love. The poem notes this
with sympathetic yet mischievous irony when Shakespeare says of her: 'She's
love, she loves, and yet she is not loved' (610). Whereas Othello is intense and
concentrated in his role as the soldier-lover, Venus is characterized by
variety, indeed 'infinite variety', as Enobarbus remarks of the dramatic
persona who most resembles her, Cleopatra. The mistake that commentators, bent on interpretation, make is to choose one or other aspect of her
behaviour and decide that this is what she means. Either that or to deplore
her different attempts at wooing Adonis as so many underhand stratagems –
even to the point of adopting Adonis's objection that she wilfully confuses
love with lust (793–810). But as Belsey points out, it is not Venus's business
to distinguish love from lust.[12] After all, why should she? They are difficult to

distinguish at the best of times. For Venus love is everything, as the poem's rhetoric demonstrates: every possible manifestation from tender concern to voracious appetite finds expression through her; and all of this is according to nature. What you will not find in her is anything so artificial as the identification of love with a man-made principle such as chastity. In this respect the world of nature (Venus) is in permanent conflict with that of reason or rational restraint (partly represented by Adonis).

Unlike Marlowe's poem, *Hero and Leander*, only one of the lovers is – as we have remarked – mortal. Venus varies between the mortal and the immortal according to what task Shakespeare at any moment asks her to perform. In her he demonstrates nature in its plenitude, as various examples illustrate. Venus gives the poet every opportunity to demonstrate what Erasmus called *copia* (or the amplification of stylistic effect creating richness of eloquence) and what Meres describes in terms approximating to *enargia* (as discussed above).[13] The poem insists on the principle of beauty, partly through Venus herself but more emphatically through her perception of Adonis, which is largely how Adonis is realized for us. Everything in the narrative sparkles with Venus's love of him, and as that love is denied, so the frustrations in love are rendered beautiful. Shakespeare adapts the truth of a traditional Petrarchan sonnet in describing how anger or contempt registers itself as becoming for the lover who suffers it mercilessly:

> At this Adonis smiles as in disdain,
> That in each cheek appears a pretty dimple;
> Love made those hollows, if himself were slain
> He might be buried in a tomb so simple,
>   Foreknowing well, if there he came to lie,
>   Why there love lived, and there he could not die.   (241–6)

We are invited to dwell on local details such as these in and for themselves, they being what the Elizabethans were pleased to call 'pretty conceits'. They would threaten to detract from the narrative were it not that they scrupulously follow the same antithetical structure that informs the poem in every aspect. Thematically the stanza just quoted has an interesting displacing effect in that it touches, however lightly, on the subject of mortality, which will contribute significantly to the poem's denouement, and varies the antithesis – which is largely and amusingly played out between improbable male chastity and unusual female importunity – by alerting us to the greater and more poignant, eventual conflict of death and love. In the meantime, the poem intends to amuse, especially throughout this early stage. As well as doing this by wordplay, it achieves the effect by inverting the customary Petrarchan mode, whereby the lady torments the lover, and has her suffer such oppression herself. The poem's use of Petrarchism, which, despite the antithetical style, often receives less critical attention than Ovid as an influence, reminds us that Adonis is constructed according to the terms of Petrarchan love: in him Shakespeare has fashioned a woman insisting on chastity in the guise of a man.

We come back now to the question of ethics which we raised at the beginning. As Vickers observes, rhetoric is closely involved with ethics: speaking well is speaking true.[14] However, in disputation, which makes the fullest use of rhetoric, ethical positions tend naturally to be subjective, which increases the element of persuasion in speech. In *Venus and Adonis* therefore, we weigh the sense of Adonis's attack on lust but we know that that is just one argument among many, and that several of Venus's debates, such as her argument for preferring procreativity over abstinence, can be put forward against it, as indeed happens in the poem continuously. Unlike the plays, where arguments come to a head, we are never obliged to choose, or more precisely, face the consequences of choice. On the contrary, to make a choice would be to destroy the antithetical structure on which everything in the poem is so finely balanced. The poignancy of the end is a way of closing the poem on an appropriate note of sorrow, but it does nothing to resolve the various arguments, for and against love, that its speakers advance throughout. It is quite wrong therefore to read the boar's killing of Adonis as symbolic of Venus's immoderate desire, as many critics have assumed.[15] As a way of *interpreting* the poem such readings completely ignore stylistic imperative. According to Hoskins, everything must be in character: it is entirely in Venus's character, as the principle of love, that she cannot imagine the boar's attentions to Adonis as being other than amorous:

> "Tis, true, 'tis true, thus was Adonis slain:
> He ran upon the boar with his sharp spear,
> Who did not whet his teeth at him again,
> But by a kiss thought to persuade him there;
>   And nuzzling in his flank, the loving swine
>   Sheathed unaware the tusk in his soft groin.'   (1111–16)

Need we point out that at this moment Venus's feelings are not immoderately sexual, even if sex markedly defines them, but tender and maternal, and prepare us subtly for the poem's final transition to a vision of Venus as mother-figure at the close?

At present a number of critics are reluctant to observe the lessons of rhetoric and seek interpretation of various kinds. In his chapter on 'Sexual Poetry', for example, Jonathan Bate makes much of the issue of incest in Shakespeare's Ovidian source and sees the fate of Myrrha, whose illicit desire for her own father resulted in the birth of Adonis, as 'an ironic darkening pre-text' for all that is transgressive in Venus and Adonis.[16] This is to set great store by a motif that hardly finds acknowledgement in Shakespeare's poem, as Anthony Mortimer points out:

> Yet if Shakespeare ever does recall Myrrha he does so in a very marginal and oblique fashion ... the allusion to 'thy mother' grows so naturally out of 'Art thou a woman's son' that one is not invited to stop and inquire who that mother might have been.[17]

Not only that but to insist on one aspect of Ovid, an aspect which doubtless appeals to the sensibility of today, ignores the more positive qualities that can also be gleaned in the Roman original. Shakespeare, a typical Elizabethan poet, tended to hold such things in balance, as his poem testifies.

The Rape of Lucrece

If the question of ethics is managed discreetly in *Venus and Adonis*, the reason for this is that no character performs an action that is truly culpable. Venus might be inclined towards promiscuity or lasciviousness in the eyes of some readers but she does nothing to harm Adonis. On the contrary, she does everything to protect him from danger, and his death results from his own determination to hunt the boar – a point that those who see her as *symbolically* destroying him need to bear in mind. *The Rape of Lucrece* contrasts greatly with the situation in the earlier poem, in that it contains two actions that may be regarded as morally culpable, and each of the major characters performs one of them. Tarquin is guilty of raping Lucrece, while she is guilty of taking her own life, suicide being regarded as sinful in the Christian culture in which Shakespeare writes the poem. Although the poem tells a Roman tale, it is clear from the way in which Lucrece reasons, both with herself and with her family who try to stay her hand, that she knows that her suicide will be judged adversely. Against this she shows a strong concern for her posthumous reputation as a chaste woman. The conflict accords with and indeed reinforces the poem's antithetical style. Within Roman society the blame attaching to her 'self-slaughter' was outweighed by admiration of her stoical purpose, since stoicism made suicide morally acceptable. Furthermore, in the story as Livy tells it, she proves an honourable sacrifice to the cause of republicanism. But Shakespeare's version of the legend came with disapproving comments by St Augustine, who insisted that no woman whose conscience was clear need fear the stigma of physical violation.[18] Shakespeare's heroine is struggling with the Augustinian objection, when, in answer to the general protest that '[h]er body's stain her mind untainted clears' (1710), she nonetheless asserts the need to secure for herself the reputation of chastity as she best understands it, and that means giving up her life. Just as she is about to die, she shows perhaps greater concern for her responsibility for the good name of women than for her obligations to God:

> 'No, no', quoth she, 'no dame hereafter living
> By my excuse shall claim excuse's giving.'   (1714–15)

All of this makes the second of Shakespeare's two long narrative poems a more sombre affair by far than the first. In *Lucrece* the erotic is entwined with guilt in a deep and pervasive way, compared with the comically guilty eroticism that appears in *Venus and Adonis*.

We must ask ourselves what, in terms of rhetorical style, is the topic of *The Rape of Lucrece*. That is to say, what gives the poem its life, or calls upon its *energia*? The answer is quite clear: the focus is on Lucrece herself and on her suffering. Shakespeare may, if he had access to a manuscript of Sidney's *Apology for Poetry* (it was not published till 1595, a year after the poem), have found his cue in the description of her given memorably there: 'the constant though lamenting look of Lucretia, when she punished in herself another's fault'. The form of the book as published in the first quarto of 1594 provides sufficient evidence. The title-page reads simply *Lucrece*, whereas *The Rape of Lucrece* appears as the running-title, editors being thus divided over whether to give the one title or the other to the poem.[19]

Lucrece then is the focus of interest and the rape she undergoes explains why she deserves such prominence. In the first part of the narrative (roughly one third of its length) she is subject to unbearable strain as the threat of rape is held over her; in the second part of the poem she suffers, if anything, the even more unbearable strain of having to endure its consequences. The chief of these is the fear that for as long as she lives she will seem guilty by association. The Augustinian insistence on clarity of conscience over bodily defilement does not help her. She is a Roman matron depicted by a poet of a Christian culture, but what emerges in Shakespeare's treatment is that her sense of herself (and that means our sense of ourselves) is not determined only by religious doctrine. The human includes the spiritual but in Shakespeare's view it is something more. This we can deduce from the fact that he, like various poets before him (Chaucer being one of the chief of these), obviously expected his audience to sympathize with his heroine and not condemn her for heresy.

The artistic problem facing the poet was how to maintain interest in a theme that for all its seriousness is poetically a good deal narrower than that of *Venus and Adonis*, and that does not admit of the variety of register, change of tone, and so on, that contribute to the vivacity of the earlier poem. Shakespeare's stylistic tactic is to produce an atmosphere of brooding intensity. We need to look at those features of the poem that show how he plans to do this; many of them indeed bear a structural similarity to those of *Venus and Adonis*.

The stanza form that Shakespeare opted for is that of rhyme royal, which Chaucer used for *Troilus and Criseyde*; it differs from that of the sixain, as used for the earlier narrative poem, in having one extra line. Of the seven, the fifth line, joining the quatrain to the end couplet, is pivotal. This not only makes the stanza slightly more spacious, it also gives a more reflective and ruminative dimension, as befits a poem whose subject, as well as its main speaker, is given to brooding on fate.

Along with the structural diversity that the metrical scheme allows, the poem also makes effective use once more of the Erasmian concept of *copia* (see above), a key characteristic of which is to vary and diversify the presentation of a topic in as many ways as possible in order to make the argument compelling. Trousdale gives an example from Hoskins on the taking of a city:

> For instead of saying, *he put the whole town to the sword*, let men reckon all ages and sorts and say:
>
> He neither saved the young men, as pitying the unripe flower of their youth, nor the aged men, as respecting their gravity, nor children, as pardoning their weakness, nor women, as having compassion upon their sex; soldier, clergyman, citizen, armed or unarmed, resisting or submitting, – all within the town destroyed with the fury of that bloody execution.[20]

Hoskins gives this passage as an example of *division*, following Erasmus' recommendation that an idea can be made emphatic by repeating its variant possibilities. In argument, persuasion may be achieved by saying the same thing any number of ways, as if to demonstrate the inescapability of the conclusion. In this passage the horrors of war are demonstrated by vividly depicting its effect on people of all stations, age, sex, etc. Shakespeare operates in precisely this way in *Henry V*, when the king gives the threatening speech to the citizens of Harfleur:

> Why, in a moment look to see
> The blind and bloody soldier with foul hand
> Defile the locks of your shrill-shrieking daughters;
> Your fathers taken by the silver beards,
> And their most reverend heads dashed to the walls;
> Your naked infants spitted upon pikes,
> Whiles the mad mothers with their howls confused
> Do break the clouds, as did the wives of Jewry
> At Herod's bloody-hunting slaughtermen.   (3.3.11–18)

This speech includes the device of accumulation or climax, but essentially it works as division according to the principles of *copia*. The main idea, the horror of war, can be divided up again and again and repeated with different examples. The argument becomes irrefutable in terms of persuasiveness but it also works artistically or poetically in terms of additional colouring, according to *enargia*. In *The Rape of Lucrece* the Night, Time, Opportunity digressions (and Erasmus has an important place for digression in so far as it amplifies the main argument and only departs from it in order to return as illustration) all repeat and contribute to the theme of the awful inevitability of the rape. Modern readers may well share the dismissive view of one of the poem's editors, F. T. Prince, who deplored the 'excesses of rhetoric',[21] but there can be no doubt that Shakespeare's first audience, weaned on such recommendations for the proper use of language as those of Erasmus and Hoskins, would have got the point. William Empson observes that '[i]n a play the audience wants the story to go forward, but here the Bard could practise rhetoric like five-finger exercises on the piano', not allowing for the fact that the speech from *Henry V* enacts the same rhetorical process as we find in the narrative poem.[22]

An understanding of the function of *copia* may help resolve differences in the narrative that modern critics often regard as irresolution, conflict, or aporia. Take the description of the moment of the rape. This occurs twice in the telling: the first time Lucrece is shown to be fighting desperately and attempting to cry out in protest ('For with the nightly linen that she wears / He pens her piteous clamours in her head', 680–1), and the second she is described as fainting away in terror (i.e. more passive, silent):

> Such danger to resistance did belong
>> That dying fear through all her body spread;
>> And who cannot abuse a body dead? (1265–7)

Realistically both of these responses (resisting and not resisting) cannot be true at the same time, but *division* in accordance with *copia* shows them contributing to the theme in contrasting and diverse ways, rhetorically reinforcing the image of female plight.

Deeper than the theme of rape itself is that of lamentation. Lucrece keens as a woman who has suffered abuse for which there can be no redress. In suffering, Lucrece, again according to the principle of division, invokes other versions of affliction to aid the portrayal of her own. Or rather Shakespeare does this for her. That is why she goes to look at the painting of the Fall of Troy. The true focal point of all the suffering she observes there is that of another woman, Hecuba, in whom she finds the greatest release for her own pain:

> To this well-painted piece is Lucrece come,
> To find a face where all distress is stelled.
> Many she sees where cares have carved some,
> But none where all distress and dolour dwelled;
> Till she despairing Hecuba beheld,
>> Staring on Priam's wounds with her old eyes,
>> Which bleeding under Pyrrhus' proud foot lies.
>
> In her the painter had anatomised
> Time's ruin, beauty's rack, and grim care's reign;
> Her cheeks with chops and wrinkles were disguised;
> Of what she was no semblance did remain.
> Her blue blood turned to black in every vein,
>> Wanting the spring that those shrunk pipes had fed,
>> Showed life imprisoned in a body dead.   (1443–56)

The suffering of Hecuba, a matron like Lucrece but one who is older and with an even greater burden of grief to bear, helps extend the degree and significance of Lucrece's own fate, as well as concentrating and intensifying the experience. The rhetorical technique of *division* develops the theme of rape, and shows how it can be applied to varied effect. Although unlike Lucrece she has not been violated in her own person, Hecuba embodies the pillage and desecration of the city, which has been betrayed by Sinon, Tarquin's counterpart in treachery.

It is important that we should see things in their proper order as the poem presents them, for many commentators have argued that the political question, especially regarding its republican aspect, is dominant not secondary or merely illustrative.[23] A good deal of the thinking along republican lines is already neatly encapsulated by Empson, who in a few provocative sentences argues that the Troy scene 'was written later as a substitute for dangerous thoughts about royalty; Lucrece when appealing to Tarquin flatters his assumptions by recalling the virtues of royalty, and the highly formal structure of the work demands that she should recognise the inadequacy of such ideals after her appeal has failed' (pp. 9–10).

On the contrary, the Troy scene has been in preparation for some time, purely in terms of the imagery, or *enargia*, which has gone into the presentation of the theme of violation, starting not just with the following lines spoken by Lucrece about her soul,

> Her house is sacked, her quiet interrupted,
> Her mansion batt'red by the enemy;
> Her sacred temple spotted, spoiled, corrupted,
> Grossly engirt with daring infamy,   (1170–3)

but also in this stanza which describes the state of mind, or specifically state of soul, of one of the protagonists immediately following the rape:

> She says her subjects with foul insurrection
> Have battered down her consecrated wall,
> And by their mortal fault brought in subjection
> Her immortality, and made her thrall
> To living death and pain perpetual;
>   Which in her prescience she controlled still,
>   But her foresight could not forestall their will.   (722–8)

This soul, feminized in accordance with the principle of violation to which it has been subjected, belongs not, as one might imagine, to Lucrece but to Tarquin. Rhetorically it is possible to switch genders with the greatest of ease, just as it is possible to exercise great flexibility in the crossing from personal to political, but we have to remember the purpose that such crossings and transfiguring serve. Tarquin's soul is in turmoil as he realises that his transgression could not have been greater. He has visited this violation on himself as well as on his victim. That is the point of his kingship (or burgeoning kingship, as he is heir to the throne); it serves to give the poem a greater sense of moment. Contrary to the Empsonian view that such behaviour by a regal person calls royalty into question, the betrayal of obligation in Tarquin's unkingly conduct works in the opposite way, dramatizing the enormity of the betrayal precisely by invoking the powerful and traditional belief in the duty of the monarch to his subjects. The stronger the ideal of royalty the better it works in terms of the image of treachery.

A Lover's Complaint

The ease with which genders may be exchanged (as the example of the soul's 'batt'red mansion' makes clear) raises a point about *A Lover's Complaint*. In that poem the wronged maid, in telling her story to the 'father' who sympathetically attends her, impersonates the voice of her abuser, so much so that she even seems to plead for him out of her own mouth. The poem performs this task according to the principle of synecdosis, whereby opposites are unexpectedly brought together, as Heather Dubrow demonstrates in her discussion of *The Rape of Lucrece* (Dubrow, pp. 80–142). Interestingly, the maid reports the young man as beginning his seductive oratory immediately after she herself has echoed the passage from *Lucrece* to which we have just referred: 'And long upon these terms I held my city/Till thus he 'gan besiege me' (176–7). In the event, the suitor addresses the object of his attention as if *he*, and not she, were the passive female, besought by so many aspiring lovers, plying him with the traditional Petrarchan gifts of trinkets and sonnets. No wonder that the lady, subject to this dizzying transfer of identities, finds herself – as if a male lover – actively pursuing what amounts to her own destruction. The poem's title, which has regularly puzzled readers and their editors, works in a dual fashion. They are *both* lovers: she pronounces the overall, controlling complaint, while he voices his complaint within hers. Whereas the rhetoric of *The Rape of Lucrece* does its best to defend the innocence of its protagonist as if she were truly uncompromised, that of *A Lover's Complaint* enters into the innermost core of the female psyche and argues relentlessly that the capacity for betrayal lies there.

Sonnet rhetoric

The Sonnets have generated endless questions over their biographical context, the problem of identification being the chief of these. Who was the 'young man right fair'? Who was the dark lady (incidentally not a collocation that ever occurs in the sequence)? Rhetorically, however, they perform a simple task with great accomplishment. The Sonnets speak of the contrasting joys and woes of love but they do so only partly within the dominant Petrarchan tradition, which places the emphasis on frustration, on hopes cut short, and on the withholding of affection by the beloved. On the contrary, we find many examples of a joy possessed, especially in the sonnets to the young man. We also find, in contrast to this, sonnets that plumb the depths of despair. The importance of such emotion is that it is grounded on real, lived experience, not merely on hope or illusion, and what gives it strength is the recognition of such experiences as love turning to hate or love betrayed, which fall strictly outside the Petrarchan mode. The sense of betrayal is indeed one of the most powerful of all feelings and it is interestingly one that is common to both the young man and dark woman sections of the Sonnets. It cuts across questions of sexuality, which have become so prevalent in discussions of the Sonnets. Sex merely speaks of kinds of love (how homoerotic? how heterosexual?), not its intensity, which is the true appeal of the poetry. Kinds of love are in fact subordinate to the theme of love's force or power, which in this sequence, especially in the sonnets to the young man, draws on feelings of love that could sometimes be better described as paternal than sexual. As in the narrative poems the Sonnets work their effect antithetically to emphasize or underscore the power of love to bring about both joy and suffering. Whatever the biographical context (which is now likely never to be known), and whatever the *nature* of the love, the intensity of feeling could not be starker or more clear, as all readers can attest by what they bring from personal experience.

Take as an example the contrasts that are expressed in Sonnet 90:

> Then hate me when thou wilt, if ever, now,
> Now while the world is bent my deeds to cross,
> Join with the spite of Fortune, make me bow,
> And do not drop in for an after-loss.
> Ah do not, when my heart hath scaped this sorrow,
> Come in the rearward of a conquered woe;
> Give not a windy night a rainy morrow,
> To linger out a purposed overthrow.
> If thou wilt leave me, do not leave me last,
> When other petty griefs have done their spite,
> But in the onset come; so shall I taste
> At first the very worst of Fortune's might.
> > And other strains of woe, which now seem woe,
> > Compared with loss of thee will not seem so.

The greatest sorrow the lover can envisage is naturally the loss of his love, since love being his whole purpose is what defines him. Other, lesser sorrows are more easily borne. The opening line gives highly dramatic expression to the theme, being so compressed in its articulation of the fear of being hated by the beloved that it carries something of John Donne's audacious intensity in his addresses to God in the Holy Sonnets: if you are going to do it, do it *now*. It is a piece of ingenuity, not to say great originality, to request that desertion by his lover be the first thing that should happen to him, when of course he really wants it to be the last. But this is how dramatic antithesis works, making use of the unexpected to gain the point.

Although the poem expresses fear of desertion and withdrawal of love, by its use of comparisons it gives precedence to love over hate in the end; and it receives help in this task by the familiar Shakespearean device of affirming through negation. The sonnet has any number of negative feelings, hatred, sorrow, woe, as well as negative grammatical imperatives, 'do not', 'do not', 'Give not', 'do not' (4, 5, 7, 9), all of which make its statements more forceful. As part of our 'pleasure' (see above), the poem demonstrates for us a strategy that we are all familiar with, that of anticipating the grief to come in order to soften the blow. That is the point of those imperatives: they show the speaker taking control of the situation. At the same time, we understand that in reality control is the last thing he is likely to achieve (yet another feature of antithesis). The climax, and the sonnet's greatest affirmation, comes not in the final couplet but in the lines just preceding:

> But in the onset come; so shall I taste
> At first the very worst of Fortune's might. (11–12)[24]

The idea reprises that of the sonnet's opening, with an important difference, and that is the careful placing of the word 'taste' with its positive connotations strategically at the end of the line. The logic of the sentence is simple enough: let me experience the worst immediately so that I can get it over with. The privileged position of 'taste', however, at the end of the line controlling and delaying the sense, inflects something of its own generally pleasing character into the statement. Supporting this is the expansive effect of the inverted verbal phrase 'Shall I' (not 'I shall'), and the subduing effect on 'very worst' of the more positive sounding 'At first' which holds the following words in a rhyming embrace. The imperative, which opens the two lines beginning 'But in the onset come', is also positive, as if taking command of the hatred to which he is subject, and its deployment is rather like that of Donne's injunction in 'Twickenham Garden', where assuming the posture of a mountebank he tries to subdue or make light of his grief:

> Hither with crystal vials, lovers come,
> And take my tears, which are love's wine.   (19–20)

The result is unexpectedly affirmative, and gives the emotion that is the theme of the sonnet its release. But none of this would be possible, were it not that so great a fear of loss of love only confirms the strength of love that the speaker experiences.

What then of context? It has been often observed, as Helen Vendler reminds us, that 'Sonnets 87–90 make up a small group which turn on the young man's repudiation of the speaker'.[25] In turn they form part of a larger group, which includes reciprocally the speaker's recriminations of the fair friend. What has caused the breach we shall never know, partly because it is in the nature of the fractured narrative of sonnet sequences to go tantalizingly silent at just those moments when our appetite has been whetted. Yet why do we need to know? It is the emotion of the thing that matters and not its contiguous causes. The rhetorical force and organization of the sonnet gives us all of that. Filling in the details behind the rift would be cumbersome and unnecessary, since we experience the emotion easily enough without them. That is all that matters. We might even go so far as to say that the fractured narrative is from this point of view convenient rather than frustrating: it gives us just what we need and no more. Information, which is delivered by implication, functions as it does in that passage of the picture illustrating the Fall of Troy in *The Rape of Lucrece*, where heroes are identified by synecdoche:

> For much imaginary work was there:
> Conceit deceitful, so compact, so kind,
> That for Achilles' image stood his spear,

Gripped in an armèd hand; himself behind
Was left unseen, save to the eye of mind:
A hand, a foot, a face, a leg, a head
Stood for the whole to be imaginèd.   (1422–8)[26]

'Imagined' by whom, if not by the reader? *We* are the context. What we bring
to the poem in terms of our own experience and understanding of the subject
it expresses enables it to function. The question of identities and kinds (who
was he/she, what sort of sex may they have had?) evaporates in the face of
this truth. We might reverse our earlier observation and say that in so far as
context exists it is something that the poetry invents or suggests in order to
give a semblance of locality to its theme. Far from presenting a disadvantage,
the gaps in a fractured narrative encourage us to piece out and imagine
what isn't there. There never was a young man or dark lady. We imagine
or *contextualize* them in accordance with rhetorical practice, which helps the
poem flesh itself out with imaginary dimensions. Context in the sense of
historically (or more recently culturally) determinable place and identity has
held too much sway over poem. In the case of the Sonnets, a proper attention
to the role of rhetoric will help redress the balance.

Conclusion: 'The Phoenix and Turtle'

I have argued here for a reading of the poems that places their rhetorical
properties above or before the contextual significance that may be derived
from them. Of course the political, historical, and social contexts of the work
of art inevitably have some bearing, but, as Russ McDonald has cogently
argued, such contexts have come to be overly dominant and detract attention
from the poetry in its proper function: 'there is no denying that the current
interest in historical conditions, political influences, gender conflicts, and
other such contextual phenomena, renewing and constructive though it is,
has necessarily diverted attention from the formal and material attributes of
words'.[27] What is more, such emphases distort the poem or find in it a purely
speculative significance, one that is supported only by the reader's determination to establish whatever meaning may be sought. Nowhere is this truer
than with 'The Phoenix and Turtle', a poem that has had more historical
analysis directed at it than just about any other in the Elizabethan canon.
Whatever plausibility may attach to the various historical–political interpretations to which the poem has been subject, none of them conveys the
pleasure and satisfaction that reading according to literary-rhetorical convention affords.[28] The virtue of applying a formal, Aristotelian reading to the
poetry lies in showing how accessible such poetry is from one age or audience

to another, whatever cultural differences may have intervened. Ethical considerations are subordinate to the poetry's rhetorical design, which principally serves one or other form of emotion: comic variety (*Venus and Adonis*), complex intensity (the Sonnets), or tragic pathos (*The Rape of Lucrece*). Lucrece's suffering, for example, is poetically more important than the motives or (political) consequences of the rape. For such reasons I have taken pains to demonstrate the fundamental importance of antithesis in both the narrative poems and the Sonnets, since not only do the poems demonstrate it undeniably (indeed, they make it their point) but they also show that antithesis is central to human experience, which finds itself readily reflected, with varying degrees of subtlety.

This is not, I should add, to resort to a New Critical insistence on antithesis as irony; on the contrary, I find little evidence of controlling irony in either the narrative poems or the Sonnets. It is to recover instead those principles of rhetoric that Shakespeare had learnt thoroughly and applied to all his poetic compositions, dramatic and non-dramatic alike. It is to return to the ancient sense of conflict in all its variant forms, hope versus disfavour, frustration versus desire, conscience versus will, love versus hate, life versus death, performed in a lighter key or register in *Venus and Adonis*, in a more reflectively solemn one in the *Rape of Lucrece*, and in varying pitches of intensity throughout the Sonnets.

NOTES

1 Vickers, 'Rhetoric and Poetics', in *The Cambridge History of Renaissance Philosophy*, ed. Charles B. Schmitt and Quentin Skinner (Cambridge University Press, 1988), p. 715.

2 Vickers, 'Rhetoric and Poetics', p. 720.

3 Aristotle, *Rhetoric* 1410b.

4 Sir Philip Sidney, *An Apology for Poetry*, ed. Geoffrey Shepherd; rev. R. W. Maslen, 3rd edn (Manchester University Press, 2002), p. 87.

5 George Puttenham, *Art of English Poesie* (1589), in *Elizabethan Critical Essays*, ed. G. Gregory Smith, 2 vols. (Oxford: Clarendon Press, 1904), II: 148.

6 *Palladis Tamia, Wits Treasury* (1598), in *Elizabethan Critical Essays*, ed. Smith, II: 315 and 317.

7 Belsey, 'Love as Trompe-l'oeil: Taxonomies of Desire in *Venus and Adonis*', in *Venus and Adonis: Critical Essays*, ed. Philip C. Kolin (New York: Garland, 1997), pp. 261–85.

8 'Upon Misprision Growing', from *Captive Victors: Shakespeare's Narrative Poems and Sonnets*; also in Kolin (ed.), *Venus and Adonis*, pp. 223–46: p. 223.

9 See *Hero and Leander* 1.93.

10 *Directions for Speech and Style* (1599), ed. H. Hudson (Princeton University Press, 1935), pp. 41–2.

11 Eliot, 'Shakespeare and the Stoicism of Seneca', in *Selected Essays* (London: Faber, 1932), pp. 130–1. Robin Headlam Wells adopts a position similar to Eliot's, though he applies it culturally rather than individually; see his chapter, '"O these men, these men"', in *Shakespeare on Masculinity* (Cambridge University Press, 2000), pp. 86–116.

12 Belsey, 'Love as Trompe-l'oeil', pp. 269–70.

13 Desiderius Erasmus' *De duplici copia verborum ac rerum* (1512). See Marion Trousdale, *Shakespeare and the Rhetoricians* (London: Scolar Press, 1982), esp. the section on 'Erasmus's De Copia' in the chapter 'The Criterion of Richness', pp. 43–55.

14 Vickers, 'Rhetoric and Poetics', p. 722.

15 Muriel Bradbrook, *Shakespeare and Elizabethan Poetry* (London: Chatto and Windus, 1951), p. 63.

16 Jonathan Bate, *Shakespeare and Ovid* (Oxford: Clarendon Press, 1993), p. 55.

17 *Variable Passions* (New York: AMS Press, 2000), pp. 67–8.

18 *City of God* 1.19.19–20.

19 The majority of editors favour *The Rape of Lucrece*. Notable exceptions are F. T. Prince (ed.), *Poems*, Arden 2nd series (London: Methuen, 1960); and Colin Burrow (ed.), *Complete Sonnets and* Poems (Oxford University Press, 2002).

20 Hoskins, *Directions for Speech and Style*, p. 23; Trousdale, *Shakespeare*, p. 49.

21 Prince (ed.), *Poems*, p. xxxiii.

22 Empson, 'The Narrative Poems', in *Essays on Shakespeare*, ed. David B. Pirie (Cambridge University Press, 1986), p. 9.

23 See variously E. P. Kuhl, 'Shakespeare's *Rape of Lucrece*', *Philological Quarterly* 20 (1941), 352–60; Michael Platt, '*The Rape of Lucrece* and the Republic for Which It Stands', *Centenniel Review* 19 (1975), 59–79 and his *Rome and Romans According to Shakespeare*, rev. edn (Lanham, MD: University Press of America, 1983), p. 35; Annabel Patterson, *Reading Between the Lines* (London: Routledge, 1993), p. 306; Andrew Hadfield, *Shakespeare and Renaissance Politics*, Arden Shakespeare (London: Thomson Learning, 2003), pp. 111–20.

24 Keats may well have had these lines in mind when he wrote the following:

> Ay, in the very temple of Delight
>   Veiled Melancholy has her Sovran shrine,
>   Though seen of none save him whose strenuous tongue
>   Can burst Joy's grape against his palate fine;
> His soul shall taste the sadness of her might,
>   And be among her cloudy trophies hung.
>
>   ('Ode on Melancholy', 25–30)

25 Vendler, *The Art of Shakespeare's Sonnets* (Cambridge, MA: Harvard University Press, 1997), p. 391.

26 E. H. Gombrich traces the concept to Philostratus' *Imagines*. See *Art and Illusion*, 4th edn (London: Phaidon, 1972), pp. 176–7.

27 McDonald, *Shakespeare and the Arts of Language* (Oxford University Press, 2001), pp. 3–4.

28 I refer the reader to the introduction to my edition of *The Poems* (Cambridge University Press, 1992; updated edn 2006), pp. 49–54.

READING LIST

Belsey, Catherine. 'Love as Trompe-l'oeil: Taxonomies of Desire in *Venus and Adonis*'. *Shakespeare Quarterly* 46 (1995), 257–76. Rpt in Kolin, *Venus and Adonis*, pp. 261–85.

Braden, Gordon. 'Shakespeare's Petrarchism'. In *Shakespeare's Sonnets*. Ed. James Schiffer. London: Routledge, 2000, pp. 163–83.

Cousins, A. D. 'Subjectivity, Exemplarity and the Establishing of Characterization in *Lucrece*'. *Studies in English Literature 1500–1900* 38 (1998), 45–60.

Dubrow, Heather. *Captive Victors: Shakespeare's Narrative Poems and Sonnets*. Ithaca: Cornell University Press, 1987.

Kerrigan, John. 'Keats and Lucrece'. In *On Shakespeare and Early Modern Literature: Essays*. Oxford University Press, 2001, pp. 41–65.

Kiernan, Pauline. 'Venus and Adonis and Ovidian Indecorous Wit'. In *Shakespeare's Ovid*. Ed. A. B. Taylor. Cambridge University Press, 2000, pp. 81–95.

Kolin, Philip C. (ed.). *Venus and Adonis: Critical Essays*. New York: Garland, 1997.

Mortimer, Anthony. *Variable Passions: A Reading of Shakespeare's 'Venus and Adonis'*. New York: AMS Press, 2000.

Trousdale, Marion. *Shakespeare and the Rhetoricians*. Cambridge, MA: Harvard University Press, 1999.

Vendler, Helen. *The Art of Shakespeare's Sonnets*. Cambridge, MA: Harvard University Press, 1997.

3

LUKAS ERNE

Print and manuscript

Introduced to England by William Caxton in the 1470s, print is the form most (though not all) of Shakespeare's literary writings assumed during or shortly after his lifetime.[1] Only the wide dissemination made possible by print guaranteed the survival of – and thus makes possible our modern engagement with – most of his works. On the other hand, the production and dissemination of literary works in manuscript was not simply superseded by print once and for all, but the two forms led a coexistence during Shakespeare's time – and well beyond. Some poets writing around the time of Shakespeare actively sought print publication, but others preferred disseminating their poetry in manuscript. A notable example of the former attitude is Edmund Spenser, who counted on print publications, from *The Shepheardes Calender* (1579) to *The Faerie Queene* (Books 1–3: 1590; Books 1–6: 1596), to shape his career as a poet-laureate. A famous instance of the latter preference is John Donne, whose poetry circulated widely in manuscript but who chose to keep most of his poetry unprinted during his own lifetime. Philip Sidney similarly did not seek print publication, and his *Astrophil and Stella*, *Arcadia*, and *Defence of Poesy* were all print-published after his death. While these authors clearly favoured one medium, print in the case of Spenser and manuscript in the cases of Donne and Sidney, Shakespeare is a somewhat more complicated and ambivalent figure, and we will need to examine in some detail his poetic output and his likely attitude as they relate to the two rival forms of dissemination.

In this examination of Shakespeare's poems at the crossroads of manuscript and print, much more is at stake than a quasi-archaeological recovery of textual origins in a far and distant past which can safely be entrusted to the care of editors and other scholars. Rather, the channels through and the form in which Shakespeare's poems first took shape can affect their meaning in fundamental ways. To understand how they do so, we first need to establish what difference the choice of channel makes in terms of author and readership. Authors who circulated their writings in manuscript 'were usually addressing the immediate audience of the scribal community, whereas print publishing authors took their places on the great stage of the world'.[2] Manuscript (or 'scribal') publication is therefore usually aimed at a relatively small, private, or semi-private community, an inner circle, as it were, within which more could be taken for granted and more was allowed than in printed books to which any purchaser had access. Certain qualities of Donne's poetry are therefore typical features of coterie poetry, such as the outrageous wit and outspokenness of his lyric poetry. Certain aspects of Spenser's poetry, by contrast, in particular the ambitious scale on which he planned and executed his career, require the print author's 'great stage of the world' to achieve their full impact.

The choice of print or manuscript as the medium for the dissemination of poetry bespeaks not only the audience the writer was addressing but also the social persona he was trying to self-fashion. While certain aristocrats did not refrain from print-publishing their literary creations, others clearly did, and scribal publication could therefore have a social prestige that print lacked. Accordingly, an author of middle-class origins like Spenser was more likely to publish in print than an aristocrat like Sidney: 'publication in print, where poems could be made available to all and sundry without any discrimination was, perhaps, construed as at the very least a lapse in gentlemanly taste and decorum'.[3]

While manuscript circulation could thus have a social cachet which print typically lacked, print conveyed on the literary text stability and fixity of a kind that manuscript poetry could not achieve. As manuscript poems circulated, they were copied, collected, excerpted, altered, abridged, expanded, or appropriated. Marlowe's poem 'The Passionate Shepherd to His Love' is a famous example, of which a number of rewritings or responses have survived, including one by Donne, entitled 'The Bait'. The kind of interaction manuscript poetry invited thus turned the circulating texts into malleable social products in contrast to the single-authored text printed in hundreds of identical copies. The rise of the *author* of lyric poetry is, unsurprisingly, a result of its print publication, as is the rise of authorial copyright. 'In a system of manuscript circulation of literature', by contrast, 'those into whose hands texts came could, in a real sense, "own" them' (Marotti, 'Literary Property', p. 143). Early modern manuscript culture, far from being a concern to which we can be indifferent, in fact 'forces us to rethink central categories of literary criticism: the author, authorship, literary and textual authority, literary property' (Roberts, p. 9).

Shakespeare in print and manuscript

This chapter now proceeds to a survey of Shakespeare's poetic creation and dissemination in the light of the material form it assumed early on in either manuscript or print. In the 1590s, Shakespeare seems to be acutely aware of the implications of both print and manuscript for the dissemination and reception of his poems. In these years, we know that Shakespeare was neither simply a print poet nor solely a manuscript poet. We know that he was both and that he distinguished between print and manuscript depending on the kind of poetry he wrote. *Venus and Adonis* first appeared in 1593 and *The Rape of Lucrece* the year after, and both were clearly intended and prepared for publication in print. Yet at the same time as these narrative poems went through some of their early editions, a number of Shakespeare's sonnets appear to have been circulating in manuscript among his friends, though there is no hope of recovering who these friends and what these sonnets precisely were.

But let us begin with what we know for certain. On 18 April 1593, the printer Richard Field who, like Shakespeare, was born and brought up in Stratford, entered *Venus and Adonis* in the Stationers' Register, which means that Field had acquired from Shakespeare a manuscript of the poem and was securing his rights in the work before going on to publish it. For Shakespeare, Field not only had the advantage of being a fellow-Stratfordian, but he was also known as a careful and reliable printer who had been entrusted with a number of significant literary texts, including John Harington's translation of *Orlando Furioso* (1591).[4] He may therefore have been an obvious choice for Shakespeare at a time when he was still little-known and unpublished. Shakespeare's choice of subject for his first venture into print is similarly astute yet unsurprising. Interest in erotic narrative poetry had been on the rise, and Shakespeare could count on an expanding market of young male readers from the universities and Inns of Court with the necessary education to appreciate and the necessary money to purchase his poem.[5] The first quarto of Shakespeare's narrative poem, which appeared not long after the text had been entered, is so carefully printed that we can safely assume that Shakespeare had prepared an impeccable copy. His name does not feature on the title page, but it does appear at the end of the dedicatory epistle to Henry Wriothesley, earl of Southampton. The dedication places the publication in the context of the discourse of patronage: Shakespeare was clearly hoping for a reward of some kind, perhaps even for employment. Just as interestingly, however, the epistle reveals an author mindful of his career (and his career as a *poet*), calling *Venus and Adonis* 'the first heir of my invention' but already announcing 'some graver labour', no doubt a reference to his work-in-progress on *Lucrece*, which was published the year after. Shakespeare's carefully prepared first appearance on the great stage of the world offered by print clearly suggests his intention to make a mark as a poet.[6]

Shakespeare refers to *Venus and Adonis* as 'the first heir of my invention' despite the fact that he had been a playwright for probably two or three years during which he may have written as many as seven plays, including one masterpiece, *Richard III*.[7] Shakespeare's authorial self-presentation begins as a poet and, more specifically, as a print-published poet. The announced 'graver' sequel to his first appearance in print must have been completed by 9 May 1594 when John Harrison entered 'a booke intituled the Ravyshement of Lucrece' in the Stationers' Register. In the following month, Harrison acquired the rights to *Venus and Adonis* from Field, and *Lucrece* was printed and *Venus and Adonis* reprinted before the end of the year, with similar ornaments on the title page, suggesting that they may well have been intended as companion volumes. Like *Venus and Adonis*, *Lucrece* was carefully printed and it, too, was dedicated to Southampton. The notably warmer rhetoric of the second dedication suggests that Shakespeare had received a reward of some kind. By the end of 1594, people browsing through the bookstalls at St Paul's Churchyard (where London's booksellers had their shops) must have realized that the poet William Shakespeare – author of a pair of narrative poems, prestigiously dedicated and handsomely printed, indeed one of them already reprinted – had arrived.

The visibility of Shakespeare's printed poems did not diminish in the following years. By 1600, *Lucrece* had reached its fourth and *Venus and Adonis* its sixth edition. By comparison, of Shakespeare's plays, only two had been reprinted more than once by 1600, *Richard II* and *1 Henry IV*, which both received three editions in the sixteenth century. While Shakespeare's printed plays thus remained less popular than his narrative poems throughout the closing years of the sixteenth century, the publication of his playbooks witnesses an important shift in the course of these years: Shakespeare's earliest playbooks had been published anonymously, but they started being printed with the author's name on the title page in 1598. The shift was sudden and decisive: before 1598, all seven Shakespearean playbooks to reach print had been published without any mention of their author's name. Yet in 1598, no fewer than four editions of Shakespeare plays appeared with the author's name on the title page, and another five followed in the next two years. All of a sudden, 'Shakespeare' was a name that sold books.

This emergence of Shakespeare, the dramatist, was not unrelated to Shakespeare, the poet. Both dramatist and poet figure prominently in Francis Meres's *Palladis Tamia* (1598) which not only mentions Shakespeare as 'among ye English ... the most excellent in both kinds for the stage', comedy and tragedy, but also praises his poems. And it is Meres's praise of

Shakespeare, the poet, which provides evidence for the circulation of his poems in manuscript:

> As the soule of *Euphorbus* was thought to liue in *Pythagoras*: so the sweete wittie soule of *Ouid* liues in mellifluous & hony-tongued *Shakespeare*, witnes his *Venus* and *Adonis*, his *Lucrece*, his sugred Sonnets among his priuate friends, &c.[8]

Shakespeare's Sonnets did not appear in print until 1609, but we thus know that more than a decade earlier sonnets of his were already in existence and circulating in manuscript. Meres's phrasing is intriguing: they did not simply circulate privately, nor simply among friends, but among 'priuate friends'. Independently of what Shakespeare's attitude was towards the publication of his Sonnets in 1609 (a topic to which we will return below), Meres's words strongly suggest that in the late 1590s, Shakespeare was consciously opting for manuscript rather than print as the right medium in which to have his sonnets read.

By the end of 1598, an up-to-date London bibliophile thus possessed the teasing knowledge of privately circulating Shakespeare sonnets and must have been aware that the name of William Shakespeare, the poet and the play-wright, was well established. All this sets the stage for a small volume which appeared in late 1598 or early 1599, a volume of poetry, 'By W. Shakespeare', according to the title page, entitled *The Passionate Pilgrim*. Only a fragment survives of the first edition, but a second edition is dated 1599, which estab-lishes that *The Passionate Pilgrim*, like Shakespeare's narrative poems, was a successful publishing venture and provides further evidence of the saleability of the 'Shakespeare' label at the close of the sixteenth century. Published by William Jaggard, this verse miscellany contains twenty poems of which only five can be attributed to Shakespeare with confidence. Only two years after Shakespeare's poems and plays were still customarily printed without being attributed to him on the title page, there is thus a volume ascribed to him, even though a part of its contents is certainly (and another part probably) not by Shakespeare. Three of the identifiable Shakespeare poems are lyrics from *Love's Labour's Lost*, but the other two are versions of Sonnets 138 and 144. Here, in other words, appear to be two of the sonnets that had been circulating among Shakespeare's 'priuate friends'. They are printed as the first and the second of the twenty sonnets of Jaggard's collection, implying that Jaggard realized what precious commodities they were. Their privileged place-ment within the miscellany and the fact that there are only two of them suggest that Meres's choice of words, 'priuate friends', was not accidental, and that his friends had indeed largely respected the privacy the author sought to preserve in the manuscript circulation of his sonnets.

What holds *The Passionate Pilgrim* together – and is likely to have been counted on for the volume's commercial success – is a number of Shakespearean intertexts: the title's 'pilgrim' calls up the conjunction of the amorous and the religious characteristic of Petrarchan poetry 'hony-tongued' Shakespeare was associated with and may have been meant, more specifically, to remind readers of the sonnet the young lovers share in *Romeo and Juliet*. The so-called 'Venus and Adonis' poems, whose author remains unidentified, establish a connection to Shakespeare's most popular work in print. The three songs and sonnets from *Love's Labour's Lost* tap into memories of readers and auditors of Shakespeare's play. And the opening sonnets may not just correspond to but also remind readers of the 'sugred Sonnets' Meres mentioned. Plays and poems, manuscript and print – Jaggard seems to have been able to draw upon a variety of sources to publish a work which was in more than one sense 'Shakespearean', even though most of the content may not in fact have been written by Shakespeare.

Although attributed to Shakespeare on the title page, *The Passionate Pilgrim* is, in a sense, Jaggard's much more than Shakespeare's, unified by commercial rather than poetic intentions. What corroborates such a view is that the 1599 title page of *The Passionate Pilgrim* points out that the volume, though published by Jaggard, is 'to be sold by W. Leake'. William Leake had obtained the rights to *Venus and Adonis* on 25 June 1596, and Jaggard clearly wanted to cash in on the great success of *Venus and Adonis* by having *The Passionate Pilgrim* sold alongside it, perhaps remembering John Harrison's similar marketing strategy in 1594 when he in effect offered to his customers *Venus and Adonis* and *Lucrece* as a Shakespearean diptych. Contrary to the narrative poems, however, *The Passionate Pilgrim* needs to be situated at the crossroads between manuscript and print: made up of poems by various hands as manuscript miscellanies usually were, yet attributed to a single author as print publications increasingly required; its most authentic pieces intended by the author for manuscript circulation among friends but nonetheless chosen by the publisher for print publication and sale to the multitude. *The Passionate Pilgrim* does not suggest a poet who presents himself through the medium of print but reflects a manuscript poet who is brought into print by others.[9]

This holds true not only for *The Passionate Pilgrim* but also for Shakespeare's 67-line 'The Phoenix and Turtle', published in 1601 among a group of fourteen poems (by Ben Jonson, John Marston, and George Chapman among others) appended to a long poem by Robert Chester, called *Love's Martyr*. Like the Shakespeare poems in *The Passionate Pilgrim*, 'The Phoenix and Turtle' forms part of a larger collection, and the characteristic form of the manuscript book – be it a miscellany, an anthology, or a journal – is a uniting of smaller units.[10] On the other hand, there is no sense that the poem reached print in spite of – rather than because of – Shakespeare, and no poems by other authors are here attributed to him. The separate title page preceding the group of poems following Chester's *Love's Martyr* suggests that a concerted effort went into the making of the miscellany:

> Poeticall Essaies on the former Sub- / iect; viz: the *Turtle* and *Phoenix*. / *Done by the best and chiefest of our* / moderne writers, with their names sub- / scribed to their particular workes: / *neuer before extant*. / And (now first) consecrated by them all generally, / *to the loue and merite of the true-noble Knight*, / Sir Iohn Salisburie.

A possible reason why some of the poets – in particular Chapman and Jonson – contributed to this volume is that in 1601, following the fall and execution of the earl of Essex, a powerful, literary patron, Salisbury may have been counted upon to fill the gap left by Essex or at least to offer an introduction to further patronage.[11] Yet what motivated the contribution by Shakespeare – who as a shareholder in his company had amassed a handsome fortune by 1601 and seems likely to have been beyond the need for Salisbury's patronage – will probably never be known.

The Passionate Pilgrim had successfully cashed in on Shakespeare's name as the publication of two editions within a year or so suggests. The volume in which 'The Phoenix and Turtle' appeared, however, does not mention Shakespeare on the title page, nor even on the separate title page prefacing the shorter poems. This may have contributed to the book's commercial failure: by 1611, still not sold out, it was reissued with a new title page and a new title, *The anuals [sic] of great Brittaine*.[12] It seems more difficult to explain why another volume similarly appears to have been a commercial failure, the 1609 quarto advertising 'SHAKE-SPEARES SONNETS' in large capital letters on the title page. Whereas *The Passionate Pilgrim* received a third edition in 1612, Shakespeare's Sonnets were not reprinted. The 1609 title page seems careful in spelling out that it contains the real thing. So what explains its apparent lack of success compared to the slight *Passionate Pilgrim* volume which is trying to capitalize on what Shakespeare's Sonnets really offers is a question that has never been satisfactorily answered. It may constitute a necessary reminder that our modern notions of authenticity and literary value did not yet exist.

The apparent lack of success as evidenced by the absence of a second edition in the following decades is of course not the only enigma surrounding Shakespeare's Sonnets. The identity of the 'young man', the 'dark lady', and the 'rival poet' has prompted countless theories and endless speculation, but they need not detain us here. More important in this context is the identity of

'Mr. W. H.' – whom the epigraph by the publisher Thomas Thorpe addresses as 'the onlie begetter of these insuing sonnets' – as it relates to the question of how the Sonnets came to be printed. If begetter means 'procurer', as some have argued, and if 'Mr. W. H.' therefore refers to the person who supplied Thorpe with a manuscript, then there is little hope of recovering to whom the initials refer. A much more straightforward answer would present itself if 'begetter' in fact refers to the author himself, and if 'W. H.' misprints Shakespeare's initials, 'W. S.' or 'W. Sh.' Most scholars have opted for neither of these views, however, but have held that the Sonnets' 'begetter' is the person who prompted Shakespeare to write them (or most of them) and is therefore to be equated with the biographical figure behind 'the young man' to whom most of the sonnets are addressed. William Herbert, earl of Pembroke, and – with the initials inverted – Henry Wriothesley, earl of Southampton, are the two main contenders, though neither of them would normally have been addressed as a mere 'Mr.' There is enough information for us to go on speculating, but not enough to arrive at a solution, and perhaps that is precisely the point. Thorpe remarks on the title page that Shakespeare's Sonnets have been 'Neuer before Imprinted', promising a reader access to what before had been confined to a circle of 'priuate friends', giving away but also withholding just enough information about this circle to keep up the curiosity. Whether or not 'W. H.' refers to a real person, the enigmatic initials may well play with this teasing promise to readers, placing them 'both inside and outside a charmed circle of knowledge'.[13]

Directly related to speculations about the identity of 'W. H.' is the question of Shakespeare's role in the publication of his Sonnets and of *A Lover's Complaint* included in the same volume following a separate title page that attributes it to Shakespeare. 'Was the 1609 Shake-speares Sonnets Really Unauthorized?', Katherine Duncan-Jones asked in an article of 1983, arguing against a long-standing consensus to suggest that it was not.[14] The debate has continued ever since, and no consensus is about to emerge. In the 1590s, Shakespeare wrote for a print readership two narrative poems which were published in 1593 and 1594, and he wrote for 'priuate friends' sonnets which circulated in manuscript. This much is clear. But whether, in the following decade, he wanted the entire Sonnet collection to be print-published or whether he wanted to keep his Sonnets in manuscript remains unclear. This considerably complicates our analysis of Shakespeare's rela-tionship towards manuscript and print. Those who believe that Shakespeare opposed the publication of the Sonnets thus think of Shakespeare primarily as a manuscript rather than a print poet, in direct opposition to those who argue that he actively sought publication.[15] Manuscript or print poet – the diametrical opposition is that between a private coterie poet like Donne or a public laureate poet like Spenser, the opposition being that which I evoked early on in this chapter.

Since it seems impossible to determine with certainty whether Shakespeare wanted his sonnets to be printed or not, we have to look instead at the sonnets themselves. If we do so, a first point that emerges is that the printed sequence, whether authorially intended or not, significantly shapes the way a reader makes sense of the sonnets. In particular, by fixing the sonnets' precise textual make-up and arranging them in a certain order, the print publication raises questions about the sequence as a whole – its design and coherence – which have figured prominently in recent scholarship.[16] In manuscript, by contrast, the sonnets must have originally existed on separate leaves (though quite possibly in small groups),[17] were detachable and adaptable, entailing a radically different relationship to the other sonnets from that in the 1609 quarto. Whether the sonnets have a plot or show a progression are questions that naturally arise in the context of a printed sequence but are less likely to pose themselves if the sonnets circulate dispersedly in time and space.

Once we examine the sonnets' propositional content, we realize that it preserves significant traces of their media of transmission. In a significant way, manuscript and print are not only the media through which the sonnets were disseminated but also what they are about. At times, it is difficult or impossible to determine whether manuscript or print is referred to: when the speaker expresses the hope 'That in black ink my love may still shine bright' (65.14), he may be referring to a handwritten or a printed page. Yet several of the poems to the young man show unmistakable signs of a relationship between a poet and a patron in which hand-written sonnets formed part of an on-going economy of exchange. Other poems, by contrast, show an authorial self-presentation and the hope for the immortality of his verse in ways which by Shakespeare's time had become closely associated with print.

Manuscript, in particular, is inscribed into a number of sonnets as their original medium of transmission.[18] Sonnet 26, for instance, refers to itself as a commodity, a hand-written epistle sent from the poet to his patron:

> Lord of my love, to whom in vassalage
> Thy merit hath my duty strongly knit,
> To thee I send this written ambassage
> To witness duty, not to show my wit.   (1–4)

The deictic 'this' in line 3 clearly refers to the poem in an earlier material form than the 1609 Sonnets. Even though the poem records its original status as a manuscript poem presented as gift to a specific patron, it survives thanks to its print publication in a book available for purchase by anyone. Other sonnets similarly point to their original manuscript status: 'if you read this line, remember not / The hand that writ it' (71.5–6), where the proximity of 'hand' to 'writ' reminds us that the former word also refers to handwriting (*Oxford English Dictionary*, n. 16); or: 'my papers (yellowed with their age)' (17.9), referring to the papers on which the poet originally wrote his sonnets.

A number of other sonnets, however, entirely remove them from the context of their early existence, expressing instead the hopes for the permanence of their reception and importance, hopes which, in Shakespeare's time, largely depended upon the dissemination made possible by print. Some of these sonnets are among the best-known, for instance 18 ('So long as men can breathe or eyes can see, / So long lives this, and this gives life to thee', 13–14) or 55 ('Not marble nor the gilded monuments / Of princes shall outlive this pow'rful rhyme', 1–2), but there are instances throughout, in particular in the first 126 Sonnets, addressed to the young man. Indeed, it seems that Shakespeare 'has written both more copiously and more memorably on this topic [i.e. poetry as immortalization] than any other sonneteer'.[19] We may be tempted to object that the idea of 'immortality through verse' was in fact voiced long before the invention of the printing press. Yet what applied to Horace and Ovid, securely aware of the lasting importance of their masterpieces, surely does not apply to Shakespeare's sonnets: not only was Shakespeare aware that lyric poetry remained relatively low on the scale of generic respectability, but he also knew that important sonnet collections of his own time, especially Sidney's *Astrophil and Stella* and Spenser's *Amoretti*, had appeared in print. Shakespeare must have known that the lasting importance of his sonnets would be bound to the printing press.

Sonnet 60 offers a particularly telling example in this context: the poet's hopes that his 'verse shall stand' (13) are voiced in a sonnet that is carefully placed within the sequence as a whole, within Shakespeare's Sonnets of 1609. Just as the number of Sonnet 12 alludes to the number of hours on the clock at the same time as it is about 'the clock that tells the time' (1), so the number of Sonnet 60 corresponds to the 'minutes' (2) that make up an hour. Indeed, the minutes that 'hasten to their end' are specifically 'our minutes', playing on 'hour minutes'. Sonnet 60 is thus emphatically not a detached or detachable sonnet pointing towards original manuscript circulation. On the contrary, it is firmly part of and occupies a specific place within a sequence of sonnets whose printing rendered possible the immortality which the sonnet itself thematizes.

Given the impossibility to determine whether Shakespeare authorized the 1609 edition or not, whether he wanted his sonnets to be printed or to remain in manuscript, it is strangely appropriate that the sonnets themselves yield ambivalent evidence regarding their relationship to manuscript or print.

While some preserve distinct traces of their original composition and transmission in manuscript, others anticipate the sequentiality and permanence of the printed collection. Oddly enough, we know a good deal about Shakespeare's attitude towards his poems in print or manuscript earlier in his career, that he wanted *Venus and Adonis* and *Lucrece* to reach print in 1593 and 1594, that he consciously kept his 'sugred Sonnets' in manuscript in the 1590s and that a small collection of lyric poetry attributed to Shakespeare, *The Passionate Pilgrim*, was printed despite and not because of Shakespeare in 1598, but the attitude of Shakespeare's Sonnets of 1609 towards manuscript and print remains inconclusive.

Poetry and print in Shakespeare's plays

I now wish to enlarge and complicate the notion of 'Shakespeare's poetry' and its various forms of publication by relating it to his dramatic works. Shakespeare wrote poems and plays, and what characterized Shakespeare's creative output is that he was a writer of both throughout his career.[20] Indeed, in the years 1593 to 1612, sixty-three quartos or octavos with plays or poems by Shakespeare were published, and twenty of them, almost one third, contained poems.[21] While the coincidence of poetic and dramatic writing throughout Shakespeare's career is undeniable – and allows a privileged angle from which to consider Shakespeare as a poet-playwright – the exact form the poems/plays coincidence takes significantly depends, however, on whether we look at it from the angle of print publication or from that of original (manuscript) composition. If we do the latter, the picture that emerges encourages us to divide the history of Shakespeare's artistic production into two periods, that up to and that after 1594. In the first period, a dramatic output of probably seven plays, of which as many as four may not be Shakespeare's unaided work,[22] is balanced by two narrative poems of some length, amounting to a total of more than 3,000 lines. In the second, by contrast, a total of thirty-one plays (of which perhaps twenty-six are of sole authorship) are complemented by a relatively meagre poetic output: the short 'Phoenix and Turtle' (67 lines), the relatively short *A Lover's Complaint* (329 lines), and the Sonnets (assuming all or at least most of them were written after 1594), amounting to little more than 2,500 lines of poetry. While the poetry–drama ratio up to 1594 is about one to five, in the period after 1594 it is closer to one to thirty-five. In the approximately twenty years after the completion of *Lucrece* during which we believe Shakespeare to have remained active as a writer, his average yearly poetic output is approximately 125 lines. Granted, numbers if cunningly handled can be made to suggest many things in many ways, and plays and narrative poetry may well require rather less writerly care than the extremely dense 'Phoenix and Turtle' or the Sonnets. Even so, there is no escaping the conclusion that Shakespeare's poetic output in the twenty-odd years after 1594 and until the end of his writing career is quite modest.

It is true that Shakespeare may still occasionally have attempted to make a mark as a poet. Burrow has suggested that the purpose of 'The Phoenix and Turtle' was 'to keep the name of Shakespeare alive and to keep it associated with new forms' (*Complete Sonnets and Poems*, p. 90). This may be so, but it makes us wonder why Shakespeare seems to have undertaken little else to uphold his reputation as an active poet. And why, if Shakespeare wished to keep his *name* alive, did he do so in a volume that does not advertise his presence in it in any significant way, not on the title page nor even on the separate title page prefacing the shorter poems? The title page of *The Passionate Pilgrim* suggests that Shakespeare the poet could have gained greater visibility for his name if he had striven for it.

In quest for an explanation as to why Shakespeare wrote little poetry after 1594, we might be tempted to advance the reverse of the plague theory with which the writing of *Venus and Adonis* and *Lucrece* has often been explained. According to the plague theory, Shakespeare became a poet – writing *Venus and Adonis* and *Lucrece* – because the theatres closed for an extended period starting in July 1592; the reverse of this theory would dictate that Shakespeare no longer wrote poems later on because he simply returned to playwrighting once the playhouses had opened again. Yet in fact, there were several lengthy periods during which the playhouses remained closed, in particular in 1598, 1599–1600, 1603–4, and August 1608 to May 1609.[23] So had Shakespeare been waiting for periods of theatrical inactivity to return to poetry, there would have been plenty of opportunities to do so. Also, Shakespeare's dramatic output in the 1600s was lower than in the 1590s, with some twenty-two plays written in the last decade of the sixteenth century compared to only fourteen in the first decade of the seventeenth. So Shakespeare could probably have written more poetry if he had wanted to.

Alternatively, is it possible that Shakespeare wrote more poetry than is extant, poetry which perhaps circulated in manuscript, like his 'sugred Sonnets' in the 1590s? Had the 1609 edition, published late in Shakespeare's life, never materialized, what would we know about the sonnets? That some had circulated in manuscript in the 1590s and that a number of those published in *The Passionate Pilgrim* are likely to be by Shakespeare (though which ones, in the absence of the 1609 quarto, might have been difficult to determine); plus a very small number might have survived in manuscript and been identified as Shakespearean.[24] It is perhaps unlikely that much Shakespearean poetry was written, existed in manuscript, did not circulate beyond the confines of a very restricted circle and – in the absence of friends who did for the poems what Heminge and Condell did for the plays – was never printed, but the possibility should not be entirely discounted.

A more likely explanation for the decrease in Shakespeare's poetic output presents itself if we think of 'Shakespeare's poetry' without opposing it to or excluding it from Shakespeare's drama. If we do so, we may realize that after 1594 Shakespeare usually did not alternate between drama and poetry by writing the one or the other but combined the two by writing drama *as* poetry. There is nothing anachronistic about this idea. On the contrary, even though modern scholarship has often opposed the poet to the playwright, 'playwright' is in fact a term that came into use after Shakespeare's writing career, and the term Elizabethans used to designate a writer of plays is precisely that of 'poet'.[25] Moreover, in the prefatory material to the 1623 quarto of *The Duchess of Malfi*, a clear distinction is made between 'the play' and 'the poem', the former designating the script as it was performed on stage, the latter referring to the dramatic text written and printed for readers. The same distinction can be related to Shakespeare's dramatic practice.[26] Once Shakespeare had become a member of the Lord Chamberlain's Men in 1594 and could exert greater control over his playtexts, he and his fellow players and shareholders seem to have adopted a consistent policy of 'publishing', as it were, both the 'play' and the 'poem', the first one in the theatre, the second one by having it printed about two years later, a practice which they seem to have applied whenever possible until the end of the century. As in the case of Webster, the difference between 'play' and 'poem' was a matter not only of publication but also of length. The title page points out that the printed text contains 'diuerse things . . . that the length of the Play would not beare in the Presentment', meaning that the play was significantly abridged in performance. At roughly 3,000 lines, *The Duchess of Malfi* is a long play ('poem' would be Webster's word), but there are two other playwrights who repeatedly wrote playtexts of a similar or even greater length: Ben Jonson, of whom we have long known that he cared more for readers than for the 'loathèd stage' and whose *Every Man Out of His Humour* (1600) was advertised on the title page as 'Containing more than hath been Publickly Spoken or Acted', and Shakespeare.

The suspicion that Shakespeare, like Webster and Jonson, distinguished between a long readerly 'poem' and an abridged theatrical 'play' is corroborated by what we know about the practice of Shakespeare's successors as playwrights for the King's Men: Francis Beaumont and John Fletcher. According to the publisher Humphrey Moseley's prefatory address in the Folio edition of Beaumont and Fletcher's plays of 1647, when their plays were performed, 'the *Actours* omitted some *Scenes* and Passages (with the

Authour's consent) as occasion led them'. Many of Shakespeare's plays are significantly longer than even the longest play in the Beaumont and Fletcher Folio, suggesting that Shakespeare wrote his long 'poems' in the knowledge that they would be reduced to the practicable performance length of 'plays'. If we wish to compare Shakespearean 'poems' to 'plays', the best evidence we have may be those plays of which short and long versions survive, in particular *Romeo and Juliet*, *Henry V*, and *Hamlet*. The second quarto of *Romeo and Juliet* (1599), the Folio text of *Henry V* (1623), and the second quarto of *Hamlet* (1604/5) are as long or even longer than *The Duchess of Malfi*. They seem to be what Webster calls 'poems', whereas the substantially shorter first quartos of *Romeo and Juliet* (1597), *Henry V* (1600), and *Hamlet* (1603) may well correspond to Webster's 'play' in that they reflect – however dimly – how these plays were performed in Shakespeare's time.

Significantly, one of the chief differences between 'poem' and 'play' resides precisely in the amount and the sophistication of poetic material. What is typically omitted in the process of abridgement are poetically elaborate passages like substantial parts of Juliet's soliloquies (for instance, all but the first six lines of her opening soliloquy in 2.5 and all but four lines of the one in 3.2), most of the Player King's long speech in 3.2 of *Hamlet*, and a long passage in Henry's speech before the gates of Harfleur. Such material does little to advance the plot and may therefore have been most liable to cutting when the texts were abridged.

It thus emerges that Shakespeare appears to have been a writer of not only lyric and narrative but also dramatic poems, of playtexts written not only with performance on stage but also with a readerly reception on the page in mind. Once we keep this in mind, we recognize the significance of the kinds of plays Shakespeare wrote in the mid-1590s, shortly after *Venus and Adonis* and *Lucrece* – *Love's Labour's Lost*, *A Midsummer Night's Dream*, *Romeo and Juliet*, and *Richard II* all fall within this period – plays, that is, which are characterized by the amount and sophistication of their poetry. In earlier accounts of Shakespeare's career, these years used to be called 'the lyric phase', and the connection in genre and chronology to the earlier narrative poems used to be recognized. Chambers thought that 'it is most reasonable to suppose that at some date Shakespeare decided to make a deliberate experiment in lyrical drama. A very natural stimulus would be afforded by his experience of lyrical work in the narrative poems.'[27] Once we are aware that Shakespeare kept writing 'poems' throughout his career, we may recognize that what Chambers calls an 'experiment' in fact marks the transition from narrative to drama as the predominant form taken by Shakespeare's poetry in the course of his career. By 1600, all four of the above-mentioned dramatic poems had appeared in print just as by 1594 both of Shakespeare's narrative poems had been published. In other words, as Shakespeare must have become aware, the fact that his plays were performed on stage did not keep them from having a second existence in the form of printed texts, making their elaborate poetry available to the reading public just as his narrative poems had been.

Shakespeare's contemporaries were clearly responsive to both kinds of poetry. Around the turn of the century, Gabriel Harvey, in a discussion of several contemporary poets, juxtaposes *Lucrece* and *Hamlet* as material fit 'to please the wiser sort'.[28] Harvey sees no generic incompatibility between the two works, but considers them both as poems on a serious subject. Similarly, William Drummond, laird of Hawthorndon, who read the second quarto of *Romeo and Juliet* (1599) in 1606, treated it much like poetry, highlighting lyric purple patches by overscoring them.[29] Montague's metaphor for dawn is representative for the kind of passage Drummond singled out: 'as the alcheering Sunne, / Should in the farthest East begin to draw, / The shadie curtaines from *Auroras* bed' (B1ʳ). Drummond's overscorings show that he read Shakespeare's playtext as a dramatic poem, not as a theatrical script that happened to have been printed.

The most telling evidence of the early reception not only of *Venus and Adonis* and *Lucrece* but also of his playtexts as poetry is provided by two literary anthologies, *England's Parnassus* and *Belvedere, or the Garden of the Muses*, both published in 1600. They compile verse passages, mostly from Elizabethan poets, passages which the title page of *England's Parnassus* calls 'The choysest Flowers of our Moderne Poets'. Both anthologies include many passages by Shakespeare, excerpted both from his narrative poems and his plays. As a consequence, lyric passages from *Richard II*, *Love's Labour's Lost*, *Romeo and Juliet*, *Richard III*, and *1 Henry IV* appear among excerpts from works by contemporary poets such as Michael Drayton, Samuel Daniel, Sidney, and Spenser, as well as among lines from Shakespeare's own *Venus and Adonis* and *Lucrece*. It appears that half-way through his career, Shakespeare, the poet, was firmly established in print as a writer of both narrative and dramatic poems.

Conclusion

This chapter has thus suggested that there are two complementary ways of looking at Shakespeare's poetic career in terms of print and manuscript: the first one stresses the continuity of Shakespeare's output of poetry in the narrow sense of this term by focusing on three periods of print publication, one early, one middle, one late: *Venus and Adonis* and *Lucrece* in 1593–4; *The Passionate Pilgrim* and 'The Phoenix and Turtle' in 1598–1601; the

Sonnets and *A Lover's Complaint* in 1609. The second distinguishes between two phases, one up to and the other from 1594. In the first phase, Shakespeare writes plays in manuscript which achieve their publication not in print but in theatrical performance, and he writes narrative poetry which is designed for and reaches print publication. In the second phase, Shakespeare keeps writing non-dramatic poetry, but far less of it, as his dramatic writings and print publications come to bridge the earlier divide between manuscript and print on the one hand and performance and reading on the other. As this second perspective suggests, after 1594, Shakespeare kept writing poetry, occasionally in free-standing poems, but mostly in his drama.

NOTES

1 *Sir Thomas More*, to which Shakespeare is usually thought to have contributed, was not printed until the nineteenth century, and *Cardenio*, a play co-authored by John Fletcher and Shakespeare according to an entry in the Stationers' Register, only survives in an eighteenth-century adaptation by Lewis Theobald.

2 Harold Love, 'Oral and Scribal Texts in Early Modern England', in John Barnard and D. F. McKenzie (eds.), *The Cambridge History of the Book in Britain: Volume IV, 1557–1695* (Cambridge University Press, 2002), p. 118.

3 Peter Beal, 'John Donne and the Circulation of Manuscripts', in Barnard and McKenzie (eds.), *Cambridge History of the Book in Britain*, p. 122.

4 See A. E. M. Kirwood, 'Richard Field, Printer, 1589–1624', *The Library* 4th series, 12 (1931), 1–39.

5 See Sasha Roberts, *Reading Shakespeare's Poems in Early Modern England*, Early Modern Literature in History (Basingstoke: Palgrave, 2003), pp. 64–5.

6 See Colin Burrow (ed.), *Complete Sonnets and Poems* (Oxford University Press, 2002), p. 9.

7 See Stanley Wells and Gary Taylor, with John Jowett and William Montgomery, *William Shakespeare: A Textual Companion* (Oxford University Press, 1987), pp. 109–15.

8 I quote from Arthur Freeman's edition, *Palladis Tamia: Wits Treasury* (New York: Garland, 1973), 281^v–282^r.

9 See Patrick Cheney, *Shakespeare, National Poet–Playwright* (Cambridge University Press, 2004), p. 143.

10 See Love, 'Oral and Scribal Texts', p. 112.

11 See Burrow (ed.), *Complete Sonnets and Poems*, pp. 88–9.

12 It has wrongly been argued that the book was reprinted, not reissued. See, for example, E. K. Chambers, *William Shakespeare: A Study of Facts and Fiction*, 2 vols. (Oxford: Clarendon Press, 1930), I: 549.

13 Burrow (ed.), *Complete Sonnets and Poems*, p. 103. See also Marotti, 'Shakespeare's Sonnets as Literary Property', in Elizabeth D. Harvey and Katharine Eisaman Maus (eds.), *Soliciting Interpretation: Literary Theory and Seventeenth-Century English Poetry* (University of Chicago Press, 1990), pp. 143–73; p. 165.

14 Duncan-Jones, 'Was the 1609 Shake-speares Sonnets Really Unauthorized?', *Review of English Studies* 34 (1983), 151–71.

15 See Cheney, *Shakespeare, Poet–Playwright*, p. 237.

16 See, in particular, Heather Dubrow, '"Incertainties now crown themselves assur'd": The Politics of Plotting Shakespeare's Sonnets', *Shakespeare Quarterly* 47 (1996), 291–305.

17 For the material form of early modern manuscript circulation of poetry, see Marotti, 'Literary Property', p. 147.

18 See Marotti, 'Literary Property'.

19 Leishman, *Themes and Variations in Shakespeare's Sonnets* (London: Hutchinson, 1961), p. 22.

20 As Cheney points out, 'the publication of Shakespeare's poems coincided throughout his career with the staging of his plays and even the printing of his plays in quartos' (*Shakespeare, Poet–Playwright*, p. 19).

21 See Lukas Erne, *Shakespeare as Literary Dramatist* (Cambridge University Press, 2003), pp. 245–9.

22 The three parts of *Henry 6* and *Titus Andronicus* all seem likely to have been written in collaboration (see Wells and Taylor, with Jowett and Montgomery, *Textual Companion*, pp. 111–15; and Brian Vickers, *Shakespeare, Co-Author* (Oxford University Press, 2003)).

23 See Cheney, *Shakespeare, Poet–Playwright*, p. 63; and Leeds Barroll, *Politics, Plague and Shakespeare's Theatre: The Stuart Years* (Ithaca: Cornell University Press, 1991).

24 On extant manuscript versions of Shakespearean sonnets, probably all dating from after Shakespeare's death, see Burrow (ed.), *Complete Sonnets and Poems*, pp. 106–7. See also Roberts, *Reading Shakespeare's Poems*.

25 The date of the earliest occurrence recorded by the *OED* (2nd edn, 1989) is 1687, but John Davies mentions it in fact as early as 1617, in *Wit's Bedlam* (F7a).

26 See Erne, *Literary Dramatist*; what follows draws on ideas developed in this study.

27 Chambers, *William Shakespeare*, I: 267.

28 G. C. Moore Smith (ed.), *Gabriel Harvey's Marginalia* (Stratford-upon-Avon: Shakespeare Head Press, 1913), p. 232.

29 See W. W. Greg's facsimile edition of Drummond's former copy of Q2 *Romeo and Juliet* in the Shakespeare Quarto Facsimile series (Oxford: Clarendon Press, 1949).

READING LIST

Barnard, John, and D. F. McKenzie (eds.). *The Cambridge History of the Book in Britain: Volume IV, 1557–1695*. Cambridge University Press, 2002.

Burrow, Colin (ed.). *Complete Sonnets and Poems*. Oxford World's Classics. Oxford University Press, 2002.

Cheney, Patrick. *Shakespeare, National Poet–Playwright*. Cambridge University Press, 2004.

Erne, Lukas. *Shakespeare as Literary Dramatist*. Cambridge University Press, 2003.

Love, Harold. *The Culture and Commerce of Texts: Scribal Publication in Seventeenth-Century England*. Amherst: University of Massachusetts Press, 1993.

Marotti, Arthur. 'Shakespeare's Sonnets as Literary Property'. In Elizabeth D. Harvey and Katharine Eisaman Maus (eds.). *Soliciting Interpretation: Literary Theory and Seventeenth-Century English Poetry.* University of Chicago Press, 1990, pp. 143–73.

Manuscript, Print, and the English Renaissance Lyric. Ithaca: Cornell University Press, 1995.

McKenzie, D. F. 'Speech, Manuscript, Print'. In Peter D. McDonald and Michael F. Suarez, S. J. (eds.). *Making Meaning: 'Printers of the Mind' and Other Essays.* Amherst: University of Massachusetts Press, 2002, pp. 237–58.

McKitterick, David. *Print, Manuscript and the Search for Order, 1450–1830.* Cambridge University Press, 2003.

Roberts, Sasha. *Reading Shakespeare's Poems in Early Modern England.* Early Modern Literature in History. Basingstoke: Palgrave, 2003.

4

COPPÉLIA KAHN

Venus and Adonis

When Shakespeare wrote this witty, sexy, sophisticated poem about a goddess's love for an alluring boy, he was a fledgling playwright in the tough competitive arena of London theatre. Some who picked up the handsomely printed quarto volume when it went on sale in mid-June of 1593 might have known him as author of the seven or eight plays that he had probably written by this date.[1] But *Venus and Adonis* was the first work that Shakespeare published under his name. Why would this actor–playwright at the beginning of a theatrical career turn to writing a long poem about a mythological love affair, appealing to an educated elite instead of the polyglot crowd of playgoers?

Several answers are possible. For centuries, this poem and *Lucrece* were regarded as sidelines from Shakespeare's 'real' theatrical calling, so scholars looked to external circumstances for an explanation of his swerve away from playwriting. They readily found one in the fact that London theatres were closed from June 1592 until June 1594 because of the plague, with only two brief periods of playing in the winters of 1593 and 1594. Deprived of his usual earnings from the Lord Chamberlain's Men, Shakespeare needed money, so this argument goes, and hoped to find it in patronage from his dedicatee, the well-connected Henry Wriothesley, earl of Southampton. Whether or not the promise of patronage – and perhaps some kind of passionate friendship with Southampton himself – induced Shakespeare to write *Venus and Adonis*, these scholars think, it was peripheral to the bent of his talent, which was first and foremost a theatrical one.[2] In contrast, it has also been argued that Shakespeare turned to poetry because he wanted his career to follow the pattern of classical poets such as Virgil and Ovid, beginning with pastoral lyrics that often focused on the vicissitudes of love, and then moving into a loftier epic style.[3]

Both the epigraph and the dedication clearly signal that Shakespeare is aiming not only at a self-consciously literary audience, but also at one with a specialized literary taste for the poetry of Ovid. He took his Latin epigraph,

Vilia miretur vulgus: mihi flavus Apollo
Pocula Castalia plena ministret aqua.

(Let the common herd be amused by worthless things, but for me let golden Apollo provide cups full of the water of the Muses.)[4]

from a poem specifically about literary ambition rather than lovemaking, in Ovid's collection of seduction poems, the *Amores*. Listing the poets whose work has immortalized them, from Hesiod and Homer to Ovid's contemporaries Virgil and Tibullus, Ovid proudly counts himself among them. The young Elizabethan writer emulates his Latin predecessor, boldly bidding for the attention of readers who consider themselves well educated, discriminating, and fashionable – young men studying law at the Inns of Court, for whom recognizing a Latin quotation was a badge of entitlement to careers of distinction. At the same time, Ovid's reputation as the poet of unbridled erotic experience, and the poem's amatory subject matter, gave *Venus and Adonis* a racy, daring tinge, making it something a young man on the loose would want to be seen reading, something both 'erotically and rhetorically sophisticated'.[5]

What hints of Shakespeare's purposes can be gleaned from his dedication of the poem to Southampton? At that time, the earl, studying law at Gray's Inn, and also attending Elizabeth at court, was known to be a playgoer. It is also known that he resisted his guardian's attempt to marry him to Elizabeth Vere, grand-daughter to William Burleigh, Queen Elizabeth's most trusted adviser. Stephen Greenblatt suggests that Shakespeare was commissioned by someone associated with the earl's mother, or by his guardian Lord Burleigh himself (who was also Lord Chancellor of England) to write the first seventeen sonnets. These poems repeatedly urge a handsome young man to marry, a theme echoed in the plot of *Venus and Adonis*, in which a beautiful boy similarly holds himself aloof from desire.[6] Colin Burrow, however, proposes a more specifically literary motive for the dedication: Shakespeare's desire to outdo the one poem already dedicated to the earl, written by John Clapham, a secretary to Burleigh. *Narcissus*, a pointedly learned, moralizing poem in Latin about another handsome youth's rejection of love, virtually invites a poet like Shakespeare to outstrip its clanking rhetorical set-pieces and Latin puns in his own expressive and potent native English. In any case, though Shakespeare went on to dedicate *The Rape of Lucrece* to the earl in 1594, in considerably warmer terms, there is no evidence that he received any reward from him or that their association continued.

Whatever Shakespeare's reasons for writing the poem, it was a stupendous success, running through sixteen editions before 1640, and remaining popular through the seventeenth century (see Chapter 14 in this volume). Few copies of these editions remain, an indication that they were much read, and by many readers. A copy of a 1595 octavo edition in the Folger Shakespeare Library measures just 5³/₈ by 3½ inches – small enough for a reader to slip into a pocket or inside a doublet. Within the year, some of those readers set out to imitate the work. Thomas Edwards wrote two poems based on Ovidian love stories, *Narcissus* and *Cephalus and Procris*, and Michael Drayton embellished his historical narrative about Edward III's love for Piers Gaveston with comparisons to 'Love-nursing *Venus*' and 'cherry-lipt *Adonis*'. The young Thomas Heywood, later to be Shakespeare's theatrical colleague, weighed in with the blatantly imitative *Oenone and Paris*.[7] In 1598, Gabriel Harvey remarked that 'The younger sort takes much delight in Shakespeare's Venus and Adonis', and allusions to the poem continue to pop up in plays well into the seventeenth century.[8] One character, a foppish gallant trying to woo his mistress with poetry, quotes the entire second stanza of *Venus and Adonis*, and rhapsodizes 'Ile worshippe sweet Master Shakespeare, and to honoure him will lay his *Venus and Adonis* under my pillowe'.[9]

Ironically, the poem's very success accounts at least partly for the fact that it has since become marginal to what most readers think of as 'Shakespeare's works' – his plays. Because *Venus and Adonis* was so marketable, printing rights would have been expensive for his fellow shareholders to obtain when they collected his plays in the 1623 Folio. Like *Lucrece* and the Sonnets, *Venus and Adonis* wasn't even published together with the plays until Rowe's 1709 edition of Shakespeare's complete works, and then it appeared in supplementary volumes with the other poems.

Why *was* the poem so successful? First of all, Shakespeare cashed in on the centuries-old popularity of the *Metamorphoses*, a compendium of classical myths written by the Latin poet Ovid during the early empire between AD 2 (or earlier) and AD 8 (see Chapter 2 in this volume). From the Middle Ages on, this vast poem had been a key text in European culture, appropriated in myriad forms for music, the visual arts, and literature of many kinds. Over time, two branches of interpretation had arisen. One, stemming from the *Ovide Moralisé* of fourteenth-century France, allegorized Ovid's pagan myths to make them exemplify Christian doctrine, changing their original meaning but incidentally preserving them as a storehouse for later writers. The other saw Ovid as the poet of unbridled sensuality, the 'archpriest of transgression', and denounced him while inadvertently acknowledging his appeal and literary artistry.[10]

In the sixteenth century, both branches remained, but at the universities and Inns of Court, where young men already well versed in Ovid sought what was provocative and new, it was the amoral, sensual side of him that seized their interest. In the 1580s, Robert Greene, John Marston, Thomas Lodge, and most notably Christopher Marlowe, who translated Ovid's erotic poems the *Amores*, began to imitate the poet's virtuosic style and mine his inventive stories of erotic passion. When Thomas Lodge's *Glaucus and Scilla* was published in 1589, its urbanely comic treatment of a grotesque love-affair based on an Ovidian story (Scilla, who repulses the sea-god Glaucus, is changed into a monster in retaliation) helped to put the emergent genre of the long mythological Ovidian poem (later termed *epyllion* or brief epic) on the literary map.[11]

Shakespeare's poem followed four years later. It was entered in the Stationers' Register on 18 April 1593, several weeks before Marlowe's sudden death on 30 May. His Ovidian poem, *Hero and Leander*, was entered the following September, just after *Venus and Adonis* was published. We cannot know which poet led the way, and which followed. If Marlowe is the 'rival poet' mentioned in the Sonnets, nowhere is that rivalry clearer than in these two poems. Both take their plots from mythological love affairs, and both adopt a highly mannered, slyly witty style, with digressive set-pieces, learned allusions, and titillating erotic episodes. But Shakespeare's is by far the more dramatic: his characters speak in their own voices, their language expressing their distinctive traits and attitudes. While Marlowe sets his poem in a pseudo-classical world, Shakespeare evokes an English rural scene. Both emulate Ovid's wit and self-conscious rhetorical play, but it is only Shakespeare who also shares Ovid's serious interest in the emotional depths of love, its risks and its costs.

The *Metamorphoses* begins with the creation of the world and ends with the stellification of Augustus, the emperor who exiled the poet to the Black Sea in mid-career. Aside from this encompassing chronological framework, the network of disparate tales is held together by the motif of metamorphosis, which is itself many-faceted and hard to summarize. While the foundational concept of the poem is the distinction between divine, human, animal, and the inanimate as basic categories of existence, through metamorphosis Ovid incessantly sabotages and plays with these categories. When the wily Lycaon is turned into a wolf, his essentially bestial nature is realized in another form; when Hecuba's personality is extinguished by her desire for vengeance against the murderer of her son, she hardens into stone.[12]

Ovid's transformations, however, don't conform to a single paradigm. The nymph Daphne, fleeing the embraces of Apollo, prays to escape him, and is turned into a laurel tree, which Apollo makes into a symbol of poetic achievement. Unlike Lycaon's metamorphosis into a wolf, Daphne's bodily change reflects nothing of her own personality or behaviour. In another respect, however, it is typical of many such changes in the poem: it is occasioned by sexual desire, Apollo's desire for her and her resistance to him. Above all, Ovid is fascinated by the many forms desire takes, and the changes it wreaks on human beings, driving them to the heights and depths of human feeling and conduct. Many tales in the *Metamorphoses* recount perverse desires that go against law and custom: Iphis, raised as a boy but actually a girl, falls in love with the bride chosen for her; Myrrha lusts for her father; the virginal Europa is charmed by the silky white bull (Jove in disguise) that amiably kneels to her. Often (as in the story of Venus and Adonis), these tales of desire are in effect tales of sexual initiation; they dramatize the mixed emotions of fear and yearning that accompany the advent of sexuality, and the desiring subject's ventures outside the self to encounter the other.[13] For Ovid, sexual desire amounts to a basic law of human existence: it cannot be avoided or resisted, and somehow or other, it will have its way, transforming us to beasts, birds, trees, rocks, flowers, monsters.

Ovid's stylistic virtuosity in depicting the capricious and overwhelming psychological changes wrought by desire, as well as its often grotesque physical mutations, is unparalleled. William Keach describes Ovid's style as a 'sustained, complex simultaneity of irony, humor, verbal wit, grotesqueness and erotic pathos'.[14] Here, for example, is Narcissus (one of several models for Shakespeare's Adonis) entranced by his own image in the pool into which he gazes:

> I burn with love for my own self; it's I
> who light the flames – the flames that scorch me then.
> What shall I do? Should I be sought or seek?
> But then, why must I seek? All that I need,
> I have: my riches mean my poverty.
> If I could just be split from my own body![15]

In this passage, Ovid renders the blind persistence of Narcissus, who vainly desires to possess his own beautiful image as though it were a lover, from the youth's point of view. Yet at the same time, the poet enables us to see the irony of the situation: how the boy's desire blots out his realization of its futility, and the perversity of his wish to split mind from body. No wonder that Shakespeare, whose capacity to inhabit villains and heroes alike, expressing their desires without overt judgement on them, has often been praised, found in Ovid a literary *alter ego*.

Though it has been shown that Shakespeare could have read Ovid in Latin, Arthur Golding's translation of the *Metamorphoses*, completed in 1567, offered him an example of how to make English do what Ovid had done.[16] Working in fourteeners (seven accented syllables to the line), Golding rendered Ovid's delicate detail in homey English idiom, yet also made his verses flow. Shakespeare was hardly the only writer to find a model in Ovid. According to Jonathan Bate, 'Extensive reading and memorizing of the *Metamorphoses* was almost universally required in sixteenth century grammar schools ... It is not an exaggeration to say that Shakespeare's first lessons in poetry were lessons in the imitation of Ovid'.[17] While scouring the *Metamorphoses* for examples of elegant Latin, Elizabethan tutors screened out his other major work, the *Amores*, as salacious and improper for pedagogical purposes. *Venus and Adonis*, however, is almost as indebted to this collection of lyrics charting the agonies of desire and the delights of seduction as it is to Ovid's mythological tales.

Shakespeare made a single change in Ovid's tale that stamped the story with his own quintessentially dramatic imagination. He altered Adonis, who in the *Metamorphoses* is passively compliant with Venus's desire, into a resistant lover who ironically rejects the goddess of love herself. At the same time, he put Venus in the male seducer's role, the role of the speaker in the *Amores* bent on arguing his way into bed, or of the Petrarchan poet-lover, yearning after an unattainable beloved. Thus he created a conflict between two wills, two equally insistent desires: to love and not to love. The more adamantly Adonis scorns the goddess of love, the more rhetorically inventive she must be, trying by turns to beg or bully her way into his affections. Yet despite the comic distance entailed in this unconventional gender reversal, Shakespeare didn't leave behind the urgency and the pathos of desire that he found in the *Metamorphoses*.

Venus

'She's love, she loves, and yet she is not loved' (610); with this elegant brevity Shakespeare's narrator sums up Venus's plight. Though the poet changed Ovid's tale to create this striking impasse, the idea that love is inherently contradictory actually lies at the heart of the *Metamorphoses*, imaged in book 1 by Cupid's twin arrows (1.470–4). The golden one smites its object with desire, while the leaden one inspires revulsion toward the one who desires. Together they represent the paradigm of eros that underlies Ovid's entire poem and that certainly drives *Venus and Adonis*: frustration, conflict, perversity.

Venus, whose desire dominates the poem (of its 1,194 lines, she speaks almost half, while Adonis has only 88), is ironically a goddess rendered powerless by the very power – love – that she represents. Unlike the gods in Ovid's poem, who can rape the women they desire, Venus's only leverage is verbal. In her shifting arguments Shakespeare shows off his mastery of rhetorical tropes and of characterization. As she tries one ploy and then another, he keeps readers 'seesawing between sympathy and judgment'.[18] The poem begins with the physical comedy of Venus actually plucking Adonis from his horse and tucking him under her arm, to prevent him from going off to the hunt (29–32), a move that broadly announces the reversal of gender roles and suggests a humorous treatment of it. Entwined with these comic effects is a concurrent satire of the conventions of love poetry. Venus uses the hyperbole, imagery, diction, and allegory that male poet-speakers use to praise and persuade their resisting mistresses, but her rhetoric seems oddly incongruent with a *male* object of desire:

> 'Thrice fairer than myself', thus she began,
> 'The field's chief flower, sweet above compare,
> Stain to all nymphs, more lovely than a man,
> More white and red than doves and roses are:
>   Nature that made thee, with herself at strife,
>   Saith that the world hath ending with thy life.'   (7–12)

Deliberately overworking the contrast of red and white already used to praise the mistress's complexion in dozens of Elizabethan lyrics, Shakespeare employs it three times in the first thirty-five lines (10, 21, and 35). Since the terms of comparison are those used for the female beloved, the effect is to feminize Adonis. No blushing sonnet mistress herself, Venus continues to take the initiative, brusquely pushing Adonis to the ground. Awkwardly, 'Each leaning on their elbows and their hips', she kisses him and 'chides' him all at once, which provokes another incongruity, 'the maiden burning of *his* cheeks' (50, my emphasis).

Then, when Venus 'murders with a kiss' Adonis's protests (54), Shakespeare changes tone with breathtaking suddenness, introducing a tension between the amusement tempered with a certain sympathy that we may already feel, and the revulsion, perhaps combined with a kind of awe, produced by the following simile:

> Even as an empty eagle, sharp by fast,
> Tires with her beak on feathers, flesh, and bone,
> Shaking her wings, devouring all in haste,
> Till either gorge be stuffed or prey be gone –
>   Even so she kissed his brow, his cheek, his chin,
>   And where she ends she doth anew begin.   (55–60)

At this moment Venus embodies desire in the Ovidian sense as a blind impersonal force that overwhelms man or woman, god or human, obliterating normal consciousness, and in mind if not in body transforming the desiring subject into an animal. The eagle is by instinct a bird of prey, and this eagle is moreover 'empty' and 'sharp by fast': impelled by natural hunger. But the eagle isn't limited to the mere satisfaction of hunger, it devours 'Till either gorge be stuffed or prey be gone'.[19] Gestures that seemed comical a few stanzas before, when Venus 'courageously' plucked Adonis from his horse, now acquire an ominous destructive potential.

A few stanzas later, Adonis still disdainful, Venus tries another tack. Thinking to impress the youth with the prestige of her previous conquests, she cites the well-known story of her affair with Mars (*Metamorphoses* 4.171–89). Here the eagle's fearsomeness mutates into sly humour. 'Yet hath he been my captain and my slave' (101), Venus brags, listing emblems of emasculation familiar to Renaissance readers:

> 'Over my altars hath he hung his lance,
> His batt'red shield, his uncontrolled crest,
> And for my sake hath learned to sport and dance,
> To toy, to wanton, dally, smile and jest' . . .   (103–6)

As Heather Dubrow notes, 'Venus repeatedly uses words of whose destructive or threatening connotations she, unlike the reader, is unaware'.[20] The disparity between the intention behind Venus' description of 'the stern and direful god of war' transformed to a lady's man, and its actual impact, undermines whatever sympathy her frustrated yearning invites. Two stanzas later, in yet another of her myriad guises, Venus abandons any hint of domination, and invites Adonis to share a kiss of enchanting tenderness and full mutuality:

> 'Touch but my lips with those fair lips of thine –
> Though mine be not so fair, yet are they red –
> The kiss shall be thine own as well as mine.
> . . .
> Look in mine eye-balls, there thy beauty lies:
> Then why not lips on lips, since eyes in eyes?'   (115–20)

In one of the poem's most famous passages, Venus again adopts a seductive tone when, comparing her body to a park, she invites Adonis to 'Feed where thou wilt, on mountain or in dale' or 'Stray lower, where the pleasant fountains lie' (232, 234). She portrays herself as a quasi-maternal source of nourishment and protection while at the same time wittily offering her body, part by part, for his sexual pleasure. The park imagery, however, has another dimension, suggested by her body language: 'lock[ing] her lily fingers one in one', she has 'hemmed' Adonis in her arms (225–30). Just as noblemen created private parks as refuges where deer were fed and protected, only in order to assure that they were available to be hunted and killed, the image implies that the goddess has imprisoned Adonis in her arms to possess and dominate rather than protect and nourish him. She would turn one kind of venery into another.[21]

Venus herself, however, represents her desire as completely 'natural'. Nature seems to agree with her when Adonis's horse breaks his rein and rushes to 'a breeding jennet', a mare that emerges just when Adonis 'hasteth to his horse' (258). While the youth seeks to escape love, his horse, as Venus notes, 'welcomes the warm approach of sweet desire' (386). Shakespeare devotes eleven stanzas to describing the imperious rearing, neighing, and bounding of the aroused horses (259–324), which generations of readers have interpreted both as a model for the recalcitrant Adonis and as the emblem of appetite uncontrolled by reason. By making both interpretations possible, the poem 'calls into question . . . the whole idea of animal behavior as something from which human beings can draw a useful lesson, whether positive or negative'.[22] Even more ambiguously, the horses act like human lovers, assuming the usual gender roles and practising the wiles of courtship (for example, the mare is 'proud, as females are', to be wooed, but 'puts on outward strangeness', 309–10). Venus, though she urges Adonis to 'learn to love' from his horse, continues to play the man's role in pursuing him.

Shakespeare builds the poem's dramatic action around the goddess's insistent desire for a kiss. In her various aspects – whether as mighty goddess, seductive woman, instinct-driven animal, or nurturing mother – she is associated with the oral pleasures of kissing or eating. At the crisis of her passion, the two kinds of imagery merge, in the kiss that devours its object, as when, in order to make his escape, Adonis finally offers her a kiss:

> Now quick desire hath caught the yielding prey,
> And glutton-like she feeds, yet never filleth.
> Her lips are conquerors, his lips obey,
> Paying what ransom the insulter willeth;
>   Whose vulture thought doth pitch the price so high
>   That she will draw his lips' rich treasure dry.   (547–52)

In contrast to the earlier eagle image, these lines convey not animal hunger, but a specifically human lust for conquest. Gluttony replaces fast, as Venus is first a military 'conqueror' and then an 'insulter,' who makes the kiss a kind of rape, a far cry from the delicate pleasure of 'lips on lips'. Yet it is her 'thought', her raging desire rather than her physical action, that is a 'vulture': she does no actual harm to Adonis. In the next stanza, Shakespeare again uses not an animal simile, but rather the conventional language for men in the height of battle, when he says, 'Her face doth reek and smoke, her blood doth boil', and ratchets up the moral costs of her passion, as she 'Forget[s] shame's pure blush and honour's wrack' (555, 558), ideals for which men, not animals, go to war.

Which is more irrational, amoral, and 'inhuman': a hungry eagle or a soldier who rapes? Is 'animal' desire such as the horses exhibit an aspect of our humanness, or foreign to it? What does it mean to be human? In the *Metamorphoses*, Ovid raises such questions not only through the sheer fiction of magical bodily transformations, but also through stories of perverse desire and the extreme emotions it provokes. In *Venus and Adonis*, Shakespeare follows Ovid in that he 'engages the question of what, given the inherent perversity of desire, constitutes "natural" sexual behavior', and 'repeatedly transgresses the discrete taxonomies of human and animal'.[23] Is it more 'natural' for Venus to satisfy desire than for Adonis to resist it? What is at stake in her desire and his resistance?

Adonis

In Ovid's story of Venus and Adonis, the hero is *iam iuvenis, iam vir*, 'now a youth, now man', implying that he is neither one nor the other, but in between, in the liminal phase of adolescence.[24] In Shakespeare's poem, Venus notes that he is still beardless (127–8), and when he speaks to her, his tone and gesture convey the sullenness of an adolescent with a 'heavy, dark, disliking eye' (182). His first words, 'The sun doth burn my face, I must remove' (186), suggest an adolescent's petulant self-centredness. These relatively precise indications of Adonis's age make it possible to see the central conflict in terms of a male rite of passage, a transition from the dependency of childhood in which women as mothers are nurturant yet controlling, to the social and sexual prerogatives of manhood, in which women become sexual objects to *be controlled* by men.[25] 'Hunting he loved, but love he laughed to scorn': in the poem's fourth line, this deft chiasmus frames Adonis's rejection of Venus as an opposition between two gender-specific domains, each a proving ground of manhood that offers a distinct mode of self-knowledge to the youth on his way to manhood.

When Adonis cries, 'Before I know myself, seek not to know me,' refusing Venus the 'carnal knowledge' of him that she seeks (525), Shakespeare links the conflict between them to a discourse of the self. Adonis means that he is too young for sexual intimacy, but in refusing the goddess of love, he refuses the very idea of love itself – Ovid's principle of eros. The alliteration linking 'know' and 'not', moreover, and the chiasmus stressing an opposition between Adonis knowing himself and Venus 'knowing' him, suggest that the real issue isn't age but rather Adonis's sense that eros is a threat to the self, against which he must defend himself. When he tells her that his heart 'will not ope the gate' to love (424), and declares,

> 'For know, my heart stands armed in mine ear,
> And will not let a false sound enter there,

Lest the deceiving harmony should run
Into the quiet closure of my breast;
And then my little heart were quite undone,
In his bed-chamber to be barred of rest.'   (779–84)

the imagery of his 'heart' as an inner sanctum to be protected and defended
at all cost suggests that he would turn away from any suitor, even one
less insistent or overbearing than Venus, because he is fearful of anything
that would disturb or change a precarious, and precious, sense of his innermost self.

Possibly, Shakespeare took the interrelated themes of self, knowledge, and
sexual initiation from the stories of Narcissus and of Hermaphroditus in the
Metamorphoses, which are closely related to that of Adonis. All three heroes
are young, strikingly beautiful, and attractive to both sexes; all reject women
who pursue them. Two die as a result of that rejection, and are metamorphosed into flowers that represent salient aspects of their human selves. The
Narcissus story begins when his mother asks Tiresias whether her son will
attain long life. ' "Yes, if he never knows himself," ' the seer replies (3.348).
The youth rejects the nymph Echo who is smitten with him, and instead falls
in love with the image of himself reflected in a pool. Eventually, he wastes
away and dies. As Anthony Mortimer remarks, the prophecy ironically turns
out to be wrong, because 'It is obsession with the self rather than true self-
knowledge that destroys Narcissus', for the image in the pool is neither the
youth himself nor another person as he takes it to be, but merely an illusion.
The story implies, then, that 'true self knowledge is only to be gained through
knowledge of others'.[26] In Ovid's terms, it is gained through acknowledging
the supremacy of eros, that which impels us to desire others, and however
much we risk, to open ourselves to them.

In a revealing stanza, Venus sarcastically compares Adonis to Narcissus:

'Is thine own heart to thine own face affected?
Can thy right hand seize upon thy left?
Then woo thyself, be of thyself rejected;
Steal thine own freedom, and complain on theft.
  Narcissus so himself himself forsook,
  And died to kiss his shadow in the brook.'   (157–62)

The repetition of 'himself' in line 161 mimics Narcissus's determination to
fasten on himself as an object to the exclusion of others, and suggests that in
loving only himself, Narcissus 'forsakes' himself by forgetting what everyone
should know: that self-love paradoxically impoverishes the self. When Venus
reproaches Adonis with refusing to reproduce, she comments similarly, 'So in
thyself thyself art made away' (763). In the first seventeen sonnets, the young

man 'contracted to [his] own bright eyes' resembles Narcissus and Adonis. The speaker calls him 'Thyself thy foe, to thy sweet self too cruel' (1.5, 8), warning that he will be 'the tomb / Of his self-love' (3.7–8), with a similar emphasis on the self-destructiveness of turning away from others to love oneself instead.[27]

From the poem's first stanza, when 'Rose-cheeked Adonis hied him to the chase', the youth is bent on hunting, while Venus strives only to detain him for the pleasures of love. Hunting is a male domain, and for the Renaissance, love is a female one. The two kinds of self-knowledge advocated by Venus and Adonis define two conceptions of the male passage to maturity that are aligned with these gender-specific pursuits. For Venus, it is carnal knowledge that ought to initiate Adonis into manhood; for Adonis, it is the hunt.[28] Both the action and the structure of the poem emphasize this opposition, for when Adonis finally succeeds in breaking away from Venus to go hunting (811–14), his departure divides the poem into two parts. The first consists of a single action, Venus's prolonged attempt to seduce him; the second, more fragmented, comprises her discovery of his corpse, her lamentation, and his metamorphosis.

While Shakespeare exploits in diverse ways the symbolic significance of Venus as the embodiment of sexual pleasure, he doesn't make explicit Adonis's reasons for preferring hunting to love. For Elizabethan readers, they would have been clear enough. Amongst the elite, hunting was 'a means of bonding adolescent males to each other and to the adult fraternity of the chase', thus initiating them into masculinity. Moreover, hunting was both celebrated and criticized 'for its capacity to initiate young men into the strategies and hardships of war' – the province of men.[29] Therefore, when Venus, horrified and frightened by Adonis's intention 'To hunt the boar with certain of his friends', throws her arms around his neck, drags him to the ground, and enters 'the very lists of love', gender boundaries are being clearly drawn (591–5). She is trying to confine him within a woman's world of words, comfort, and pleasure, while he seeks initiation into a man's world of deeds, competition, and danger.

The boar

It isn't hunting *per se* that throws Venus into a panic, though; it is hunting the boar. Suggestively, when Adonis declared his aversion to love – 'I know not love, nor will not know it' – he added what seemed a joking exception: 'Unless it be a boar, and then I chase it' (409–10). In medieval and Renaissance tradition, the boar, 'A mortal butcher bent to kill', is the most aggressive and dangerous animal hunted, and moreover 'a symbol' of 'overbearing masculinity in love and war'.[30] As Venus's three-stanza description makes clear, every part of the boar's body constitutes a weapon (615–36), especially its tusks, which point downward, so that in its foraging the boar unintentionally 'digs sepulchres where'er he goes' (622). There are more specific reasons for Venus to fear the boar, however. Unlike the deer or the hare which she suggests to Adonis as more suitable prey, the boar is so aggressive that hunting it is 'a supreme test of manhood', in which 'The youth becomes a man by taking on the boar's virility', in the form of 'an aggressive adult masculinity'.[31] Ovid's narrator, commenting on Venus's attempt to dissuade Adonis from boar hunting, says, 'But daring [Lat. *virtus*, manliness] is not keen to heed such warnings'. He specifies that the boar 'sinks his long tusks/into Adonis' groin', making it clear that in this conflict, the youth's masculinity is at stake (10.714–15). Again, Shakespeare makes the conflict between the goddess and the youth a gender-specific struggle between female- and male-oriented forms of initiation into manhood.

At the same time, the boar can be seen not as Venus's opposite but rather as a surrogate for her that mirrors and carries out the destructive aspects of her desire, its 'vulture thought' and 'blindfold fury' (551, 554).[32] In Edward Topsell's *The History of Foure-Footed Beasts* (1607), the best-known bestiary of the English Renaissance, the boar is described as a strikingly libidinous animal: 'inflamed with venereal rage, he so fretteth upright the bristles of his neck ... then champeth he with his mouth, grateth and gnasheth his teeth one against another, and breathing forth his boyling spirit, ... he desireth nothing but copulation'.[33] It is Venus who first describes the beast; with an odd tenderness, she imagines it killing Adonis, and taking her place by murdering him with a kiss:

> If he did see his face, why then I know
> He thought to kiss him, and hath killed him so
> . . .
> But by a kiss thought to persuade him there;
> And nuzzling in his flank, the loving swine
> Sheathed unaware the tusk in his soft groin.
>
> (1109–10, 1114–16)

Blind to the grotesque mixture of affection and brutality in this picture, she reinforces it: 'Had I been toothed like him, I must confess, / With kissing him I should have killed him first' (1117–18). The boar's fatal penetration of the youth suggests several kinds of 'perverse' desire. Not only does the boar play a masculine role that echoes Venus's assumption of the male's role in courtship – it also parodies Sir Edward Coke's legal 1644 definition of bestiality (sexual intercourse with animals), in which 'the least penetration maketh it carnall knowledge'.[34] Finally, Venus's fantasy of the masculine boar kissing

Adonis portrays them as a homoerotic couple committing sodomy, an affront to political and moral order.[35] As mentioned earlier, these kinds of transgressive desire – crossing the boundaries between human and animal, violating gender roles – connect the poem with a philosophical discourse that questions basic ontological and social categories.

Prophecy and metamorphosis

The final moments of the poem dramatize two actions: Venus's prophecy and the metamorphosis of Adonis. In Ovid's version, these moments are relatively brief, taking up only seventeen lines. Shakespeare expands them considerably, enriching the ironies and contradictions that have previously marked his treatment of Venus's transgressive love and Adonis's resistance to it.

Ovid's Venus doesn't 'prophesy' at all. Rather, she changes Adonis to a flower, an action that she intends as an eternal remembrance of him, and establishes an annual feast that will bear his name, an allusion to the Adonia, the annual commemoration of Adonis's death celebrated in the ancient world (*Metamorphoses* 10. 724–7). In contrast, Venus's prophecy sounds much like an act of revenge: '*Since* thou art dead', she says, 'lo, here I prophesy, / Sorrow on love hereafter shall attend' (1135–6, emphasis mine). Five stanzas follow, describing the contrariness of love, reading like an inventory of the vicissitudes providing the obstacles and momentum that drive love-story plots (1135–65), and anticipating the briefer list chimed by Hermia and Lysander in *A Midsummer Night's Dream* (1.1.134–9). Venus's tally of love's 'sorrow' includes jealousy, inequality of rank and difference in age, infidelity, deception, and most of all extreme and contradictory emotions that make lovers 'sparing, and too full of riot,' 'raging mad and silly mild', 'merciful, and too severe'. Ironically, this copious list implies that before Adonis died, desire was unproblematic, but the whole poem dramatizes Venus's infatuation with someone who is oblivious to her charms. As Cupid's gold and lead arrows of desire and revulsion mentioned earlier indicate, however, in Ovid's world disappointment is inherent in desire, which is bound to bring sorrow in its wake.[36] From the beginning, Shakespeare has made Venus sound unpredictably like a goddess in one stanza and a mere mortal in the next. In these final moments, she seems to be both at once: her prophecy suggests the prescience of a divinity but also the rancor of a mere woman, who is much more true to the concept of desire that she represents than she herself realizes.

Shakespeare makes Adonis's metamorphosis tender and moving. Yet it also reiterates elements of perversity already present in his relations with Venus.

In Ovid's story, Venus sprinkles nectar on Adonis's blood, from which spring flowers the colour of pomegranates, a fruit associated with fertility; thus the flowers hint at the youth's regeneration. In contrast, the metamorphosis in Shakespeare's poem occurs without any action on Venus's part at all:

> By this the boy that by her side lay killed
> Was melted like a vapour from her sight,
> And in his blood that on the ground lay spilled
> A purple flower sprung up, check'red with white,
>   Resembling well his pale cheeks and the blood
>   Which in round drops upon their whiteness stood.   (1165–70)

Nor does this transformation carry the hopeful associations of the original story. Venus imagines the flower as Adonis's child ('Sweet issue of a sweet-smelling sire', 1178), and thus as the image of its father, whom she sees as both her child and her lover:

> 'Here was thy father's bed, here in my breast;
> Thou art the next of blood, and 'tis thy right.
> Lo, in this hollow cradle take thy rest,
> My throbbing heart shall rock thee day and night;
>   There shall not be one minute in an hour
>   Wherein I will not kiss my sweet love's flower.'   (1183–8)

Thus the metamorphosis hints of incest, for in these gestures of cradling and kissing Adonis, Venus sees herself as both his mother and his lover. It also reminds us of the youth's actual parentage. As the issue of his mother's incestuous relationship with her father Cinyras, who is Venus's son, he is his mother's sister, his grandfather's son, etc.: a confusion of normal kinship relations that mirrors the ambiguity of his relations with Venus.[37]

Piling further intimations of perversity on to the flower image, Shakespeare has Venus say, after she 'crops the stalk' of the flower that now represents the flower-like, 'feminine' beauty of the dead youth (1175),

> To grow unto himself was his desire,
>   And so 'tis thine, but know it is as good
>   To wither in my breast as in his blood.   (1180–2)

Cropping the flower (an action Shakespeare adds to Ovid's original), then placing it in her bosom like a nursing child, only to let it 'wither', Venus recapitulates something of the unintentionally annihilating qualities of her desire that were imaged in the devouring eagle. The youth who, like Narcissus, wanted only 'to grow unto himself' is now completely fused with the goddess whose desire for him was represented as insatiable.

Moreover, as a flower that Venus says she will kiss every 'minute in an hour' he is also 'an object of cultivation', something like the potted plants known as 'Gardens of Adonis', which became popular in Elizabethan England.[38] His status confounds the boundary between nature and culture, as Venus's love for him confounds the boundary between the maternal and the erotic, as his own flower-like self-regard confounded the distinction between self and other.

In terms of the initiation into manhood at the core of the story, though Adonis successfully fights off Venus's sexual demands, when he is gored by the boar he loses more than manhood. He dies defending himself against eros, yet by the standards of the Renaissance or the classical world, it is a manly death. Then, as the flower that Venus 'crops', he is reduced to a mere image, Venus's fiction of him. Yet the image is deeply ambiguous. She possesses him totally – but only as a flower, symbolically. Withering in her bosom, he seems to have surrendered to her all-embracing love, but in another sense, he dominates her totally: she kisses him 'every minute in an hour'. Though Shakespeare has transformed Ovid's story, he has also remained true to Ovid's conception of eros as a paradox, a mystery: inexorable yet finally ambiguous and elusive.

NOTES

1 See Cheney, *Shakespeare, National Poet–Playwright* (Cambridge University Press, 2004), p. 78, for a list of plays probably written by the time Shakespeare published *Venus and Adonis*.

2 On the poem's publication and dedication, see Burrow (ed.), *Complete Sonnets and Poems* (Oxford University Press, 2002), pp. 6–15.

3 Cheney sees this two-step pattern in *Venus and Adonis*, in the contrast between the pastoral world that Venus invokes in her wooing, and the vigorous, traditionally masculine hunt that Adonis embraces. See Cheney, *Shakespeare, National Poet–Playwright*, pp. 81–108.

4 Translated by John Roe (ed.), *The Poems* (Cambridge University Press, 1992), p. 78.

5 Anthony Mortimer, *Variable Passions: A Reading of Shakespeare's 'Venus and Adonis'* (New York: AMS Press, 2000), p. 2.

6 Stephen Greenblatt, *Will in the World: How Shakespeare Became Shakespeare* (New York: Norton, 2004), pp. 28–9.

7 Katherine Duncan-Jones, 'Much Ado with Red and White: The Earliest Readers of Shakespeare's *Venus and Adonis*', *Review of English Studies*, ns 44 (1993), 480–501.

8 C. M. Ingleby, *et al.* (compilers), *The Shakespere Allusion-Book: A Collection of Allusions to Shakespere from 1591 to 1700*, 2 vols. (London: Oxford University Press, 1932), I: 56.

9 Anon., *The First Part of the Return from Parnassus* 995–1000, 1201–2, in J. B. Leishman (ed.), *The Three Parnassus Plays 1598–1601* (London: Ivor Nicholson & Watson, 1949).

10 Jeremy Dimmick, 'Ovid in the Middle Ages: Authority and Poetry', in Philip Hardie (ed.), *The Cambridge Companion to Ovid* (Cambridge University Press, 2002), pp. 264–87.

11 For a fine study of Ovidian narrative poetry in Renaissance England, see William Keach, *Elizabethan Erotic Narratives: Irony and Pathos in the Ovidian Poetry of Shakespeare, Marlowe, and their Contemporaries* (New Brunswick, NJ: Rutgers University Press, 1977).

12 As Leonard Barkan says, 'Often the business of metamorphosis . . . is to make flesh of metaphors', by turning human flesh into the form that the human soul most resembles' (*The Gods Made Flesh: Metamorphosis and the Pursuit of Paganism* (New Haven: Yale University Press, 1986), p. 23).

13 For a fine discussion of the tale of Europa and the bull as a paradigm of sexual initiation, and metamorphosis as a 'figure for all the fears and necessities of exogamy', see Barkan, *The Gods*, pp. 13–15.

14 Keach, *Elizabethan Erotic Narratives*, p. 24.

15 *The Metamorphoses of Ovid*, trans. Allen Mandelbaum (New York: Harcourt, 1993), 3.464–9. Hereafter all quotations in English from the *Metamorphoses* will be taken from this translation.

16 See T. W. Baldwin, *Shakspere's Small Latine and Lesse Greeke*, 2 vols. (Urbana: University of Illinois Press, 1944), II: 417–55, for evidence that Shakespeare read the *Metamorphoses* in Latin; for excellent discussions of Golding's translation, see Gordon Braden, *The Classics in English Renaissance Poetry* (New Haven: Yale University Press, 1978), pp. 1–54; and Jonathan Bate, *Shakespeare and Ovid* (Oxford: Clarendon Press, 1993), pp. 1–47.

17 For an extensive discussion of the pedagogical, literary, and dramatic contexts in which Shakespeare would have known Ovid, see Bate, *Shakespeare and Ovid*, pp. 1–47.

18 Heather Dubrow, *Captive Victors: Shakespeare's Narrative Poems and Sonnets* (Ithaca: Cornell University Press, 1987), p. 42.

19 For an interpretation of this and other passages in the light of the psychoanalytic concept of narcissism, see Coppélia Kahn, *Man's Estate: Masculine Identity in Shakespeare* (Berkeley: University of California Press, 1981), pp. 21–46.

20 Dubrow, *Captive Victors*, p. 70.

21 Edward I. Berry, *Shakespeare and the Hunt: A Cultural and Social Study* (Cambridge University Press, 2002), p. 55.

22 Mortimer, *Variable Passions*, p. 78.

23 Dympna Callaghan, '(Un)natural Loving: Swine, Pets, and Flowers in *Venus and Adonis*', in *Textures of Renaissance Knowledge*, ed. Philippa Berry and Margaret Tudeau-Clayton (Manchester University Press, 2003), p. 75.

24 Ovid, *Metamorphoses*, trans. Frank Justus Miller, 2nd edn, 2 vols. (Cambridge, MA: Harvard University Press; and London: Heinemann, 1966), 10.523.

25 On the poem's action as a rite of passage, see Kahn, *Man's Estate*, pp. 21–46.

26 Mortimer, *Variable Passions*, p. 64.

27 See Kahn, *Man's Estate*, pp. 31–3, on the representation of self in the stories of Narcissus and of Hermaphroditus.

28 Specifically, Berry explains, 'For him, self-knowledge precedes sexual experience; for her, self-knowledge and sexual experience occur at the same time' (*Shakespeare and the Hunt*, p. 42).

29 Berry, *Shakespeare and the Hunt*, pp. 43, 45.

30 A. T. Hatto, '*Venus and Adonis* – and the Boar," *MLR* 41 (1946), 55–6.

31 Berry, *Shakespeare and the Hunt*, pp. 45, 47.

32 For a different view, see Mortimer, *Variable Passions*, pp. 155–6. Noting that the boar's 'kiss' dates to a late Greek poem that Shakespeare could have known, Mortimer argues that Venus intends 'to make the boar innocent by association with herself'.

33 Qtd in Callaghan, '(Un)natural Loving', pp. 62–3.

34 Qtd in Callaghan, '(Un)natural Loving', p. 60.

35 Callaghan, '(Un)natural Loving', p. 61.

36 For a compelling interpretation of the poem as a study in the illusory and frustrating nature of desire, see Belsey, 'Love as Trompe-l'oeil'. As Keach comments, 'Venus's erotic illusions have blinded her to the disorder and conflict inherent in the love of which she is the goddess. ... Yet these erotic illusions are themselves an essential aspect of the view of love enacted in the poem' (*Elizabethan Erotic Narratives*, p. 81).

37 See Ovid, *Metamorphoses* 10. 298–518. See also Bate, *Shakespeare and Ovid*, pp. 51, 54–5, for a discussion of how this story exerts a 'contextual pressure' on Shakespeare's poem.

38 Callaghan, '(Un)natural Loving', p. 74.

READING LIST

Barkan, Leonard. *The Gods Made Flesh: Metamorphosis and the Pursuit of Paganism*. New Haven: Yale University Press, 1986.

Belsey, Catherine. 'Love as Trompe-l'oeil: Taxonomies of Desire in *Venus and Adonis*'. *Shakespeare Quarterly* 46 (1995), 251–76.

Berry, Edward I. *Shakespeare and the Hunt: A Cultural and Social Study*. Cambridge University Press, 2002.

Burrow, Colin (ed.). 'Introduction: *Venus and Adonis*', *The Oxford Shakespeare: Complete Sonnets and Poems*. Oxford University Press, 2002, pp. 6–40.

Callaghan, Dympna. '(Un)natural Loving: Swine, Pets, and Flowers in *Venus and Adonis*'. In *Textures of Renaissance Knowledge*. Ed. Philippa Berry and Margaret Tudeau-Clayton. Manchester University Press, 2003, pp. 58–78.

Dubrow, Heather. *Captive Victors: Shakespeare's Narrative Poems and Sonnets*. Ithaca: Cornell University Press, 1987.

Kahn, Coppélia. 'Self and Eros in *Venus and Adonis*'. *Man's Estate: Masculine Identity in Shakespeare*. Berkeley: University of California Press, 1981, pp. 21–46.

Keach, William. *Elizabethan Erotic Narratives: Irony and Pathos in the Ovidian Poetry of Shakespeare, Marlowe, and Their Contemporaries*. New Brunswick, NJ: Rutgers University Press, 1977.

Mortimer, Anthony. *Variable Passions: A Reading of Shakespeare's 'Venus and Adonis'*. New York: AMS Press, 2000.

Ovid. *The Metamorphoses of Ovid*. Trans. Allen Mandelbaum. New York: Harcourt, 1993.

5

CATHERINE BELSEY

The Rape of Lucrece

Shakespeare's second narrative poem, printed in 1594, links non-consensual sex with a tyrannical regime: Tarquin's violation of his friend's wife not only damages her but also shows him unfit to govern the state. *Lucrece* is almost certainly the 'graver labour' promised in the dedication to *Venus and Adonis*,[1] and its mode of address is appropriately elegiac, as well as rhetorically complex, characterized by intricate wordplay and elaborate conceits. These features, admired then, less appealing now, have often deterred modern readers. Is there, even so, a ready way through a text that has proved puzzling or alienating in our own time?

Tarquin's rape of Lucrece also goes on to haunt the margins of Shakespeare's plays. As a point of reference for later works, the story is repeatedly invoked at moments of dramatic tension, with the effect of bringing out the significance of the action. In Shakespeare's own epoch Lucrece's tragic tale and its political implications were already widely current, and the legendary names alone would have alerted a substantial proportion of the audience to specific resemblances. In addition, the exceptional popularity of Shakespeare's poem itself must have reinforced the familiarity of its subject matter. If the chaste Lucrece had come to stand as a byword for marital fidelity, Tarquin's name evoked the violent abuse of power. Their story carried a variety of resonances in the early modern period, so that by citing the events he had already recounted in one genre, Shakespeare could extend in another the range of meanings available to his audience.

Time and cultural change have a way, however, of modifying tastes. In the twenty-first century many people know Shakespeare's plays better than the poem, so that it is perhaps easier for us to put the original practice of citation into reverse. Possibly, then, the dramatic invocations of events the poem records can help us to single out aspects of a text that an earlier generation of critics often found prolix, repetitious, or just plain baffling. In the plays, while *Cymbeline* identifies Tarquin as invading the sanctity of the home,

Macbeth cites him as a knowing predator, aware of his own culpability. In *Julius Caesar*, meanwhile, Tarquin appears as a political oppressor, and the play alludes to the public consequences of his private crime. All three of these concerns are already delineated by the poem itself.

Like Lucrece, the heroine of *Cymbeline* welcomes a stranger who brings news of her absent husband, and like Lucrece, Imogen trustingly falls asleep in her own bed, that most vulnerable of all places, precisely because it should be the safest. Imogen's bedroom, like Lucrece's, is at the mercy of the duplicitous guest-turned-intruder, who creeps towards her sleeping body in the manner of his Roman predecessor: 'Our Tarquin thus / Did softly press the rushes, ere he wakened / The chastity he wounded' (*Cymbeline* 2.2.12–14). Iachimo does not disturb Imogen, however: he has other villainy in view. But the brief parallel with Lucrece's story alerts the audience to the possibility of rape, while Iachimo, in much the manner of Tarquin, pruriently studies the details of Imogen's sleeping body, before returning to his secret hiding-place in his own trunk. In each case it is the innocence of the woman that lays her open to deception. Imogen believes Iachimo when he pretends his sexual advances have been no more than a test of her fidelity; an inexperienced 'reader', Lucrece cannot draw the erotic inferences that would give meaning and point to Tarquin's admiring gaze (*Lucrece* 99–102). Iachimo's incursion into the privacy of Imogen's bedchamber endangers her reputation and in due course her life; Tarquin's violation of Lucrece's chastity threatens her honour and leads to her death. That aftermath forms the primary matter of more than half the poem.

It is not rape Macbeth has in mind, on the other hand, but regicide, and in this instance the precedent he invokes is Tarquin's surreptitious but remorseless tread, as he makes his way through the house at dead of night towards his prey. While evil dreams haunt sleepers in their curtained beds, Macbeth's own waking thought, whose murder still remains fantastical, generates a personified version of this intent:

> withered murder,
> Alarumed by his sentinel, the wolf,
> Whose howl's his watch, thus with his stealthy pace,
> With Tarquin's ravishing strides, towards his design
> Moves like a ghost.   (*Macbeth* 2.1.52–6)

The lawless Tarquin forces locks to reach Lucrece; his crime breaks the rules of hospitality and comradeship, as well as marriage. Macbeth's murder of Duncan repudiates the social obligations of hospitality, kinship, and allegiance. Each is fully aware of the implications of his criminal design; and each is driven by a destructive will to power that overcomes all moral scruples.

Macbeth dies in defence of the crown for which he has paid so high a price and which seems to give him, in the event, so little pleasure. Sextus Tarquinius, his desire slaked, if not gratified, slinks away from Lucrece's bed, and never comes to inherit the Roman kingdom. Instead, the entire Tarquin clan are banished for his deed, and monarchy gives way to the Republic at the instigation of Lucius Junius Brutus. Deliberating on the implications of Julius Caesar's apparent imperial ambitions, a later Brutus remembers his illustrious forebear: 'My ancestors did from the streets of Rome / The Tarquin drive when he was called a king' (*Julius Caesar* 2.1.53–4).[2] This time, however, the parallel is not exact. The first Brutus parades Lucrece's dead body through those same streets as evidence of Tarquin's crime; visual images of the time relate his oration to her death, as he incites the Romans to overthrow the Tarquin regime.[3] His descendant, by contrast, can do no more than make assumptions about Caesar's tyrannical purposes, 'since the quarrel / Will bear no colour for the thing he is' (2.1.28–9). Unlike Tarquin's, Caesar's wrongdoing is not available for all to see. On the contrary, this time it is the hero's opponent, Antony, who puts the victim's body on display in the marketplace, enlisting the citizens in civil war against the assassins. The irony would have been available to the play's audience. By citing the exile of the Tarquins as a heroic precedent for the murder of Caesar, Marcus Brutus reveals, in spite of himself, the nature of the deception practised on his own political naivety. His wilier predecessor had had the acumen to lie low until Lucrece offered a palpable and unifying cause for action.

These three issues, the personal implications of the rape for Lucrece, Tarquin's abuse of power, and the public consequences of the event for Rome, are held together in a narrative poem which begins in sexual politics and ends with the redistribution of rule in the state. At the same time, while the poem unfolds with the leisure available to a text designed to be read, it also reveals itself as the work of a dramatist, a poet–playwright who understands the distinct capabilities of each genre, but also permits a trace of each to appear in the other.

Rape and shame

Though she resists with all her might, Lucrece experiences the rape as shameful. There is no question that Tarquin takes possession of Lucrece's body by violence and against her will. She pleads and reasons, but her eloquence does not deter him.[4] Instead, he interrupts her in mid-sentence, stamps on the light, and gags her with her smock to prevent her crying out:

> The wolf hath seized his prey, the poor lamb cries,
> > Till with her own white fleece her voice controlled
> > Entombs her outcry in her lips' sweet fold.
>
> For with the nightly linen that she wears
> He pens her piteous clamours in her head,
> Cooling his hot face in the chastest tears
> That ever modest eyes with sorrow shed.   (677–83)

In a text replete with ambiguities this moment, at least, seems unequivocal. The association of whiteness with innocence and the dark with evil goes back a long way in textual history. So does the image of the wolf destroying the flock. In one of the classical sources Ovid compares Lucretia with a little lamb caught by a wolf, but for Shakespeare's readers the image would also carry biblical connotations.[5] Lucrece is decisively depicted here as faithful, pure, and helpless to resist Tarquin's tyrannical action. Later, the text will add that she was paralyzed with fear (1261–7).

Moreover, she has given Tarquin no excuse. Convinced by his praise of Collatine, incapable of suspecting his real purpose, Lucrece proffers the welcome appropriate to her husband's friend. When she wakes to find him in her bedchamber, she nonetheless musters every possible argument against what he intends. But Tarquin, driven by an imperative he himself hardly understands, is not amenable to reason, and Lucrece is left to bear the consequences of a crime she did not commit.

Even so, she feels ashamed. Tarquin's act leaves her blood ineradicably 'stained', like her bed, 'The spots whereof could weeping purify, / Her tears should drop on them perpetually' (685–6). Her body is ' "spotted, spoiled, corrupted" ' (1172). Although the ' "disgrace" ' is necessarily ' "invisible" ' (827), Lucrece feels as if her ignominy must be on display: even the daylight, when it comes, seems to be peering accusingly at her. One anonymous contemporary evidently admired this perception. A page of jottings, consisting mainly of Shakespeare's name in various forms, includes the titles of *Richard II* and *Richard III*, as well as the beginning of a single slight misquotation from *The Rape of Lucrece*.[6] In modern spelling and true to the printed poem, the lines read: 'Revealing day through every cranny spies, / And seems to point her out where she sits weeping' (1086–7). Shortly afterwards, in an episode that foreshadows the tragedies by verging on a comic interlude in this otherwise unremitting poem, the guileless servant who comes to take her letter to Collatine blushes at finding himself in her presence. Lucrece, convinced that he must know her secret, blushes in return, causing him to blush still more deeply, and the two face each other in embarrassed silence. Lucrece perceives herself as ' "guilty" ' (841); somehow the ' "trespass" ', the ' "sin" ', and the ' "crime" ' are hers, as well as Tarquin's (1070, 1074, 931). In the end, she concludes, only death, administered by her own hand in the high Roman fashion, can restore her integrity: ' "My life's foul deed, my life's fair end shall free it" ' (1208).

Commentators have found this odd. In experiencing her own position as shameful, however, she shares an understanding with other textual victims of rape familiar in the early modern period. Ovid's Lucretia yields in response to Tarquin's threat to leave her dead body in her bed with a slave, and is afterwards ashamed to face her husband and her father (*Fasti* 2.819). Chaucer's Lucrece, derived in general from Ovid's, differs in that she faints for the duration of the rape itself. We might think that this would exonerate her decisively, but thereafter she cannot speak to her friends for 'shame' (1835), and resolves that her husband shall not suffer for her 'gylt' (1844).[7] Moreover, Shakespeare's poem compares Lucrece with Ovid's Philomela, raped in the woods by her sister's husband. After the deed, Philomela vows to reveal his crime despite her shame (*Metamorphoses* 6.544–5), wishing Tereus had killed her first to leave her ghost free from blame (540–1).[8] When in 1576 George Gascoigne develops Ovid's account (and Chaucer's) of this story, his Phylomene speaks to her rapist of ' "my faulte, thy facte" ' (deed, line 261), as if the two were inextricable, just as they are for Lucrece.[9]

Gascoigne's Phylomene adds a wish: ' "oh that death (before this gilte) / Had overcome my will" ' (271–2). There is no suggestion that Phylomene is complicit in any way with her rapist. On the contrary. But, since both guilt and shame are apparently the inevitable concomitants of rape, death is consistently to be preferred. Chaucer also popularized a third related classical story: Livy's Verginia was threatened with rape by the judge, Appius, and to avert this catastrophe, her father cut off his daughter's head.[10] Chaucer's Virginius sees two options for the daughter he loves, either death or shame. Despite his anguish, he decides that he must kill her, and a tearful Virginia reluctantly concurs with this judgement: ' "Yif me my deeth, er that I have a shame" ' (249).[11] When R. B. publishes his version of this story as a moral play in 1575, it is Virginia who takes the initiative:

> Thou knowest, O my father, if I be once spotted,
> My name and my kindred then forth wilbe blotted;
> And if thou my father should die for my cause
> The world would accompt me as gilty in cause.   (794–7)[12]

Even though Virginius would gladly die to protect her, his death would not avert her shame and the world's view of her as guilty. Evidently, only an uncertain boundary divides what Virginia and her father know from others' opinion of the case. And she continues, 'Then rather, deare father, if it be thy pleasure, / Graunt me the death; then keepe I my treasure' (798–9).

In instances where death cannot prevent rape, it remains the only honourable outcome. Shakespeare's Titus Andronicus explicitly takes his cue from Virginius when he executes his own raped daughter, Lavinia, whose story also both draws on and exceeds Philomela's (5.3.36–44). Virginia offers a precedent, he avers, and a warrant for his own action: 'Die, die, Lavinia, and thy shame with thee, / And with thy shame thy father's sorrow die' (45–6).

Lavinia shares her plea for death and oblivion rather than rape (2.3.168–78) with both Philomela and Virginia. At the same time, the fate of Lucrece represents a recurring intertextual presence in this play that almost certainly dates from about the same period as the poem. Very nearly the whole story of *The Rape of Lucrece* appears in miniature in the margins of *Titus Andronicus*. Like Lucrece, but unlike Philomela and Virginia, Lavinia is already married when Chiron and Demetrius rape her in the woods. Even Aaron acknowledges that 'Lucrece was not more chaste / Than this Lavinia' (2.1.108–9). After the rape, Titus is anxious to know who perpetrated the crime. He suspects the new emperor: 'slunk not Saturnine, as Tarquin erst, / That left the camp to sin in Lucrece's bed?' (4.1.63–4). Marcus urges the Andronici to swear vengeance for Lavinia, just as, with *her* kindred, 'Lord Junius Brutus swore for Lucrece's rape' (4.1.91). Lucius has already vowed to drive out the imperial couple, 'like Tarquin and his queen' (3.1.297).[13]

Shakespeare does not repeat himself. Lavinia, her tongue cut out like Philomela's, cannot speak to explain her plight; Lucrece speaks copiously to define hers. It is not surprising, therefore, that cross-references should deepen the pathos as well as the authority of *Titus*. The early modern textual imbrication of these Roman heroines is more than purely Shakespearean, however. Gascoigne, faithful in general to Ovid's story of Philomela, had already amplified his own narrative by invoking lines from Ovid's (and Chaucer's) account of Lucrece.[14] If Titus claims Virginius as his precedent for killing Lavinia, R. B.'s villainous Judge Apius claims Tarquin as *his* pattern for raping Virginia.[15] Since these rape victims evidently formed a kind of intertextual support network, it must be legitimate to invoke the parallels between them in accounting for Lucrece's feelings of guilt and shame.

Only Shakespeare's poem, however, explores these feelings in detail. Modern rapists also leave their victims feeling contaminated by the crime they did not commit. Were they in some way complicit with the act? Did they unconsciously encourage it? What about the consequences, pregnancy, or disease? But while there is inevitably considerable overlap between these anxieties and the early modern response to rape, there are historical differences too. Lucrece's identity depends on her fidelity to her husband: from the beginning she is named as 'Lucrece the chaste' (7). If the place of wife and mother in the dynastic family seems to us a narrow one, it remains precious to its holder. The raped Lucrece both is and is not chaste: ' "I was a loyal wife: / So am I now – O no, that cannot be; / Of that true type hath Tarquin rifled me" ' (1048–50). Tarquin has stolen the justification of her good name and with it, in a world that does not distinguish as rigidly as we do between individual and family, inner and outer, personal and public, the meaning of what she is. Her legacy to succeeding ages, she fears, will be as an instance of scandal:

> 'The nurse to still her child will tell my story,
> And fright her crying babe with Tarquin's name.
> The orator to deck his oratory
> Will couple my reproach to Tarquin's shame.
> Feast-finding minstrels, tuning my defame,
>   Will tie the hearers to attend each line,
>   How Tarquin wrongèd me, I Collatine.'   (813–19)

If she is pregnant, no bastard, she resolves, must ever be born to ' "pollute" ' Collatine's lineage (1063);[16] she will not leave Tarquin in a position to laugh at her cuckolded husband (1065–6); nor will she stoop to conceal what has happened (1074–5). Lucrece believes she cannot live as the thing she has become; only death can demonstrate her true fidelity to the husband she loves. But in case this seems to modern eyes like a slavish subservience to *his* ' "crest" ' (828)[17] and *his* ' "stock" ' (1063), it is worth noting that she herself takes her decision, as the result of a long process of reasoning, and in her own name:

> 'For me, I am the mistress of my fate,
>   And with my trespass never will dispense,
>   Till life to death acquit my forced offence.'   (1069–71)

The paradox of her shame remains even in this resounding affirmation of sovereignty: her ' "offence" ' was ' "forced" ', and thus, we might want to argue, no ' "trespass" ' at all. But Lucrece would not agree. At her death the Roman men make clear that they see Lucrece as innocent. Does duress exonerate her, she asks: ' "May my pure mind with the foul act dispense?" ' (1704). 'With this they all at once began to say, / Her body's stain her mind untainted clears' (1709–10). But Lucrece is not persuaded by this rigorous separation of mind and body. Instead, she turns away a face 'which deep impression bears / Of hard misfortune, carved in it with tears' (1712–13). Her drawn countenance and her tears register in physiological form a psychological distress, calling into question the dualist view that separates consciousness from the flesh it inhabits.

Rape necessarily deconstructs that dualist opposition. Rape differs from common assault to the degree that it involves sexual intrusion and humiliation, with repercussions for both mind and body. Neither purely physiological – it breaks taboos and mortifies the victim – nor purely psychological – as physical violence, it is experienced physiologically and can issue in physical consequences – rape calls into question all comfortable certainties that a clear conscience puts everything right.

Indeed, the sexual act itself disturbs any such dualism. Arguably, its success or failure has as much to do with perception, imagination, fantasy, as with the physiology of the event itself. Is sexual desire a state of mind or body? Both, surely. The poem registers the overlap between the two in a succession of ambiguities concerning the imperative that drives Tarquin. 'Will' in the period can mean 'penis', as well as 'intent'. When Tarquin's ' "will is strong, past reason's weak removing" ' (243), does the poem describe a psychological state or a physiological one? (And is there necessarily in this context any significant difference?) Is Tarquin's 'hot burning will' (247) a state of mind or body? (And does it matter?) The text maintains a similar equivocation when, 'with more than admiration' (418), he gazes at her sleeping body, and this causes new mutiny in his 'veins', which 'Swell in their pride' (426–32). After the rape, Tarquin turns away disgusted: 'His taste delicious, in digestion souring, / Devours his will that lived by foul devouring' (699–700). Is it shame or detumescence that goes on to deflate the personification of desire?

> And then with lank and lean discoloured cheek,
> With heavy eye, knit brow, and strengthless pace,
> Feeble Desire, all recreant, poor and meek,
> Like to a bankrupt beggar wails his case.
> The flesh being proud, Desire doth fight with Grace,
>   For there it revels, and when that decays,
>   The guilty rebel for remission prays.   (708–14)

Mind–body dualism has come in our own period to identify the person with consciousness, and the utterance that 'expresses' it. *The Rape of Lucrece*, however, offers a more complex model of human identity. Tarquin silences Lucrece's arguments as he assaults her body. Moreover, it is not her speech alone, nor the display of her corpse alone, but the conjunction of the two that brings about a change in Rome's mode of government. In a culture that has not yet settled irreversibly into a dualist perception of what constitutes a person, the violation of the flesh troubles the soul (1167–76), and it is at least intelligible that this distress can be expunged by suicide. Lucrece sees death by her own hand as a deliberate repudiation of dishonour in a reclamation of sovereignty that destroys a polluted body: ' "For in my death I murder shameful scorn; / My shame so dead, mine honour is new born" ' (1189–90).

The abuse of power

The poem tells Lucrece's story, and Lucrece herself is named as a model of propriety in a number of Shakespeare's plays (*The Taming of the Shrew* 2.1.285; *As You Like It* 3.3.123). The reclusive Olivia has Lucrece's image on her seal (*Twelfth Night* 2.5.78). On the other hand, it is Tarquin who features in *Cymbeline, Macbeth*, and *Julius Caesar* as the type of the oppressor: stealthy, treacherous, remorseless, tyrannical. There is a certain symmetry between Lucrece's deliberations and Tarquin's. She finds reason out of a turmoil of emotion; Tarquin allows his feelings to prevail over rationality. But he knows, the poem makes clear, exactly what he is doing. In that he anticipates Iachimo, but also, and most strikingly, Macbeth.

What exactly elicits Tarquin's desire? The poem is evasive. Is it the challenge of Lucrece's incorruptible reputation (8–9), or her pre-eminence (36–7)? Or is it, perhaps, a sense of rivalry with his comrade-in-arms, a resentment provoked by Collatine's claim to 'possess' what a prince does not (15–21)?

> Perchance that envy of so rich a thing,
> Braving compare, disdainfully did sting
>   His high-pitched thoughts, that meaner men should vaunt
>   That golden hap which their superiors want.   (39–42)

Taking his cue from her husband, Tarquin treats Lucrece as property which, if it can be owned, can also be stolen. Her beauty only confirms the desire evoked in the first instance by Collatine's praise.[18]

As he prepares to seek her out, Tarquin acknowledges all the reasons why he should not destroy Lucrece's chastity. Like Macbeth, Tarquin experiences a proper fear of the outcome. The deed will bring disgrace on him as a soldier and dishonour his family name; his children will be ashamed to claim him as their father; these consequences are not worth a fleeting moment of pleasure; surely Collatine will seek revenge? But all such rational thoughts give way to what Tarquin calls ' "affection" ' (271), an equivocal term in the period, capable of embracing a range of emotions from pure love to uncontrolled and disgraceful passion. ' "Desire my pilot is" ', Tarquin affirms (279):

> 'I have debated even in my soul
> What wrong, what shame, what sorrow I shall breed;
> But nothing can affection's course control
> Or stop the headlong fury of his speed.
> I know repentant tears ensue the deed,
>   Reproach, disdain, and deadly enmity;
>   Yet strive I to embrace mine infamy.'   (498–504)

The narrative voice, however, tells a slightly different story. Here power constitutes the driving force, not love in any of its forms. The imagery consistently identifies Tarquin as a predator rather than a lover (342): he is a night-owl to catch a dove (360), a 'lurking serpent' (362), a 'grim lion' fawning over his prey (421), a 'gripe' holding a doe in its sharp claws (543). Editors worry over the precise meaning of 'gripe', but the word itself vividly conveys, by association with 'grip', the nature of the relationship between the poem's protagonists. Tarquin 'stalks' (365) his victim, and delays only as a 'foul night-waking cat' holds a 'mouse' with its paw (554–5). Moreover, he surveys Lucrece's sleeping body from the point of view of a would-be conqueror. Her breasts, like worlds, reinforce this 'ambition' in Tarquin, 'Who like a foul usurper went about / From this fair throne to heave the owner out' (412–13). The poem defines his approach to Lucrece in a sustained metaphor comparing his action to a military exploit: her chastity is a 'fort' he scales (481–2); she herself is a 'city' he enters (469).

In other words, the poem consistently implies a parallel between this private act of expropriation and the ruthless wars notoriously conducted by the Tarquin family against Rome's neighbours. In addition, the text makes clear, the rape of Lucrece is specifically the action of a tyrant. Doing her best to restore Tarquin to reason, Lucrece appeals to the laws of knighthood, hospitality, friendship, and pity. When these arguments fail, she dwells in some detail on the obligations of the heir to the throne, putting to Tarquin the advice for princes conventional in the period. He will ruin his own reputation; the deeds of kings cannot long be concealed. Above all, his action will turn him into an oppressor, ruling by terror, while good government depends on the consent of the governed: ' "This deed will make thee only loved for fear, / But happy monarchs still are feared for love" ' (610–11). Lawless behaviour in the monarch breeds lawlessness in subjects: how can they punish offences they themselves commit (612–21)? Kings should behave like gods (602), and his intended victim begs Tarquin to become what the heir apparent should be: ' "I sue for exiled majesty's repeal" ' (640).

Her words anticipate the end of the story, figuratively linking the rape of Lucrece with the banishment of the Tarquins. And as if to confirm the justice of the outcome, Tarquin responds like a tyrant refusing good counsel: ' "Have done", quoth he, "my uncontrollèd tide / Turns not, but swells the higher by this let" ' (645–6). When Lucrece tries again, urging Tarquin, as a future king, to command his own impulses, he silences her with violence: ' "No more", quoth he. "By heaven, I will not hear thee!" ' (667). Tyrannical force overrides at once her entitlement to speak and her control of her own body. In its account of the rape itself, the narrative thus keeps in view the relationship between Lucrece's personal tragedy and the politics of the state: even in the bedchamber itself, it is made clear that the implications of Tarquin's crime extend beyond the family to the realm.

Troy story

Even so, for the next 600 lines the focus narrows again to Lucrece's personal anguish. While the Argument that precedes the poem depends primarily on Livy's account of the story and, like Livy, emphasizes in prose the historical and political events, the poem itself relies most heavily on Ovid, poet of intense emotion, and dwells in verse on the feelings of its main protagonist. These issue in an act of self-sacrifice which is at the same time an affirmation of autonomy, and which changes the mode of government in Rome for good. As a bridge for the reader between the claustrophobic domestic space, where Lucrece struggles to make sense of her position, and the marketplace, where Brutus draws the inferences for Rome, the poem interpolates the picture of the Trojan War. In the case of Helen's rape, too, ' "private pleasure" ' can become ' "public plague" ' (1478–9). Tarquin intrudes by a subterfuge into the home of Lucrece, invades her body like a city and destroys her (469); by duplicity the Greeks sent the wooden horse into the city of Troy and sacked it; to avenge the death of Lucrece, the city of Rome will reverse the process, driving out the treacherous tyrant who has disgraced its values.

Ecphrasis, the literary description of a work of visual art, was a favourite device of the period. *Ecphrasis* allows one story to cite another, linking two narratives chronologically or thematically. In the course, for example, of convincing the innocent Imogen's husband that he has spent the night with her, Iachimo mentions the tapestry in her bedchamber: 'the story / Proud Cleopatra when she met her Roman, / And Cydnus swelled above the banks' (*Cymbeline* 2.4.69–71). His brief evocation of this image of the sexual relationship between the Egyptian queen and *her* Italian guest by the engorged river is designed not only to prove his knowledge of Imogen's bedroom, but also to eroticize that knowledge in the mind of his dupe, her husband. At a time when Shakespeare had just published *Venus and Adonis*, two examples of *ecphrasis* in the work of other narrative poets might particularly have appealed to him. A tapestry in Spenser's Castle Joyous depicts the story of Venus and Adonis in four panels;[19] meanwhile, the sleeves of Marlowe's Hero are embroidered with miniature images of the naked goddess, who strives 'To please the carelesse and disdainfull eies / Of proud Adonis'.[20]

The Troy story rendered as *ecphrasis* has a 'graver' lineage, however. In Virgil's epic account of the journey of Aeneas, the hero begins to look back on his escape from a burning Troy as he sees through his tears images on a Carthaginian temple of the Trojan War and the defeat of his heroic comrades. It is here that Dido first finds him, and at her feast that night Aeneas will be induced to tell the rest of the sad tale. The fall of Troy represented the grandest of all stories: rich, towering palaces, 'cloud-kissing Ilion' (*Lucrece* 1370), destroyed by fire when Sinon's treachery enabled the Greeks to bring into the city the wooden horse concealing their own soldiers. Ultimately, however, a new civilization comes out of loss, and Aeneas goes on to found the city of Rome as a second Troy. In Shakespeare's poem, too, personal tragedy issues in political renewal,[21] when Rome opts for a new kind of government, based this time on consent.[22]

Since the Middle Ages the story of the Trojan War, recounted in Lydgate's *Troy Book* and again in William Caxton's popular *Recuyell of the Historyes of Troye*, had come to play an increasing part in the mythological history of Britain, too. Geoffrey of Monmouth had named Brute, great-grandson of Aeneas, as the founder of Britain, and linked London's earlier name of Trinovantum with Troynovantum, identifying London as a third Troy. In Spenser's epic Britomart is moved by the pitiful story of Troy's fall, and she goes on to make the imperial claim that while, as the second Troy, Rome held all the world under its sway, Troynovant will equal both its predecessors in glory.[23]

Taking their cue directly from Virgil himself, successive English poets established their own credentials by recounting the fall of Troy specifically as *ecphrasis*. Thomas Sackville's Induction to the 1563 edition of the popular *Mirror for Magistrates* locates the story on the painted shield of War personified: 'The hugie horse within thy walles is brought: / Thy turrets fall' (452–3).[24] Chaucer had already found it depicted on the walls of the temple in *The House of Fame*, and his account begins with Sinon's lies (151–6), which induced the Trojans to let in the wooden horse.[25]

In interpolating the Troy story as *ecphrasis*, *The Rape of Lucrece* thus confirms its own gravity and the importance of its subject matter. Uniquely among these instances, Shakespeare's poem describes the painting from two

distinct points of view.[26] On the one hand, the generalized account emphasizes the artistic skill that has gone to make the painting and the life-like
effects this creates; on the other, just as Aeneas is moved by images with no
substance (*Aeneid* 1.464),[27] Lucrece as viewer 'feelingly' 'weeps Troy's
painted woes' (1492). Dwelling on the resemblances to her own situation,
she is ready to scratch out the eyes of the Greeks who have caused Hecuba's
sorrow, or to tear the images of the ' "strumpet" ' Helen (1471) and the
' "false" ' Sinon (1560) with her fingernails.

Lucrece finds her own similitude in Priam's widow, and perhaps all the
'forlorn' of Troy (1500), but it is the figure of Sinon that holds her attention.
Shakespeare probably derived the parallel between Sinon and Tarquin from
an annotated version of his Ovidian source.[28] Both were intruders who
secured the confidence of their hosts by craft; both appeared deceptively
innocent; both destroyed something inestimably precious. At the heart of this
long *ecphrasis, The Rape of Lucrece* summarizes Sinon's part in the fall of
Troy, and at the same time both names and demonstrates art's role in giving
it life:

> The well-skilled workman this mild image drew
> For perjured Sinon, whose enchanting story
> The credulous old Priam after slew;
> Whose words like wild-fire burnt the shining glory
> Of rich-built Ilion. (1520–4)

If the analogy between Sinon and Tarquin indicates the magnitude of their
respective crimes for both individuals and states, it also implies a promise of
renewal through Aeneas-Lucrece, at the same time investing Shakespeare's
protagonist with heroic stature. Meanwhile, the affirmation of artistic skill
in such a context lays claim to epic grandeur for the poem's own power to
keep alive the ideal of consent in human relations, whether private or public.

A narrative by a poet–playwright

One intermediary between Shakespeare's text and Virgil's seems to have
been Marlowe's early play, *Dido, Queen of Carthage*. Here, as in Virgil,
Aeneas recounts Troy's tragic tale to Dido. But Marlowe's play and
Shakespeare's poem differ from Virgil's account in shared details. Virgil's
Aeneas, for example, records in Sinon's own voice the speeches that
deceive Priam, while Marlowe's Aeneas and Shakespeare's *ecphrasis*
both reduce them to a third-person mention of Sinon's 'inchaunting' words
(*Dido* 2.1.161).[29] Virgil's Trojans pity the lying Sinon (2.145); Marlowe's
Priam, however, is 'overcome' by his pitiful tale (*Dido* 2.1.157), while

Shakespeare's weeps in response to Sinon's story (1548–9). Moreover, some of Shakespeare's phrases directly echo Marlowe's Aeneas, who similarly records the outcome as including the 'wilde fire' (2.1.217), 'wherewith rich *Ilion* burnt' (2.1.264).[30]

The story of Troy also represents a consistent point of reference in *Titus* (3.1.69; 3.2.27–8; 5.3.79–86), while 'Aeneas' tale to Dido' would recur, of course, in *Hamlet* (2.2.404–75). A narrative detail of the speech Hamlet so fondly remembers is attributable directly to *Dido, Queen of Carthage* (*Hamlet* 2.2.431–2; *Dido* 2.1.253–4); the rest constitutes an affectionate parody of Marlowe's mighty line, heroic, graphic, 'more handsome than fine' (more ample than intricate, 403–4).

These interactions between the poem and drama confirm the closeness of the relationship between the two genres that Patrick Cheney identifies in *Shakespeare, National Poet–Playwright* and in this volume. So, indeed, does Lucrece's reproach to Night as ' "Black stage for tragedies and murders fell" ' (766). In addition, as Macbeth himself reminds us, there are clear resemblances between Tarquin and the heroes of the tragedies: if Tarquin were portrayed with more sympathy, if, in other words, we saw more of the action from his point of view, he himself might qualify as a tragic hero. But the depiction of Tarquin also looks back to the moral plays, whose protagonists tend to seem altogether more obtuse, more blindly bent on the pursuit of their own immediate pleasures in the face of the arguments presented by personified abstractions representing virtue.

Indeed, Tarquin explains his own resolution to act in terms of this long tradition of popular entertainment: ' "My part is youth" ', he insists (278). This affirmation represents the conclusion of an ethical debate, conducted in soliloquy, in which fear/conscience contends with desire/will for control of Tarquin. He eventually resolves the dispute in favour of desire, dismissing the claims of a personified coward-conscience: ' "Then childish fear avaunt" '. Moreover, he is now ready to put an end to the whole discussion: ' "debating die!" ' (274). He defers two further abstractions until later: ' "Respect and reason wait on wrinkled age!" ' (275). In conclusion, ' "Sad pause and deep regard beseems the sage; / My part is youth, and beats these from the stage" ' (277–8).

Tarquin's reference is exact. *The Interlude of Youth*, which probably dates back to the early years of the sixteenth century, shows its flamboyant protagonist choosing to keep company with Riot, Pride, and Lady Lechery, while Humility and Charity do their best to reclaim him for Christian values. During most of the play they fail. Impervious to their moral counsel, which he does not seem to understand, Youth, like the equally arrogant and pitiless Tarquin, struts and threatens with his dagger, until, with the help of his companions, he puts Charity in the stocks. Pride assures him that 'It is tyme inoughe to be good / Whan that ye be olde' (637–8).[31] As unwise and as wayward as Tarquin, the young man claims entitlement to his own will on the grounds of his supremacy: 'For I am promoted to hye degree; / By ryght I am kinge eternal' (583–4). But Youth is also unstable (544) and, in accordance with the conventions of the moral play, he eventually repents and is renamed Good Contrition. Tarquin's remorse is as sudden, but less redemptive. He steals away, 'a heavy convertite' (penitent) (743), and does not reappear except to be banished at the end of the poem.

The anonymous *Interlude of Youth* was evidently popular in the sixteenth century: five editions had appeared by 1562. Nor was it an isolated case. *Youth* shares common ground with *Hickscorner* (c. 1513) and with R. Wever's Protestant revision, *Lusty Juventus* (1550), where the hero's English name is also Youth. Eventually, following the example of the Prodigal Son, Lusty Juventus yields to God's Merciful Promises, and urges his peers to repent: 'Your bodies subdue unto virtue, delight not in vanity; / Say not "I am young, I shall live long," lest your days shortened be' (1144–5).[32] Ironically, while Tarquin knows the arguments, he fails to profit from the examples of the predecessors he invokes.

Although it includes a good deal of dialogue, *The Rape of Lucrece* is palpably not drama, and it takes advantage of its own genre to allow its protagonist in particular to deliberate at length and in detail. No play could permit such rhetorical expansiveness, of course. Nevertheless, as Frank Kermode has pointed out, Shakespeare's early works for the stage include speeches 'as elaborately structured' as Lucrece's. In Kermode's view, it was not until about 1600 that the playwright developed the remarkable combination of reticence and density, the austere 'compaction of language', that we have come to regard as characteristically Shakespearean. This 'new way of representing turbulent thinking' is apparent, for instance, in Macbeth's kaleidoscopic 'If it were done' soliloquy, with its compressed word-play and allusive imagery, ranging from the domestic context to the Last Judgement (1.7.1–28).[33]

But if his later manner changes to suit the developing requirements of stage audiences or, indeed, the constraints of the sonnet form, nowhere else does Shakespeare explicitly invest a female protagonist with the eloquence of that greatest of all poets, Orpheus (552–3), and the Renaissance type of the lyric poet, Philomela, the nightingale (1128–48).[34] As a display of poetic skill, *Lucrece* delivers an overt challenge, in the voice of a woman, to the most authoritative practitioners of Elizabethan verse, both narrative and dramatic,[35] while at the same time foregrounding her contribution to the process of changing the course of history for the better.

NOTES

1 The title of the poem given on the title page of the first edition in 1594 is *Lucrece*; the half-title and the running heads call it *The Rape of Lucrece*. I have varied the titles with a view to drawing attention either to the protagonist or the act. 'A book entitled *The Ravishment of Lucrece*' was entered in the Stationers' Register in May 1594 (Colin Burrow (ed.), *The Complete Sonnets and Poems* (Oxford University Press, 2002), pp. 40–3).

2 The messenger who reports the retreat of Coriolanus also remembers the joy at the expulsion of the Tarquins (*Coriolanus* 5.4.38–9).

3 Diane Wolfthal, *Images of Rape: The 'Heroic' Tradition and its Alternatives* (Cambridge University Press, 1999), Figure 42; see also Figures 41 and 113.

4 The reference to 'Her modest eloquence' is ambiguous (563). Are we to understand her articulacy as self-effacing, or limited? At this stage, she stutters under the pressure of circumstances; later, her rhetorical skill is not in doubt.

5 Ovid, *Fasti* 2.800. Rpt and trans. in F. T. Prince (ed.), *The Poems*, Arden Shakespeare (London: Methuen, 1960), pp. 196–201. Compare, for example, Luke 10.3, where Jesus, sending out disciples, warns them, 'I send you forth as lambs among wolves'.

6 The jottings appear on the title page of the Duke of Northumberland's manuscript of some of Francis Bacon's writings (*The Shakspere Allusion-Book*, ed. C. M. Ingleby, L. Toulmin-Smith and F. J. Furnivall, 2 vols. (London: Oxford University Press, 1932), I: 40).

7 Geoffrey Chaucer, 'The Legend of Lucrece', *The Legend of Good Women*, *The Works of Geoffrey Chaucer*, ed. F. N. Robinson (London: Oxford University Press, 1957), pp. 507–9.

8 Ovid, *Metamorphoses* 6. 438–674, trans. Frank Justus Miller, revised by G. P. Goold, 2 vols. (Cambridge, MA: Harvard University Press, 1977). Since Philomela and her sister Procne secured their revenge by inducing Tereus to eat his young son, it is tempting to think that the story might have influenced both *The Rape of Lucrece* and *Titus Andronicus* when it was staged as an example of lechery in *The Seven Deadly Sins* in the early 1590s. However, now that David Kathman has produced convincing evidence for reassigning to the late 1590s the 'plot', or casting-chart, which is all that remains of this work, there is no evidence that Richard Tarlton's play was revived at this time. (See David Kathman, 'Reconsidering *The Seven Deadly Sins*', *Early Theatre* 7 (2004), 13–44.) The story of Philomela was extremely widely cited.

9 *George Gascoigne's 'The Steele Glas' and 'The Complainte of Phylomene'*, ed. William L. Wallace (Salzburg: Institut für Englische Sprache und Literatur, Universität Salzburg, 1975).

10 Livy himself links this story with Lucretia's (*Ab Urbe Condita*, 3.44.1 in *Livy*, vol. II, trans. B. O. Foster (London: William Heinemann, 1967). In addition, Gower tells Virginia's story immediately after Lucrece's (*Confessio Amantis* 7.5131–306, in *The Complete Works of John Gower*, ed. G. C. Macauley 4 vols. (Oxford: Clarendon Press, 1901), vol. III).

11 Chaucer, 'The Physician's Tale', *Works*, pp. 145–7.

12 R. B., *Apius and Virginia*, *Tudor Interludes*, ed. Peter Happé (London: Penguin, 1972), pp. 271–317.

13 In the sources Tarquin is married, though Shakespeare's poem ignores this complication.

14 '*What could the virgine doe? / She could not runne away ... Ahlas what should she fight? ... It booted not to crie. ...*' (Gascoigne, *Phylomene* 209–20). Cf. 'Quid faciat? pugnet? .../ Clamet? .../ Effugiat?' (Ovid, *Fasti* 2.801–3); 'To whom shal she compleyne, or make mone? / What! shal she fyghte with an hardy knyght? / Wel wot men that a woman hath no myght. / What! shal she crye ...?' (Chaucer, 'Legend of Lucrece' 1,799–1,802).

15 'For looke how Torquin Lucres faire by force did once oppresse, / Even so will I Virginia use' (558–9).

16 I can find no justification in the text itself for the view, based on medical and legal opinion of the time, that her fear of pregnancy implies her sexual pleasure, and that this in turn explains her shame. Chaucer's Lucrece was unconscious, and she too feels shame and guilt. But for a forceful argument that Lucrece's involuntary 'consent' is the 'prurient secret at the heart of this text' see Barbara J. Baines, 'Effacing Rape in Early Modern Representation', *ELH* 65 (1998), 69–98 (p. 89).

17 In an influential essay Nancy Vickers argues that the heraldic imagery that repeatedly defines Lucrece displays the prestige of the men who compete for possession of her body, effectively excluding the possibility of self-determination for the woman who is nominally at the centre of the text (' "The Blazon of Sweet Beauty's Best": Shakespeare's *Lucrece*', in *Shakespeare and the Question of Theory*, ed. Patricia Parker and Geoffrey Hartman (New York: Methuen, 1985), pp. 95–115). For a respectful counter-argument, see Enterline, ' "Poor Instruments" '.

18 In the Argument, as in the sources, Collatine boasts of his wife's virtue, and the soldiers ride to Rome to check. Shakespeare's poem, however, might be read as indicating that Tarquin is aroused purely by Collatine's words.

19 *The Faerie Queene* 3.1.34–8 (ed. A. C. Hamilton (London: Longman, 1977)). Books 1–3 were published in 1590.

20 *Hero and Leander* (1593), in *The Complete Works of Christopher Marlowe*, vol. I, ed. Roma Gill (Oxford: Clarendon Press, 1987), pp. 175–209, lines 14–16.

21 Cf. Cheney, *Shakespeare, National Poet–Playwright*, p. 136.

22 Catherine Belsey, 'Tarquin Dispossessed: Expropriation and Consent in *The Rape of Lucrece*', *Shakespeare Quarterly* 52 (2001), 315–35.

23 *The Faerie Queene* 3.9.38–9; 44–5.

24 Lily B. Campbell (ed.), *The Mirror for Magistrates* (Cambridge University Press, 1938), pp. 297–317.

25 Chaucer, *Works*, lines 280–302.

26 Burrow (ed.), *Complete Sonnets and Poems*, pp. 61–2.

27 Virgil, *Works*, trans. H. Rushton Fairclough, rev. G. P. Goold, 2 vols. (Cambridge, MA: Harvard University Press, 1999).

28 T. W. Baldwin, *On the Literary Genetics of Shakspere's Poems and Sonnets* (Urbana: University of Illinois Press, 1950), p. 145.

29 *Complete Works*, 1: 113–74.

30 Marlowe's Aeneas attributes to 'false *Sinon*' (*Dido* 2.1.143; *Lucrece* 1560) 'craft and perjurie' (*Dido* 2.1.144; *Lucrece* 1517). While Virgil's shepherds are 'Dardan' (2.59), Marlowe's Aeneas has Sinon led by 'Phrigian shepherds', his hands 'bound' (*Dido* 2.1.153, 151; *Lucrece* 1501–2). Both Dido and Lucrece call

Helen a 'strumpet' (2.1.300; 1471). There is no direct warrant for most of these precise phrases in Virgil or in the standard sixteenth-century translation (Steven Lally (ed.), *The 'Aeneid' of Thomas Phaer and Thomas Twyne* (New York: Garland, 1987)).

31 *Tudor Interludes*, lines 113–38.

32 J. A. B. Somerset (ed.), *Four Tudor Interludes* (London: Athlone, 1974), lines 97–127.

33 Frank Kermode, *Shakespeare's Language* (London: Penguin, 2001), pp. 16, 27–8, 208.

34 Lynn Enterline, ' "Poor Instruments" and Unspeakable Events in *The Rape of Lucrece*', in *The Rhetoric of the Body from Ovid to Shakespeare* (Cambridge University Press, 2000), pp. 168–9.

35 Cheney, *Poet–Playwright*, pp. 130–34. See also Chapter 1 in this volume.

READING LIST

Bashar, Nazife. 'Rape in England between 1550 and 1700'. In *The Sexual Dynamics of History: Men's Power, Women's Resistance*, ed. The London Feminist History Group. London: Pluto, 1983, pp. 28–42.

Belsey, Catherine. 'Tarquin Dispossessed: Expropriation and Consent in *The Rape of Lucrece*'. *Shakespeare Quarterly* 52 (2001), 315–35.

Bowers, A. Robin. 'Iconography and Rhetoric in Shakespeare's *Lucrece*'. *Shakespeare Studies* 14 (1981), 1–21.

Burrow, Colin (ed.). *The Complete Sonnets and Poems*. The Oxford Shakespeare. Oxford University Press, 2002.

Cheney, Patrick. *Shakespeare, National Poet–Playwright*. Cambridge University Press, 2004.

Dubrow, Heather. ' "Full of Forged Lies": *The Rape of Lucrece* '. In *Captive Victors: Shakespeare's Narrative Poems and Sonnets*. Ithaca: Cornell University Press, pp. 80–168.

Enterline, Lynn. ' "Poor Instruments" and Unspeakable Events in *The Rape of Lucrece*'. In *The Rhetoric of the Body from Ovid to Shakespeare*. Cambridge University Press, 2000, pp. 152–97.

Kermode, Frank. *Shakespeare's Language*. London: Penguin, 2001.

Wolfthal, Diane. *Images of Rape: The 'Heroic' Tradition and its Alternatives*. Cambridge University Press, 1999.

6

JAMES P. BEDNARZ

The Passionate Pilgrim and 'The Phoenix and Turtle'

In the long interim between the publication of *Lucrece* (1594) and *The Sonnets* (1609), Shakespeare's poetry was featured in two verse miscellanies, *The Passionate Pilgrim* (printed twice between September 1598 and 1599, then expanded in 1612) and *Love's Martyr* (published in 1601 and reissued as *The Annals of Great Britain* in 1611), that testify, albeit in different ways, to his dual literary reputation as a lyric poet and commercial dramatist. For while *The Passionate Pilgrim* is most valuable as an historical document registering Shakespeare's contemporary popularity, *Love's Martyr*, which includes his mysterious unnamed elegy sometimes known as 'The Phoenix and Turtle', not only affords a glimpse of the conditions that shaped his emergent reputation, but also indicates how his ongoing involvement with the hybrid theatrical/literary culture of late Elizabethan England contributed to the creation of this enigmatic lyric masterpiece.

The Passionate Pilgrim

Attributed on its title page to 'W. Shakespeare', *The Passionate Pilgrim*, published by William Jaggard, who would later print the First Folio, is a short octavo edition that might be called the first anthology of Shakespeare's verse with one major qualification: most of the poems are not his. In 1598 Francis Meres in *Palladis Tamia* tantalized readers with a reference to Shakespeare's 'sugared Sonnets' circulated 'among his private friends'. Having secured copies of two of these poems (an inferior version of what was later printed as 138 along with a more accurate transcription of 144), Jaggard set out to supply them to an audience that had already made *Venus and Adonis* a bestseller. But of the twenty poems he originally included in *The Passionate Pilgrim*, only five (conventionally numbered 1, 2, 3, 5, and 16) are clearly Shakespeare's: the two sonnets that open the volume and the three slightly rewritten lyrics from *Love's Labour's Lost* (4.3.58–71; 4.2.105–18; 4.3.99–118 without lines 112–13) that fill it out. Of the fifteen remaining poems: Richard Barnfield wrote 8, 20, and possibly 17; Bartholomew Griffin composed a version of 11 and possibly 4, 6, and 9 (the four 'Venus and Adonis sonnets'); Thomas Deloney might have penned 12 (as part of a longer poem); and Christopher Marlowe and probably Sir Walter Ralegh were remotely responsible for 19, Jaggard's butchered conflation of a four-stanza version of 'Come live with me and be my love' (bereft of its opening word) with a single-stanza reply.[1] And although counter-attributions for 7, 10, 13, 14, 15, and 18 have never been posited, it is unlikely that Shakespeare wrote these pleasant weak poems.

John Benson's collection of Shakespeare's *Poems* in 1640, which included all of the 1612 *Passionate Pilgrim*, facilitated its problematic incorporation into the canon. Yet when considering the history of the volume's reception, it is important to remember that Nicholas Ling had already begun to distinguish between the authentic and inauthentic attributions of *The Passionate Pilgrim* in his rival miscellany *England's Helicon* (1600). The concluding section of six poems (15–20) in the 1599 *Passionate Pilgrim* was printed with an internal title page calling it *Sonnets to Sundry Notes of Music*, and it is from this section that Ling selected four poems (16, 17, 19, and 20), ignoring only the two weakest (15 and 18). But rather than attributing all four to Shakespeare, he makes crucial differentiations among them. In a signal act of authentication, he correctly identifies 'W. Shakespeare' as the author of 'On a Day' (16), the one genuine poem he reprints. But he simultaneously challenges three of Jaggard's incorrect ascriptions (17, 19, and 20) and substitutes two superior texts for 19. He consequently reprints 17 ('My Flocks feed not') and 20 ('As it fell upon a Day') immediately after the validated 16, as adjacent anonymous poems entitled '*The unknown Shepherd's complaint*' and '*Another of the same Shepherd's*' (without the didactic conclusion of lines 27–56) and signed 'Ignoto'. Ling did not know that Barnfield had written 20, but he was confident that Shakespeare had not. Finally, in response to Jaggard's ascription of 'Live with me and be my Love' and 'Love's Reply' (19) to Shakespeare, he offers more accurate complete transcriptions of the six-stanza 'Come live with me, and be my love' and a perfectly balanced six-stanza response 'If all the world and love were young' that remain the standard versions. For the first time in print they are reproduced as separate poems, entitled '*The passionate Shepherd to his love*' and '*The Nymph's reply to the Shepherd*', with Shakespeare's authorship rejected in favour of Marlowe and Ralegh (whose name was, however, later changed to 'Ignoto').[2] Here, given a proper publication, these lyrics provide attributive and textual correctives to *The Passionate Pilgrim* as they are jettisoned from the Shakespeare canon.

Ling's greater accuracy in assigning authorial credit constitutes a foundational act in Shakespeare bibliography that must have been difficult to judge at the time. Print culture not only inherited the loose ascription habits of manuscript circulation but added a new market-driven incentive to be deliberately deceptive by fraudulently advertising a famous author's name to boost sales. Indirectly targeting Jaggard's practice, Ling, in his prefatory letter, declares that 'The names of Poets have been placed with the names of the greatest Princes of the world, by the most authentic and worthiest judgments' (A4^v). Unwilling to take his responsibility lightly but admitting his limitations, he announces that 'If any man hath been defrauded of anything by him composed, by another man's title put to the same, he hath this benefit by this collection, freely to challenge his own in public, where else he might be robbed of his proper due'. Nothing had been placed by 'the Collector' (as he calls himself) 'under any man's name, but as it was delivered by some especial copy coming to his hands' (A4^r).

Ling, however, takes for granted his right to alter texts and invent titles to strengthen the volume's main theme, so that the name of Marlowe's most famous poem '*The passionate Shepherd to his love*', which first appears in this collection, seems to have been the work of this pastoralizing editor familiar with its prior publication in *The Passionate Pilgrim*.[3] (One wonders if Ling knew that in *As You Like It*, a play blocked for publication on the same day, 4 August 1600, that *England's Helicon* was registered, Shakespeare had eulogized Marlowe as the 'dead Shepherd', mainly for having written this poem.) Ling's copy of Shakespeare's untitled 'On a day, (alack the day)', which closely follows Jaggard's text (even omitting the same two lines present in *Love's Labour's Lost*), similarly became, using Jaggard's epithet, '*The passionate Shepherd's Song*'. It is possible but not provable that Jaggard printed some of his inauthentic poems from a manuscript miscellany or commonplace book and that he honestly assumed they were Shakespeare's. But it is just as possible that he recognized which were genuine. He certainly knew that Shakespeare had not composed 'If music and sweet poetry agree' (8) and 'As it fell upon a Day' (20), because they had originally been published by his brother John in 1598 under the titles 'To His Friend Master R. L. In Praise of Music and Poetry' and 'An Ode' in *Poems in Divers Humours*, a short collection of poems appended to *The Encomion of Lady Pecunia, or the Praise of Money*. The title page of *Lady Pecunia* advertises that it was written by Richard Barnfield, 'Graduate in Oxford', and since there are no significant variations between the versions of these two poems in *Lady Pecunia* and *The Passionate Pilgrim*, William apparently used John Jaggard's edition for his copy. Although print technology guaranteed the stability of Barnfield's text, it effaced the sign of his authorship by substituting 'W. Shakespeare' for his less vendible name. In 'A Remembrance of Some English Poets' (the second of two lyrics in *Poems in Divers Humours* printed between those Jaggard had copied for 8 and 20), Barnfield lists Shakespeare, whose 'Name' has been enrolled 'in fame's immortal Book' (line 16) as the author of *Venus and Adonis* and *Lucrece*, with Edmund Spenser, Samuel Daniel, and Michael Drayton as one of the four greatest living writers. Since Jaggard saw this poem when applying Shakespeare's name to *The Passionate Pilgrim*, Barnfield's literary enthusiasm for Shakespeare seems to have contributed, ironically, to his own erasure. Jaggard, suspecting that most readers would not be familiar enough with Barnfield's verse to distinguish it from Shakespeare's, apparently counted on this fact to conceal his own devotion to Lady Pecunia.

That there is no early record of his protest does not mean that Shakespeare was not irritated by Jaggard's aggressive misuse of his name by 1599. His anger is, however, revealed in Thomas Heywood's open letter to the printer Nicholas Okes at the end of *An Apology for Actors* (1612), which states that Shakespeare was 'much offended with M. Jaggard', who without his consent had 'presumed to make so bold with his name'.[4] The source of his annoyance in 1612 was the third octavo that Jaggard issued to attract new readers, after Thomas Thorpe's edition of the Sonnets in 1609 had eliminated one source of his collection's novelty. The newly designed title now read: 'THE PASSIONATE PILGRIM, OR *Certain Amorous Sonnets, between Venus and Adonis, newly corrected and augmented, By W. Shakespeare*. Whereunto is newly added two Love-Epistles, the first From *Paris* to *Helen*, and *Helen's* answer back again to *Paris*'. Jaggard had faith in his revised edition's potential to lure readers who still enjoyed *Venus and Adonis* and might even be led to believe that his enlarged volume complemented the Sonnets. But he did nothing new to reinforce this theme. He merely employs it on the title page as a marketing tool to invite readers to view his new edition as a sampling of Shakespeare's Ovidian 'Love-Epistles'. Ovid's *Heroides*, rather than the *Metamorphoses*, now shaped Jaggard's last version of Shakespeare, the passionate pilgrim. Here, Jaggard imagines Venus and Adonis writing sonnet-letters to each other, just as the male lovers had done to their mistresses in *Love's Labour's Lost*. What is equally deceptive is the title page's suggestion that Shakespeare had corrected and augmented the volume with the epistles between Paris and Helen duplicating the sonnets purportedly written by Venus and Adonis. But the book, strictly speaking, does not contain sonnets between Venus and Adonis, and the two new epistles between Paris and Helen, as well as the seven other new verses unmentioned on the title page, were not Shakespeare's. They were instead translations by Thomas Heywood, mainly from Ovid's *Heroides*, *Art of Love*, and *Remedies of Love*. Jaggard knew that all of these poems were Heywood's work because he had published them under Heywood's name in *Troia Britannica* (1609) three years earlier.

We consequently learn of Shakespeare's distress through Heywood who complains to Okes about Jaggard's incompetence and unscrupulousness. Jaggard, Heywood protests, had not only done a bad job printing *Troia Britannica* and had refused to add a list of errata, but he then published part of it as Shakespeare's in the expanded third edition of *The Passionate Pilgrim*. Heywood was particularly troubled, he tells Okes, that 'the world' might be led to believe that he had plagiarized the Paris–Helen epistles in *Troia Britannica* from Shakespeare, and that Shakespeare had then 'published them in his own name' in *The Passionate Pilgrim*, three years later, to counter Heywood's attempt to 'steal them'. Heywood, however, humbly acknowledges that his own lines were 'not worthy' of being attributed to the greater poet. Together the two writers were united, he tells Okes, in their outrage at Jaggard, who had 'offended' both poets with his failure to accord them what Heywood emphatically calls the author's 'rights of the press' (G4^r), by which he means the implicit moral contract – based on ethics not law – between publisher and writer not to violate the latter's assumed privileges of just representation and correct attribution. Even if what Jaggard did was not technically illegal, he nevertheless submitted to the social pressure, the personal remonstrance, levied by Heywood and perhaps Shakespeare, when he printed a second title page without the latter's name. 'Jaggard, whatever his original intention in designing the title-page, recognized the justice of Heywood's attack', Hyder Rollins concludes. The 'improprieties referred to by contemporaries were not simply legal ones', observes Adrian Johns. 'They permeated the domains of print, occupying the far more amorphous territory of civility.'[5]

From the start, Jaggard was so hobbled by his inability to secure enough genuine Shakespeare material to fill out *The Passionate Pilgrim* in 1598/9 that he padded his slender volume with plausible counterfeits. He had so few poems that he had them printed only on the recto sides of his book's small pages (until belatedly deciding to compress the last three to save paper), with ornamental borders above and below the short texts. Acting as a secret collaborator, he created a multifaceted version of 'Shakespeare' as a witty, passionate, self-divided sonneteer, pastoral poet, ballad and song writer, the imitator of Ovid, the admirer of Edmund Spenser, and Marlowe and Ralegh's equal. Central to Jaggard's project was the conviction he shared with Meres that Shakespeare's literary achievement was equally demonstrated in his dramatic and non-dramatic works, in plays, narrative poems, and sonnets, which he treats as analogous poetic media. Indeed, Jaggard's 'Shakespeare' collection is a prime example of the hybrid quality of Elizabethan theatrical/literary culture. Nowhere, in this sense, is Jaggard's counterfeiting more creative than in his evocative title, *The Passionate*

Pilgrim, a phrase based on the playfully sublime dialogue in *Romeo and Juliet* in which, when the lovers first meet, Romeo apologizes for the sacrilege of having touched the saint-like Juliet's hand and promises to atone for his rudeness: 'My lips, two blushing pilgrims, ready stand / To smooth that rough touch with a tender kiss' (1.5.93–9). Responding to the witty passionate rhetoric of the religion of love, Juliet consequently identifies Romeo as a 'Good pilgrim' whose gesture shows an appropriate devotion to his sexual saint. The title of Jaggard's collection names both the volume and its imputed author, who is imagined as his most eloquent and intense erotic hero. Jaggard's Shakespeare is Romeo, the passionate pilgrim, the poet Meres similarly describes as being 'passionate in bewailing the perplexities of love' in his then unpublished Sonnets.[6] John Marston indicates that *Romeo and Juliet* was so popular in 1598 that the obsessive theatregoer Luscus, who has seen it at the Curtain theatre, keeps quoting it in conversation, as from his lips 'doth flow / Naught but pure *Juliet* and *Romeo*'.[7] Jaggard's marketing strategy was to lure theatregoers and readers acquainted with Shakespeare's drama and eager to read more of his poetry, and his primary inspiration was either the 1597 or 1599 quartos of *Romeo and Juliet*, which he evidently recognized as being Shakespeare's work, even though neither version bore the author's name. He might have been particularly attracted to Romeo and Juliet's brilliant dialogue because it contains an improvised sonnet (1.4.93–106) whose metrical form matched the two manuscript sonnets he possessed.

As in most Elizabethan miscellanies and sonnet sequences, the collection is allowed remarkable freedom to explore variable attitudes and ideas about love. Whatever artistic coherence it possesses comes from its network of formal, thematic, and verbal analogues secured by its four primary Shakespeare intertexts: the unpublished Sonnets, *Love's Labour's Lost*, *Venus and Adonis*, and *Romeo and Juliet*. All but one of Jaggard's poems fit three metrical patterns that Shakespeare prominently employed – sonnet, sixain, and tetrameter – which emerge sequentially in the volume as signature forms, as is illustrated (with known Shakespeare poems in bold numbers) by the following chart.[8]

Sonnet:	**1 2 3 4 5** 6 8 9* 11 12*			
Venus and Adonis sixain:	7 10 13 14 18			
Tetrameter variations:	**16** 17 19 20			
Ballad:	15			

Within this metrical structure, secured at both ends by genuine poems, the form and content of its Shakespeare components freely mingle, as the story of Venus and Adonis is, for instance, made explicit only in Sonnets 4, 6, 9, and 11, not in its original sixains. Recently, Patrick Cheney has drawn attention to Jaggard's marketing of 'Shakespeare' as a 'failed pilgrim of passion', an Ovidian poet who provocatively moves 'the sensual into the religious sphere'. Cheney and John Roe before him have shown how the title's numinous eroticism reverberates through the volume in the good and bad angels of poem 2, the 'heavenly rhetoric' of 3 (line 1), the classical mythology of 4, and praise of the 'Celestial' lover (line 13) in 5. It is in the context of this religion of love that the volume's obsession with oath-breaking (1, 2, 3, 5, 7) modulates into the lewd caprice of the Venus and Adonis sonnets (4, 6, 9, 11) and the melancholy of the poems on beauty and time (10, 12, 13). These three thematic clusters, however, further overlap in their discussion of youth and age (1, 4, 9, 11, 12, 13), their recurrent pastoral settings (10, 12, 14, 16, 17, 19, 20), and interest in music (8), which broadens in the volume's concluding song lyrics (15–20). One of the elements that hold this diverse volume together is, as Cheney observes, 'the first-person voice' used in 'fifteen of the twenty poems', which encourages readers 'to identify *The Passionate Pilgrim* with "W. Shakespeare"'.[9]

Key differences of phrasing in the first poem, 'When my Love swears that she is made of truth', and the version printed in 1609 have led some scholars to speculate that Jaggard's printing preserves an earlier authoritative transcription of what would later become Sonnet 138. It is more probable, however, in light of the collection's bad provenance and inferior copy, that *The Passionate Pilgrim* opens with a corrupted transcription of the same sonnet that Thorpe published more accurately a decade later. The collection begins, in any case, with the amorous perplexities and moral accommodations of the final Sonnets: with a tenuous union based on mutual lies and the passionate triangle that binds the poet to a woman 'devil' and an 'angel' man in 'Two Loves I have, of Comfort and Despair', subsequently printed as 144. The three poems from *Love's Labour's Lost* consequently match the opening sonnets' paradoxical union of the sacred and transgressive. In Longaville's 'Did not the heavenly Rhetoric of thine eye' (3), the perjured lover claims that he has broken an earthly vow for a goddess whose 'grace' can cure 'all disgrace in me' (line 8). Who would not 'break an Oath', he asks, 'to win a Paradise?' (line 14). In reprinting this poem, Jaggard apparently ignored Berowne's critique that Longaville's 'idolatry' makes 'flesh a deity' and 'a green goose' [i.e., a prostitute] 'a goddess' (4.3.72–3). We can only imagine what Shakespeare would have thought about seeing himself equated with Longaville. After poem 4 introduces the first of the Venus and Adonis sonnets, Berowne's 'If Love make me forsworn' (5) repeats the poet's admission of oath-breaking and similarly justifies his error by claiming that 'all those pleasures … that Art can comprehend' (line 6) are discovered in his mistress, whose angry eyes flash

'Jove's lightning' (line 11). Finally, the last genuine poem, Dumaine's brief trochaic lyric 'On a day' (16) appears among the songs (singularly stripped of its two lines of self-rebuke for oath-breaking) to help enliven its conclusion.

A strong incentive for readers to buy *The Passionate Pilgrim* was that it offered sonnets that complemented *Venus and Adonis*, Shakespeare's most successful publication. To optimize the possibility that the readers who had made Shakespeare's Ovidian narrative poem so popular would purchase *The Passionate Pilgrim*, Jaggard even had it distributed by William Leake at the sign of the Greyhound in St Paul's Churchyard, the same bookseller who offered *Venus and Adonis*. The main problem with the Venus and Adonis sonnets (4, 6, 9, and 11), however, is that although we cannot be certain that Bartholomew Griffin wrote all four, Colin Burrow plausibly states that they 'read like reflections at one remove' of the 'story as told by Shakespeare' and suggest 'a pastiche' of his work.[10] Since a version of 'Venus and Adonis sitting by her' (11) was previously printed in Griffin's *Fidessa, More Chaste than Kind* (1596), the three others ('Sweet Cytherea, sitting by a brook', 'Scarce had the sun dried up the dewy morn', and 'Fair was the morn when the fair queen of love') might be his as well. 'Crabbed age and youth cannot live together' (12), which was probably derived from the first stanza of 'A Maiden's Choice twixt Age and Youth' in Thomas Deloney's *Garland of Good Will* (registered on 5 March 1593), even provides a kind of resolution to these poems of mismatched love.[11] If the Venus and Adonis sonnets gave the impression that Shakespearean form and content were in hand, they also attested to the reputation Shakespeare had secured as a master of Ovidian narrative. It was in this genre that Shakespeare rivalled Spenser's use of the Adonis myth as one of the central leitmotifs of Book Three of *The Faerie Queene* (1590). And since, in poem 8, 'Shakespeare' explains that Spenser's 'deep Conceit is such, / As passing all conceit, needs no defense' (lines 7–8), readers of *The Passionate Pilgrim* were implicitly encouraged to link the poets. Indeed, Barnfield, who actually wrote this praise of Spenser, had already assumed their parity in 'A Remembrance of Some English Poets'.

Further expanding its potential customer base, the volume's last part, *Sonnets to Sundry Notes of Music*, serves as a songbook (without musical settings) that allows readers to collaborate in re-making 'Shakespeare' through their own voices and musicianship. The Renaissance Orphic tradition customarily represented poetry as song, and for Elizabethans singing was a favourite recreation. We do not know if all these poems had been set to melodies. Ling's designation of Shakespeare's 'On a day' as '*The Passionate Shepherd's Song*' in *England's Helicon* might be based solely on the authority of *The Passionate Pilgrim*. But it is possible that as the poem migrated from literary recitation in a play to both dramatic and non-dramatic publication, it became a song. Early modern songbooks occasionally printed lyrics without suggestions for tunes, and two other poems in this section had already been arranged. 'My flocks feed not' (17) had been featured as the second song in three parts in Thomas Weelkes's *Madrigals to 3, 4, 5, and 6 voices* (1597), and Marlowe's 'Come live with me' was a familiar ayre that Sir Hugh sang to himself the same year in *The Merry Wives of Windsor* (3.1.17–29).

The Passionate Pilgrim is a register of perplexities and frustration that moves from the paradoxes of amused self-deception (1), through the shepherd-poet's painful declaration that 'Love is dead' (17, line 32) and his debate on desire in 'Live with me and be my Love' and 'Love's answer' (19), to sympathy with the nightingale's grief in 'As it fell upon a Day' (20). The endings of the two parts of *The Passionate Pilgrim* are simultaneously coordinated. 'Good night, good rest' (14) closes the first section with anxious expectation, and the volume ends with the poet's lament for the nightingale, whose mythological origin as Philomela Shakespeare had retold from Ovid in *Lucrece* and *Titus Andronicus*. Caroline Spurgeon notes that aside from references to 'the human body', Shakespeare's 'images from birds are by far the largest section drawn from any single class of objects'.[12] But in the only new non-dramatic verse he subsequently published during the Elizabethan period, Shakespeare would surpass even his own song of the cuckoo and owl in *Love's Labour's Lost* and evocation of the nightingale and lark in *Romeo and Juliet* with his short allegorical masterpiece on the mystical union of the phoenix and turtle-dove.

'The Phoenix and Turtle'

This exquisite untitled short lyric – sometimes called 'The Phoenix and Turtle' – first appeared with an attribution to 'W. Shakespeare' in a special collection of verses appended to Robert Chester's *Love's Martyr, or Rosalin's Complaint, Allegorically Shadowing the Truth of Love, in the Constant Fate of the Phoenix and Turtle*, published in 1601. It seems likely, as Carleton Brown speculates, that Sir John Salusbury, to whom the volume is dedicated and in whose service Chester seems to have been employed, commissioned the verses through Ben Jonson. Jonson and probably also John Marston knew Salusbury, but holograph copies of two of Jonson's poems have been discovered among his family's papers. Salusbury, an Esquire to the Body of the Queen and a member of the Middle Temple, had just been knighted, and he probably asked Jonson to secure the service of three other famous poet–playwrights, Shakespeare, Marston, and George Chapman, to provide *Love's Martyr* with literary credibility. The book's title page hints that the volume includes 'new compositions' by 'several modern Writers whose names are subscribed to their several works', and the collection's internal title page reveals their formidable reputations: *Hereafter Follow Diverse Poetical Essays on the former Subject; viz: the Turtle and Phoenix. Done by the best and chiefest of our modern writers, with their names subscribed to their particular works: never before extant.* This section contains fourteen poems: two attributed to the group as 'Vatum Chorus' (chorus of poets); two by Ignoto; Shakespeare's lyric; four linked verses by Marston; one by Chapman; and four by Jonson. Sir Philip Sidney in *An Apology for Poetry* had pointed out that the Latin word for 'poet' – '*vates*' – means 'diviner, foreseer, or prophet' in appreciation of his 'divine force'.[13] So that when 'the best . . . modern writers' describe themselves as 'Vatum Chorus', they claim the highest dignity their vocation affords them: as a chorus of secular prophets engaged in a philosophical debate on the question of ideal love.

Shakespeare might have agreed to contribute to the volume for several reasons. He might have wanted to indicate his allegiance to Salusbury as a political gesture in the wake of the earl of Essex's execution on 25 February, since Salusbury had been knighted in June of 1601, having opposed the earl's revolt. Shakespeare might also have enjoyed collaborating with and competing against Jonson, Marston, and Chapman on this project in which he symbolically took back control of his name as a poet in print. By 1601, each of these four poet–playwrights had established imposing theatrical/ literary reputations, and three of them – Shakespeare, Jonson, and Marston – were currently engaged in a theatrical debate on the meaning and function of drama that Thomas Dekker in *Satiromastix* called the '*poetomachia*'.[14] Although printed as a miscellany, the 'Poetical Essays' assumes the appearance of a theatrical performance, framed by a dramatic chorus that elicits Shakespeare, Marston, Chapman, and Jonson, respectively, to present their verses as if they were being recited or sung. Following Ignoto, the first named poet to step forward is 'W. Shakespeare', whose contribution, the sole masterpiece in the collection, with its odd balance of ritualized austerity and playful wit, together with its poignant ontological paradoxes – that *two are one* and *one is none* – is the first great published 'metaphysical' poem. One might conceive of their coactive engagement with each other in composing the 'Poetical Essays' as a kind of test (assay) or contest to determine who could most eloquently respond – by 'allegorically shadowing the truth of love' – to Chester's fascinating myth.

In *England's Helicon*, Ling had differentiated Shakespeare's 'On a day' from Barnfield's two other tetrameter poems, as well as from Marlowe and Ralegh's tetrameter pastorals. He had also printed Shakespeare's poem in the same collection as 'In a grove most rich of shade', the eighth song of Sidney's *Astrophil and Stella*, which is widely recognized as one of his models. Recent scholarship has demonstrated that Shakespeare twice drew inspiration from Sidney's song, first, in the early 1590s when he composed Dumaine's 'On a day (alack the day)' for *Love's Labour's Lost* and, then, in 1601 when he wrote 'The Phoenix and Turtle'. What has gone unobserved, however, is their interconnected publishing history. H. R. Woudhuysen, who notes that Dumaine's poem is 'reminiscent in tone and setting' of Sidney's song, observes that both 'take place in the open air in May and meditate on the wind's freedom to kiss whom it wants', while 'exposing their speakers to a certain amount of comic ridicule'. In a play saturated with his influence, it not only pays 'homage' to Sidney, Woudhuysen contends, but shows that Shakespeare 'can surpass him'.[15] Shakespeare again returned to its subtle trochaic rhythms, as John Roe and Barbara Everett maintain, in 'The Phoenix and Turtle', for an even more decisive victory in a work that registers a fundamental change in the nature of late Elizabethan poetry. Alert to new possibilities concerning what a short poem might be, Shakespeare keyed his verse to the philosophically inflected baroque arguments on questions of love that had originated in coterie manuscript circulation of the late 1590s, which would go on to inspire some of the best lyrics of the seventeenth century.[16]

Shakespeare's reaction to the publication history of his poetry is coded in the metrical idiom of trochaic tetrameter that represented him in *England's Helicon* and that he now deployed in *Love's Martyr* to re-define himself in print, by availing himself of the most avant-garde poetic style in manuscript circulation and linking his work with that of three of the most erudite 'modern' poet–playwrights. Indeed, when Shakespeare wrote 'The Phoenix and Turtle' in 1601, 'On a day' was his most frequently published lyric, having been reprinted five times (at least four times with his name) between 1597 and 1600: in the two editions each of *Love's Labour's Lost* (only the second of which is extant) and *The Passionate Pilgrim*, and in *England's Helicon*, where it is his sole poem. It is hard to imagine that Shakespeare would not have appreciated Ling's diligence in distinguishing his work from Barnfield's and Marlowe's. Shakespeare might even have taken pride in having his lyric published in the same anthology that included Sidney's eighth song. So that when he returned to Sidney's trochaic rhythms in 1601 for his contribution to *Love's Martyr*, the poetic medium he employed had a special symbolic valence, based on its prior textual history as a site of contestation between the editors of *The Passionate Pilgrim* and *England's Helicon* concerning the question of what constituted a legitimate 'Shakespeare' text. Shakespeare intervened in his own ongoing textualization by attaching his name to an entirely different kind of poetic discourse, but one that was symbolically resonant of his own prior as well as his predecessor's acoustic worlds. Transforming the poetic formula that had defined him in *England's Helicon*, Shakespeare created a new and different poetic persona to substitute for Jaggard's representation of him in *The Passionate Pilgrim* as the erotically obsessed author of *Love's Labour's Lost*, *Romeo and Juliet*, and *Venus and Adonis*. Through his contribution to *Love's Martyr*, Shakespeare appropriated the terms of the religious eroticism of *The Passionate Pilgrim* to serve a new and very different conception of poetry, as he used the signature metrics of trochaic tetrameter to assume the voice of a priest in the religion of love. Here both *Venus and Adonis* and *Lucrece* might be seen as being superseded by an even 'graver labour', as the Ovidian poetics of *The Passionate Pilgrim* and *England's Helicon* were superseded by an idiosyncratic Neoplatonism, qualified by scholastic philosophy, that defines ideal love as a sacrificial act of mutual recognition and self-denial.

Formally conveying the mystical state in which two might be one, while remaining distinct, the structure of Shakespeare's untitled poem of 67 lines can be read in two ways. As a single work, it has three parts, with the second embedded in the first and the third embedded in the second. The poet thus instructs the unknowable 'bird of loudest lay' (line 1) to summon three allegorically symbolic birds (the eagle, swan, and crow) to the funeral of the phoenix and turtle-dove (stanzas 1–5), whose miraculous devotion to each other is celebrated in an 'anthem' (or 'funeral song') commemorating their ideal love (stanzas 6–13) that describes how Reason has capitulated to Love and composed the concluding 'Threnos' (or 'dirge') (stanzas 14–18). But the same verses can also be taken as comprising two connected poems: thirteen *untitled* stanzas of heptasyllabic trochaic tetrameter quatrains (with a few variations of accent) rhyming *abba*, followed by a *titled* poem, 'Threnos', written in five stanzas of heptasyllabic trochaic tetrameter tercets rhyming *aaa*, printed on a separate page above the author's name, between ornamental borders. In the first case, Reason's Threnos emerges as a song within a song (the anthem) within a poem, and in the second, it arises as a theatrical 'chorus' commenting on the poem's tragic 'scene' (line 52).

The effect of this structural doubling is to create a generic rebus that flouts categorical distinctions between drama, poetry, and song, while echoing the conceit of a 'Vatum Chorus' that frames the collection as a programme of theatrical/literary performances by poets who recite or sing their poems to their patron Salusbury *in print*. The elegy begins audaciously with the poet-maker summoning his universe into being with an echo of divine fiat:

> Let the bird of loudest lay,
> On the sole Arabian tree,
> Herald sad and trumpet be:
> To whose sound chaste wings obey.   (lines 1–4)

Apart from this enigmatic trumpeter, whose identity is left strategically obscure, only three other mourners, the eagle, swan, and crow, are called to attend, while the screech owl, 'foul precurrer of the fiend', and other raptors, 'fowl of tyrant wing' (lines 6 and 10), are banned. The 'anthem' they either sing or hear performed by the "death-divining" swan idealizes the union of the female phoenix and male turtle:

> So between them love did shine
> That the Turtle saw his right
> Flaming in the Phoenix' sight;
> Either was the other's mine.   (lines 33–6)

Written in a stately, visually arresting, and allusive style, Shakespeare's poem meditates on the mystery of reciprocal self-perception, an ideal state through which lovers overcome their individual isolation to become one, while still apparently remaining biologically distinct. The phoenix and turtle loved 'in twain' but had one 'essence' (lines 25–6). They were separate but united: 'Two distincts, division none', so that in being *both two and one*, 'Number there in love was slain' (lines 27–8). Although their hearts might be 'remote', they were never 'asunder', because their intersubjectivity proved that 'Distance' lacked 'space' (lines 29–30). The Turtle perceives himself in the Phoenix's flaming vision in which he is both idealized and annihilated. Through their reciprocal love, 'Either was the other's mine' (line 36), they become both treasurer and treasury. But their baffling union, based on Trinitarian doctrine, destabilizes materiality, and the guardians of that order, the allegorical figures of Property and Reason, alerted to this crisis of ontology, lose their authority because of it. Property (whose name is based on the Latin word *proprietas*, the principle of individuation) is 'appalled / That the self was not the same; / Single nature's double name / Neither two nor one was called' (lines 37–40), as the phoenix–turtle union cancels the concept of autonomy. Under these conditions, the most reasonable thing Reason can do is surrender its identity, conceding that 'Love hath reason, Reason none, / If what parts, can so remain' (lines 47–8).

Reading 'The Phoenix and Turtle' is complicated by its literary resonances, which include tomb inscriptions, bird elegies, and religious psalms, and range from Lactantius' *Carmen de Phoenice*, through John Skelton's 'Philip Sparrow', to Matthew Roydon's and Nicholas Breton's poems in *The Phoenix Nest* (1593). And although he adapts the Chaucerian allegorical love-vision of *The Parliament of Fowls*, Shakespeare's insistence on demonstrating his waking power to conjure the poetic scene into being through a speech act – as its maker – rather than depicting himself as the passive dreamer who records mysterious somatic impressions is new. Most fascinating of all is the question of whether or not Shakespeare by 1601 had read John Donne's poetry in manuscript. Had the 'frequenter of plays', whose style is often described as being dramatic, influenced the playwright? Jonson claimed that Donne had written 'all his best pieces' before he turned twenty-five in 1597. Yet it is Donne who seems to be echoing 'The Phoenix and Turtle' in 'The Canonization' (written after 1603), when he writes that 'The phoenix riddle hath more wit / By us; we two, being one, are it' (lines 23–4).

From the end of the nineteenth century, scholars have read Shakespeare's poem as an historical allegory, but no current consensus has been established. In light of this unavoidable irresolution, it might be wiser to heed G. Wilson Knight's suggestion that the phoenix and turtle in Shakespeare's poem 'indicate really not so much persons, as a kind of *relationship*', through which their 'difficult, tragic, and yet victorious experience' reveals 'multi-faceted potentialities' of interpretation.[17] Chester invented his myth of the phoenix and turtle to remedy anxieties about 'rebirth', the period's most enduring trope. Because even though early modern poets continued to view the phoenix as a paradigm of uniqueness, endurance, and resurrection, they also began to consider the possibility of its endangerment or extinction. Petrarch in *Canzonieri* 323 describes how, after Laura's death, lightning strikes a laurel tree filled with singing birds and the Muses' spring is destroyed by an earthquake, after which the phoenix in sorrow stabs itself and dies. Spenser's first published poems, in Jan Van der Noot's *Theatre for Voluptuous Worldlings* (1569), included an English translation of this passage (through Marot's French version), along with a woodcut of the phoenix's suicide, and he later retranslated it for inclusion among 'The Visions of Petrarch' in *Complaints* (1591). There, brooding on the phoenix's extinction, he sadly observes that 'each thing at last we see / Doth passe away' (lines 62–3). Chester, in contrast, proposed that the phoenix was only endangered and might still be reborn through a turtle-dove's act of selfless devotion. *Love's Martyr* is a poetic failure, lacking the structural armature required to unify its tangential excursions into myth and history that occasionally mimic a Spenserian model. But Shakespeare had a knack for developing other writers' ideas, and in the wreckage of Chester's plot, he discovered this curious fable of the phoenix and turtle's ideal act of mutual recognition.

What is different about Shakespeare's poem, however, is the fact that it uses Chester's myth of the marriage/funeral of the phoenix and turtle to emphasize the intersubjectivity of a fully realized love, even though it denies the biological regeneration it was supposed to foster: 'Death is now the Phoenix' nest, / And the Turtle's loyal breast / To eternity doth rest' (56–8). Did Shakespeare deliberately add a melancholy Petrarchan twist to

Chester's sanguine myth of rebirth? Marston read Shakespeare's poem in this manner, when he admired its 'Threnos' (its 'Epiceduim' or 'funeral song') but questioned its conclusion:

> O 'twas a moving *Epiceduim*!
> Can Fire? Can Time? Can blackest Fate consume
> So rare creation? No; 'tis thwart to sense,
> Corruption quakes to touch such excellence.   (lines 1–4)

In the 'cinders' of Shakespeare's poem, Marston finds a 'glorious issue', that 'most wondrous creature' fated to arise from the phoenix and turtle's ashes, because 'Ought into nought can never remigrate' (line 6). And he seeks divine assistance in meditating on a state of ideality that he calls 'this same *Metaphysical* / God, Man, nor Woman, but elix'd of all' (lines 23–4), using the very word that would come to characterize the new species of poetry Shakespeare auditioned in *Love's Martyr*. When Samuel Johnson later wrote that 'about the beginning of the seventeenth century appeared a race of writers that may be termed the metaphysical poets', he consequently reiterated Marston's epithet but without his enthusiasm.[18]

Those who find a mode of consolation in Shakespeare's epithalamion/ dirge, however, emphasize the symbolic presence of the phoenix and turtle in the ceremony that commemorates their self-sacrifice. If 'the bird of loudest lay / On the sole Arabian tree' (lines 1–2) in the poem's opening stanza is the phoenix, then, despite what Reason concludes in the Threnos, the realized ideal still figuratively beckons the turtle-dove's 'chaste wings' (line 4) in the flock that answers its call, as the allegorized mourners instantiate the virtues of the 'dead birds' (line 67) they memorialize. Contrasted with the ominous owl that haunts death and the predators of 'tyrant wing' that destroy life, they include the kingly eagle who attests to the rite's propriety, the swan who joyfully sings at death, and the crow whose legendary long life (three times a man's) and reproduction without sex (by an exchange of breath) reflect aspects of the idealized Neoplatonic lovers they mourn. But such a reading depends upon a deliberately obscure epithet – 'the bird of loudest lay' – that has been as confidently identified as a nightingale, crane, and cock, as it has been spotted as the phoenix. The phrase's mannered obscurity speaks to the mystery of Shakespeare's riddle. The poem's provocative speculation, propelled by Shakespeare's desire to revise his print persona away from *The Passionate Pilgrim*, positioned beside the work of Marston, Chapman, and Jonson, the most learned poet–playwrights of the day, set a standard of literary achievement that none matched. Unique in the canon, it was written during a period of rapid political, social, philosophical, and literary change and continues to enthrall readers with its surreal allegory and oracular pronouncements through which nothing or everything is revealed. Here, Shakespeare, the poet–playwright, reclaimed and readjusted his voice in print, assuming authority to express the crisis of the new century in an archetype poised between comic and tragic alternatives that paradoxically mirrored the time's darkest hope and brightest fear.

NOTES

1 For print and manuscript sources and parallels, see the notes on *The Passionate Pilgrim* in Rollins (ed.), *Variorum Poems*; John Roe (ed.), *The Poems*, The New Cambridge Shakespeare (Cambridge University Press, 1992); and Colin Burrow (ed.), *Complete Sonnets and Poems*, The Oxford Shakespeare (Oxford University Press, 2002).

2 If Ralegh actually penned '*The Nymph's Reply*', he persuaded the publisher to paste printed cancel slips marked 'Ignoto' over his name to avoid the stigma of print.

3 Ling worked under the direction of John Bodenham, and because he left shortly before the volume was complete it is possible that I overstate his importance.

4 Thomas Heywood, *An Apology for Actors* (London, 1612), G4^{r-v}.

5 Rollins (ed.), *The Passionate Pilgrim*, p. xvi; and Adrian Johns, *The Nature of the Book* (University of Chicago Press, 1998), p. 162.

6 Francis Meres, *Palladis Tamia, Wit's Treasury* (London, 1598), p. 283.

7 *The Scourge of Villainy*, 2.37–8, qtd from *The Poems of John Marston*, ed. Arnold Davenport (Liverpool University Press, 1961).

8 The two poems marked by asterisks appear incomplete: 9 is missing its second line and 12 (written in hexameter, similar to Shakespeare's genuine poem 5) lacks a concluding couplet.

9 Patrick Cheney, *Shakespeare, National Poet–Playwright* (Cambridge University Press, 2004), p. 159.

10 Burrow (ed.), *Complete Sonnets and Poems*, p. 80; see also Roe (ed.), *Poems*, pp. 56–8.

11 The first extant edition of *The Garland of Good Will*, however, was published in 1628, and Deloney did not write all the poems in this collection.

12 Spurgeon, *Shakespeare's Imagery* (Cambridge University Press, 1965), p. 48.

13 Sidney, *An Apology for Poetry*, ed. Forrest G. Robinson (Indianapolis: Bobbs-Merrill, 1970), p. 11.

14 See James P. Bednarz, *Shakespeare and the Poets' War* (New York: Columbia University Press, 2001), pp. 198–200.

15 H. R. Woudhuysen (ed.), Introduction to *Love's Labour's Lost* (London: Thompson, 1998), pp. 12–13.

16 Roe (ed.), *Poems*, p. 48; and Barbara Everett, 'Set Upon a Golden Bough to Sing: Shakespeare's Debt to Sidney in "The Phoenix and Turtle"', *Times Literary Supplement*, 16 February 2001, pp. 13–15.

17 Knight, *The Mutual Flame: On Shakespeare's 'Sonnets' and 'The Phoenix and the Turtle'* (London: Methuen, 1962), p. 155.

18 Johnson, 'Life of Cowley', in *Lives of the English Poets*, 2 vols. (Oxford University Press, 1964), I:14.

READING LIST

Adams, Joseph Quincy (ed.). *The Passionate Pilgrim*. New York: Scribner's, 1939.

Brown, Carleton (ed.). *Poems by Sir John Salusbury and Robert Chester*. Early English Text Society. London: K. Paul, Trench, Trübner, 1914.

Burrow, Colin (ed.). *Complete Sonnets and Poems*. The Oxford Shakespeare. Oxford University Press, 2002.

Cheney, Patrick. *Shakespeare, National Poet–Playwright*. Cambridge University Press, 2004.

Crane, D. E. L. (ed.). *England's Helicon*. London: Scolar Press, 1973.

Cunningham, J. V. '"Essence' and "The Phoenix and Turtle"'. *ELH* 19 (1952), 256–76.

Everett, Barbara. 'Set Upon a Golden Bough to Sing: Shakespeare's Debt to Sidney in "The Phoenix and Turtle"'. *Times Literary Supplement*, 16 February 2001: 13–15.

Grosart, Alexander B. (ed.). *Robert Chester's Love's Martyr*. New Shakespeare Society. London, 1878.

Matchett, William. *The Phoenix and the Turtle*. The Hague: Mouton, 1965.

Roe, John (ed.). *The Poems*. The New Cambridge Shakespeare. Cambridge University Press, 1992.

Rollins, Hyder (ed.). *The Passionate Pilgrim, by William Shakespeare (1612)*. New York: Scribner's, 1940.

A New Variorum Edition: The Poems. Philadelphia: J.B. Lippincott, 1938.

7

MICHAEL SCHOENFELDT

The Sonnets

Shake-speares Sonnets have over time proved a remarkably attractive yet profoundly intractable document. Concealing as much as they reveal, and sharing intimacies only in the most detached manner, the Sonnets have frequently functioned as a mirror in which cultures reveal their own critical presuppositions about the nature of poetic creation and the comparative instabilities of gender, race, and class. Entering the world in a publication that may or may not be authorized, the Sonnets are surrounded by veils of inscrutability that have stirred the curiosity of readers since their initial publication. Although the Sonnets have proven particularly amenable to some of the central developments of late twentieth-century modes of criticism – particularly feminism and gender and gay studies – they continue to be richer and more complex than anything that can be said about them. As they approach their 400th birthday, the Sonnets have in fact aged quite well.

Perhaps this chronic inscrutability is why editing has proven to be such a rich area of enquiry for recent scholarly engagement with the Sonnets. Since Stephen Booth's marvellous and prize-winning edition of 1977, the Sonnets have been edited by John Kerrigan (1986), G. B. Evans (1996), Katherine Duncan-Jones (1997), Helen Vendler (1997), and most recently, Colin Burrow (2002).[1] Each of these editions has been a work of criticism and scholarship at least as much as of editing, since the textual problems are for the most part rather straightforward (there is only one early edition, possibly authorized, but no manuscripts, no competing early editions, and relatively few typographical conundrums). The issue in each of these editions has been: how do we read the Sonnets? What is the most significant unit of meaning – the sequence, the individual poem, the quatrain, the sentence, or the word? Do we annotate the poems in order to record all possible meanings and inferences, or do we point to constellations of meaning and coherence? Should we emphasize contemporaneous references, the poems' creative adaptations of earlier poetry, their historical embeddedness, or their formal accomplishment? What editorial practices might best represent the remarkable aesthetic achievement of these enduring lyrics?

The poems are first published in Shakespeare's lifetime, possibly many years after their composition, and dedicated to a mysterious 'Mr W. H.' with an elusive utterance signed not by the poet but by the printer Thomas Thorpe:

TO.THE.ONLIE.BEGETTER.OF.
THESE.INSVING.SONNETS.
M^r.W. H. ALL.HAPPINESSE.
AND.THAT.ETERNITIE.
PROMISED.
BY.
OVR.EVER-LIVING.POET.
WISHETH.
THE.WELL-WISHING.
ADVENTVRER.IN.
SETTING.
FORTH.
T. T.

The volume may have been pirated by Thorpe, or the edition may have been completely authorized by the poet, or it may inhabit some grey area between these possibilities. We are not even sure what 'begetter' means here – does it refer to the patron of the poems, or to the inspirer of the poems, or to the person who helped Thorpe obtain a copy of the poems, or even to the poet himself? Various candidates for Mr. W. H. exist. He may have been Henry Wriothesley, the earl of Southampton, whose initials may have been accidentally transposed by an otherwise careful printer, or deliberately transposed by an intentionally cagey printer. The curious italicization of rose in the second line of Sonnet 1 – 'From fairest creatures we desire increase, / That thereby beauties *Rose* might never die' – would then refer to Wriothesley, whose name was probably pronounced 'rose-ly'. Shakespeare had already dedicated his two other major non-dramatic publications, *Venus and Adonis* and *The Rape of Lucrece*, to Southampton. Nine years younger than Shakespeare, Southampton possesses an age and status that match that of the putative young man addressed in Sonnets 1–126. Sonnets 1–17 urging the young man to marry, moreover, resemble the arguments Venus uses to attempt to seduce a reluctant Adonis in *Venus and Adonis*. Mr. W. H., though, may also refer to William Herbert, the third earl of Pembroke, co-dedicatee of the First Folio of Shakespeare's plays. A life-long bachelor and a wealthy patron, Pembroke was sixteen years younger than Shakespeare. For both aristocrats, though, the term 'Mr' seems inadequate to convey their exalted social status, particularly in a volume so concerned with registering class markers. It is even possible that either Thorpe or Shakespeare was exploiting a deliberate ambiguity with these initials in order to ingratiate two or more patrons with one dedication.

We do know that some of the poems circulated in manuscript before their publication – the clergyman Francis Meres in *Palladis Tamia* (1598) asserts that 'the sweet witty soul of Ovid lives in mellifluous and honey-tongued Shakespeare, witness his *Venus and Adonis*, his *Lucrece*, his sugared Sonnets among his private friends, etc.'[2] Sonnets 138 and 144 are published in a variant form in a popular anthology, *The Passionate Pilgrim*, in 1599, ten years before *Shake-speares Sonnets* is published. Although the 1609 edition was published in Shakespeare's lifetime, seven years before he died, he certainly did not rush into print with his own authorized edition in response, as so many authors did when an unauthorized version of their poems appeared. The volume seems not to have been a major hit; a second edition did not appear until 1640, and then in a highly revised and reordered edition, John Benson's *Poems: Written by Wil. Shakespeare. Gent.*[3]

There is something at once belated and revolutionary in the 1609 sequence. Numerous sonnet sequences were published in England in the 1590s, including Sir Philip Sidney's *Astrophil and Stella* (1591), Samuel Daniel's *Delia* (1592), and Edmund Spenser's *Amoretti* (1595).[4] But by 1609, when Shakespeare's collection was published, the fashion had waned; sonnet sequences were no longer a central form for literary and courtly aspiration. When one reads the opening sonnet of the 1609 sequence, in which one male urges another to procreate in order to preserve his beauty, we realize that we are in very different territory from that inhabited by typical Elizabethan sonnet sequences. Rather than the conventional idealization of a distant female beloved, we confront a casual misogyny, in which women are useful as incubators for aristocratic males who wish to reproduce their beauty, but not as objects of emotional attachment or intellectual companionship. As Sonnet 1 declares:

> From fairest creatures we desire increase,
> That thereby beauty's rose might never die,
> But as the riper should by time decease,
> His tender heir might bear his memory:
> But thou, contracted to thine own bright eyes,
> Feed'st thy light's flame with self-substantial fuel,
> Making a famine where abundance lies,
> Thyself thy foe, to thy sweet self too cruel.
> Thou that art now the world's fresh ornament
> And only herald to the gaudy spring,

> Within thine own bud buriest thy content,
> And, tender churl, mak'st waste in niggarding.
>   Pity the world, or else this glutton be,
>   To eat the world's due, by the grave and thee.

The poem takes the conventional praise of chaste beauty, and turns it on its head – the young man's beauty burdens him with the responsibility to reproduce, a responsibility he is currently shirking. In a fascinating and unexpected ethical reversal, the speaker does not engage in stock exaltation of the chastity of the beloved, but instead accuses the young man of gluttonous self-consumption in his refusal to produce a 'tender heir' who would continue his beauty beyond the inexorable decay of aging.

Shakespeare, then, makes the sonnet cycle something more ethically complex, and yet more narratively diffuse, than anything previous writers had produced. The collection is divided into two large sequences: Sonnets 1–126, which are written to a beautiful young man, and Sonnets 127–52, which are written to a 'dark lady'. Throughout the collection, moreover, there are many small sequences: Sonnets 1–17 urge the young man to reproduce, and also meditate on poetry as a mode of reproduction and immortality. Sonnets 78–90 describe a rival poet and lover, in which literary patronage and erotic relations are blurred. Sonnets 91–6 suggest that the poet and the young man have reconciled. In Sonnets 100–20 the poet apologizes for his truant muse, and his inability to be constant. Sonnets 133–4 depict the dark lady being unfaithful with the young man, while Sonnets 135, 136, and 143 develop puns on the poet's name – 'Will' – and his desire, or 'will'. Sonnets 153 and 154, the last sonnets in the collection, are poems on the power of Cupid, and depict the inability of any human action to 'cure' the disease of love. The 1609 sequence concludes with *A Lover's Complaint*, a cynical response to Spenser's glorious celebration of the consummation of his erotic desire in the *Epithalamion* that follows his *Amoretti*.

Beginning with a putatively male speaker imploring a beautiful young man to reproduce, and concluding with a series of poems – the dark lady poems – that affiliate consummated heterosexual passion with incurable disease, Shakespeare's Sonnets radically and deliberately disrupt the conventional heterosexual narrative of erotic courtship. Women are not rhapsodic objects of erotic aspiration, but either a necessary means of biological reproduction or the trigger of intemperate lust. The vagaries of male friendship in all of its forms, from the affably respectful to the erotically ardent, absorb the energies of heterosexual idealization and impassioned intimacy that inhabit most traditional sonnet sequences. Sonnet 127, the first of the dark lady poems, signals a direct and intentional violation of literary convention.

> In the old age black was not counted fair,
> Or if it were, it bore not beauty's name;
> But now is black beauty's successive heir,
> And beauty slandered with a bastard shame:
> For since each hand hath put on Nature's power,
> Fairing the foul with art's false borrowed face,
> Sweet beauty hath no name, no holy bower,
> But is profaned, if not lives in disgrace.
> Therefore my mistress' eyes are raven black,
> Her eyes so suited, and they mourners seem
> At such who not born fair no beauty lack,
> Sland'ring creation with a false esteem:
>> Yet so they mourn, becoming of their woe,
>> That every tongue says beauty should look so.

The force of the 'now' in line 3 demarcates a novel aesthetic the poet is forthwith articulating and practising, one that challenges the conventional equation of beauty with a fair, or light, complexion even as it sustains the conventional deployment of class-specific terms ('bastard shame') to demarcate erotic attraction and repulsion. This aesthetic could issue in playful flauntings of convention – Sonnet 130, 'My mistress' eyes are nothing like the sun', is the most famous. But it could also issue in a radically divided consciousness, experiencing erotic desire for an unconventional beauty as a kind of perjury against the self and its better knowledge.[5]

Sonnets 127–52 are famously written to a purported 'dark lady', but we do not know what darkness means in this collection – is she simply a Caucasian woman with dark hair and eyes, or a woman with a dark Mediterranean complexion, or a woman from Africa? Or is she simply Shakespeare's variation on the Renaissance poetic game of finding ways to praise 'brown beauty' in a lyric discourse that traditionally preferred lightness and fairness? Regardless, the poems certainly deploy a hierarchy of colour that underpins, and predates, Western racism.[6] The central concern of such poems is not the identity of the mistress but rather the ingenuity of the poet. Nevertheless, candidates have been proposed for this role, including Amelia Lanyer, a former mistress to the Lord Chamberlain (the patron of Shakespeare's company), and author of the *Salve Deus Rex Iudaeorum* (1611); Mary Fitton, whom William Herbert, the earl of Pembroke, impregnated; and Jane Davenant, mother of William Davenant, a writer who liked to claim that he was the illegitimate offspring of Shakespeare.[7]

The poems are all the more tantalizing because they seem to be our only chance to hear Shakespeare, the consummate dramatist, speak with something like his own voice. We know that the poems contain some overt puns on Shakespeare's first name, *Will*; Sonnets 135 and 136 pun promiscuously on the felicitous fact that the poet's first name can also designate sexual desire and even the sexual organs:

[135]
Whoever hath her wish, thou hast thy Will,
And Will to boot, and Will in overplus;
More than enough am I that vex thee still,
To thy sweet will making addition thus.
Wilt thou, whose will is large and spacious,
Not once vouchsafe to hide my will in thine?
Shall will in others seem right gracious,
And in my will no fair acceptance shine?
The sea all water, yet receives rain still,
And in abundance addeth to his store;
So thou, being rich in Will add to thy Will
One will of mine, to make thy large Will more.
   Let no unkind, no fair beseechers kill;
   Think all but one, and me in that one Will.

[136]
If thy soul check thee that I come so near,
Swear to thy blind soul that I was thy Will,
And will, thy soul knows is admitted there;
Thus far for love, my love-suit, sweet, fulfil.
Will will fulfil the treasure of thy love,
Ay, fill it full with wills, and my will one.
In things of great receipt with ease we prove
Among a number one is reckon'd none:
Then in the number let me pass untold,
Though in thy stores' account I one must be;
For nothing hold me, so it please thee hold
That nothing me, a something sweet to thee.
   Make but my name thy love, and love that still,
   And then thou lovest me, for my name is Will.

These sonnets combine word play and erotic play, connecting the proliferation of lovers in a scenario of erotic betrayal to the proliferation of meaning in puns. They also signal a series of erotic anxieties, as the speaker reveals his fears about the promiscuity of the beloved, and about the possible dissociation of physical and emotional attachment, of identity and desire. Since *Will* can designate the poet, his penis, his lust, his beloved, his beloved's lust, and his beloved's genitalia, the poems enquire whether individual identity and romantic love are simply fictions laminated on a series of undifferentiated erotic appetites. Is sexual desire, the poems ask, an opportunity for emotional intimacy, or simply an undifferentiated hunger for largely interchangeable objects?

Another sonnet seems to contain a pun drawn directly from Shakespeare's life. There is a probable play on the name of Shakespeare's wife, Ann Hathaway (pronounced 'hate-away'), in Sonnet 145, which along with its unique tetrameter line has led some critics to surmise that this was the first sonnet Shakespeare wrote:

> Those lips that Love's own hand did make
> Breathed forth the sound that said 'I hate'
> To me that languished for her sake;
> But when she saw my woeful state,
> Straight in her heart did mercy come,
> Chiding that tongue that ever sweet
> Was used in giving gentle doom,
> And taught it thus anew to greet:
> 'I hate' she altered with an end,
> That follow'd it as gentle day
> Doth follow night, who like a fiend
> From heaven to hell is flown away:
>   'I hate' from hate away she threw,
>   And saved my life, saying 'not you'.

Cleverly opening with a stated antipathy that we learn in the last two words is not directed at the speaker, the poem uses syntactic suspense to depict erotic anxiety. Along with the 'Will' sonnets, the poem tempts us to locate the drama of the collection in Shakespeare's own experience. In all three poems, the drama of erotic attraction and repulsion is made to hinge on our knowledge of the names of the protagonists.

Writing of the Sonnets, William Wordsworth, the co-founder of English Romanticism, suggested that 'with this key, / Shakespeare unlocked his heart'. Robert Browning, though, the Victorian exemplar of the dramatic monologue, responded to Wordsworth's mawkish reading of the poems by remarking, 'Did Shakespeare? If so, the less Shakespeare he'.[8] It is typical of responses to the Sonnets in literary history that they supply the occasion on which two poets articulate and defend absolutely opposite poetic principles. Where Wordsworth assumes that the Sonnets were composed romantically, like his own verse, in a spontaneous overflow of powerful emotion, perhaps rhymed and ordered metrically in tranquillity, Browning counters that the poems were the product of a deliberate assumption of a dramatic role in a specific situation, much like the composition of drama, or of Browning's own dramatic monologues.

However we read Shakespeare's Sonnets, we must acknowledge the pull of both perspectives. We must also acknowledge some sense of the inevitable tension between the integrity of an individual poem and the narrative and thematic contexts in which it exists. Some readers want to read the Sonnets as a kind of flipbook with some pages missing; if one moves through them quickly enough, a story will emerge. Other readers, though, want to focus on the artifice of individual sonnets. When reading a sonnet sequence, there is an inexorable pull between the part and the whole, between the highly wrought quanta of lyric energy that is a sonnet and the loosely suggestive vectors of theme, imagery, and narrative that connect individual poems. Whether we base our interpretations on obvious biographical correlatives or not, we read the collection, and individual sonnets, by creating little narratives and dramas; whether we are conscious of it or not, these poems demand that we locate them amid an imagined conversation among four central players – the speaker, the young man, the rival poet, the dark lady. In these necessary acts of provisional explication, the subtle prejudices and covert presuppositions of a reader, or a culture, are inevitably writ large. A remarkable study in the seductive allure of inference and innuendo, the poems at once whet and frustrate our corollary drives for narrative shape and aesthetic closure.

Certain themes, though, cut across the various narratives of the collection. The troubling economy of sexual reproduction stalks both the poems to the young man and the poems about the dark lady. Contemporaneous medical theory claimed that each orgasm shortened one's life; this medical 'fact' troubled Shakespeare, as it worried his contemporary John Donne, who writes succinctly in *The First Anniversary*, 'We kill ourselves, to propagate our kind'.[9] This physiological doctrine only intensifies the paradox explored in Sonnets 1–19 that in order to reproduce, and so save yourself, you must give of yourself. Because beauty cannot sustain its own value over time, the young man is repeatedly urged to procreate, to engage in the wise investment of seminal fluid that would pay the long-term interest of progeny (Sonnet 16):

> But wherefore do not you a mightier way
> Make war upon this bloody tyrant Time?
> And fortify yourself in your decay
> With means more blessed than my barren rhyme?
> Now stand you on the top of happy hours,
> And many maiden gardens yet unset
> With virtuous wish would bear your living flowers,
> Much liker than your painted counterfeit:
> So should the lines of life that life repair,
> Which this, Time's pencil, or my pupil pen

> Neither in inward worth nor outward fair
> Can make you live yourself in eyes of men:
>> To give away yourself keeps yourself still,
>> And you must live, drawn by your own sweet skill.

Women here are imagined as fertile gardens eagerly awaiting the young man's seed, so that they can bear his 'living flowers', that is, children. Comparing sexual reproduction to two modes of aesthetic reproduction – visual art and poetry – the speaker encourages the young man to create the self-portrait of progeny.

The dark lady poems express similar worries about the economies of sexual reproduction. But in these desperate poems, there is no mention of the possible consolation of progeny, just the self-destructive compulsions of lust. The poems depict the agonizing entropy of love frustrated, and the equally disturbing entropy of love fulfilled. Sonnet 129 may be the first English poem to describe orgasm, the physical consummation ostensibly sought by so many previous love poets, and the picture is not pretty:

> Th'expense of spirit in a waste of shame
> Is lust in action, and till action, lust
> Is perjured, murd'rous, bloody, full of blame,
> Savage, extreme, rude, cruel, not to trust,
> Enjoyed no sooner but despised straight,
> Past reason hunted, and no sooner had,
> Past reason hated, as a swallowed bait
> On purpose laid to make the taker mad;
> Mad in pursuit, and in possession so,
> Had, having, and in quest to have, extreme,
> A bliss in proof, and proved, a very woe;
> Before, a joy proposed; behind, a dream.
>> All this the world well knows, yet none knows well
>> To shun the heaven that leads men to this hell.

Sounding more like a fire-and-brimstone preacher than a devout poetic lover, the speaker is as far from the traditional idealization of the beloved as one can imagine. The headlong syntax and rushed enjambment brilliantly enact the rash, impulsive action the poem describes. The emphatic but progressively exhausted stresses of line 4 effectively produce one of Shakespeare's least metrical lines. The pun in line 1 on *waste* and *waist* underscores the poem's unflinching account of the inexorable dissipations of erotic desire. Where Sonnet 16 tells the young man that 'To give away yourself keeps your self still', Sonnet 129 tells all lovers that they desire what will ultimately destroy them, morally and physically.

This theme is continued in Sonnet 147, 'My love is as a fever', which identifies erotic desire as a sexual disease that destroys its carrier:

> My love is as a fever, longing still
> For that which longer nurseth the disease,
> Feeding on that which doth preserve the ill,
> Th'uncertain sickly appetite to please.
> My reason, the physician to my love,
> Angry that his prescriptions are not kept,
> Hath left me, and I desperate now approve
> Desire is death, which physic did except.
> Past cure I am, now reason is past care,
> And, frantic-mad with evermore unrest,
> My thoughts and my discourse as madmen's are,
> At random from the truth vainly expressed:
>   For I have sworn thee fair and thought thee bright,
>   Who art as black as hell, as dark as night.

The speaker is a patient who refuses to follow the prescriptions of his frustrated physician, reason. He confesses that he desires precisely what precipitates and prolongs his illness. His profoundly divided sensibility provokes a kind of insanity in which erotic desire is not a refuge from the ravages of time but rather a venue for hastening time's grievous mortal effects: 'desire is death'.[10]

This bleak portrait of desire as a disease allied to death leads Shakespeare to explore in two signal sonnets the potentially salutary aspects of rigorous self-control. In Sonnet 146, the sonnet that immediately precedes 'My love is as a fever' in the 1609 sequence, Shakespeare explicates the abiding tension between the hedonistic demands of the body and the exalted aspirations of the soul.

> Poor soul, the centre of my sinful earth,
> [...] these rebel pow'rs that thee array;
> Why dost thou pine within and suffer dearth
> Painting thy outward walls so costly gay?
> Why so large cost, having so short a lease,
> Dost thou upon thy fading mansion spend?
> Shall worms, inheritors of this excess,
> Eat up thy charge? Is this thy body's end?
> Then, soul, live thou upon thy servant's loss,
> And let that pine to aggravate thy store;
> Buy terms divine in selling hours of dross;
> Within be fed, without be rich no more:
>   So shalt thou feed on Death, that feeds on men,
>   And Death once dead, there's no more dying then.

The soul is imagined as a figure of precarious authority surrounded by 'rebel pow'rs', the body and its passions, which can only be kept under control through a regimen of deliberate starvation. The second line contains one of the few textual cruces in the 1609 edition – the first three words simply repeat the last three words of the previous line ('My sinful earth').[11] The poem deftly uses assonance to develop a cogent contrast between the precarious defences of the *poor* soul and the shrewd incursions of the 'rebel *pow'rs*'. The poem proposes that the predatory demands of Death – a continuing preoccupation of the Sonnets – can be curbed by carefully disciplining the insatiable appetites of the body.

Sonnet 146 suggests that one response to the troubling entropy of erotic desire identified in Sonnets 129 and 147 is ascetic self-denial. Separating the body from the soul in a way that is at once Platonic and Pauline, the poem endorses a kind of moralized anorexia that idealizes stringent self-control. Sonnet 94 extends this emphasis on the importance of absolute self-control into the conjoined arenas of social and medical practice. Like Sonnets 146 and 129, it is a generalized sonnet, spoken in the third person, as if enacting its rigid regimen of self-denial in its decidedly detached mode of address. Indeed, Sonnet 94 is one of the most cryptic poems in this deeply enigmatic sequence, revealing at once the moral premium placed on the fastidious control of desire and the potential liabilities of such control.

> They that have pow'r to hurt, and will do none,
> That do not do the thing they most do show,
> Who, moving others, are themselves as stone,
> Unmoved, cold, and to temptation slow –
> They rightly do inherit heaven's graces,
> And husband nature's riches from expense;
> They are the lords and owners of their faces,
> Others but stewards of their excellence.
> The summer's flow'r is to the summer sweet,
> Though to itself it only live and die,
> But if that flow'r with base infection meet,
> The basest weed outbraves his dignity:
>   For sweetest things turn sourest by their deeds;
>   Lilies that fester smell far worse than weeds.

Troubled by the disparity between the emotional coldness of the figures being praised and the divine reward these figures are said to merit, readers have argued about whether Sonnet 94 is an ironic indictment of social hypocrisy or a necessary prophylactic against toxic desire from within and base infection from without.[12] The poem's urgent if equivocal endorsement of cool stability can best be understood as a response, however constraining, to the volatile, combustible self depicted in poems such as Sonnet 129, 'Th'expense of spirit', and 147, 'My love is as a fever'. The capacity to resist temptation, Sonnet 94 suggests, entails economic as well as moral concerns; by being unmoved, one manages to 'husband nature's riches from expense'. The poem, moreover, suggests that cool self-control inoculates one against the omnipresent social and medical hazard of 'base infection'. At issue in our response to the poem is whether we imagine personal authenticity to emerge from the scrupulous regulation of emotion or from the expression of unfettered passion. I would argue that whereas we in the twenty-first century tend to privilege the latter, early moderns tended to privilege the former. The poem offers an elaborate endorsement of the signal early modern virtue: temperance. This virtue, at once classical and Christian, entails the deliberate balance between emotional extremes that was seen as the only reliable avenue to moral and physical health. Sonnet 94 suggests that the rigid demands of classical Stoicism (becoming 'as stone / Unmoved, cold') can provide a path to Christian salvation ('They rightly do inherit heaven's graces'). In yet another example of his remarkably creative adaptation of convention, Shakespeare here transforms the sonnet – a form traditionally dedicated to the articulation of precipitous desire and the ventilation of extreme emotion – into a vehicle for advocating the social and medical benefits of dispassionate self-control.

Other sonnets, though, attend to the contingent delights of emotional commitment, and offer kinder, gentler accounts of the pleasures and comforts of human intimacy. Sonnet 18, 'Shall I compare thee', has proven to be one of the most popular of Shakespeare's poems, largely because its emphasis on impermanence is as genial as the opening comparison, and becomes a provocation for aspiration rather than despair:

> Shall I compare thee to a summer's day?
> Thou art more lovely and more temperate:
> Rough winds do shake the darling buds of May,
> And summer's lease hath all too short a date;
> Sometime too hot the eye of heaven shines,
> And often is his gold complexion dimmed;
> And every fair from fair sometime declines,
> By chance or nature's changing course untrimmed:
> But thy eternal summer shall not fade,
> Nor lose possession of that fair thou ow'st;
> Nor shall Death brag thou wand'rest in his shade,
> When in eternal lines to time thou grow'st.
> > So long as men can breathe or eyes can see,
> > So long lives this and this gives life to thee.

This sonnet, which was featured prominently in the film *Shakespeare in Love*, boldly suggests that the climatological impossibility of an eternal summer can in fact be attained in the idealizing verse of the poet. As we read the lines, we reaffirm their promise of eternal life via aesthetic representation.

In the film *Shakespeare in Love*, Shakespeare the poet is imagined to compose the verse after being smitten by a beautiful woman, Viola de Lesseps, played by Gwyneth Paltrow.[13] Yet the poem comes to us in a group of poems written to the young man, and its air of gentle eroticism and temporal anxiety perfectly matches the tone of those poems. Like so many of the Sonnets, though, the poem bears no overt markers of the gender of its addressee. A poem that does indelibly and uneasily flaunt such marks is Sonnet 20:

> A woman's face with Nature's own hand painted
> Hast thou, the master-mistress of my passion;
> A woman's gentle heart, but not acquainted
> With shifting change, as is false women's fashion;
> An eye more bright than theirs, less false in rolling,
> Gilding the object whereupon it gazeth;
> A man in hue, all hues in his controlling,
> Much steals men's eyes and women's souls amazeth.
> And for a woman wert thou first created;
> Till Nature as she wrought thee fell a-doting,
> And by addition me of thee defeated,
> By adding one thing to my purpose nothing.
>> But since she pricked thee out for women's pleasure,
>> Mine be thy love, and thy love's use their treasure.

The casual misogyny of the Sonnets is here turned to the praise of the young man – he is more beautiful but less false, less changeable, than women. The various bawdy puns on 'prick' and 'quaint' (an early version of the vulgar 'cunt', and used freely by Chaucer's Wife of Bath) preclude any comfortable refuge in the discourse of non-physical male friendship. Cleverly, this poem about the complex genesis of same-sex love, is written entirely in the unaccented final syllable that the Renaissance, and we, call 'feminine rhymes'. This poem, which has been used as evidence for both Shakespeare's heterosexual and same-sex commitments, instead signals the fungibility of all sexual identity and desire.[14] Significantly, both Nature and the speaker experience an originary same-sex desire, and both find this desire to be the source of some frustration: where nature first makes the 'master-mistress' a woman, but falls in love and gives him a penis ('adding one thing') so that her desire will have a heterosexual outlet, the speaker finds this addition to be a kind of subtraction ('adding one thing to my purpose nothing'). The speaker concedes that the added prick is largely 'for women's pleasure', but is not willing to renounce his erotic love for the male so easily. The final couplet instead separates out a kind of love that could be involved in 'use', or usury – the heterosexual copulation for the purposes of progeny to which the first 19 poems are dedicated – with a kind of love that yields other 'treasures'. But it never suggests that one love is physical and the other Platonic.

A similar but far more ominous love triangle is explored in a poem from the dark lady sequence, 'Two loves I have'. The off-handed misogyny of Sonnet 20 – assuming that women are, unlike the young man, intrinsically changeable and false – is in Sonnet 144 amplified into the material of paranoia and nightmare. This is all the more pronounced in a genre that fetishizes the constancy of the lover and the beloved. In Sonnet 144, we see a speaker divided between same-sex and opposite-sex erotic commitments:

> Two loves I have, of comfort and despair,
> Which like two spirits do suggest me still:
> The better angel is a man right fair;
> The worser spirit a woman coloured ill.
> To win me soon to hell my female evil
> Tempteth my better angel from my side,
> And would corrupt my saint to be a devil,
> Wooing his purity with her foul pride.
> And whether that my angel be turned fiend
> Suspect I may, yet not directly tell,
> But being both from me, both to each friend,
> I guess one angel in another's hell.
>   Yet this shall I ne'er know, but live in doubt,
>   Till my bad angel fire my good one out.

Like a figure from a medieval morality play or from Christopher Marlowe's *Doctor Faustus*, the speaker is torn between the persuasions of two angels, one good and one bad. Here, though, the bad angel is a female, representing the relationship we would term heterosexual, while the good angel is a male, and exemplary of same-sex love. The poem profoundly reverses the terms of a culture which tends to idealize heterosexuality and scorn homosexuality. Shakespeare, the great creator of pathologically jealous males from Othello through Leontes, imagines a speaker haunted by the possibility that the dark lady might corrupt the young man. The only relief imagined from such excruciating doubt is the even more troubling evidence of their intercourse. Venereal disease, a malady of love likened in Sonnet 147 to the fires of passion that transmit it, would be spread from his bad angel to his good angel, and so 'fire' him out. In this turgid emotional universe, no exculpating evidence of fidelity is possible; like Shakespeare's dramatic protagonists of jealousy, the tortured speaker wilfully banishes any possibility of faith in another's constancy.

The Sonnets, then, convey a frequently despairing account of human relationships. The speaker of these poems is distressed by the periodicity of erotic desire – the way that desire inevitably waxes and wanes, either in frustration or satiation. Sonnet 75 explicitly links the alternating absence and presence of the beloved to the cyclic and quotidian need to consume food:

> So are you to my thoughts as food to life,
> Or as sweet seasoned showers are to the ground;
> And for the peace of you I hold such strife
> As 'twixt a miser and his wealth is found:
> Now proud as an enjoyer, and anon
> Doubting the filching age will steal his treasure;
> Now counting best to be with you alone,
> Then bettered that the world may see my pleasure:
> Sometime all full with feasting on your sight
> And by and by clean starved for a look;
> Possessing or pursuing no delight,
> Save what is had or must from you be took.
>   Thus do I pine and surfeit day by day,
>   Or gluttoning on all, or all away.

The speaker reels between satiation ('all full with feasting') and starvation ('clean starved for a look'). He fears that a kind of erotic bulimia – either 'gluttoning on all, or all away' – will also dictate the schedule of emotional commitment.

Various poems struggle to find something that will indeed abide amid the inexorable entropies of erotic desire and physical decay. As we have seen, many of the early poems to the young man suggest that progeny might offer a kind of fragile, vicarious immortality; 'Make thee another self for love of me', urges the speaker of Sonnet 10. Other poems such as Sonnet 55 suggest that the medium of poetry itself might survive the degradation that destroys even the most perdurable of materials: 'Not marble nor the gilded monuments / Of princes, shall outlive this pow'rful rhyme'. This is a claim that is validated every time the poems are read. The sequence as a whole is tormented by the transience of desire, and of those things that are desired. If, as the speaker of Sonnet 15 laments, 'every thing that grows / Holds in perfection but a little moment', what, the poems continually ask, can abide of value amid 'this inconstant stay'?

Sonnet 19 boldly tells 'Devouring Time' that poetry and love may together blunt his predatory reach: 'despite thy wrong, / My love shall in my verse ever live young'. The dual possessives – my love and my verse – declare a desperate faith in the ability of versified affection to function as a possible bulwark against the ruination of time. Various poems assert the power of lyric passion to defeat time, and so to achieve a kind of immortality. Among the most famous and beloved of these is Sonnet 30, a poem that establishes a different economy of emotional expenditure from either the sonnets urging the young man to reproduce, or the sonnets lamenting the wastes of lust:

> When to the sessions of sweet silent thought
> I summon up remembrance of things past,
> I sigh the lack of many a thing I sought,
> And with old woes new wail my dear time's waste;
> Then can I drown an eye (unused to flow)
> For precious friends hid in death's dateless night,
> And weep afresh love's long since cancelled woe,
> And moan th'expense of many a vanished sight;
> Then can I grieve at grievances foregone,
> And heavily from woe to woe tell o'er
> The sad account of fore-bemoaned moan,
> Which I new pay as if not paid before:
>   But if the while I think on thee (dear friend)
>   All losses are restored, and sorrows end.

The poem begins by finding in the contemplation of loss the occasion of further loss, and concludes by arguing that thinking about the friend, unlike all other thought, produces restoration and gain, not loss. The poem performs a kind of magical accounting, by which the melancholy medium of loss becomes the joyous matter of gain. The form of the sonnet is structurally synchronized with the quatrain-based units of argumentative thought ('When ... Then ... Then ... But'), so that the final assertion of meditative restoration is accepted with epigrammatic certainty that is unearned logically, but formally convincing. The solution proves temporary, of course, but provides a valuable form of comfort nonetheless.

There is, then, no happy ending in Shakespeare's Sonnets – just a series of provisional and partial efforts to stave off in different media the tortuous temporality of existence through an expression of the profundity of emotional attachment or through an assertion of the immortalizing power of poetry. The last two Sonnets use the myth of Cupid to demonstrate the contagious and incurable nature of 'love's fire'. The last sonnet in particular shows how in the universe of Shakespeare's Sonnets, the effort to contain or cure love just offers further opportunities for its proliferation:

> The little Love-god lying once asleep
> Laid by his side his heart-inflaming brand,
> Whilst many nymphs that vowed chaste life to keep
> Came tripping by; but in her maiden hand
> The fairest votary took up that fire
> Which many legions of true hearts had warmed,
> And so the general of hot desire
> Was sleeping by a virgin hand disarm'd.
> This brand she quenched in a cool well by,
> Which from Love's fire took heat perpetual,
> Growing a bath and healthful remedy
> For men diseased; but I, my mistress' thrall,
> > Came there for cure, and this by that I prove:
> > Love's fire heats water, water cools not love.

Love, Shakespeare suggests, is a kind of universal solvent, corroding what is supposed to contain it. It is, moreover, a highly contagious disease, and one that spreads through the very therapies intended to cure it. This bleak sonnet is followed by *A Lover's Complaint*, the grief-stricken lament of an abandoned lover, who confesses in the poem's final line that she would do it all again if given the chance. The melancholic tone of the complaint provides an apt conclusion to the sonnet sequence, underscoring the internal agonies, obsessive behaviours, and ephemeral joys of love (see Chapter 8 in this volume on *A Lover's Complaint*).

For all of its accidental and willed mysteries, Shakespeare's sequence achieves a remarkably consistent play of light and dark, of idealism and cynicism. The poems demonstrate the feverish horrors of giving in to love, and the chilling nausea of remaining indifferent to its pleasures; they dwell on the distressing transience of existence, and argue that this transience at once makes things more valuable and drains them of meaning. The Sonnets carefully record the accommodations and compromises required to fulfil erotic and emotional desire, even as they reveal these desires to be fleeting, and ultimately unsatisfying. A kind of lyric chiaroscuro, the Sonnets offer a studied alternation of love and despair that infers the exalted promises and elusive mysteries of human erotic attachment.

NOTES

1 Stephen Booth (ed.), *Shakespeare's Sonnets* (New Haven: Yale University Press, 1977); John Kerrigan (ed.), *The Sonnets and A Lover's Complaint* (Harmondsworth: Penguin, 1986); G. B. Evans (ed.), *The New Cambridge*

Shakespeare: The Sonnets (Cambridge University Press, 1996); Katherine Duncan-Jones (ed.), *Shakespeare's Sonnets*, Arden Shakespeare (Nashville: Nelson, 1997); Helen Vendler, *The Art of Shakespeare's Sonnets* (Cambridge: Harvard University Press, 1997); Colin Burrow (ed.), *The Oxford Shakespeare: Complete Sonnets and Poems* (Oxford University Press, 2002).

2 Meres, *Palladis Tamia, or Wit's Treasury* (London, 1598), cited in *The Shakespere Allusion-Book*, ed. J. Munro, 2 vols. (Oxford University Press, 1932), I:46–8. The full force of the comparison to Ovid as a poet and playwright is explored by Patrick Cheney, *Shakespeare, National Poet–Playwright* (Cambridge University Press, 2004).

3 Benson claims that his edition, which frequently combines several sonnets into a single poem to which he devotes a thematic title, and which mingles those conglomerate poems with poems that are not by Shakespeare from an anthology entitled *The Passionate Pilgrim* (1612), allows the poems finally to 'appeare of the same purity, the Author himselfe then living avouched' (John Benson, (ed.), *Poems: Written by Wil. Shakespeare. Gent.* (London, 1640)). For a fuller discussion of the manuscript and print publication history of the Sonnets, see Chapter 3 by Lukas Erne in this collection.

4 See Hallett Smith, *Elizabethan Poetry: A Study in Conventions, Meaning, and Expression* (Cambridge: Harvard University Press, 1952); J. W. Lever, *The Elizabethan Love Sonnet* (London: Methuen, 1974); Anne Ferry, *The Inward Language: Sonnets of Wyatt, Sidney, Shakespeare, Donne* (University of Chicago Press, 1983); Heather Dubrow, *Echoes of Desire: English Petrarchism and its Counterdiscourses* (Ithaca: Cornell University Press, 1995); Paul Innes, *Shakespeare and the English Renaissance Sonnet: Verses of Feigning Love* (New York: St Martin's Press, 1997); and Chapter 1 by William Kennedy in this collection.

5 This theme is explored powerfully by Joel Fineman, *Shakespeare's Perjured Eye: The Invention of Poetic Subjectivity in the Sonnets* (Berkeley: University of California Press, 1986).

6 On the complex issue of colour and race in Shakespeare, see Kim Hall, *Things of Darkness: Economies of Race and Gender in Early Modern England* (Ithaca: Cornell University Press, 1995); Ania Loomba, *Shakespeare, Race, and Colonialism* (Oxford University Press, 2002); and Mary Floyd-Wilson, *English Ethnicity and Race in Early Modern Drama* (Cambridge University Press, 2003).

7 On the various candidates for dark lady, see Marvin Hunt, 'Be Dark but Not Too Dark: Shakespeare's Dark Lady as a Sign of Color', in James Schiffer (ed.), *Shakespeare's Sonnets: Critical Essays* (New York: Garland, 2000), pp. 369–90; and David Bevington, 'A. L. Rowse's Dark Lady', *Aemilia Lanyer: Gender, Genre, and the Canon*, ed. Marshall Grossman (Lexington: University Press of Kentucky, 1998), pp. 10–28.

8 William Wordsworth, 'Scorn not the Sonnet'; Robert Browning, 'House'.

9 *John Donne: Complete English Poems*, ed. A. J. Smith (Harmondsworth: Penguin, 1971), p. 273, line 111.

10 In *Bodies and Selves in Early Modern England: Physiology and Inwardness in Spenser, Shakespeare, Herbert, and Milton* (Cambridge University Press, 1999), I explore the connections between desire and disease in early modern physiology. The same connection is parsed in terms of contemporary theory in

Jonathan Dollimore, *Death, Desire and Loss in Western Culture* (London: Penguin, 1998).

11 Suggestions for the elided phrase are myriad, and include 'Pressed by', 'Lord of', 'Thrall to', 'Feeding', 'Fool'd by', and 'Starv'd by'.

12 See for example John Crowe Ransom, 'Shakespeare at Sonnets', in *The World's Body* (New York: Scribner's, 1938); Edward Hubler, *The Sense of Shakespeare's Sonnets* (Princeton University Press, 1952); William Empson, 'They That Have Power: Twist of Heroic-Pastoral Ideas into an Ironical Acceptance of Aristocracy', in *Some Versions of Pastoral* (London: Chatto & Windus, 1935), pp. 89–115; Stephen Booth, *An Essay on Shakespeare's Sonnets* (New Haven: Yale University Press, 1969), pp. 152–68; and my *Bodies and Selves in Early Modern England*, pp. 82–95.

13 *Shakespeare in Love* (1998), written by Marc Norman and Tom Stoppard, directed by John Madden.

14 Joseph Pequigney, *Such is My Love: A Study of Shakespeare's Sonnets* (University of Chicago Press, 1985); Bruce Smith, *Homosexual Desire in Shakespeare's England* (University of Chicago Press, 1991); Alan Bray, *Homosexualiy in Renaissance England* (London: Gay Men's Press, 1982); Eve Kosofsky Sedgwick, *Between Men: English Literature and Male Homosocial Desire* (New York: Columbia University Press, 1985); Richard Halpern, *Shakespeare's Perfume: Sodomy and Sublimity in the Sonnets, Wilde, Freud, and Lacan* (Philadelphia: University of Pennsylvania Press, 2002); and Paul Hammond, *Figuring Sex between Men from Shakespeare to Rochester* (Oxford: Clarendon Press, 2002).

READING LIST

Booth, Stephen. *An Essay on Shakespeare's Sonnets*. New Haven: Yale University Press, 1969.

Dubrow, Heather. *Captive Victors: Shakespeare's Narrative Poems and Sonnets*. Ithaca: Cornell University Press, 1987.

Edmundson, Paul, and Stanley Wells. *Oxford Shakespeare Topics: Shakespeare's Sonnets*. Oxford University Press, 2004.

Greenblatt, Stephen. *Will in the World: How Shakespeare Became Shakespeare*. New York: Norton, 2004.

Hyland, Peter. *An Introduction to Shakespeare's Poems*. Basingstoke: Palgrave Macmillan, 2003.

Kay, Dennis. *William Shakespeare: Sonnets and Poems*. New York: Twayne, 1998.

Roberts, Sasha. *Reading Shakespeare's Poems in Early Modern England*. New York: Palgrave Macmillan, 2003.

Schiffer, James (ed.). *Shakespeare's Sonnets: Critical Essays*. New York: Garland Publishing, 1999.

Schoenfeldt, Michael (ed.). *A Companion to Shakespeare's Sonnets*. Oxford: Blackwell, 2006.

Schalkwyk, David. *Speech and Performance in Shakespeare's Sonnets and Plays*. Cambridge University Press, 2002.

8

KATHERINE ROWE

A Lover's Complaint

This intense, artful poem opens voyeuristically, with an unnamed narrator overhearing the complaints of a weeping maiden. She wanders alone beside a river, her hair intriguingly loose and her cheeks 'pale and pinèd', tearing up old love-letters and other mementos or 'favours' (32, 36). Within a few stanzas she is joined by a second listener: a 'reverend' man retired from the bluster of court and city, who invites her to pour out her sorrows so that he 'may her suffering ecstasy assuage' (69). The maiden takes up his invitation, describing her resistance and eventual surrender to a deceitful young courtier while the reverend man, narrator, and readers of the poem listen in. As her dramatic monologue unfolds, however, it takes a peculiar turn and she begins to ventriloquize her deceiver in a way that proves far from easing her feelings. Indeed, she conjures his seductions so powerfully that they ' "Would yet again betray the fore-betrayed, / And new pervert a reconcilèd maid!" ' (328–9). The seductions themselves turn out to be equally perverse. What tempted her then and what she relives 'now', in these final lines, is his detailed account of how he ensnared other women, with passionate performances he then turned on her. Like her, these other lovers fell so enchanted with him they ' "dialogued for him what he would say, / Asked their own wills, and made their wills obey" ' (132–3). Such passionate speech itself – conjuring powerful feelings in the self and others – turns out to be as much the subject of the poem as the maiden's confession.

The essentially theatrical dynamics of overheard confession provide the poem's central actions, as different states of feeling (grief, regret, love, triumph, scorn, dispassion, and more) are called forth and performed by these three characters. But there is a second kind of action in the poem as well: the verbal action of highly wrought, self-conscious language, reworking established poetic conventions. This play with received forms will be central to the poem, as we learn in its opening lines when the 'plaintful story' comes to us in 'double voice', 'reworded' not only by the landscape but also implicitly by the poem's narrator. The evocative idea of 'rewording' another's speech resonates throughout what follows. Renaissance readers (for whom the renovation of literary models was a basic feature of any good fiction) would expect such rewording to involve play with a variety of literary sources. The sources concentrated in this small piece range remarkably widely: from courtly poetry, to stage plays, popular ballads, and criminal confessions, as well as classical poetry. Indeed, the rural landscape itself – a valley populated with weeping maiden, cattle, retired man of the city, and a narrator who lies down to listen (like a melancholy nobleman or a weary shepherd) – would be familiar as an explicitly fictional environment. In such pastoral settings numerous poems have been given voice since the classical period.[1] The valley announces itself as a 'concave womb', an acoustic mirror that returns echoes of older forms, recreated and transformed.

Of the literary conventions 'reworded' – reprised and remade – in this fictional environment, perhaps the most familiar remains amorous complaint itself. The basic formula of complaint – 'I loved him and this is why I still do, although I know he done me wrong' – is still repeated in popular lyrics, from the blues to country music. Many of the other conventions being reworked here are likely to be less familiar to modern readers. So the connections between the poem's self-reflexive verbal play and its emotional dramas may seem obscure. To help make sense of these connections this chapter will sketch the literary context of Renaissance complaints and explore the poem's characteristically contrary approach to inherited materials – closing with a discussion of one particular literary resource, the discourse of blason and counter-blason. These contexts, together with some sense of English Renaissance theories of emotion, help explain the powerful but enigmatic transfers of feeling conjured in the poem.

'Reworded' art

The genre of amorous complaint is remarkably long-lived. *A Lover's Complaint* reworks conventions that look back to Petrarch, to medieval ballads, and to the classical poets, especially Virgil and Ovid. Complaints were particularly in vogue in England during the 1590s, when poets such as Samuel Daniel and Thomas Lodge paired female-voiced laments with sonnet sequences, as if to counter-balance the almost exclusively male voices of the Petrarchan sonnet tradition. *A Lover's Complaint* was first printed with *Shake-speres Sonnets*, in 1609, offering counterpoint male and female voices on this model (Kerrigan, pp. 13–15). But poetic laments were not exclusively amorous in this period. Sixteenth-century European writers applied the genre widely, to political and social concerns, and laments circulated in popular broadside as well as in courtly venues (Kerrigan,

p. 14). As Katherine Craik has shown, *A Lover's Complaint* draws on a specific popular tradition that flourished in the 1590s, ballads that retold the confessions of female criminals.

The way the poem reworks this popular tradition illustrates how complex and charged an apparently simple 'rewording' can be. Confessional ballad-laments dealt in sensation, purporting to be the first-person accounts of women accused of murder, treason, witchcraft, infanticide, adultery, and other crimes. As with popular murder pamphlets, these ballads testified to the power of the Crown and the law courts, whose actions in restoring order were justified by the very fact of confession.[2] In this way, ballad-laments provide the pleasures of intimate access to shocking events – and to an apparently authentic, female experience – while at the same time serving the interests of state control (Craik, p. 439). *A Lover's Complaint* conforms to the basic fictional structure of ballad-laments: its female speaker confesses to sexual transgression, offers sensational details in her own defence, and follows this with a male antagonist's counter-defence (Craik, p. 445). Legal language proliferates in the poem, evoking the forensic context of ballad-laments: 'register', 'witness', 'grounds and motives', 'grievance', 'injury', 'judgment', 'fee-simple', and so on. Yet the poem literally 'rewords' the form by making it clear that these confessions come to us via a hidden audience with its own (obscure, unarticulated) interests. As Craik observes, this makes it radically unclear on whose behalf this ventriloquized female voice speaks and even about the 'facts' conveyed by her confessions. As a result, the poem raises questions about the biases that motivate any confession or defence transmitted through multiple speakers. Certainly the male antagonist of *A Lover's Complaint* seems as culpable as he is persuasive, offering the familiar but ugly excuse, 'they asked for it': they 'sought their shame that so their shame did find' (Craik, p. 187). In these ways, the poem resists the kind of political closure ballad-laments usually provide, closing with its complications unresolved and its narrative frame open. The maid ceases to speak just at the moment when, in a ballad, we would expect her to repent. Essentially, the poem rewords the popular ballad structures in a way that exposes rather than hides the different interests the confessional form serves. In this contrary turn, *A Lover's Complaint* more closely resembles Shakespeare's use of the female complaint in his plays, especially *Hamlet* (1602), than it does popular pamphlets; we find something similar in the despairing accusations of Ophelia's mad lament, in 4.5, and in her flowers, love-letters, and drowning stream (Craik, p. 444).

If *A Lover's Complaint* seems particularly Shakespearean in its contrary spin on popular material, many readers have found its verse style atypical. Indeed, some scholars find the language so compacted and mannered that they attribute the poem to other writers. Before exploring the poem further, then, it is worth briefly addressing the question of authorship. As so often in the Renaissance, the documentary evidence is scant. Thomas Thorpe, the publisher who printed *A Lover's Complaint* with the Sonnets, provides the only attribution to Shakespeare, in a separate title page that precedes the poem. The Sonnets themselves are generally accepted as Shakespeare's work but the 1609 volume is usually thought to have been pirated, published without his oversight or permission.[3] Accordingly, scholarly challenges to Shakespeare's authorship of *A Lover's Complaint* have been frequent. As authorship studies have become more statistical and computer-based, the poem is regularly used to test new computer models.[4]

By including *A Lover's Complaint* in its canon, this volume aligns itself with those who attribute the poem to William Shakespeare of Stratford and London. The reasons for this choice have as much to do with changing notions of how Renaissance writers worked as with the lack of compelling evidence to the contrary. For many years, authorship studies have applied new technologies to an old passion: the obsession with filling in the shadowy figure of the Bard, an obsession that became pressing in the eighteenth century as English writers became more committed to the myth of their national poet.[5] Many studies of authorship still see particular texts as sources of biographical evidence, providing the keys to fictionally encoded secrets. For example, Ward Elliott and Robert Valenza explain that 'authorship matters' because the determination that a given work was written by Shakespeare can make a 'major difference as to how we would judge' the artist's 'tastes, contacts, stylistic range' (p. 196). If Shakespeare wrote *A Funeral Elegy* (as critics used to think), the argument goes, then the poem would tell us something about the man who wrote it and 'perhaps we would have a clue to the identities of the Fair Youth and Dark Lady of the *Sonnets*' (p. 197).

Authorship study in this mode – as private detection into the life and character of a great man – seems increasingly narrow. In the first place, it requires us to imagine creative works reductively, as encoded biography rather than as artistic inventions in a full sense. In the second place, it assumes, inaccurately, that the writing and publishing of poetry and drama was primarily a solo project. Recent research into the collaborative world of English Renaissance bookmaking makes it clear that works such as the 1609 collection of the Sonnets and *A Lover's Complaint* involved many hands, at different stages of the printing process and sometimes in the creative process.[6] It is not that authorship did not matter to Renaissance writers: many writers strove to establish reputations for themselves and some were particularly careful about the way their work circulated, both in print and manuscript. But what authorship studies typically assume about artistic composition, the material production of texts, and even the property relations claimed for an 'author' in the Renaissance can be misleading. It may be especially misleading in the case of a poem that begins with an echo, tells a 'reworded' story, and recycles familiar conventions and characters. *A Lover's Complaint* invites us to think about categories such as author, voice, and style as fictional effects, rather than historical facts or personal attributes. Indeed this poem so artfully rewords the different styles and preoccupations of contemporary writers that it can be read as a fiction of authorship: characters in a Spenserian landscape play out Marlovian seductions using Petrarchan devices; each of these fictional elements reworks earlier Virgilian and Ovidian models in ways that are characteristic of these writers, who used the earlier models to define the trajectories of a poetic career. At the same time, the poem stages the convergence of two artistic modes: the theatre (' "tragic shows" ' that are 'material, performative, and external') and lyric ('deep-brained sonnets' that are 'subjective, mental, and internal').[7] It remains unclear what computer-aided testing can tell us about Renaissance imitations and pastiches, or about the specific arts of echo in a highly allusive poem such as this.

With these contexts in mind, we can turn to look more closely at the language of the poem and the many arts of echo it employs. From its opening line, *A Lover's Complaint* announces its interest in reported and repeated speech, the 'double voice' of the maid's lament, 'reworded' by the landscape. Rewording is a creative rather than a merely reflective process, as suggested by the feminine qualities of the 'concave womb' that creates the echo. That force works directly on those listening. The narrator's 'spirits' 'attend' and conform to the echo, as we learn from the telling rhyme, 'accorded' (1–3). We will return in a moment to look closely at the connections here between psychology ('spirits') and landscape. For now it is helpful to observe that the valley is not a simple acoustic mirror. To 'accord' means not only to feel similarly or to agree, but also musically to align different intervals, as in a well-tuned chord. These echoes turn out to be 'sad-tuned', of course, suggesting that they harmoniously align emotions as well as sounds (4).

Thus 'rewording' means not simply retelling speech but multiplying its effects across different listeners and refracting those effects in surprising ways, as we have seen the poem does with ballad-laments. This multiplication of emotional effects repeats throughout the poem. The maid is not the first woman the young man has seduced. A trail of 'broken bosoms' follows him and even pleads his case to her: ' " 'Now all these hearts that do on mine depend, / Feeling it break, with bleeding groans they pine, / And supplicant their sighs to you extend' " ' (274–6). Similarly, the 'reverend' man who sits so 'comely distant' beside the maid serves as a stand-in for the listening narrator, his eagerness to hear her story a cover for that narrator's own desires and for ours in turn. Even to narrate is to multiply roles. Thus the young maid plays, among other roles, storyteller, complainant, witness, impersonator, commentator, poet, and an impassioned audience, caught up ecstatically in her own story.

The opening lines of the poem tune our ears not only to repetitions within the dramatic scene but also to multiple meanings in the language. The poem is full of compact verbal constructions that expand almost unmanageably when one begins to unpack their meaning. The brief description of the reverend man makes a good example. He may be 'sometime a blusterer' (58) but he is still it seems a performer: aware enough of the proprieties to sit 'comely distant' from the maid as he offers a comforting ear. The peculiar phrase 'comely distant' suggests he is behaving properly, but it also implies that he feels the need to behave properly. 'Blusterer' (menacing braggart) links him to Spenser's Braggadochio, a crude boaster who peeps through the bushes at the innocent Belphoebe and would rape her were he not so craven.[8] Thus the old man resolves into a parody of such dirty old men from Spenser or Ariosto, a hypocritical *senex* with the unholy interests of Spenser's Archimago (Cheney, p. 247). Of course it is the narrator who offers this description, suggesting that the listener observes this self-consciousness or perhaps projects it on to the old man. In this way, the single, enigmatic phrase 'comely distant' evokes a host of questions about hidden motives. Might the old man's eagerness to hear the story spring from more prurient interests than sympathy? Is he a little too close? Is the narrator as well, by implication, intruding for his or her own pleasure? Are we? A little pressure on this phrase opens up these questions and reminds us that what appears here to be private speech serves the needs of its auditors and by implication the culture at large – which retells this kind of story for its own purposes. The long account of the young man's beauties and seductions, which follows, substantiates the hint that both homoerotic and heteroerotic pleasures are on offer. A powerful appeal of *A Lover's Complaint* is the emotional and physical detail of these twice-overheard confessions of sexual wandering: the pleasure of seduction spoken aloud and artfully replayed, whether for sympathetic sharing or erotic entertainment.

The poem's compact language can make us uncertain who is the source of a particular observation and even what actually happened. We cannot be sure who wrote the papers ('schedules' and 'deep-brained sonnets') the maid tears up, though they are linked in different ways to the young man, his other lovers, and the maid herself. We know little of the narrator, though that listener is linked in several ways to the old man, notably his voyeurism and posture. And the poem calls our attention directly to such problems of knowledge, personified in the young man. We learn that he is a consummate performer who ' "Did livery falseness in a pride of truth" ' (105). (Actors, called 'players' in the Renaissance, often wore cast-off livery, clothing from the noble household that supported them.) This description appears straight-forward enough: he uses the appearance of frankness to cover up his real interests, a kind of verbal cross-dressing that disguises falseness with ostentatious displays of truthfulness (the maid gives us many examples). Yet the clothing metaphor develops in a way that further complicates the picture. If to 'livery' is to dress in official clothing, typically the clothing of a servant, then to 'livery falseness in the pride of truth' is to dress it up so that the sin appears to be properly subordinate to the virtue. Yet the virtue itself is compromised by the phrase that modifies it, including that second negative term, 'pride'. When paired so closely with 'livery', the word 'pride' seems to mean 'proud attire', or 'ostentation'. What should be an absolute – 'truth' – becomes something that can be qualified, modified, and manipu-lated for artistic and seductive effect. If truth can be so easily enlisted to do the work of falseness, if truth can supply ostentatious costumes, then the proper order of things is clearly disrupted. We may begin to wonder to what degree all the performances in the poem – including the young maid's confessions of passion and regret – are strategic and crafted rather than spontaneous and authentic. Most confusingly, this line suggests that the maiden is never wholly deceived. For all she implies she is 'young and simple' (320) she appears to know from the start that the young man is a player.

Arts of emotion

The young man is a player, the poem suggests, in both the idiomatic modern sense that he controls his social scene and the technical Renaissance sense that he is skilled at stagecraft. His 'art of craft', or deceit, is explicitly theatrical. Like a good actor, he can call up the external signs of emotion at will, change them with Protean speed, and impress them on his auditors.[9] ' "Of burning blushes, or of weeping water, / Or sounding pale-ness; and he takes and leaves, / In either's aptness, as it best deceives" ' (304–6). He does this in perfect accord with contemporary stage conven-tions: ' "To blush at speeches rank, to weep at woes, / Or to turn white and sound at tragic shows" ' (307–8). Indeed, he represents a perfect night-mare of feigned emotions that contemporary anti-theatrical pamphlets feared most. These Puritan attacks on the theatre warned that playgoers would experience exactly what the young maid endures: corruption of innocence, bodily transformation by illness, and even madness. Yet the poem is far from simply anti-theatrical. It demonstrates the transformative power of theatrical audition quite effectively. And it uses stage-conventions to call attention to devices that might otherwise (as in the case of ballad-laments) remain hidden. By recasting a female confession in the mode of dramatic soliloquy, for example, it reminds us that the illusion of privacy and intimate access to her mind is being conjured within a public context of multiple listeners, for whose pleasure and profit the story unfolds.

What the poem has in common with Shakespeare's plays, more precisely, is an interest in how passionate speech and 'shows' may be used to manage emotions in the self and others.[10] The English public theatre was understood as a space for experimenting with the management of emotion in this way.[11] And the young man of the poem seems to have learned his passionate arts from several stage idioms: shame goes with 'rank' or bawdy speech; sorrow goes with 'woes' or sentimental spectacles; amazement or horror goes with 'tragic shows' (307–8). *A Lover's Complaint* shares an interest in tools and environments for conjuring emotion. And like Shakespeare's plays, it presents both extreme emotional discipline (the young man's) and extreme emotional impressibility (the young maid's) as dangers to be avoided. Yet these concerns do not derive exclusively from the theatre. Arguments about the emotions – their benefits and dangers, best practices for managing them – cross many different kinds of writings in the English Renaissance.

For modern readers, early modern discussions of emotion display a mixture of familiar and strange attitudes towards feelings, reflecting the historically composite nature of our own concepts of emotion.[12] To make sense of the passionate transactions that take place in this poem, therefore, a few points of background are helpful. First, while the young man's capacity to remain unmoved by 'affections hot' (218) is clearly a negative thing in this poem, such coldness was often seen as a gentlemanly virtue, a form of self-control highly valued by neo-Stoic writers. The young man of the Sonnets, for example, displays a similar aloof coldness that appears much more positively there.[13] Renaissance subjects were differentiated by their capacity to moderate their passions; women, old men, and young men were proverbially understood to be more variable and less able to control the fluid internal environment of 'affections and humors'.[14] Thus, although the young man in *A Lover's Complaint* is feminized in a number of ways – pale-skinned, 'maiden-tongued', with 'small show of man' on his chin (100, 92) – his self-discipline is as masterful and masculine as his riding.[15]

The general admiration for the way he handles his horse (so often, in Petrarchan lyric, a figure for amorous impulses), reflects neo-Stoic values of gentlemanly self-discipline.[16]

Second, modern readers usually come to Renaissance expressions of emotion having been taught, by the Romantics, to value spontaneous, overflowing feeling. Yet the qualities of openness and impressionability were often understood in the Renaissance to be negative ones. And in the Renaissance (as in the Romantic period) transformative openness is an especially feminized quality. For *A Lover's Complaint*, the subtext that allows these connections is Ovid's myth of 'Echo and Narcissus', retold in Arthur Golding's translation of *The Metamorphoses* (1567). Ovid recounts the damaging transformations that result from too receptive, too open a mode of audition: the nymph Echo, cursed by Jove to speak only through repetition, pursues a young man mortally obsessed with his own image. The story gives voice both to an extreme narcissism that loves only its own capacity for control and an extreme impressibility that conforms to and ventriloquizes the passions of another.

Yet by the turn of the seventeenth century, the kinds of arguments English writers were making about emotions, their causes and uses, were becoming increasingly complicated. Along with theorists of emotion, such as Thomas Wright, Shakespeare and his contemporaries engaged in a nationalist recuperation of stereotypically northern and feminized qualities, including emotional impressibility.[17] Re-describing the ability to be swayed by outside impressions as a native virtue, they used anti-Stoic arguments about the moral and ethical uses of authentic emotion to denigrate the kind of hyper-civilized, skilful, emotional deceptions they associated with southern Europeans. In *A Lover's Complaint* we find both strains of thought at work, unresolved: anti-Stoic suspicion of the effete young man's pathological dispassion and neo-Stoic warnings about the dangers of being excessively moved by emotion.

To be 'moved' is not only a metaphor, in this period, but also a literal description of how emotions were understood to work. 'Motion' was the Renaissance synonym for emotion (along with 'affection' and 'passion'); emotions were conceived as alterations in the body's balance of fluid 'humours' and movements of its animal 'spirits' (thinner, but still material substances communicating between the external senses and inward faculties such as imagination, will, and memory).[18] Physical changes such as paleness, blushing, and sighs were the external signs of such motions. The way *A Lover's Complaint* evokes emotional changes – as pooling and flowing fluids and exchanges of heat and cold – reflects this Renaissance model of an embodied mind. Female passions pour into the young man, who stores them up for future use while remaining unmoved himself:

> ' "The broken bosoms that to me belong
> Have emptied all their fountains in my well,
> And mine I pour your ocean all among:
> I strong o'er them, and you o'er me being strong." ' (254–7)

This conceit ends in a classically humoural moment of congealing liquids, transforming the maid's body as they pour into it: ' " 'I strong o'er them, and you o'er me being strong, / Must for your victory us all congest, / As compound love to physic your cold breast' " ' (257–9). That medicinal 'physic', however, has unequal effects on their differently constituted bodies: ' "All melting; though our drops this diff'rence bore, / His poisoned me, and mine did him restore" ' (300–1). This fluid regulation of inputs and outputs might in theory be healthy or unhealthy, depending on the current temper of a given body. What makes the transaction so negative here is its amorous context, which requires reciprocity: a feedback loop in which lovers respond to the workings of their own affections on their beloved, and spirits 'accord'.

Thus emotions were meaningful in the Renaissance not only as internal events but as transactions between the body and its social and material environment; the work of a civil subject involved regulating such transactions, through changes in diet, sleep, air, exercize, elimination, but also through such social practices as hearing a play, praying, and so on.[19] Thus a nun, the poem tells us, might be ' " 'disciplined, ay, dieted, in grace' " ' (261), a figure that captures the intimate transactions that constitute an ensouled body or embodied soul.[20] This material psychology changes how we may interpret one of the central generic conceits of complaint, the reflection of inner and outer states. Thus, when Spenser's heroine Britomart complains by the sea-coast, lashing wind and waves reflect the thoughts raging inside her: a ' "Huge sea of sorrow, and tempestuous griefe, / Wherein my feeble barke is tossed long" '.[21] Similarly, the young maid of *A Lover's Complaint* wanders the 'weeping margent' of a river, 'Storming her world with sorrow's wind and rain' (39, 7). It is usual for critics to describe this motif in terms of the 'pathetic fallacy', a phrase coined by John Ruskin in 1856 to describe what he saw as the irrational ascription of human feelings to nature, an 'error ... which the mind admits when affected strongly by emotion'.[22] Ruskin asks us to see the natural and human world, the rational mind and the body, as ideally separate. Yet Renaissance psychology (perhaps closer to modern cognitive theory than to Victorian rationalism) did not admit to a full separation of natural and human, or mind and body. And indeed, the entire action of *A Lover's Complaint* is premised on the receptiveness of the narrator's 'spirits' to conform themselves to external impressions – sounds and emotions – that have been already reconformed by the landscape and that will by implication be refracted again, as the 'plaintful story' passes through this listener to us (2–3).

'Craft of will'

No possibility of a well regulated emotional transaction exists between the lovers in this poem; but a different transaction does takes place, with the forms of poetic utterance. While the poem offers only negative extremes of emotional control and impressibility, it also offers an extended demonstration of the ways in which speech, particularly poetic forms of speech such as the lyric blason, might be used to affect passionate alterations. In this poetic action the poem illustrates some possibility for transforming, if not completely mastering, the forms of passionate speech so that they not only powerfully mediate internal states but record the unequal costs, sometimes traumatic, of that mediation.

Renaissance blasons are short, epigrammatic verses in praise of a beautiful lady, one's own or the king's mistress perhaps. The typical pattern of blason is a catalogue of body parts (though some blasons focus on single parts – such as the eyebrow, or lips), elaborately comparing each to a precious object (gems, artwork, instruments) or to natural beauties (stars, the sun, honey, flowers). A stanza from Spenser's blason of Belphoebe, from Book 2 of *The Faerie Queene*, provides a good example:

> Her ivorie forhead, full of bountie brave,
>   Like a broad table did it self dispred,
>   For Love his loftie triumphes to engrave,
>   And write the battels of his great godhed:
>   All good and honour might therein be red:
>   For there their dwelling was. And when she spake,
>   Sweet words, like dropping honny she did shed,
>   And twixt the perles and rubins softly brake
> A silver sound, that heavenly musicke seem'd to make.   (2.3.24)

The pattern is easy to imitate and by the mid sixteenth century the form had become a popular mode of courtly competition in Europe. The use of such elaborate similes, crafted to prove the speaker's ingenuity more than his affection, easily slips into absurdity, exposing blason's tendency to objectify scattered parts rather than presenting its female figures as whole subjects.[23] Thus mock blasons proliferated, literalizing the excessive hyperboles of the form.[24] And counter-blasons (*contreblasons*), such as Clément Marot's

'*Epigramme du Laid Tétin*' ('The Ugly Breast', 1536), offered wittily dis-
gusting catalogues of faults, while anti-blasons exposed the shortcomings of
simile as a mode of description.²⁵ In this mode, Shakespeare's contrarian
Sonnet 130 offers a particularly witty send-up of the failings of comparison
as a mode of praise, 'My mistress' eyes are nothing like the sun; / Coral is far
more red than her lips' red'. Earlier, in the discussion of ballad-laments, such
exposure of affective craft, 'baring of the device', seemed a particularly
Shakespearean turn. But blason is a form dedicated from the start to self-
conscious display of an artfulness that serves multiple interests (celebrating
my lady, showing off wit, advancement at court). While Spenser's narrator
blasons Belphoebe, moving slowly down her body, Braggadochio and his
sidekick Trompart look greedily on. That the blason comes to us triangulated
in this way merely foregrounds a performative context that is always present
with this form.

A Lover's Complaint starts with these devices of 'scattered rhyme' fully
bared. We meet the young maid literally scattering items we would expect
to find in blason: 'amber', 'crystal', 'jet', 'gold', 'bone' (ivory), 'favours' her
lover wooed her with (36–45). The poem proceeds through several transformations of the form. First we learn how these love-tokens came to her:
through the young man's seductive deconstruction, marshalled in a catalogue of favours that (in the mode of Sonnet 130) exposes the inadequacy of its
very devices in the face of her power and beauty. ' " 'O, then, advance of
yours that phraseless hand,' " ' he pleads, ' " 'Whose white weighs down the
airy scale of praise; / Take all these similes to your own command' " '
(225–7). ' " 'When thou impressest, what are precepts worth / Of stale
example?' " ' (267–8).

This seduction goes even further than the conventions of anti-blason – and
in quite the opposite direction from Sonnet 130 – by reducing blason to its
most objectifying and triumphal impulses. The young man's former lovers
and their now stale emotions emerge in his redescription only as a collection
of trophies:

> ' "Look here, what tributes wounded fancies sent me,
> Of pallid pearls and rubies red as blood;
> Figuring that they their passions likewise lent me
> Of grief and blushes, aptly understood . . ." '.   (197–200)

While he recognizes that each gem 'figures' or symbolizes passions and easily
glosses the familiar code, the young man remains so unmoved that he
reverses the usual direction of simile. Grief and blushes are reduced to
descriptive terms, vehicles for describing the gems rather than vice versa, as
in conventional blason. This pattern continues as the young man shifts into a

catalogue of praise for the gems themselves – a blason so diminished that its central interest seems to be only these objects, reducing those who sent them to figures of description: ' " 'each several stone, / With wit well blazoned, smiled or made some moan' " ' (216–17). This mode of blason might be said to turn the form inside out, making its ostensible motive force – the alterations of spirit and humour signified by paleness or blushing – merely a system for cataloguing things.

Mysteriously, even while dismantled and turned inside out in this way, the young man's blason seems to do its work, binding two parties to each other over the amorous display of another (or in this case many others). This seeming paradox can be partly explained by returning again to the organic transactions that dominate the poem's language of emotion, and by looking at related uses of blason in prose and on stage. When the young man uses blason as a tool of seduction he rehearses the commonplace understanding that literary forms might be used to titrate – alter and regulate – specific emotion states as effectively as other disciplines. Experts as diverse as Henry Peacham, Sir Thomas Elyot, and Richard Mulcaster advised their readers to use verbal exercises – *vociferatio* – as a means of tempering (or as the reverend man suggests 'assuaging') their humours. The Jesuit Thomas Wright, author of a popular manual of emotional discipline, *The Passions of the Minde in Generall* (1604), works through a variety of kinds – from oratory to meditation to the specific formulas of elegy and blason – as recipes for governing the passions in the self and others.[26]

For such writers the highly codified nature of forms such as blason is what makes them particularly usable as recipes, and a tendency to 'bare the device' contributes to, rather than detracts from their effectiveness. The point of any recipe is not that it allows unmediated transfers of experience or perfectly reduplicates internal states from one subject to another, but that its mediations are legible and potentially repeatable. Wright's use of blason conventions makes a good example. He turns to them in the fifth book of his manual, the section that treats ways to move the passions. Beginning with an account of how the senses move the passions, Wright explains how to manage passions by music and by 'action' (theatrical gesture), how to move them by reason, and finally, how to bring oneself to love God. In this last section the discussion shifts from third person description into a meditation addressed directly to God. This meditation serves both as a catalogue of motives to love God and a demonstration of how to use that catalogue, which includes a blason-like anatomy of the beauties of Divinity. The meditation offers itself as just one more exercise in reapplying familiar techniques for working with the senses and affections – a technique any gentlemanly reader interested in conjuring love-of-God in himself might use. Yet Wright is engaged here in an uncertain if not downright dangerous undertaking for a Jesuit in Protestant England: covert transmission of Catholic devotional scripts. As cover, he carefully emphasizes the paradox of adapting secular devices (anatomizing, listing) to describe a beauty that 'neither hast body nor parts' and that transcends 'grossie, massie, terrene corruptible' (pp. 197–8). We might think that the devices of blason are being misapplied here, but in fact such meditational strategies belong to a long devotional tradition. For Wright's purposes, blason conventions work both as professional cover and as spiritual guide precisely because they bare their devices and in doing so, speak with the double voice of advice and ministry.

As Wright's meditation shifts into second person address, a devotional 'thou' more intimate than most amorous blasons, it invites the reader to craft for him or herself a programme of reading that produces a particular and repeatable configuration of body and soul.[27] It is not that the conventions of devotional blason offer or withhold direct access to a certain kind of experience (love of God).[28] What they offer is mediation of material inter-actions between body and soul – movements that are, by virtue of their very materiality, constantly altering and therefore in need of remediation. Shakespearean characters turn to amorous blason seeking similar media-tions, but in a way that tends, for female characters at least, to record trauma rather than transport. In a particularly striking moment in *The Two Noble Kinsmen* (5.3), for example, Emelye is asked to choose between two identical lovers, for whom she feels nothing, so she blasons their beauties in an attempt to create some sense of affection for one or the other. In fact Emelye has no real choice to make; the lesson of this scene is to record that fact and to illustrate that her affections conform to structural rather than individual interests – the interests of the state of Athens and the gods.

As with any recipe, then, repetition of a poetic form involves a kind of feedback loop that remains only partly within the control of those using it: expectation that it will have a certain effect, unexpected effects, the require-ment of a new experiment with an altered recipe. It is this mutability of the form itself, reflecting the traces of its uses, to which *A Lover's Complaint* shifts its attention and with which it leaves us in its final movement. In the last stanza the maid rewords the form, counter-blasoning the 'craft of will' in which the young man catches 'all passions' (126). As she lists his theatrical deceptions, they work contagiously on her, returning the poem to woeful echoes like those with which it opened:

> 'O, that infected moisture of his eye,
> O, that false fire which in his cheek so glowed,
> O, that forced thunder from his heart did fly,

O, that sad breath his spongy lungs bestowed,
O, all that borrowed motion, seeming owed ['owned' and 'due'],
Would yet again betray the fore-betrayed,
And new pervert a reconcilèd maid!'   (323–9)

The trajectory of these descriptions moves progressively outward: physical changes (moisture, infection) prompt bodily expressions that aim towards the listener, as the sequence of verbs suggests. 'Glowed' begins the movement outward, 'fly' reaches further and faster, 'bestowed' arrives, and 'owed' settles there (if it means 'owned') or perhaps sets out on the return journey (if it means 'due'). Though these 'motions' are identified as performative – forced, borrowed – they are also profoundly effectual, internalized by their imaginary auditor, the maid. But that process of internalization involves the repetition of the form in a new register: where the young man blasons the objects that typically serve as vehicles of simile, she counter-blasons the affects that such similes typically signify, recording and testifying to their injurious potential. To the extent that this is an affirmation of the power of artifice to move auditors viscerally even when – like the nymph Echo and this maid – they are all too aware it is artifice, the experience of giving oneself up to such artifice appears both transporting and also traumatizing.[29] With its repetitions of that enigmatic 'O', what this final movement of blason claims for performative poetry is the capacity to register the convergence of trauma and transport in the passage of rewording.

NOTES

1 For portraits of this classic melancholy pose, a Renaissance vogue for noblemen, see Roy Strong, 'The Elizabethan Malady: Melancholy in Elizabethan and Jacobean Portraiture', *Apollo* 79 (April 1964), 264–9.

2 See Peter Lake and Michael Questier's discussion of murder pamphlets in *The Antichrist's Lewd Hat: Protestants, Papists and Players in Post-Reformation England* (New Haven: Yale University Press, 2002).

3 Katherine Duncan-Jones argues the contrary in 'Was the 1609 Shake-speares Sonnets Really Unauthorized?' *Review of English Studies* 34 (1983), 151–71.

4 Ward E. Y. Elliott and Robert J. Valenza survey recent computer-aided tests and conclude with a case against Shakespearean authorship; see 'Glass Slippers and Seven-League Boots: C-Prompted Doubts about Ascribing *A Funeral Elegy* and *A Lover's Complaint* to Shakespeare', *Shakespeare Quarterly* 48 (1997), 177–207. MacD. P. Jackson counters using a different mode of database analysis in '*A Lover's Complaint* Revisited', *Shakespeare Studies* 32 (2004), 267–94. Brian Vickers argues the case for John Davies in ' "A Rum Do" ': The Likely Authorship of *A Lover's Complaint*', *Times Literary Supplement*, 5 December 2003, pp. 13–15.

5 See Michael Dobson, *The Making of the National Poet: Shakespeare, Adaptation and Authorship, 1660–1769* (Oxford University Press, 1992).

6 See Jeffrey Masten's study of collaboration in the theatre, *Textual Intercourse: Collaboration, Authorship, and Sexualities in Renaissance Drama* (Cambridge University Press, 1997). On questions of authorship and female voice invoked by the ventriloquism in this poem, see Wendy Wall, *The Imprint of Gender: Authorship and Publication in the English Renaissance* (Ithaca: Cornell University Press, 1993), pp. 250–69.

7 See Patrick Cheney, *Shakespeare, National Poet–Playwright* (Cambridge University Press, 2004), Chapter 8 (pp. 242ff) for a discussion of the fictions of authorship in the poem.

8 *The Faerie Queene* 3.4.

9 On Renaissance theories of acting and emotion, see Joseph Roach, *The Player's Passion: Studies in the Science of Acting* (Ann Arbor: University of Michigan Press, 1993).

10 See Craik and Kerrigan for discussions of theatricality in this poem, in terms of audition and performativity, and Senecan stylings, respectively. Harry Berger discusses the larger critical stakes for a method that draws connections between page and stage in this way, in *Imaginary Audition: Shakespeare on Stage and Page* (Berkeley: University of California Press, 1989). On the theatrical management of emotion, see Katherine Rowe, 'Shakespearean Tragic Emotions', in *A Companion to Shakespeare's Works*, Vol. I, ed. Richard Dutton and Jean Howard (Oxford: Blackwell, 2003), pp. 47–72.

11 Steven Mullaney, 'Mourning and Misogyny: *Hamlet, The Revenger's Tragedy*, and the Final Progress of Elizabeth I, 1600–1607', in *Centuries' Ends, Narrative Means*, ed. Robert Newman (Stanford University Press, 1996), pp. 238–60.

12 See Rowe, 'Shakespearean Tragic Emotions', p. 52.

13 Michael C. Schoenfeldt, *Bodies and Selves in Early Modern England: Physiology and Inwardness in Spenser, Shakespeare, Herbert, and Milton* (Cambridge University Press, 1999), p. 17. See also Schoenfeldt's chapter in this volume, Chapter 7, esp. with respect to Sonnet 94.

14 See Gail Kern Paster, 'The Unbearable Coldness of Female Being: Women's Imperfection and the Humoral Economy', *English Literary Renaissance* 28 (1998), 416–40.

15 On the humoral language of gender and skin colour in Renaissance portraiture, see Zirka Filipczak, *Hot Dry Men, Cold, We Women: The Theory of Humors in Western European Art*, exhibition catalogue (New York: American Federation of Arts, 1997).

16 See, for example, Sonnet 49 in Philip Sidney's *Astrophil and Stella* (c. 1582).

17 On the nationalist discourse of emotion in Renaissance England, see Mary Floyd-Wilson, *English Ethnicity and Race in Early Modern Drama* (Cambridge University Press, 2003).

18 For a full discussion of this material psychology, see Gail Kern Paster et al. (eds.), 'Introduction', *Reading the Early Modern Passions: Essays in the Cultural History of Emotion* (Philadelphia: University of Pennsylvania Press, 2004), pp. 1–20.

19 On emotions as 'transactions', see Floyd-Wilson, *English Ethnicity*.

20 See Gail Kern Paster's comments, 'Shakespeare and Embodiment, an E-Conversation', in *Blackwell Literature Compass* online (Oxford: Blackwell, 2005).

21 Spenser, *The Faerie Queene* 3.4.8, in *The Faerie Queene*, ed. Thomas P. Roche, Jr (London: Penguin Books, 1978).

22 Ruskin, *Modern Painters* 3.12 (London, 1873).
23 See Nancy Vickers, 'Diana Described: Scattered Women and Scattered Rhyme', in *Feminism and Renaissance Studies*, ed. Lorna Hutson (Oxford University Press, 1999), pp. 233–48, on the complex poetics and politics of blason.
24 Spenser's portrait of the False Florimell, in *The Faerie Queene* 3.8.5–8.
25 These labels are rather loosely applied in criticism but the distinctions are useful in practice.
26 Thomas Wright, *The Passions of the Mind in General*, ed. William Webster Newbold (1601; rpt New York and London: Garland, 1986). Manuals teaching the gentlemanly management of emotions, such as Wright's, were part of that larger movement of neo-Stoic disciplines of the civil subject in Renaissance England described by Schoenfeldt, Paster, and Floyd-Wilson.
27 See Julian Yates' comments, 'Shakespeare and Embodiment, an E-Conversation', *Blackwell Literature Compass* online (Oxford: Blackwell, 2005).
28 This is both to extend and qualify Colin Burrow's observation that in Shakespeare's verse 'objects do not reveal emotions; they encrypt them intriguingly, and start his readers on a quest for mind. An object is held up as something which offers a point of access to an experience, but the experience which it signifies, and whatever those mysterious "deep-brained sonnets" actually relate, is withheld from us' ('Life and Work in Shakespeare's Poems', Chatterton Lecture on Poetry, *Proceedings of the British Academy* 97 (1998), p. 28. Rpt in *Shakespeare's Poems*, ed. Sean Keilen and Stephen Orgel (New York: Garland, 2000)).
29 On Ovid's myth of Echo and Narcissus and the political and psychological dynamics of trauma, see Lynn Enterline, *Tears of Narcissus: Melancholia and Masculinity in Early Modern Writing* (Stanford University Press, 1995).

READING LIST

Cheney, Patrick. ' "Deep-brain'd sonnets" and "tragic shows": Shakespeare's Late Ovidian Art in *A Lover's Complaint*'. In Shirley Zisser (ed.), *Critical Essays on Shakespeare's 'A Lover's Complaint'* (Aldershot, Hants: Ashgate Press, 2006), pp. 55–77.
Craik, Katharine. 'Shakespeare's *A Lover's Complaint* and Early Modern Criminal Confession'. *Shakespeare Quarterly* 53 (2002), 437–59.
Dubrow, Heather. *Echoes of Desire: English Petrarchism and its Counterdiscourses*. Ithaca: Cornell University Press, 1995.
Hyland, Peter. *An Introduction to Shakespeare's Poems*. Basingstoke: Palgrave Macmillan, 2003.
Kerrigan, John. *Motives of Woe: Shakespeare and 'Female Complaint': A Critical Anthology*. Oxford: Clarendon Press, 1991.
Paster, Gail Kern, Katherine Rowe, and Mary Floyd-Wilson (eds.). 'Introduction'. *Reading the Early Modern Passions: Essays in the Cultural History of Emotion*. Philadelphia: University of Pennsylvania Press, 2004, pp. 1–20.
Vickers, Nancy. 'Diana Described: Scattered Women and Scattered Rhyme'. In *Feminism and Renaissance Studies*. Ed. Lorna Hutson (Oxford University Press, 1999), pp. 233–48.
Zisser, Shirley (ed.). *Critical Essays on Shakespeare's 'A Lover's Complaint'* (Aldershot, Hants: Ashgate Press, 2006).

9

ANDREW HADFIELD

Poetry, politics, and religion

How should we read Shakespeare's poetry in terms of early modern English political ideas and religious beliefs? Shakespeare must have had political views, although there is a long critical tradition of assuming that his works exist as monuments for all time, beyond the exigencies of their moment of production.[1] He also must have had some form of religious upbringing and, perhaps, adhered to a particular religious belief in his adult life.[2] The problem is how to relate what we suspect were Shakespeare's views and beliefs to the poems. Or, to open out the question rather more carefully, how to read the works in terms of the religious and political ideas, images, and discourses that were in circulation in the late sixteenth and early seventeenth centuries. Shakespeare's poems may have had meanings that he did not, or could not, fully control.

Scholars of early modern politics and religion constantly warn readers that separating beliefs is a complicated task from the literary evidence that survives. Often Protestant and Catholic writers used the same conventions, making it hard to tell them apart as easily as we would like.[3] Writers borrowed conventions, such as that of weeping as a form of religious ecstasy; imitated dominant poetic styles and models associated with one particular form of religious persuasion (especially that of Spenser, the pre-eminent Protestant poet of Elizabethan England); and often sought to minimize differences in the hope of religious unity, rather than emphasize the fact that the church had split apart. Moreover, Catholic writers frequently sought to disguise their beliefs so that they could be read only by readers of the same faith, suggesting that an absence of overtly Christian words and images does not necessarily indicate an absence of religious faith.

Similar – but not identical – issues complicate our understanding of early modern political differences. Again, it is clear that there were substantial differences between those who supported the right of the monarchy to exist above the law, and those who argued that the monarch was only legitimate within a parliamentary tradition. A familiar reading of early modern English history is that these two factions, roughly speaking, what developed into 'court' and 'country' parties, eventually grew so far apart that civil war became inevitable when the king seized too many powers for himself.[4] However, it is no longer agreed that such differences were so straightfor-wardly articulated, especially in the Elizabethan period, or that history can be read as teleologically as this 'Whig' model of history suggests. Many historians now argue that Shakespeare was writing at a time when both 'constitutional' and 'absolutist' arguments shared the same languages and underlying beliefs, making them, like their religious counterparts, hard to prise apart with any certainty.[5]

For the sake of convenience, this chapter divides into two halves. The first part will discuss Shakespeare's more overtly political poems, *Venus and Adonis* and *The Rape of Lucrece*, in terms of the political issues outlined. The second will examine the religious language and imagery in the Sonnets, in order to explore how Shakespeare's poems can be situated in terms of a religious literary tradition. Of course, separating politics and religion com-pletely in the early modern period is also a problematic enterprise, but degrees of emphasis and focus are often made clear enough, Shakespeare's poems being, in fact, a good case in point.

The Politics of *Venus and Adonis* and *The Rape of Lucrece*

In the second half of Elizabeth's reign many of her subjects began to become extremely anxious about the problem of the succession. In 1587 Elizabeth was relatively old by Renaissance standards; she was fifty-four, only two years younger than her father, Henry VIII, was when he died – when she finally bowed to the pressure of her influential Protestant subjects and had Mary Stuart, Queen of Scots, executed for treason. This event, more than the celebrated defeat of the Spanish Armada in the following year, characterizes the final years of Elizabeth's rule and overshadows the early stages of Shakespeare's career. It was now clear that Elizabeth could not produce an heir and that the Tudor dynasty would end, most people expecting this to happen rather sooner than 1603. The candidates for the next English mon-arch were not likely to fill an anxious nation full of hope or expectation of a glorious new dawn. There were the weak claims of the earls of Huntington and Suffolk and the duke of Clarence, none of them major forces in the political hierarchy; the rather stronger claim of Isabella, the Spanish infanta – the daughter of the king and queen, unable to inherit the Spanish throne – opposed by many because she was a Catholic; but the strongest claim of all was that of Elizabeth's eventual successor, James VI of Scotland, who was now the son of an executed traitor. Although James was brought up as a

Protestant in Scotland, it is clear that many south of the border were afraid that they might be ruled by a foreign Catholic king. If the normal English practice of primogeniture was followed, the country could be plunged into a disastrous civil war, perhaps as serious as the recent religious wars in France (represented on the stage in Marlowe's *The Massacre at Paris* (c.1589)), or the protracted dynastic struggle, the Wars of the Roses (represented on stage by Shakespeare and his collaborators in the three *Henry VI* plays and *Richard III* (early 1590s, possibly late 1580s)).[6]

In such circumstances many powerful subjects started to explore alternative political models, turning especially to the history of the Roman republic and other constitutional forms that enabled the succession to be settled by choice, election, or other means not dependent on the mystical body of the monarch.[7] How serious many were is open to question, but it is notable that many republican writings–literary, historical, and constitutional – as well as translations of classical works, appeared in the 1590s. Given that the question of the succession could not easily be discussed – Elizabeth was, understandably, not keen to have the issue aired in public – it is hardly surprising that various literary genres were employed by writers to perform this task. One of the most obviously disaffected of Elizabeth's powerful subjects was Robert Devereux, second earl of Essex (1566–1601), who showed a keen interest in learning about republicanism. Among his clients was Henry Wriothesley, third earl of Southampton (1573–1624), Shakespeare's first known patron, to whom both Shakespeare's narrative poems were dedicated.[8] Indeed, given this political background, it is hard not to read *The Rape of Lucrece* in particular as an intervention into late Elizabethan political culture.[9]

The story of the rape of Lucrece, at the hands of Tarquinus Sextus, the selfish son of the last tyrannical king of Rome, Tarquinus Superbus, was known by everyone who had benefited from a grammar school education. The story of Lucrece is an important context for our understanding of *Venus and Adonis*. Even though *Venus* is not an explicitly political work, being more obviously mythical and sexual in focus, as other chapters in this volume make clear, it does have significant political resonances, which become clear when it is read as a companion piece to *Lucrece*. Tarquin's brutal violation of Lucrece leads to a cataclysmic political transformation of Rome, from monarchy to republic. In pointed contrast, Venus's failed comic rape of Adonis results in the sexual energy of the first half dissolving into the bleak deathliness of the second. If we read Venus as a type of Elizabeth, an older woman who proves unable to procreate and so causes a disruption in the natural order, then the relationship between the poetry and the politics becomes evident.[10]

Venus is spared few indignities as she aggressively woos Adonis. The goddess's humiliation culminates in her throwing him to the ground in a desperate and futile attempt to arouse him when she learns that he plans to hunt the boar:

> whereat a sudden pale,
> Like lawn being spread upon the blushing rose,
> Usurps her cheek; she trembles at his tale,
> And on his neck her yoking arms she throws.
>> She sinketh down, still hanging by his neck;
>> He on her belly falls, she on her back.

> Now is she in the very lists of love,
> Her champion mounted for the hot encounter.
> All is imaginary she doth prove;
> He will not manage her, although he mount her:
>> That worse than Tantalus' is her annoy,
>> To clip Elizium and to lack her joy.   (589–600)

These lines are, of course, richly and cruelly comic, the balanced caesura of the last line of each stanza – a noted feature of the poem's showy rhetorical style – emphasizes the undignified and unqueenly behaviour of the enamoured goddess of love. The point is hardly subtle and if we do read Venus as Elizabeth they constitute a stinging attack on her inability to produce an heir, suggesting that her cult of virginity was seen as a failure by many of her subjects, one that made her ridiculous and un-natural. In the early 1590s Shakespeare was by no means alone in his fears that the chastity of Elizabeth was a source of considerable frustration.[11]

The strategically placed use of 'usurps' further hints at a political significance that will become clearer in the second half of the poem: the Tudors' right to rule was seen by many as a usurpation and it was more than likely that many would see Elizabeth's successor, whoever that might be, in the same light. And these lines are invested with a more tragic meaning as the mood in the second half of the poem changes and the political themes are developed. When Adonis announces his decision to depart, Venus is given a long speech on the transitory nature of the world which contains numerous reflections that could apply to other contexts rather closer to home, as her concluding lines demonstrate:

> 'What is thy body but a swallowing grave,
> Seeming to bury that posterity,
> Which by the rights of time thou needs must have,
> If thou destroy them not in dark obscurity?
>> If so, the world will hold thee in disdain,
>> Sith in thy pride so fair a hope is slain.

> 'So in thyself thyself art made away;
> A mischief worse than civil home-bred strife,
> Or theirs whose desperate hands themselves do slay,
> Or butcher sire that reaves his son of life.
>   Foul cank'ring rust the hidden treasure frets,
>   But gold that's put to use more gold begets.' (757–68)

Venus's speech has an importance that ranges far beyond her own situation in the poem, the words carefully chosen so that they can be applied to the more public, political situation of England ruled by Elizabeth in the 1590s. The notion of the body as a 'swallowing grave', which buries its own posterity, is an eloquent image of human decay, but also functions as a comment on the impending death of the queen who was about to expire without leaving behind any posterity. Elizabeth, Shakespeare allegorically suggests, has neglected the rights of stable succession that her subjects expect, destroying them in a 'dark obscurity', perhaps a reference to her refusal to allow the question of the next monarch to be discussed.[12]

The final stanza expresses the common fear of the consequences of Elizabeth's failure, namely civil war. Venus claims that Adonis's frigid chastity is worse than 'civil home-bred strife', a forceful comment, especially given Shakespeare's leading role in the composition of the *Henry VI* plays, two parts of which were about to be published. Elizabeth stands condemned by the goddess of love for failing to see that the consequences of her virginity are more serious than she can possibly have imagined. The stanzas express a variation on the familiar *carpe diem* motif in Western literature, a demand that urgent action be taken before the onset of inevitable decay and death. Here, we know that Venus's desires are doomed to failure and that she is quite right to feel despair, as her loss is everyone's loss.

Venus ends the poem retreating into herself, 'weary of the world' (1189), like Elizabeth in 1593, and waiting for death, a striking contrast to her earlier vigorous attempt to force the unwilling Adonis into having sex with her:

> Now quick desire hath caught the yielding prey,
> And glutton-like she feeds, yet never filleth.
> Her lips are conquerors, his lips obey,
> Paying what ransom the insulter willeth;
>   Whose vulture thought doth pitch the price so high
>   That she will draw his lips' rich treasure dry.
>
> And having felt the sweetness of the spoil,
> With blindfold fury she begins to forage;
> Her face doth reek and smoke, her blood doth boil,
> And careless lust stirs up a desperate courage,

> Planting oblivion, beating reason back,
> Forgetting shame's pure blush and honour's wrack.   (547–58)

As Coppélia Kahn has noted, the imagery used here bears a striking resemblance 'to that describing Tarquin when he is about to rape Lucrece'.[13] Tarquin and Venus are here related as sexually predatory tyrants.[14] Tarquin leaning over the innocent sleeping body of Lucrece is described in suitably bestial terms:

> As the grim lion fawneth o'er his prey,
> Sharp hunger by the conquest satisfied;
> So o'er this sleeping soul doth Tarquin stay,
> His rage of lust gazing qualified –
> Slak'd not suppress'd, for standing by her side,
>   His eye which late this mutiny restrains,
>   Unto a greater uproar tempts his veins.   (421–7)

> Yet, foul night-waking cat, he doth but dally,
> While in his hold-fast foot his weak mouse panteth.
> Her sad behaviour feeds his vulture folly,
> A swallowing gulf that even in plenty wanteth.
> His ear her prayer admits, but his heart granteth
>   No penetrable entrance to her plaining:
>   Tears harden lust, though marble wear with raining.   (554–60)

There are many links that can be made between the two descriptions. Both cast the act of sex in similar fashion, suggesting that Shakespeare has transformed Venus – albeit briefly – into a rapist. Each poem represents the aggressor as a carnivore stalking a prey, Venus as a vulture, Tarquin as a lion, then a vulture, and finally a cat stalking a mouse. The sexual act is seen in terms of appetite (Venus is 'glutton-like', Tarquin is driven on by 'sharp hunger'). Both have their sexual urges inflamed by the prospect of success and the lack of resistance of the sex object; Venus feels 'careless lust', Tarquin, 'a rage of lust'. Both experience a rush of blood to the head: Venus's 'face doth reek and smoke, her blood doth boil', Tarquin experiences a 'greater uproar' that 'tempts his veins'. Both lose control of reason and are quite indifferent to the consequences of their actions. And, most significantly of all, the emphasis on the political nature of the language of rape in *Venus and Adonis* (Venus's lips are 'conquerors', forcing Adonis to pay 'what ransom the insulter willeth') forges a connection to the other most political of all rapes.

Venus/Elizabeth's failure to complete the sex act places the realm in danger. Shakespeare seems to be drawing a pointed contrast between Venus/Elizabeth and the virtuous Lucrece, a truly noble woman whose actions benefit her fellow citizens, a significance that is latent in *Venus and Adonis* itself, and becomes obvious if we read the two narrative poems together. Elizabeth/ Venus's repellent virginity – achieved despite her vigorous efforts – is shown up by the virtuous chastity of Lucrece. *The Rape of Lucrece* shows us the development of Lucrece from pliant subject to potential king-killer in her long speeches that make up the bulk of the poem's narrative once Tarquin has entered her chamber. Tarquin surrenders to his personal lust and neglects to act as a prince. Lucrece chooses to kill herself, but the poem forces us to ask: 'What if Lucrece had resolved to kill Tarquin rather than herself?'[15]

The Rape of Lucrece differs from earlier versions of the story in placing such emphasis on the character of Lucrece.[16] The tradition of the story either made a political point, following Livy, which saw the rape as the prelude to the establishment of the republic by Brutus, and so minimized the role of Lucrece. Or, following Saint Augustine, criticized Lucrece for her pride in killing herself because she could not bear the stigma of the rape. Shakespeare's poem is a new departure within a literary tradition, one that is explicitly related to contemporary political concerns. Given that great emphasis is placed on Lucrece herself, and that she narrates more lines than any other speaker, *The Rape of Lucrece* can also be seen as part of the fashionable genre of female complaint, as we see events through the development of her consciousness.[17] We follow Lucrece's journey from servile subject of the king to an outspoken critic of the excesses of monarchy, prepared to use violence, progress that absorbs the political transformation which she had traditionally been seen to cause. There is little need for Brutus in Shakespeare's version because Lucrece has already done all the work for the reader. In transferring the political significance of her violation to the victim herself, Shakespeare refashions and combines two distinct poetic traditions. Furthermore, in doing so, he establishes the virtuous, beautiful, politically agile and literate Lucrece as a pointed contrast to the self-absorbed and unattractive Venus/Elizabeth. The countering of one form of anti-feminism is cleverly used to establish another.

The most politically charged section of the poem is the verbal confrontation between Tarquin and Lucrece immediately prior to the rape (Hadfield, *Shakespeare and Politics*, ch. 3). The lines are replete with political language, ideas, and imagery. As they argue, it becomes apparent that both protagonists accept that a limited monarchy is a desirable political form. The problem is that Tarquin cannot confine his appetites within the boundaries established, and Lucrece is consequently forced to consider more revolutionary action. Tarquin is represented as a tyrant, admitting to himself that his 'will is strong past reason's weak removing' (244). The narrator elaborates on this clash between reason and appetite, referring to Tarquin as a traitor, whose 'greedy eyeballs' commit 'high treason' in misleading his heart (369–70). While still attempting to persuade Lucrece to commit adultery, he proposes a means of circumventing the law that will satisfy his desires, confirm his real power, and leave the constitution intact:

> 'But if thou yield, I rest thy secret friend;
> The fault unknown is as a thought unacted.
> A little harm done to a great good end
> For lawful policy remains enacted'. (526–9)

Tarquin's argument is that Lucrece should submit to him as a means of preserving Roman liberty; the barely suppressed threat is that if she does not yield to him he will undermine the state when he becomes king.[18] Tarquin's reason informs him that he is acting in a manner ill-befitting the heir to the throne, but his will is too strong for him to control. Any monarch who cannot limit his appetites is a tyrant who must be overthrown in the interests of the people. In a discussion about kings who seize kingdoms 'by violence and without the consent of the people', the influential political theorist and tutor of James VI, George Buchanan, argues that tyrants often disguise their true natures because they are aware of the consequences of their actions, 'For the hatred aroused by a single misdeed loses them all gratitude for their ostentatious generosity.' Their aim is to act 'for the sake of their own absolute power rather than the advantage of the people' and to 'enjoy their own pleasures' rather than governing in the interests of the people they are supposed to serve.[19] This dishonest and closed form of government encourages the further vice of bad rule, flattery, the 'nurse of tyranny and the most grievous plague of lawful kingship'.[20]

Lucrece refuses to remain silent and dares to challenge Tarquin. His desire to separate his private act from his public person produces a corresponding division in Lucrece's understanding of him: 'In Tarquin's likeness I did entertain thee: / Hast thou put on his shape to do him shame?' (596–7). Initially, Lucrece tries to separate the private from the public body of the future king. She then explores the consequences of Tarquin's as yet uncommitted crime in lines that show her political ideas changing before our eyes:

> 'Thou seem'st not what thou art, a god, a king:
> For kings like gods should govern everything.
>
> 'How will thy shame be seeded in thine age,
> When thus thy vices bud before thy spring?
> If in thy hope thou dar'st do such outrage,
> What dar'st thou not when once thou art a king?
> O be remember'd, no outrageous thing

From vassal actors can be wip'd away:
Then kings' misdeeds cannot be hid in clay.

'This deed will make thee only lov'd for fear;
But happy monarchs still are fear'd for love.'   (601–11)

Lucrece stands as the ideal subject in these lines, perhaps even transforming herself into a Roman citizen when threatened by the illegal actions of the son of the monarch, a role that prefigures her representation as the body politic itself when Tarquin rapes her. In the first lines cited here she sees kings as god's representatives on earth, able to govern everything, the familiar statement of absolutist theory in Europe, and an interpretation of the role of the monarch within the English constitution which the Tudors intermittently asserted as theirs.[21] In the second stanza she develops her ideas, speculating on what Tarquin might do when he has become king if he is prepared to act so badly before he has assumed power. The implications of this train of thought undermine the premise with which she started. If kings need to be suitable for their office, then they have no absolute right to rule. If they rule to serve the people, then the people have a right to expect proper regal behaviour.

Lucrece explains that she sues for 'exil'd majesty's repeal' (640), and her pleas are unsuccessful. Nevertheless, the lines point to a very different future. Lucrece means here, in line with her earlier separation of the office and person of the king, that Tarquin is exiled from himself in his duty as king. But we all know that Tarquin and his line really are banished from Rome at the end of the poem, and that even a protracted war with the newly established republican armies fails to restore the dynasty. The eventual effect of Tarquin's base desires is to make Romans value their freedom even more. Lucrece's failure at this stage does not imply that resistance to Machiavellian tyrants is futile; rather, it suggests that the rhetoric of counsel may have to be abandoned in favour of more drastic measures.

Eventually, Lucrece concludes that her suffering cannot be redressed by legal means and that her attempt to argue with Tarquin has been a waste of time: 'For me, I force not argument a straw, / Since that my case is past the help of law' (1021–2). This statement – without precedence in any source – shows that Lucrece feels that the means of feasible redress are closed to her. Given that we have seen that her attempts at advising Tarquin through the adoption of the rhetoric of counsel have been brushed aside, we surely conclude that she is right to dismiss the legal route. She also argues that the sins of the royal family should not remain secret and so be visited on the people:

'Why should the private pleasure of some one
Become the public plague of many moe?

> Let sin alone committed, light alone
> Upon his head that hath transgressed so;
> Let guiltless souls be freed from guilty woe:
>   For one's offence why should so many fall,
>   To plague a private sin in general?'   (1478–84)

All of which suggests that Lucrece's suicide can be read as a displaced assassination of the tyrant. In fact, she does ask Collatine to kill the king's son before she kills herself:

> 'And for my sake, when I might charm thee so,
> For she that was thy Lucrece, now attend me:
> Be suddenly revenged on my foe, –
> Thine, mine, his own. Suppose that thou dost defend me
> From what is past: the help that thou shalt lend me
>   Comes all too late, yet let the traitor die,
>   For sparing justice feeds iniquity.'   (1681–7)

It is hard to imagine a more direct request for political assassination. The phrase 'suddenly revenged' can only mean one thing, especially when supplemented by the elaboration that Tarquin is the enemy of everyone, including himself. The connection made in the last two lines between the death of the treacherous son of the king and the need to implement justice, therefore, has to be read as a defence of tyrannicide when the law cannot be applied.

What political message might we glean from the two poems? My suggestion is that in his early career Shakespeare was keen to be seen as a radical political writer, either through conviction or opportunism, given the intellectual climate of the 1590s. The virtue of Lucrece stands as a pointed contrast to the lustful and selfish tyranny of the monarchs represented in the two poems dedicated to Southampton, Tarquin, and Venus. Together, they form a composite picture of the perils of monarchy, each showing that inside every monarch lurks a tyrant waiting to escape. Furthermore, neither manages to produce an heir, despite their attention to the sexual act, a failure that highlights the dangers of their personal rule. Lucrece stands as the body politic, abused as a possession by the monarch, who fails to see that the people who make up the state have voices and rights as well as corporeal existence, as Lucrece's articulate speech proves.

Religion and the Sonnets

Shakespeare wrote very little poetry that can be described as 'religious'. Of course, there are exceptions, such as Sonnet 146, which is explicitly theological in subject and style. There are also works that employ biblical imagery and language, a usage that may or may not be incidental.[22] And there is 'The Phoenix and Turtle', which is a mysterious Neoplatonic allegory that no one has successfully decoded, and which could be classified as religious in nature.[23] However, compared to other major poets such as Sidney, Spenser, Chapman, Donne, and Drayton, Shakespeare's poetry is remarkable for its apparent lack of interest in religion. Shakespeare writes about classical legend and mythology in his Ovidian narrative poems, and constancy and love in his Sonnets. Perhaps only Christopher Marlowe, who wrote much more obviously about religion in his plays than Shakespeare did, shows an equal ostensible indifference to religious matters in his poetry.

But the reason for this absence may not be quite as easy to interpret as it seems. There is a growing conviction among many scholars that Shakespeare was actually either a Catholic by choice, or one by birth, and that his adult life was haunted by the need to disguise his beliefs or his connections with Catholics.[24] The fact that he avoided writing about religion is a sign of his constant awareness of its importance, either because he still held the beliefs instilled in him in childhood; because he was trying to find an alternative outlet for his energies; or, because he was aware of the danger that such views posed.

There are many problems with such arguments that require comment. First, the evidence provided is wholly circumstantial or open to dispute: the copy of the Catholic testimony discovered in the attic of John Shakespeare's house has to be assumed to be genuine; the 'William Shakeshafte' who was associated with Houghton Tower has to be a pseudonym of Shakespeare, meaning that Shakespeare spent his 'lost years' in Lancashire as tutor to a Catholic family, rather than as an apprentice playwright and actor in London[25]; and the links between Shakespeare and Catholic members of his family, including those who took part in the Gunpowder Plot, have to be of great significance. All of these connections are, of course, possible. But there is no real evidence in the plays and poems that Shakespeare was a Catholic or that he employed notably Catholic language and imagery that readers in the know would have detected. In short, the argument is biographical rather than textual, and depends upon an ability to anchor evidence outside the plays and poems which can then be used to unlock their secrets. As yet, no such certainty exists.

Moreover, recent studies of early modern religion in England have tended to complicate our understanding of religious belief and adherence. The traditional history of the Reformation in England argued that late medieval Catholicism was hopelessly corrupt and that the country was ripe for reform and a break from the tyranny of Rome. A reaction to this simplistic narrative launched the counter argument that the true picture pointed in the opposite direction: far from being moribund in the fifteenth and early sixteenth centuries, the church was in a healthy state, popular and serving the people well. Only Henry VIII's desperate need for a male successor and the opportunism of a well-organised band of Protestant zealots led a reluctant nation away from its natural affiliation to European Christendom. The reign of Mary Tudor was not the aberration that historians have often assumed it to be, but was actually a welcome return to traditional life for most Englishmen and women.[26]

However, these diametrically opposed narratives may well distort the evidence in ways that suggest that trying to work out whether Shakespeare was a Protestant or a Catholic is an even more problematic task than has been assumed in the discussion so far. Not all Catholics were the same. The Catholic community could be divided into those conformists who longed for England to be a Catholic country – or to return to the certainties of late medieval piety – but who did not feel strongly enough to take any action against the status quo; and those who, following Pope Pius V's bull of 1570 excommunicating Elizabeth and pardoning any of her subjects who took up arms against her in the Catholic cause, felt that their religion overrode any loyalty they had to their state and sovereign. Furthermore, Catholics were not necessarily consistent in their beliefs: they might view matters in strict terms of black and white at one point and then see shades of grey at another. The same applies to Protestants who could be divided along similar lines into Anglicans and puritans. Separating out religious belief from political discourse and more popular forms of thinking is a dubious enterprise.[27]

And there is a further complication. Shakespeare did not write his poetry in a vacuum, but conceived his work in relation to other writers, most importantly for our purposes here the dominant Protestant poet in print in the 1590s, Edmund Spenser.[28] Spenser's sonnet sequence, the *Amoretti* (published 1595) along with the *Epithalamion*, is a fictional record of his courtship of his second wife, Elizabeth Boyle, and their marriage on 11 June 1594. The sonnets are explicitly religious in nature, the sequence being based on the liturgical calendar of the Christian year, to which key sonnets allude, making use of the text that would have been read in churches throughout Elizabeth's dominions on a particular day as decreed by the *Book of Common Prayer*.[29] A connection is made between the progress of the poet's suit and Christian belief. Sonnet 38, for example, compares the lover's suffering to that of Christ, employing language derived from Luke 10, the text used on 27 February. Sonnet 64, which can be dated to the Wednesday before Easter in 1594 (March 27), consists of a series of complex allusions that make sense in terms of an acknowledged understanding of biblical references:

> Comming to kisse her lyps (such grace I found)
> Me seemd I smelt a gardin of sweet flowres:
> that dainty odours from them threw around

> for damzels fir to decke their lovers bowres.
> Her lips did smell lyke unto Gillyflowers,
> her ruddy cheekes lyke unto Roses red:
> her snowy browes lyke budded Bellamoures,
> her lovely eyes lyke Pincks but newly spred,
> Her goodly bosome lyke to a bounch of Cullambynes:
> her brest lyke lilyes, ere theyr leaves be shed,
> her nipples lyke yong blossomd Iessemynes:
> Such fragrant flowres doe give most odorous smell,
> but her sweet odour did them all excell.

The sonnet describes the lady as a natural beauty, imagining her in terms of a paradise of beautiful flowers. Spenser alludes to a series of religious contexts. The reference to the kiss in the opening line refers to Judas's kiss in the Garden of Gethsemane before he betrayed Christ (Luke 22), a striking contrast to the kiss of Spenser and his future wife (the reference to Iessemynes (jasmines) in line 12, undoubtedly puns on Gethsemane). The references to the Garden refer to Hosea 13 and 14, when the prophet, having condemned his false rivals, sings of a lovely garden, a verse traditionally connected to the more famous description in the Song of Songs.[30]

It is likely that Shakespeare had this sonnet in mind when he wrote his own Sonnet 130, 'My mistress' eyes are nothing like the sun'. That poem has, quite rightly, been read as a parody of the *blazon* of a mistress, a poem that described the body of the lady in question.[31] Commentators have found parallels for many of the details in Shakespeare's poem in other works by Henry Constable, Samuel Daniel, Barnaby Barnes, and others: the coral lips, red cheeks, and golden hair. But it might seem that Shakespeare's poem is deliberately written with the imagery of the *Song of Songs* in mind, which emphasizes the perfume of the beloved, her lovely breasts, as well as the beauty of her face and hair, all details that are contained in Spenser's sonnet. Shakespeare constructs his mistress as a striking contrast:

> If snow be white, why then her breast are dun;
> If hairs be wires, black wires grow on her head.
> I have seen roses damasked, red and white,
> But no such roses see I in her cheeks,
> And in some perfumes is there more delight
> Than in the breath that from my mistress reeks.   (3–8)

Line 8 places heavy emphasis on his mistress's foul smell, demonstrating that she is a world away from Spenser's floral lady. The concluding couplet introduces a commonplace religious comparison: 'And yet, *by heaven*, I think my love as rare / As any she belied with false compare' (my emphasis).

Shakespeare's sonnet can be read as a cheeky response to the intricately wrought religious language of the great Protestant poet, as well as a satire of the general conventions of Elizabethan love poetry. Elizabethan poetic conventions encouraged writers to interact with each other, writing, parodying, and rewriting the work of other poets, as Walter Ralegh's 'The Nymph's Reply' responded to Christopher Marlowe's 'The Passionate Shepherd to His Love'. Nowhere was such intricate intextertuality more important than in the vogue for sonnet sequences, most of which try to score points off each other. Accordingly, Spenser's praise of courtship and married love can be read as a response to Sidney's *Astrophil and Stella*, which dealt with the frustrated love of a failed suitor for a lady who marries someone else. In turn, Shakespeare's Sonnets seem carefully designed to subvert Spenser's sequence, as they detail the poet's twin passion for a younger man of higher social status and a lascivious, unconventionally attractive lady, which culminates in a complicated love triangle when the two 'angels' have sex with each other in Sonnet 144. Shakespeare further comments that he will only know definitely of this relationship if he is able to detect the sexually transmitted diseases they pass on to each other: 'Yet this shall I ne'er know, but live in doubt, / Till my bad angel fire my good one out' (which then poses the question of how they might have got the diseases in the first place: perhaps from the poet himself?).[32] It is hard to imagine an amorous relationship more calculated to undermine the sanctity of marriage.

This is a highly speculative reading of the Sonnets, and we are certainly hampered by the problem that we do not know when they were written, nor whether their order is one authorized by the author or imposed on the material by the publisher. Nevertheless, the anti-Spenserian nature of the poems is frequently in evidence, as Shakespeare undermines and parodies the religious style of the *Amoretti*. Spenser's Sonnet 82, for example, written to celebrate the feast of Ascension, emphasizes the heavenly name of his lady which the poet vows to make permanent through the use of his talents:

> For had the equall heuvns so much you graced
> in this as in the rest, ye mote invent
> som hevenly wit, whose verse could have enchased
> your glorious name in *golden moniment*.
> But since ye deigned so goodly to relent
> to me your thrall, in whom is little worth,
> that little that I am, shall all be spent
> in setting your immortall prayses forth.   (Emphasis added)

Spenser's lines argue that the poet needs to supplement the work of heaven in order to give the lady her just reward. They are an echo of Sonnet 69, which makes substantially the same point:

> What trophee then shall I most fit devize,
> in which I may record the memory
> of my loves conquest, peerlesse beauties prise,
> adorn'd with honour, love, and chastity?
> Even this verse vowd to eternity,
> shall be thereof *immortall moniment*:
> and tell her prayse to all posterity,
> that may admire such worlds rare wonderment.
>
> (Emphasis added)

The sonnet is written to coincide with Easter Monday, when the liturgical theme was the sepulchre, the monument from which Christ arose.[33] Elizabeth Boyle assumes a heavenly identity as she is seen to be sanctioned by Christ for the poet, her name designed to live on through the verse, linked to her future husband as well as Christ in a holy love triangle.

Shakespeare's Sonnets contain a long section of poems on the ability of the poet to immortalize the young man, the most celebrated of which is Sonnet 55:

> Not marble, nor the gilded monuments
> Of princes shall outlive this pow'rful rhyme,
> But you shall shine more bright in these contents
> Than unswept stone besmeared with sluttish time.　　(1–4)

The second half of the poem makes a series of allusions to the Last Judgement ('That wear this world out to the ending doom' (Line 12)), suggesting that the poet's power goes beyond that of religion and opens up a new space for the eternal preservation of mankind.[34] But the thrust of the argument is as much against, rather than in terms of, the religious comparisons that Spenser makes between his love and Christ. These are replaced by an apparent faith in the abilities of the poet alone to conquer the vicissitudes of time and fortune. If there is any triangular relationship in Shakespeare's Sonnets, it is the very earthly one between the poet and his two loves, a man and a woman. The image in the final line cited above, and the carefully chosen use of the word 'sluttish', stands as yet another pointed contrast to Spenser's use of 'honour, love, and chastity' (especially, of course, the last word).

This reading of Shakespeare's Sonnets presents us with a number of ways of thinking about the meaning and significance of Renaissance verse. Poems exist within a complex web of discourses, both literary and non-literary, and it is hard to extract them and then read them back against what we might like to see as unchanging and fixed series of beliefs. The Sonnets appear to be situated in terms of a dominant Protestant poetic, but how exactly should we then read them? Are they Catholic poems, hostile to a mode of writing that they are keen to undermine, without stating an alternative case? The most famous Elizabethan Catholic poet was the martyr Robert Southwell (1561?–95), who was, in fact, a distant relative of Shakespeare, and it is not implausible to argue that Shakespeare would have been wary of imitating Southwell's style.[35] Or are they simply the work of an ambitious young poet–playwright who was keen to forge an identity and a career for himself by showing that he could imitate and refigure the styles and modes of his most prominent peers? After all, the discipline of the theatre, with the intense rivalry between companies, also encouraged writers to produce work that was distinct from that of their competitors.[36]

It is hard to give an answer with any certainty, and the reason why Shakespeare wrote so little religious verse is an important question that warrants further study. Shakespeare's political beliefs are not easy to extract from his work, but the direction that he follows in his early writings gives us more clues than they do of his religious affiliation. But this is only what we might expect given that the Elizabethan authorities reacted far more savagely to obvious religious as opposed to 'political' transgression in print (a point that should also make us wary of separating religion and politics in this period).[37] Shakespeare did have his brushes with the law, notably when the Chamberlain's Men performed *Richard II* – probably his play – for Essex's supporters on the eve of the Essex uprising in 1601. Yet, compared to other dramatists and writers – Ben Jonson, Thomas Nashe, Thomas Dekker, George Chapman, John Marston – he was the very soul of discretion.

Shakespeare did write one overtly religious poem, Sonnet 146, a meditation on the relationship between the soul and the body which resembles those written by Sidney, Donne, and later Marvell:

> Poor soul, the centre of my sinful earth,
> Spoiled by these rebel powers that thee array,
> Why dost thou pine within and suffer dearth,
> Painting thy outward walls so costly gay?
> Why so large a cost, having so short a lease,
> Dost thou upon thy fading mansion spend?
> Shall worms, inheritors of this excess,
> Eat up thy charge? Is this thy body's end?
> Then, soul, live thou upon thy servant's loss,
> And let that pine to aggravate thy store;
> Buy terms divine in selling hours of dross;
> Within be fed, without be rich no more.
>   So shall thou feed on Death, that feeds on men,
>   And Death once dead, there's no more dying then.

This is one of the few sonnets that makes no reference to a love-object and the last line recalls 1 Corinthians 15.26, 'The last enemie that shall bee destroyed is death' (Geneva translation), which does make the sonnet stand out as unusual in the sequence. But we might also point out that it can be linked to the wider discussion of time and eternity in the poems, one factor that might explain its seemingly anomalous presence. The poem is sandwiched between 'Those lips that love's own hand did make', the only sonnet in octosyllabic lines, which seems to refer to Anne Hathaway and so is probably a piece of juvenilia incorporated into the text, and 'My love is as a fever', which sits more comfortably with the themes and conventions of the 'dark lady' sonnets. Its position might suggest that it is an early poem incorporated into the sequence, possibly by the printer rather than the author. Whatever the case may be, Sonnet 146 does little to help us solve the enigma of Shakespeare's religious beliefs.

The evidence would seem to suggest that Shakespeare was far more interested in politics than religion in his poems, as he was in his plays. But it may be that we are jumping to conclusions too readily in assuming this relative balance of his concerns. It was safer, after all, to write about politics without religion. Perhaps it was just good sense to disguise one's religious beliefs in the fraught and complicated period of later Tudor and early Stuart England. Moreover, politics was clearly sound business, as the success of the *Henry VI* plays indicates.[38] Shakespeare might have been more interested in writing and/or money. Despite the wealth of current speculation, we will probably never know for certain.

NOTES

1 See, for example, Blair Worden, 'Shakespeare and Politics', *Shakespeare Survey* 44 (1991), 1–15.

2 Although, of course, his major precursor in the theatre, Christopher Marlowe, probably did not: see David Riggs, *The World of Christopher Marlowe* (London: Faber, 2004), pp. 166–8, *passim*.

3 Alison Shell, *Catholicism, Controversy and the English Literacy Imagination, 1558–1660* (Cambridge University Press, 1999).

4 See, for example, G.R. Elton, 'A High Road to Civil War?', in *From the Renaissance to the Counter-Reformation: Essays in Honour of Garrett Mattingly*, ed. Charles H. Carter (New York: Random House, 1965), pp. 325–47.

5 Kevin Sharpe, *Remapping Early Modern England: The Culture of Seventeenth-Century Politics* (Cambridge University Press, 2000), pt 1. For an alternative reading, see J.P. Sommerville, *Politics and Ideology in England, 1603–1640* (Harlow: Longman, 1996).

6 Andrew Hadfield, *Shakespeare and Republicanism* (Cambridge University Press, 2005), ch. 3.

7 Patrick Collinson, 'The Monarchical Republic of Queen Elizabeth I', in *Elizabethans* (Hambledon: London, 2003), pp. 31–58; Markku Peltonen, *Classical Humanism*

and Republicanism in English Political Thought, 1570–1640 (Cambridge University Press, 1995), ch. 2.

8 On Essex's political connections, see Paul E. J. Hammer, *The Polarisation of Elizabethan Politics: The Political Career of Robert Devereux, 2nd Earl of Essex, 1585–1597* (Cambridge University Press, 1999), ch. 7; Dzelzainis, 'Shakespeare and Political Thought' in *A Companion to Shakespeare*, ed. David Scott Kastan (Oxford: Blackwell, 1999), p. 107.

9 For a more sceptical reading, see Colin Burrow (ed.), *The Complete Sonnets and Poems* (Oxford University Press, 2002), Introduction, pp. 45–66.

10 At least one contemporary did read Venus as Elizabeth: see Katherine Duncan-Jones, 'Much Ado with Red and White: The Earliest Readers of Shakespeare's *Venus and Adonis*', *Review of English Studies* ns 44 (1993), 480–501.

11 See Helen Hackett, *Virgin Mother, Maiden Queen: Elizabeth I and the Cult of the Virgin Mary* (Basingstoke: Macmillan, 1995), ch. 6–7.

12 Janet Clare, *'Art made tongue-tied by authority': Elizabethan and Jacobean Dramatic Censorship*, 2nd edn (Manchester University Press, 1990), ch. 2.

13 Coppélia Kahn, 'Self and Eros in *Venus and Adonis*', *Centennial Review* 20 (1976), 351–71: 363.

14 On the relationship between sex and tyranny, see Rebecca Bushnell, *Tragedies of Tyrants: Political Thought and Theater in the English Renaissance* (Ithaca: Cornell University Press, 1990).

15 Katherine Eisman Maus, 'Taking Tropes Seriously: Language and Violence in Shakespeare's *Rape of Lucrece*', *Shakespeare Quarterly* 37 (1996), 67.

16 For an overview, see Ian Donaldson, *The Rapes of Lucrece: A Myth and its Transformations* (Oxford: Clarendon Press, 1982).

17 See John Kerrigan (ed.), *Motives of Woe: Shakespeare and 'Female Complaint', A Critical Anthology* (Oxford: Clarendon Press, 1991).

18 On the political implications of disguise in the poem, see Dzelzainis, 'Shakespeare and Political Thought', pp. 111–13.

19 George Buchanan, *A Dialogue on the Law of Kingship among the Scots: A Critical Edition and Translation of George Buchanan's 'De Jure Regni apud Scotos Dialogus'*, ed. and trans. Roger A. Mason and Martin S. Smith (Aldershot: Ashgate, 2003), pp. 85–7.

20 Buchanan, *Law of Kingship*, p. 3.

21 J. P. Sommerville, 'Absolutism and Royalism', in Burns and Goldie (eds.), *Cambridge History of Political Thought, 1450–1700* (Cambridge University Press, 1991), pp. 347–73.

22 See David Daniell, 'Shakespeare and the Protestant Mind', *Shakespeare Survey* 54 (2001), 1–12.

23 For an overview of criticism, see Richard Allan Underwood, *Shakespeare's 'The Phoenix and Turtle': A Survey of Scholarship* (Salzburg: University of Salzburg, 1974).

24 See Richard Wilson, *Secret Shakespeare: Studies in Theatre, Religion and Resistance* (Manchester University Press, 2004); Michael Wood, *In Search of Shakespeare* (London: BBC, 2003); Stephen Greenblatt, *Will in the World: How Shakespeare Became Shakespeare* (New York: Norton, 2004).

25 See E. A. J. Honigmann, *Shakespeare: The 'Lost Years'*, rev. edn (Manchester University Press, 1998).

26 For the classic statement of the former narrative, see A. G. Dickens, *The English Reformation* (London: Batsford, 1964); for the latter, see Eamon Duffy, *The Stripping of the Altars: Traditional Religion in England, 1400–1580* (New Haven: Yale University Press, 1992).

27 For discussion, see Ethan Shagan (ed.), *Catholics and the 'Protestant Nation': Religious Politics and Identity in Early Modern England* (Manchester University Press, 2005); Peter Lake with Michael Questier, *The Antichrist's Lewd Hat: Protestants, Papists and Players in Post-Reformation England* (New Haven: Yale University Press, 2002). The division of Protestants into 'Anglicans' and 'puritans' is, needless to say, problematic.

28 See the extensive and persuasive discussion in Patrick Cheney, *Shakespeare, National Poet–Playwright* (Cambridge University Press, 2004).

29 See *Edmund Spenser's 'Amoretti' and 'Epithalamion': A Critical Edition*, ed. Kenneth J. Larsen (Tempe, AZ: MRTS, 1997).

30 *Edmund Spenser's 'Amoretti' and 'Epithalamion'*, pp. 194–5.

31 See *The Sonnets and A Lover's Complaint*, ed. John Kerrigan (Harmondsworth: Penguin, 1986), pp. 359–60. Kerrigan notes comparisons with the *Amoretti*, but not this poem.

32 For comment, see *Sonnets*, ed. Kerrigan, p. 60. More generally, see Paul Hammond, *Figuring Sex between Men from Shakespeare to Rochester* (Oxford University Press, 2002), pp. 62–87; Margreta de Grazia, 'The Scandal of Shakespeare's Sonnets', *Shakespeare Survey* 46 (1994), 35–50.

33 *Edmund Spenser's 'Amoretti' and 'Epithalamion'*, p. 202.

34 See Cheney, *Shakespeare, National Poet–Playwright*, pp. 226–7, for discussion.

35 Wilson, *Secret Shakespeare*, ch. 5; *The Poems of Robert Southwell, S. J.*, ed. James H. McDonald and Nancy Pollard Brown (Oxford: Clarendon Press, 1967).

36 See James P. Bednarz, *Shakespeare & the Poets' War* (New York: Columbia University Press, 2001).

37 See Janet Clare, *'Art made tongue-tied by authority'*; and Cyndia Clegg, *Press Censorship in Elizabethan England* (Cambridge University Press, 1997).

38 Hadfield, *Shakespeare and Republicanism*, ch. 3.

READING LIST

Burns, J. H., and Mark Goldie (eds.). *The Cambridge History of Political Thought, 1450–1700*. Cambridge University Press, 1991.

Dzelzainis, Martin. 'Shakespeare and Political Thought'. In *A Companion to Shakespeare*. Ed. David Scott Kastan. Oxford: Blackwell, 1999, pp. 100–16.

Hadfield, Andrew. *Shakespeare and Renaissance Politics*. Arden Critical Companions. London: Thomson, 2004.

Shakespeare and Republicanism. Cambridge University Press, 2005.

Maus, Katharine Eisman. 'Taking Tropes Seriously: Language and Violence in Shakespeare's *Rape of Lucrece*'. *Shakespeare Quarterly* 37 (1996), 66–82.

Riggs, David. *The World of Christopher Marlowe*. London: Faber, 2004.

Shagan, Ethan, (ed.). *Catholics and the 'Protestant Nation': Religious Politics and Identity in Early Modern England*. Manchester University Press, 2005.

Sharpe, Kevin. *Remapping Early Modern England: The Culture of Seventeenth-Century Politics*. Cambridge University Press, 2000.

Shell, Alison. *Catholicism, Controversy and the English Literary Imagination, 1558–1660*. Cambridge University Press, 1999.

Worden, Blair. 'Shakespeare and Politics'. *Shakespeare Survey* 44 (1991), 1–15.

IO

DANIELLE CLARKE

Love, beauty, and sexuality

Shakespeare's poems have had a long and complex literary afterlife, but these are essentially pre-modern poems. The categories that they deploy, invoke, and disrupt are not those that construct modern notions of love, desire, or sexuality, however much they may seem to resemble them. These notions are in flux, in the process of arriving at their modern formations. Yet these complex and intriguing texts are capable of effective time travel and transcending the specific conditions of their production. They are not an easy read, and consistently confound any attempt to reduce them to bland sentimentality. They have proved themselves amenable to endless appropriation and re-appropriation, as successive generations of readers have found in them expressive analogues for highly personalized states of desire and emotion. Love, for Shakespeare, is rarely an unequivocally pleasant condition; it is not even a single emotion, but rather a nexus of oppositional and often competing impulses and drives. Love is multi-faceted, emotionally complex, and involves its sufferer in a complex web of desires and deceptions. Yet love, fuelled by perceptions of beauty, and having its ultimate fleeting expression in sexual desire is, for Shakespeare, at the heart of human life. It is simultaneously origin and destination, an exhaustion of youth and vitality and a potent reminder of death, a spur to self-realization, and the potential destruction of that self.

The main poems in Shakespeare's canon consider the destructive effects of love on the self, in ways analogous to, although not identical with, the treatment of love in the plays, where it is inflected profoundly by genre.[1] The price of Tarquin's satisfaction of lust is Lucrece's self-immolation; that of Venus's rapacious desire the death and transformation of Adonis into a 'purple flower' (1,168); the maiden in *A Lover's Complaint* bewails the loss of her maidenhead and personhood; the speaker of the Sonnets finds himself ashamed, betrayed, alone. In each text, the lover finds himself or herself trapped within a situation, and a discourse, that she or he cannot completely control. We seldom find a reciprocal mutuality between lover and beloved – on the rare occasions that this can be glimpsed, it is ruthlessly revealed as a delusion, a self-deception of the most damaging kind, or a fleeting state, subject to destructive, external forces, a lost ideal to be mourned: 'Beauty, truth, and rarity, / Grace in all simplicity, / Here enclosed, in cinders lie' ('The Phoenix and Turtle', 53–5). Love and desire thrive on inequality; the beloved withholds or grants favour in arbitrary and callous ways, whilst the lover attempts to manipulate from a position of dispossession, with the poetry itself as an unstable and frequently impotent vehicle.

Although Shakespeare transforms the literary models for love that he inherits, nevertheless this notion of erotic inequality shapes both Ovidian representations of love, as well as that of Petrarchanism, both precedents that Shakespeare relies upon at the same time as he subjects them to ruthless scrutiny and metamorphosis (see Chapters 1 and 11 in this volume, respectively). Hovering in the background are the more obviously socially conditioned inequalities underlying marriage and sexual reputation, conditions that are played out to their logical conclusions in the closure of the comedies, a form of closure resolutely denied in the poems. This inequality produces a solipsistic scrutiny of the self, with the flattering delusions that this entails. The boundaries of the self are revealed to be fragile, at risk of being redefined by the love object whose responses and repudiations are incorporated into the speaker's sense of self; the dividing line between subject and object, self and other, is fluid, sometimes dangerously so, in ways that recall the dissolution of the subject/object distinction suffered by Shakespeare's tragic heroes.[2] Equally frangible are those distinctions that apparently structure our experience: male/female, homosexual/heterosexual, age/youth, lust/chastity. Desire may embolden the speaker, but in the face of non-reciprocation it can lead to the collapse of the boundaries of the self. Desire in Shakespeare's poems is no respecter of convention or respectability, as the speaker of the Sonnets, and the figure of Lucrece prove. Neither is desire the exclusive preserve of patriarchal heterosexuality, but it is articulated through a variety of potentially transgressive scenarios, to which literary precedents and conventions are jaggedly and creatively appropriated.

For Shakespeare, sexuality is much more than an erotic relationship structured by social norms, and he chooses scenarios that permit him to delineate its fluid and unpredictable effects. *A Lover's Complaint* narrates the personal and social damage inflicted by a serial lothario, whose beauty and sweetness of speech blind his victims to consequence: ' "His qualities were beauteous as his form, / For maiden-tongued he was, and thereof free" ' (99–100). *Venus and Adonis* inverts the structure of the *epyllion* by having a mature female pursue and attempt to entrap a younger man in a correlative to more abstract debates about the relationship between Love and Lust, Age and Youth,

Beauty and Art. *The Rape of Lucrece* explores the forced violation of married chastity within the context of ideals of hospitality and republican politics.[3] The Sonnets are mostly preoccupied with desire for and love of a beautiful young man, explicitly articulated as such through the layering and juxtaposition of discourses more conventionally reserved for hetero-sexual desire.

Each of Shakespeare's poems adopts a particular generic framework, and each brings its own textual complexities, but – as in the plays – it is the case that interpretation and the representation of love are inflected by the choice of form, even though there are semantic fields that are brought into play over the course of nearly two decades of attempting to write desire – nature, expenditure, the power of the gaze, the limits to representation. Because of their generic affinity, and because of questions of dating, this chapter will first consider *Venus and Adonis* and *The Rape of Lucrece*, and then discuss the Sonnets, with brief mention of *A Lover's Complaint*.[4]

Hunting for love in *Venus and Adonis*

Venus and Adonis and *The Rape of Lucrece* traverse narrative territory familiar to Shakespeare's readers, although each poem acknowledges a quite distinct classical tradition: *Venus and Adonis* being primarily Ovidian in character, and *Lucrece* deriving from Livy's and Ovid's interest in the form of complaint, and unleavened by the comedy of Adonis's prosaic refusal both of Venus, and the hyperbolic states of desire that she represents. That both texts recount and replay stories familiar to early modern readers allows Shakespeare a certain liberty; just as the central characters are literally and fatally transformed by the unpredictable playing out of desire, so Shakespeare transforms his sources through narrative. The emphasis falls on questions of rhetoric, representation, and the relationship between speech, desire, and interpretation: this can occasionally seem contrived or oppressive, but Shakespeare's poetry struggles to maintain any kind of work-able distinction between love and its articulation, insistently returning to questions of how language copes with the complexities of desire and sexu-ality. Equally, language is a potent but unreliable tool in lovers' mouths, and often functions both metaphorically and metonymically for the nature of desire itself.

These texts reveal an interest in the relationship between the verbal and the visual, drawing directly upon the rhetorical category of *ecphrasis*, and posit-ing the relationship between lover and beloved as a dialectic between subject and object.[5] After Lucrece has been raped, she famously reads 'a piece / Of skilful painting' (1366–7) depicting the fall of Troy, looking for emotions analogous to those she has found herself unable to articulate ('more is felt than one hath power to tell' (1288)) and in a highly self-conscious literary moment, she seeks a precedent for her suffering. Lucrece's rape destroys her selfhood, a vestige of which she seeks in the two-dimensional figures represented in the 'painting' – she can only read herself in the other: 'To this well-painted piece is Lucrece come, / To find a face where all distress is stelled' (1443–4). Lucrece literally subjects herself to repesentation, in an ironic echo of the way Tarquin objectifies her. Lucrece's chastity is beyond reproach, her body apparently a closed monument to marital fidelity, an idea reinforced by the seemingly secure and closed chamber in which she sleeps: 'The locks between her chamber and his will, / Each one by him enforced retires his ward' (302–3). This is a cruelly ambiguous image in its proleptic power, as it anticipates the future action through its deployment of double meanings, yet suggests that this action cannot be averted. Lucrece is represented through discursive frameworks that suggest her absence, her negation – a necessary tactic, if she is to be seen as innocent and free from complicity. Tarquin's desire, and determined expectation that it is his right to fulfil it, warps perception, inverts categories. Lucrece's chaste beauty is misread: 'Her hair like golden threads played with her breath, / O modest wantons, wanton modesty!' (400–1). Watched, as she sleeps, Lucrece unknowingly subjects herself to Tarquin's gaze and feeds his desire: 'So o'er this sleeping soul doth Tarquin stay, / His rage of lust by gazing qualified; / Slacked, not suppressed' (423–5). Lust, like love, is a form of disorder, which brings death and destruction in its wake; in *Lucrece* the price of sexual consummation is literally death, for both parties.[6]

Venus and Adonis and *Lucrece* are poetic dilations of a non-consensual sexual act – unconsummated in the case of *Venus and Adonis* – and responses to classical *topoi*. In *Lucrece* this is, superficially, relatively straightforward: Tarquin's lust is inflamed by Lucrece's chaste reputation ('Haply that name of "chaste" unhapp'ly set / This bateless edge on his keen appetite' (8–9)), *and* by her beauty. That beauty can both embody an ideal conjunction of body and soul, an apotheosis of nature's bounty, *and* elicit sinful or transgressive, dark, and violent responses, is one of the central paradoxes of Shakespeare's aesthetic. The 'sexuality' of *Venus and Adonis* is less straightforward, because of Venus's fatal confusion of love with lust. The poem's central conflict is between beauty and love, as Adonis (beauty) persists in the repudiation of Venus (love), but the poem also stages an argument between passion and reason, pitting self-governance against giving emotion free reign. It is tempting to see Venus and Adonis's respective positions as confirming contemporary gender ideologies ('Look how he can, she cannot choose but love' (79)), but this would be to oversimplify. *Eros* and the forms it takes do not map neatly on to sexed roles: Venus is older than the somewhat femin-ized Adonis, whose addiction to the hunt might be read as marking the threshold of adult masculinity; she is a goddess who has held Mars as 'my captive and my slave' (101); she is enthralled by Adonis's beauty as the apotheosis of nature, whilst he inhabits a universe where nature is marked not by its beauty, but by its utility and capacity for sport.

Given his non-compliance with Venus's will, her love becomes a form of self-consumption, of solipsism, and despite Venus's attempts to argue the contrary, there is nothing uplifting or transcendent about her desire for Adonis. It is a misguided attempt at self-fulfilment that turns out to be destructive and debasing, and in a reworking of a favourite classical *locus*, a kind of tragic narcissism:[7]

> And now she beats her heart, whereat it groans,
> That all the neighbour caves, as seeming troubled,
> Make verbal repetition of her moans;
> Passion on passion deeply is redoubled:
>   'Ay me', she cries, and twenty times, 'Woe, woe',
>   And twenty echoes twenty times cry so.   (829–34)

The Ovidian story of Echo and Narcissus is an analogue for the endlessly repetitive nature of unfulfilled desire, as well as suggesting how this all-consuming state collapses established hierarchies and oppositions. The unwillingness of the beloved to accede to the lover's desire mobilizes a favourite argument of Shakespeare's, which is that exceptional beauty is tied to use, that it should be shared, and that to deny it to another is to 'waste' it. *Waste* carries implications of loss, self-consumption, ingratitude, selfishness and sexual expenditure without return, yet allies beauty unequi-vocally with nature. Beauty is nature's art ('Nature that made thee, with herself at strife' (11)) and must be put to use; even if the price is exhausting its source in reproduction.

In *Venus and Adonis* reproduction is cast aside in favour of transforma-tion, which comes at a heavy price. The selfishness of the withholding beloved is again presented through the refracted image of Ovid's Narcissus, where self-love ultimately produces self-negation, without the compensation of an other:

> 'Is thine own heart to thine own face affected?
> Can thy right hand seize love upon thy left?
> Then woo thyself, be of thyself rejected;
> Steal thine own freedom, and complain on theft.
>   Narcissus so himself himself forsook,
>   And died to kiss his shadow in the brook.'   (157–62)

Adonis's refusal of Venus's approaches is presented by him as being due to a *deficit* of self-knowledge, 'Before I know myself, seek not to know me' (525), yet his insistence on the role of active pursuer, rather than passive receptacle of Venus's erotic hunt ('quick desire hath caught the yielding prey, / And glutton-like she feeds, yet never filleth' (547–8)), leads to his dissolution, just as Narcissus' self-consuming passion does. As in Sonnets 1–17, beauty's obligation is to reproduce itself, 'Thou wast begot, to get it is thy *duty*' (168) and 'By *law* of nature thou art *bound* to breed' (171).

Throughout the poem Venus is a supplicant, a pursuer, inverting the hunting metaphor that structures much of the poem; Adonis sets off to chase the boar, yet it is he who is hunted, both physically and rhetorically. It is not simply love that Adonis rejects, but its articulation. This suggests that rhetorical struggle lies at the heart of desire and sexuality, and Shakespeare's poems – like his plays – reveal a preoccupation with the relationship between oratorical power and eroticism, the terms in which this is expressed, and its effect upon its intended object. Speech and language are key elements in Venus's attempted seduction of Adonis; however, these arguments amount to more than the physical, as Venus's interventions attempt to turn Adonis from masculine, homosocial activity to mature sexuality ('Hunting he loved, but love he laughed to scorn' (4)) within the crucible of an untriangulated relationship between Venus and Adonis, which it is the intention of Venus to forge, create, and control. Throughout, Venus is the primary agent of speech, the originator of utterance, although she does not always remain in control of its effects. Shakespeare selects language that threatens through its tendency to impose and project Venus's own – culturally conditioned – version of love and desire. Venus will '*smother* thee with kisses' (18), 'she *seizeth* on his sweating palm' (25), 'She *feedeth* on the steam as on a *prey*' (63), but even her denials suggest danger: 'And yet not *cloy* thy lips with loathed *satiety*, / But rather *famish* them amid their plenty' (19–20; all emphases added). The language is that of excess, an overwhelming quickness of desire in contrast to Adonis's petulant withdrawal, he 'blushed and pouted in a dull disdain, / With leaden appetite, unapt to toy' (33–4).

This formless relationship is marked by fundamental inequalities, of age, of sex, of will: 'Backward she pushed him, as she would be thrust, / And governed him in strength, though not in lust' (41–2). It falls to Venus to give her desire articulate form, and to attempt to mould Adonis to her will: 'Make use of time, let not advantage slip; / Beauty within itself should not be wasted' (129–30). His refusal is presented as self-destruction, even where this destruction comes, ironically, directly from the activity that Adonis chooses in preference to love: ' "So in thyself thyself art made away" ' (763). The form that this attempt at persuasion takes is two-fold, although semantically and conceptually entwined – physicality and verbosity, as demonstrated by Venus's first approach:

> now doth he frown
> And gins to chide, but soon she stops his lips,
>   And kissing speaks, with lustful language broken,
>   'If thou wilt chide, thy lips shall never open.'   (45–8)

Venus's language suggests the plasticity of boundaries and categories, and the way in which lust is a form of disorder, albeit a highly creative one which might alter a thing into its opposite: 'He saith she is immodest, blames her miss; / What follows more she murders with a kiss' (53–4). This is certainly true of *Venus and Adonis*'s structuring trope of hunter and hunted, as pursuit is figured as entrapment – Adonis is 'fastened in her arms', like a bird 'tangled in a net' (68, 67), yet this enforcement does not finally answer Venus's desire, prompting a further turn to rhetoric: 'Still she *entreats*, and *prettily entreats*, / For to a *pretty* ear she tunes her tale' (73–4; emphasis added). As Venus's language fails to convince, she retreats into what are the cultural defaults for female speech: entreating, imitative, lamenting, repetitive.

The attempt to persuade the beloved permits the speaking subject (and the poet) to meditate upon language, words, images, and the limits to representation. Speech and language are crucial to the working out of desire, to its being rendered as part of a power relationship rather than as inchoate and directionless, yet *Venus and Adonis* returns insistently to the failure of language to effect the fulfilment of desire: 'Now which way shall she turn? What shall she say? / Her words are done, her woes the more increasing; / The time is spent, her object will away' (253–5). Venus's language is ultimately a failed speech-act, a set of performative utterances that fail because of the non-receptive nature of the recipient.[8] Adonis is a resisting reader, not only of Venus, but of the argument about putting beauty to use, to submit to love, leading to Venus's own repudiation of the principle that she embodies. Yet the failure of language to produce the desired effect is part of the genius of Shakespeare's poem, as the complexities and ambiguities of articulation effectively map the poem's dynamic binaries, but simultaneously acknowledge their failure. Passion dissolves the very boundary that Adonis wishes to maintain, 'The kiss shall be thine own as well as mine' (117), yet these boundaries consistently reassert themselves in renewed ways. Adonis's bids for escape re-entrap him, and drive him into the arms of an enemy far more destructive than love, because of its lack of regenerative power, and its inability to acknowledge the ennobling power of his beauty.

Just as Shakespeare's poem is preoccupied with the principle of reproduction (Adonis's beauty might be read as the consummate example of

Nature's generative power, to which he is returned), so his poetics are concerned with the attempt to generate *copia*, a principle of style that is both generative and transformative. Adonis utilizes accusations of stylistic torpor to explain his resistance to Venus's oft-trumpeted charms, suggesting that her themes are tired and her language weak. He accuses her of deploying an 'idle over-handled theme' (770), and asserts his ability to resist her language:

> 'If love have lent you twenty thousand tongues,
> And every tongue more moving than your own,
> Bewitching like the wanton mermaid's songs,
> Yet from mine ear the tempting tune is blown;
> For know, my heart stands armèd in mine ear,
> And will not let a false sound enter there.' (775–80)

Adonis, by and large, eschews rhetoric in favour of an integrity that does not require expression (' "More I could tell, but more I dare not say; / The text is old, the orator too green" ' (805–6)); it is the female speaker who runs to language, importuning, lamenting, cursing, yet without an audience: 'Their copious stories, oftentimes begun, / End without audience, and are never done' (845–6). Venus's language is inventive, mobile, and witty, yet finally, impotent, unable to reach the object towards which it constantly gestures, but floundering in a vortex of self-consuming echoes: 'She says, "'Tis so", they answer all, "'Tis so", / And would say after her if she said "No" ' (851–2). Venus's lament mirrors her situation, condemned to repeat rather than to generate.

Violent rhetoric: *The Rape of Lucrece*

The Rape of Lucrece is *not* a poem about love. Like *Venus and Adonis*, *Lucrece* represents a non-consensual sexual act. Its view of love and sexuality is distinct – obviously indebted to the republican classicism of its sources – but concerned with the social and cultural context of sexuality: marriage, family honour, and femininity. Sex in *Lucrece* is unequivocally transgressive, dark, and cruel, with none of the playfulness found in *Venus and Adonis*, and might more fruitfully be compared to the late romances than to the comedies.[9] Its mood and style is more restrained, more *classical* than *Venus and Adonis*, but no less interested in what sexual desire is, its relation to the senses, and its potentially devastating consequences. One innovation of Shakespeare's is to focus on the dynamics of the relationship between Lucrece and Tarquin, looking at self and other, and the scopic economy of the gaze that constructs Lucrece as a 'virtuous monument' (391). The poem shares rhetorical and stylistic ground with *Venus and Adonis*, not least in terms of its deployment of recurrent discourses, hardly surprising given the proximity of the two poems' composition. Here too, passion is seen as essentially disordered but as paradoxically provoked by beauty and virtue, as well as a set of emotions produced by, and productive of, a fundamental power inequality. The form of passion enacted in *Lucrece* is unequivocally non-generative; it is an act of sexual violence, falsely construed by Tarquin as desire in a misguided attempt at self-justification. Tarquin's motivation is not sexual; it is prompted by male competition, and it is a power struggle, not so much with Lucrece herself, but with her husband Collatine, to whom she 'belongs'. From the beginning of the poem, the double sense of *raptus*, as theft and as sexual violation, is implicit; throughout it is rendered explicit through the language of conquest ('Rude ram to batter such an ivory wall' (464)), of entrapment ('do not then ensnare me' (584)), and of material and personal possession ('but she is not her own' (241)). It is Lucrece's credulousness and innocence, together with cultural constructions of femininity and homosociality, that facilitate the rape, and determine its self-negating consequences. Rhetoric here is less an attempt at persuasion, but an extended exercise in imitation and embellishment, in effect a lengthy dilation of the defining act that is the absent centre of the text. Language is an instrument of force, as it registers the inescapable logic of Tarquin's dark desire, and is a wholly inadequate vehicle for the expression of Lucrece's grief at the loss of her chastity, her honour, her self.

The narrative of *The Rape of Lucrece* depends upon a conventional understanding of male and female sexuality. Tarquin is driven by masculine forces that he cannot – or will not – control, as evinced in his frequent acknowledgement that what he desires is wrong, whilst he wilfully reads Lucrece's every word and posture as a kind of collusion in his own dark sexual economy. At the heart of the poem is the staging of moral struggle between the notion that beauty can be read simultaneously as a form of extreme provocation, prompting homosocial competition based in ideas of ownership, and as the outward embodiment of an inner virtue that cannot be compromised by its violation. Whilst Lucrece is seen, and sees herself, as being socially damaged (the idea of honour), the poem makes it clear that Lucrece is innocent. Yet this underlying truth is brought into question by the vulnerability of Lucrece *as a woman*. The only way for her to assert her innocence is to deny agency and selfhood; to speak of what has happened to her is to acknowledge that she is a sexual being, and to take ownership of that being. This undermines the suppositions on which her virtue and innocence are based; that she belongs to her husband Collatine, and that her sexuality is also his possession. Her innocence both marks her virtue and renders that virtue vulnerable to assault. Prior to the rape, she is posited as a naive reader, unable to decipher, or even perceive, the threat that Tarquin poses:

> But she that never coped with stranger eyes,
> Could pick no meaning from their parling looks,
> Nor read the subtle shining secrecies
> Writ in the glassy margents of such books. (99–102)

The poem repeatedly casts Lucrece in relation to material objects – heraldry, treasure, stone, jewels – which alienates her from the events that shape her destiny, and casts these events in a wider social and political frame. The price exacted for Lucrece's indirect agency (the transformation of Rome from monarchy to republic) is the loss of her selfhood.

One of *Lucrece's* prevailing tropes is the inexpressibility *topos*, and in this, the poem reflects and shapes the discourses and consequences surrounding early modern rape. Carolyn D. Williams argues that 'Renaissance presentation of rape victims follows classical tradition in making the victim's body, living or dead, communicate with an eloquence and credibility beyond the range of words'.[10] Yet the only way in which rape can be known – at least within early modern understandings of rape – is through what is *said* about it.[11] The difficulty for Lucrece lies in this process of making known.[12] In the case of *Lucrece*, the situation appears to be relatively unambiguous; the reader is shown the process by which the crime unfolds: intent on the part of Tarquin is clearly established. As in early modern legal definitions of rape, though, the innocence of Lucrece, whilst well established in terms of natural justice, is more ambiguous. The threats that Tarquin deploys to force her to accede to his will are indicative of the double bind that she finds herself in: ' "this night I must enjoy thee. / If thou deny, then force must work my way" ' (512–13). Tarquin's silence is the price of Lucrece's consent, but whilst he can persuade himself that '[t]he fault unknown is as a thought unacted' (527), Lucrece knows that her reputation and social standing depend upon her sexual purity. What for Tarquin is a predetermined act with its own self-fulfilling logic, as he effects a pathological dissociation from the consequences of his actions by projecting the 'fault' on to Lucrece, and by extension on to all women ('The fault is thine'; 'Thy beauty hath ensnared thee to this night' (482, 485)), is for Lucrece the loss not only of her honour, but of her *self*; shortly before she kills herself, she refers to 'she that *was* thy Lucrece' (1682; emphasis added).

To convey the gravity of what has happened to her, Lucrece deploys what might be termed a corporeal rhetoric. Her attempts to speak of her loss of self concentrate upon the bodily, but the bodily as inscribed in language. Once again, this is a question of her lack of agency, and her prior definition as a monument, a body, whether compellingly beautiful and whole, or shattered, broken, and lost. This betrays Lucrece's inability to control how her body makes meaning, and the extent to which this is constructed by others, and by social expectations and norms. Yet this conceptual manoeuvre is necessary for Lucrece's innocence to be incontrovertibly established:

> For men have marble, women waxen minds,
> And therefore are they formed as marble will.
> . . .
> Then call them not the authors of their ill,
>   No more than wax shall be accounted evil
>   Wherein is stamped the semblance of a devil.   (1240–6)

The denial of responsibility is the loss of agency, which explains why Lucrece turns to the classical conventions for lament and grieving in mourning the loss of her self, as well as the violation of her chastity – the concept upon which her social standing, through marriage, rests. As she puts it, she is 'rifled' of the 'true type' of 'loyal wife' (1048–50), thus coalescing the semantic doubleness of the word 'rape', both as theft and as sexual violation. Shakespeare consistently converts one meaning into the other, as Lucrece's chastity is figured as a 'treasure' framed by the 'guiltless casket' of her body (1056–7). Language is represented as inadequate, 'idle words', 'unprofitable sounds, weak arbitrators' (1016–17), necessitating that her violation be written on and through the body.[13]

Shakespeare draws on classical precedent, appropriating the conventions of grief that structure loss of female selfhood, particularly in Ovid. *The Rape of Lucrece* strains after a discourse appropriate to its heroine's calamity, and in true Renaissance fashion, Shakespeare calls upon familiar but resonant parallels, that of Philomela in particular. Philomela's rape by Tereus is also based upon a grim deception and a perversion of hospitality, and concretizes the dilemma of articulation through the figure of the dismembered tongue.[14] Lucrece's tongue is not cut out, but her discourse is compromised, and like Philomela, other means of articulation are sought, not least the disclosure of meaning through Lucrece's dead, self-immolated body. Just as Tarquin's penetration of her body amounts to the loss of self, Lucrece's penetration of her body with the knife results in the loss of life and her transformation into a resonant symbol of male rivalry played out upon the site of the female body; equally, Lucrece's dead body figures forth Tarquin's crime in a way that her words, seemingly, cannot.[15] Lucrece weeps, her eyes 'like sluices' (1076), '[l]ike ivory conduits coral cisterns filling' (1234), wearing away the monument of her body, leading ultimately to the moment of dissolution.

Just as tears are signs that may signify and multiply, Lucrece's words remain elusive, allusive, and cryptic, because she is unable to disclose what has befallen her, even to her maid, her social inferior:

> 'if it should be told,
> The repetition cannot make it less;
> For more it is than I can well express,'   (1284–6)

Lucrece adopts a strategy that allows her to disclose her meaning without directly articulating it; her letter to Collatine announces her as 'that unworthy wife' (1304), and deploys the language of legality that framed early modern responses to the crime of rape. Prior to this scene, Lucrece outlines her bequest, framed by metaphors suggesting that she is violated property: 'Her house is sacked', 'Her sacred temple spotted, spoiled, corrupted', a 'blemished fort' (1170, 1172, 1175). Her resolution to die is presented through legal discourse:

> 'My stainèd blood to Tarquin I'll *bequeath*,
> Which by him tainted shall for him be spent,
> And as his due writ in my *testament*.'
> (1181–3; emphasis added)

Her blood is a 'legacy' (1192), 'my will' (1198). This is not a legal document, but a way of framing the sign that her body will become: '[h]ow Tarquin must be used, *read it in me*' (1195; emphasis added). Lucrece anticipates that the only form of articulation available to her lies in the transformation of her body into a resonant sign, in an ironic reprise of Tarquin's earlier threat that her 'crime' will stain succeeding generations, and that Lucrece '[s]halt have thy trespass cited up in rhymes / And sung by children in succeeding times' (524–5).

This transformation of grief and sorrow into the corporeal finds its most powerful parallel in Shakespeare's description of the pictorial representation of the siege of Troy, which places Lucrece's resolve in a heroic, epic dimension. Her casting around for an adequate vehicle for her grief is an attempt to find an appropriately elevated precedent for the act she is about to commit. It is presented as a means by which Lucrece can find a form of mourning consonant with her loss: 'she her plaints a little while doth stay, / Pausing for means to mourn some newer way' (1364–5). Just as she has lost her life in losing her chastity, the visual narrative she sees gives grief and sorrow a permanent form, 'in scorn of nature, art gave liveless life' (1374). Pronoun shifts make the reader complicit, rather than the detached, voyeuristic observer of the earlier parts of the poem: '[t]here might *you* see' (1380), '*You* might behold' (1388), 'there pleading might *you* see' (1401; emphasis added). She identifies with the tragically resonant figure of Hecuba, who bears 'so much grief and not a tongue' (1463), but it is not Hecuba who is the pivotal figure, but the apotheosis of treachery, Sinon. For Lucrece, Sinon represents the fatal disjunction between inner and outer that led Lucrece not to suspect Tarquin; yet, as she rails against the pictorial representation of Sinon, the futility of her actions suggest her powerlessness to act.

Shortly after the rape, Lucrece begs for daylight not to come:

> 'Make me not object to the tell-tale Day:
> The light will show, charactered in my brow,
> The story of sweet chastity's decay,
> The impious breach of holy wedlock vow.
> Yea, the illiterate, that know not how
>   To cipher what is writ in learnèd books,
>   Will quote my loathsome trespass in my looks.'   (806–12)

When Collatine returns, her suffering has been resolved into narrative, as she retells her rape, often echoing Tarquin's words; just as her sexuality is not her own, neither are the discourses available to describe it. Her weakness is her defence, but Tarquin's lust has undermined the idea that external beauty embodies purity of soul, as this idea is inverted: 'Though my gross blood be stained with this abuse, / Immaculate and spotless is my mind' (1655–6). Whilst Lucrece embodies honour, it is only when the wrong done to her is disclosed that action can be taken, and the true significance of the language of assault and siege becomes clear; at the moment of her death, Lucrece is translated from potent symbol of female suffering and disempowerment into a resonant site of political meaning. Her bleeding body is 'like a late-sacked island' (1740), and represents the natural order in chaos: 'If children predecease progenitors, / We are their offspring, and they none of ours' (1756–7).

You live in this: the Sonnets, poetry, and immortality

Shakespeare's Sonnets are contested texts, and one of the key areas of controversy has been the question of sexuality.[16] Too often, this question has been approached as if it were possible to determine the sexuality of a text, and thus that of its author. Yet as a sustained analysis of the poems quickly reveals, their verbal inventiveness undermines any crude reduction to one sexual orientation or another. Generations of readers have found themselves puzzled, challenged, or offended by Shakespeare's representation of a homoerotic attachment; others have discovered with delight the inscription of desires and urges consonant with their own. The variety of responses suggests something fundamental about the Sonnets, namely the degree to which the reader is involved in the making of meaning, and is imagined to guarantee the immortality of both poems and lover through continual re-creation and rehearsal: 'Your monument shall be my gentle verse, / Which eyes not yet created shall o'er-read, / And tongues to be your being shall rehearse' (Sonnet 81, lines 9–11). The fact that Shakespeare is liberated from the demands of a pre-existing narrative means that the poems reside in a realm of abstraction, which, whilst certainly present in his other poems, does not dominate to the same degree – although it is a feature of many of his greatest dramatic speeches, soliloquies in particular.[17] This is not to say that the Sonnets are immured to the cultural and literary context in which they were shaped; but that they approximate and construct an intimacy often lacking from the narrative poems that can mislead the reader into thinking that these most literary of texts are intensely personal, an illusion sustained by Shakespeare's subtle and shifting usage of the early modern distinction between the pronouns 'thou' and 'you'.[18] Unlike *Venus and Adonis* and *The Rape of Lucrece*, the Sonnets foreground, almost obsessively, the subjectivity and sexuality of the speaker, casting a forensic eye on the effects of desire at the same time as deploying it rhetorically in order to win over the beloved. While the Sonnets are a complete work of art in themselves, one aspect of this artistry is the games of perception that Shakespeare plays with the boundaries between life and art, continually gesturing to an outside that it is left to the reader to construct. Critics have indulged this impulse, positing a range of scenarios external to the poems that are somehow scripted there.[19]

The linguistic virtuosity of Shakespeare's Sonnets can blind the reader to parallels with the other poems, in particular the way that Shakespeare uses the idea of beauty centrally to mark a transition from reproduction as natural and physical to verbal and poetic, such that the poems displace and overwrite their object, rather than supplementing it. The concept of *copia* that provides the stylistic and rhetorical bedrock on which the Sonnets rest presupposes a stable point of reference, whether idea, phrase, or object, that is to be varied and reproduced. Yet Shakespeare significantly extends this idea, so that it is the subject himself who is copious in his beauty; thus verbal ingenuity and variation is the only appropriate response, and these become the reality of love, lover, and beloved. *Copia verborum* is not a means to an end, but fundamental to the aesthetic of the poems, and the ideas of immortality and constancy in variation found there, 'I teach thee how / To make him seem long hence as he shows now' (101.13–14).[20] The Sonnets open with conventional arguments about the obligation of beauty to reproduce itself, in order to transcend age, time, and decay. The promise of immortality is dangled before the reader–lover, and the spectre of self-consuming narcissism hovers over Sonnets 1–17, 'Die single, and thine image dies with thee' (3.14). But this is more complex than a natural obligation to beauty; the lover's obligation is quickly redacted into a power relationship with the speaker, 'Make thee another self for love of me' (10.13), an attenuated way of addressing the non-reproductive character of the sexual desire that the speaker has for the young man. This is represented through a continual verbal undertow of sexual suggestion, and more specifically, sexual shame: *spend, use, waste, abuse* (4). These early Sonnets establish a conventional position, but do so in a proleptic way, establishing the parameters by which the speaker, despite repeated protestations to the contrary, attempts to establish his egotistical monopoly over the beloved's image.

Language and rhetoric are unreliable and plastic media for registering the complexities of desire, beauty, and sexuality, media that the poet struggles to control as the focus shifts from physical to poetic reproduction. This transition is registered through the redeployment of established discourses. In Sonnet 16 the language of sexual reproduction used to convince the young man is dramatically re-crafted to turn poetry into a vehicle for the re-production of the beloved's image. The poet's role is seamlessly grafted on to that of the desiring lover, overturning the separation of object and subject; in constantly recreating the object (and writing becomes a form of fragile and increasingly convoluted constancy) the poet possesses and controls the object; yet the poet relentlessly reflects upon himself and the effects of his words (Sonnets 22 and 24). This collapse of self into other centres on the effort to maintain control over the beloved's image, and the distortions that desire effects: ''Tis thee (my self) that for myself I praise, / Painting my age with beauty of thy days' (62.13–14).[21]

The desire to possess the beloved translates into a desire to control his image, to fuse desire and poetry together to represent a love that transcends time, death, decay. Claiming that 'this time's pencil or my pupil pen / Neither in inward worth nor outward fair / Can make you live yourself in eyes of men' (16.10–12), Shakespeare deploys the humility *topos*, not only to elevate the beauty and desirability of the beloved, but his own skill at depicting these. Shakespeare continually re-imagines this relationship, working up to an ideal of poetic immortality that has *his* verse as its object , 'So long lives this, and this gives life to thee' (18.14). Poetry becomes a kind of prophylactic against time and the decay of beauty, imaged as the loving attentions of future readers: 'His beauty shall in these black lines be seen, / And they shall live, and he in them still green' (63.13–14). The idea of the Sonnets as an enduring monument depends upon an imagined audience beyond the triangle of poet–friend–lover; yet also requires that the lover's image remains in excess of the poet's capacity to represent it. The poet's task is framed not in terms solely of *ars*, the craft of making, but in terms of the emotional sincerity of the speaker: 'O let me, true in love, but truly write, / And then believe me' (21.9–10).[22] The Sonnets envisage a reader who will accede to the poet's vision and collude in his assertion of the beloved's exceptional beauty; the reader is positioned so as to dilate and preserve the young man's image, and thus is intrinsic to the Sonnets' method.

The uniqueness of the beloved creates an extraordinary pressure on representation, such that issues relating to poetry are virtually co-extensive with sexual desire itself. This is manifested through language and scenarios that can signify and multiply. In Sonnet 76, for example, the language of reproduction that dominates the early part of the sequence is reworked. The alleged monotony of the poet's idiom ('Why is my verse so barren of new pride?' (76.1)) is marshalled to the end of constancy. Poetic reproduction is likened to sexual reproduction:

> Why write I still all one, ever the same,
> And keep invention in a noted weed,
> That every word almost doth tell my name,
> Showing their birth, and where they did proceed?   (76.5–8)[23]

The exhaustion of the medium of poetry is paralleled with sexual exhaustion and expenditure, 'So all my best is dressing old words new, / Spending again what is already spent' (76.11–12). The poems addressing rival poets also constitute a form of mimetic possession, as the poet reasserts his superior claim to the beloved: 'be most proud of that which I compile, / Whose influence is thine, and born of thee' (78.9–10), often through paradox or contradiction. The poet presents *his* work in terms of primacy and proximity; *their* efforts are faulty copies that steal from the beloved without adequate return:

> Yet what of thee thy poet doth invent
> He robs thee of, and pays it thee again:
> He lends thee virtue, and he stole that word
> From thy behaviour.   (79.7–10)

Articulation, repetition, and silence are stances, marshalled to the end of proclaiming the poet's superiority in love, and suggest an interiority that remains in excess of the poet's capacity to represent it: 'I love not less, though less the show appear: / That love is merchandised whose rich esteeming / The owner's tongue doth publish every where' (102.2–4).

The articulations of love in the Sonnets relate more to the effects of sexuality than to sexuality itself. The sequence is remarkably unconcerned with the poet's choice of love-object, concentrating instead on the meanings and agonies of desire.[24] The Sonnets unequivocally posit the speaker as male, and the object of his affections as also male: even in the dark lady sonnets, the primary love-object is the young man: 'The better angel is a man right fair; / The worser spirit a woman coloured ill' (144.3–4). The terms that are used to describe him tap into the early modern lexicon surrounding sodomitical relationships, and participate in the slippery definitions and distinctions that attempted to both articulate and demarcate such relationships: youth, friend, dear, my love, slave, lord, sovereign, 'deceivèd husband' (93.2).[25] Like other writers who attempted to write of homoerotic desire, Shakespeare's language wheels away into a wider set of discourses; yet the ambiguity of reference permits Shakespeare to elevate this desire into a transcendent aesthetic force. The Sonnets reveal a great deal of ambivalence in relation to desire, and sexual desire in particular; yet the expression of sexual shame usually relates more to how it makes the poet behave than to the posited object of desire – Shakespeare's famous sonnet on the corrosive effects of lust (129) is found in the midst of the dark lady sonnets. The poet's concern for the beloved's reputation, as well as his own, suggests less that love is a source of shame, but a struggle to fully encompass the beloved's virtues, virtues that are primarily but not exclusively aesthetic. As Shakespeare imagines his lover's view of him after his death, there is an ambivalent drive towards both assertion and denial that serves to impress upon the reader the virtues of the beloved: 'you in me can nothing worthy prove, / Unless you would devise some virtuous lie / To do more for me than mine own desert' (72.4–6).

A Lover's Complaint is linked to, but generically distinct from the Sonnets, and explores the negative effects of desire in the context of the sexual vulnerability of a young woman. The poem reveals a telling interest in the complexities of voicing and narration, and looks at the conventions surrounding love and its articulation with a critical cynicism. The maiden's powerlessness and loss of status are structurally figured through a series of framing narrators, such that just as the maiden finds herself subjected to the spurious persuasions of the young man, her words fail to find unmediated expression. Like many other complaint poems – a popular form in the Renaissance – *A Lover's Complaint* narrates the effects for a woman of the loss of reputation contingent upon abandonment. As in the narrative poems, loss and grief take conventional forms: tears, dishevelment, a focus on the material remains of a broken relationship. The maiden throws away '[a] thousand favours' (36), tears up written tokens of love: 'Of folded schedules had she many a one, / Which she perused, sighed, tore, and gave the flood' (43–4). Yet such abjection also seeks an audience; love, even thwarted love, requires articulation. In *A Lover's Complaint* much of the focus is on the appropriate context in which such an audience might be found; her interlocutor is a secular father–confessor, a reformed man atoning for his own misspent youth. It is crucial to the telling of the tale that appropriate decorum is observed: 'comely distant sits he by her side' (65). Her story, then, is multiply framed: the narrator of the poem ('down I laid to list the sad-tuned tale' (4)); the 'reverend man' (57), and her complaint is a cautionary tale about the deleterious effects of the rhetoric of love. As such, it is of a piece with Shakespeare's repeated scrutiny of the language of desire, and serves – to an extent – to destabilize and undermine some of the structuring assumptions of the Sonnets.

In *A Lover's Complaint* the reader once again encounters a beautiful youth: 'Each eye that saw him did enchant the mind, / For on his visage was in little drawn / What largeness thinks in Paradise was sawn' (89–91). The youth's undoubted beauty is augmented by charm to the extent that both men and women abdicate their will to him: 'Consents bewitched, ere he desire, have granted, / And dialogued for him what he would say, / Asked their own wills, and made their wills obey' (131–3). As such, the poem is a cautionary tale about the deceptions of beauty, and the dangers of assuming a consonance between outer appearance and inner reality. Equally, the poem suggests the way in which desire makes the lover construct the love-object subjectively, and delusionally: ' "So many have ... / Sweetly *supposed* them mistress of his heart" ' (141–2; emphasis added). The maiden knows, rationally, of the youth's reputation, but her desire leads her to believe his own protestations that ' "All my offences that abroad you see / Are errors of the blood, none of the mind" ' (183–4), allying the poem both with the self-deceptions of the speaker of the Sonnets, and with Tarquin's attempts to dissociate himself from his crime. The youth might be read as an ironic counterpoint to the young man in the Sonnets, as he boasts of the love tokens and trophies he has received, including 'deep-brained sonnets' (209). He callously echoes the arguments of the Sonnets as he suggests that '[n]ature hath charged me that I hoard them [the desires of others] not, / But yield them up where I myself must render' (220–1), and manipulates the language of love to his own short-term advantage, flattering the maiden with the fleeting illusion of his own subjection to her, 'you o'er me being strong' (257). *A Lover's Complaint* is a complex text that distils the multiple discourses of Shakespeare's love poetry into a devastating critique of the effects of the language of love.

Conclusion

Shakespeare's poems are not a unified body of work; they are generically and stylistically varied, whilst deploying a distinctive lexicon for love and desire

Love, beauty, and sexuality

that is to some extent present in the dramatic corpus as well. They are not unequivocally love poems, seeking instead to register the vagaries and agonies of states of desire for the delight or edification of readers who are envisaged as central to the process of making meaning. These texts are often strange, quirky, and quixotic, yet able to speak to readers whatever their experience. The Sonnets have proved more sympathetic to modern minds – *Venus and Adonis* and *The Rape of Lucrece* are more obviously marked by the conventions and assumptions of their time. It is important to register how daringly radical Shakespeare's poems actually are; at the same time as they thoroughly acknowledge, and indeed depend on, the prevalent discourses of the early modern period, they are refreshingly non-institutional. None of the sexual relationships depicted are marital, not all of them are even conventionally heterosexual; Shakespeare pushes at the boundaries of what it means to love, to perceive beauty, and what love and beauty do to both lover and beloved.

Equally unconventional is what Shakespeare does with inherited assumptions structuring the creation of poetry; instead of mere imitation (a particular problem in relation to sonnet sequences and *epyllia*) Shakespeare radicalizes his medium, turning love itself into a representational problem. The slipperiness and fragility of love and desire are not simply described or even depicted here; rather they structure the very act of representation, which may be one of the many reasons why Shakespeare's love poems have been so amenable to repeated reincarnation, such that time is turned on its head, and memory becomes, paradoxically, eternally present in the minds and hearts of readers:

> So all their praises are but prophecies
> Of this our time, all you prefiguring, ...
> ... For we, which now behold these present days
> Have eyes to wonder, but lack tongues to praise.
>
> (106.9–10, 13–14)

NOTES

1 See essays by Valerie Traub in *The Cambridge Companion to Shakespeare*, ed. Margreta de Grazia (Cambridge University Press, 2001); by Catherine Bates and Barbara Hogden in *The Cambridge Companion to Shakespearean Comedy*, ed. Alexander Leggatt (Cambridge University Press, 2001); and by Catherine Belsey on 'Gender and the Family' in *The Cambridge Companion to Shakespearean Tragedy*, ed. Claire McEachern (Cambridge University Press, 2003).

2 For example, Macbeth's repeated over-reading of the signs of nature as interpretive of, and prophetic of, his own destiny.

3 See Stephanie Jed, *Chaste Thinking: 'The Rape of Lucretia' and the Birth of Humanism* (Bloomington: Indiana University Press, 1989).

4 Space prohibits further discussion of 'The Phoenix and Turtle'. For dating and publication history, see Roe (ed.), *The Poems*; and for the Sonnets, see *Shakespeare's Sonnets*, ed. Katherine Duncan-Jones, Arden 3rd series (London: Thomas Nelson, 1997), pp. 1–28.

5 See Murray Krieger, *Ecphrasis: The Illusion of the Natural Sign* (Baltimore: Johns Hopkins University Press, 1992).

6 Useful comparisons can be drawn with Shakespeare's representation of the moral, verbal, and political consequences of rape in *Titus Andronicus* and of the *idea* of rape in *Cymbeline*.

7 See Ovid, *Metamorphoses*, trans. Arthur Golding, ed. Madeleine Forey (Harmondsworth: Penguin, 2002), Book 3. See Jonathan Bate, *Shakespeare and Ovid* (Oxford: Clarendon Press, 1994), ch. 2.

8 See J. L. Austin, *How to Do Things with Words* (Oxford: Clarendon Press, 1962).

9 *Cymbeline* and *The Winter's Tale*, for example.

10 ' "Silence, like a Lucrece knife": Shakespeare and the Meanings of Rape', *Yearbook of English Studies* 23 (1993), 92–110: pp. 106–7.

11 See the comments of Matthew Hale, in *Pleas of the Crown*, quoted in Deborah G. Burks, ' "I'll want my will else": *The Changeling* and Women's Complicity with their Rapists', *ELH* 62 (1995), 759–90: p. 789 n. 41.

12 See Laura Gowing, *Common Bodies: Women, Touch and Power in Seventeenth-Century England* (New Haven: Yale University Press, 2003), ch. 3.

13 See Page de Bois, *Sowing the Body: Psychoanalysis and Ancient Representations of Women* (University of Chicago Press, 1988).

14 See Book 6, in Ovid, *Metamorphoses*.

15 See, for an illuminating reading of Philomela's rape, Jane O. Newman, ' "And let mild women to him lose their mildness": Philomela, Female Violence, and Shakespeare's *The Rape of Lucrece*', *Shakespeare Quarterly* 45 (1994), 304–26.

16 For informed and balanced accounts, see Duncan-Jones (ed.), *Shakespeare's Sonnets*, 45–69; John Kerrigan (ed.), *'The Sonnets' and 'A Lover's Complaint'* (Harmondsworth: Penguin, 1986); and G. Blakemore Evans (ed.), *The Sonnets* (Cambridge University Press, 1996), pp. 15–18. See also Peter Stallybrass, 'Editing as Cultural Formation: The Sexing of Shakespeare's Sonnets', *Modern Language Quarterly* 54 (1993), 91–103. More recent 'queer' reclamations of Shakespeare include Bruce R. Smith, *Homosexual Desire in Shakespeare's England: A Cultural Poetics* (University of Chicago Press, 1991), pp. 226–70; and Gregory W. Bredbeck, *Sodomy and Interpretation: Marlowe to Milton* (Ithaca: Cornell University Press, 1991), pp. 167–80.

17 E.g. *Lear*, parts of *Hamlet*, *Cymbeline*.

18 See Roger Lass, *The Cambridge History of the English Language*, 6 vols. (Cambridge University Press, 1999), III: 148–55.

19 A. L. Rowse (ed.), *Shakespeare's Sonnets* (London: Macmillan, 1973), is probably the most famous example.

20 See George Pigman III, 'Versions of Imitation in the Renaissance', *Renaissance Quarterly* 33 (1980), 1–32.

21 See also Sonnets 40, 133–4.

22 See also Sonnet 32.7, 14: 'Reserve them for my love, not for their rhyme'; 'Theirs for their style I'll read, his for his love'.

23 On this common Renaissance trope, found in the opening sonnet of Sidney's *Astrophil and Stella*, see Katharine Eisaman Maus, 'A Womb of His Own: Male Renaissance Poets in the Female Body', in *Sexuality and Gender in Early Modern Europe: Institutions, Texts, Images*, ed. James Grantham Turner (Cambridge University Press, 1993), pp. 266–88.

24 This frankness has caused great discomfort to generations of readers, necessitating a series of complex explanations, interventions, and editorial meddlings – see Duncan-Jones (ed.), *Shakespeare's Sonnets*, pp. 29–45.

25 See Danielle Clarke, ' "The sovereign's vice begets the subject's error" ', in Tom Betteridge (ed.), *Sodomy in Early Modern Europe* (Manchester University Press, 2002), pp. 46–64.

READING LIST

Belsey, Catherine. 'Tarquin Dispossessed: Expropriation and Consent in *The Rape of Lucrece*'. *Shakespeare Quarterly* 52 (2001), 315–35.

Booth, Stephen. *An Essay on Shakespeare's Sonnets*. New Haven: Yale University Press, 1969.

Dubrow, Heather. *Captive Victors: Shakespeare's Narrative Poems and Sonnets*. Ithaca: Cornell University Press, 1987.

Duncan-Jones, Katherine (ed.). *Shakespeare's Sonnets*. Arden 3rd series. London: Thomas Nelson, 1997.

Felperin, Howard. *The Uses of the Canon: Elizabethan Literature and Contemporary Theory*. Oxford: Clarendon Press, 1990.

Fineman, Joel. *Shakespeare's Perjured Eye: The Invention of Poetic Subjectivity in the Sonnets*. Berkeley: University of California Press, 1986.

Kerrigan, John (ed.). *'The Sonnets' and 'A Lover's Complaint'*. Harmondsworth: Penguin, 1986.

Maus, Katharine Eisaman. 'Taking Tropes Seriously: Language and Violence in Shakespeare's *Rape of Lucrece*'. *Renaissance Quarterly* 37 (1986), 66–82.

Newman, Jane O. '"And let mild women to him lose their mildness": Philomela, Female Violence, and Shakespeare's *The Rape of Lucrece*'. *Shakespeare Quarterly* 45 (1994), 304–26.

Stallybrass, Peter. 'Editing as Cultural Formation: The Sexing of Shakespeare's Sonnets'. *Modern Language Quarterly* 54 (1993), 91–103.

Vendler, Helen. *The Art of Shakespeare's Sonnets*. Cambridge, MA: Harvard University Press, 1997.

11

HEATHER JAMES

Shakespeare and classicism

According to one of the great commonplaces of Shakespeare studies, we owe *Venus and Adonis, The Rape of Lucrece*, and possibly Shakespeare's first thoughts of the Sonnets to an outbreak of the plague: the city officials of London, ever hostile to the theatres, leapt to close down the playhouses in 1592, leaving Shakespeare to seek alternative ways to earn his living. The plague that closed the theatres is a matter of historical record, and yet its prominence in accounts of the poetic origins of *Venus and Adonis* and *The Rape of Lucrece* betrays a curious hint of embarrassment about the narrative poems. This story of creative origins fuels a critical suspicion that Shakespeare was never entirely at home with a poetic genre that is studded with classical learning and rhetorical artifice; he only fully thrived when the quarantine was lifted and he was able to exchange the legendary and mythological figures of the past for live actors. The Sonnets, which efface their debts to classical models, seem to confirm the point that overt classicism constricted Shakespeare's creative genius. By modern standards, the narrative poems fail where his other genres prosper: they lack the frank charm of the Sonnets and the imaginative scope of the plays. They do, however, win the consolation prize of undeniable historical importance: *Venus and Adonis* went through nine lifetime editions, while *The Rape of Lucrece* went through five.

Recent criticism has done much to defend the narrative poems on the grounds of their thematic variety, rhetorical ingenuity, and power to move the minds and senses of readers. Shakespeare's commitment to classicism, however, has not received a similarly careful re-evaluation. Reasons for such critical neglect are not far to seek. The classicizing imagination has yet to recover fully from two blows dealt by literary history: the neoclassical penchant for regulating literary and dramatic forms (at the expense of invention) and the subsequent rejection of prescriptive traditions in the Romantic period. Classicism continues to labour under the suspicion that it is more likely to inhibit than inspire creative innovation. This concept, however, was alien to London of the 1590s, when young and witty intellectuals were reaching for the classics and especially for the 'counter-classical' love poet, Ovid, in a self-conscious effort to transform the literary scene. Classicism held the key to a new rather than an old aesthetic, one based on bold experimentation with poetic conventions.[1]

The result was an outpouring of narrative poems that rejected a straightforward identification with moral purpose and took Ovidian themes as their point of departure. Poems such as Thomas Lodge's *Scyllaes Metamorphosis*, Christopher Marlowe's sensual *Hero and Leander*, Thomas Nashe's bawdy *Choice of Valentines*, and John Marston's sensational *Metamorphosis of Pigmalion's Image* flaunted their 'toying' and 'trifling' status. The point was not to trivialize poetry. To the contrary, the poets of the Elizabethan avant-garde sought to revisit the foundational rules of poetry and revive elements of its persuasive powers. They raised searching questions about the rules and prerogatives of poetry: what subjects made for a good poem, what style or form made for compelling representation, and how far might poets go in testing the bounds of decorum?

In short, they asked the same questions that the Roman poet Horace had posed in his celebrated *Art of Poetry* and, led by their commitment to Ovid as an innovator in poetic form, came to somewhat different conclusions. Horace affirmed the duty of poetry to instruct and delight, a proposal that Elizabethans readily endorsed, although they did not share a uniform understanding of the nature and ideal balance of the two. Horace simultaneously urged a rationalization of poetic form, encouraging poets to give up the monstrosities of the archaic imagination (such as the centaurs and sirens of Homeric myth) and cultivate an aesthetic based on verisimilitude. Rather than passively accepting the Horatian ideal of decorum as it had come down through the centuries, the Elizabethan poets of the 1590s approached it in the spirit of audacious play associated with Ovid, whose poetry tested the boundaries of form and, in the *Metamorphoses*, eschewed realism to focus on the wondrous and strange.

In view of the ambitious and imaginative uses to which the younger Elizabethans put classicism, it seems unlikely that Shakespeare was casting about for an alternative to drama when the plague broke out and closed the theatres. He may have been looking for an excuse to try his hand at narrative poetry in the classical style. By publishing *Venus and Adonis* in 1593, he was ahead of the curve. Only the poems by Lodge and Marlowe were already in circulation. Shakespeare, in short, helped to place classicism at the heart of debates over the scope and limits of poetic imagination and expression.

The anti-classical prejudice

The vogue for wanton versions of classical poetry and myth had multiple sources. One impetus came, with delicious irony, from the rise of strenuous opposition among moral conservatives to the presence of pagan themes in the schoolroom, on the poetic page, and on the stage. To understand why the classics were seen as dangerous – especially to boys and women – we might consider the case of a youth in *Eunuchus*, a Roman comedy by Terence, who was a mainstay of the humanist curriculum. The youth, Chaerea, disguises himself as a eunuch in order to infiltrate the company of courtesans and get close to a young woman, whom he mistakenly believes is a prostitute. Chaerea finds his chance and he rapes her, led (as he says) by his contemplation of a picture on a mythological subject that happened to be in the room where he and the young woman sat: the subject of the painting was the rape of Danäe, a mortal woman to whom Jove came as a shower of gold. Inspired by the god's example, Chaerea followed precedent.

In Shakespeare's day, this troubling scene illustrated all too vividly that the classics held a dangerous sway over the imagination and were thus far more likely to erode than build up moral principles in schoolboys. Terence does not propose the youth as a model: his Chaerea manifestly abuses the ideal of education through imitation. But Terence's pedagogical meditations do him no good in the Renaissance, since his textual and theatrical medium participates in the corruption of morals. His play, whether it is put on stage or read in the classroom, gathers together the powers of visual and rhetorical figures in a manner calculated to seduce young men. Terence's text illustrates the effects of the careless disregard in which both the theatre and classical rhetoric seem to hold the truth, for both are concerned with persuasion rather than truth-telling. The sensational displays of the theatre have their counterpart in the figural language of classical rhetoric, which cultivates social agency through the use of persuasive tropes or figures of speech. This reading found support from St Augustine, who saw the rape of Danae as an analogue for Chaerea's seduction by divinely potent language.

If saints wrestled with the classics, what chance did schoolboys have? It was far from clear how schoolmasters might train boys to use classical resources but withstand their seductive force. In 1578, for example, the schoolmaster John Stockwood complained about 'what horrible beastly Authors are taught in some schooles' and urged censorship: he informed Elizabethan parents (in words he lived to regret) that 'you had I think rather see your children murthered and slaine before your eyes, then that ... their tender minds shoulde be noursled up and infected with such lothsome filth [and] deadly poison' (K5^v).[2] Stockwood feared the boldness with which pagan writers exposed 'things most secret in man and woman' (K5ᵛ) and suggested they be sent back to Italy, the home of seduction: 'let *Tibullus, Catullus, Propertius, Gallus, Martialis*, a greate parte of *Ouid*, with the most horrible beastlines of *Priapus* ioyned too the end of euery *Virgil*, togither withal other filthy *Poets* & comedies, be sent again to Rome fro[m] whe[n]ce they firste came' (K6ʳ). Although Stockwood's fears sound extreme to modern ears, the Privy Council of 1582 seemed to agree, where one of the offending poets was concerned, and it issued a ban on teaching Ovid's more scandalous poems in the schools'.[3] In 1585, complaints about the 'unprofitable and idell pamphlets, leud and wanton discourse of love, prophane ballades [and] lying historie[s]' associated with the classics were heard even in parliament, and Ovid was again singled out for blame.[4]

It is tempting to dismiss the extremes of anti-classical sentiment, especially when one contrasts them with the moderation or advocacy of Roger Asham, Sir Thomas Elyot, William Webbe, and Sir Philip Sidney. Even a Calvinist such as Arthur Golding found it possible to translate Ovid, arguing that readers are responsible for looking past the 'strange and delectable' fables that outwardly compose Ovid's *Metamorphoses* for the 'wholesome hestes and precepts' that constitute its interior and allegorical life.[5] But the laments of cantankerous Elizabethans also turn up in more private and plangent forms, such as diaries. Samuel Woodford, the poet and translator of the psalms, looked back with shame and regret on his education in the classics, which he confessed he preferred to 'more serious studies ... of the holy scriptures & other good bookes' and associated with 'the greatest extrauagances imaginable' in his university days.[6] In retrospect, the exposure to classical influences helped him to realize 'how dangerous liberty was' and to long for more restraints. Woodford's self-reproach is a far cry from the hectoring pamphlets of the Elizabethan period. But his view of the classics is consistent with that of Philip Stubbes, who regarded them all as 'Hethenicall pamphlets of toyes and bableries ... to corrupt mens mindes, pervert good wits, allure to Bawdry, induce to whoredome, suppresse vertue and erect vice'.[7]

Once out of the schoolroom, Londoners were nowhere more at risk than in the playhouses: pamphleteers such as Stubbes, Stephen Gosson, and William Prynne objected in the strongest terms to the theatre, which distracted the populace with 'vain' and 'idle' entertainments and, just as dangerously, created a public space in which men and women, as well as the various social classes, mingled promiscuously.[8] It appalled moral reformers that the playhouses drew larger assemblies than the parish churches, even on Sundays. It was worse to contemplate the wanton scenarios spread out on the stage: the theatre could seduce the masses with a pagan myth, such as the tale of

Bacchus' courtship of Ariadne.[9] As the pamphleteers reveal, the anti-theatrical prejudice intersects with an anti-classical prejudice. The very name of London's first playhouse received special notice for its pagan roots: it was 'The Theatre', named 'euen after the maner of the olde heathenish Theatre at Rome, a shew place of al beastly & filthye matters'.[10] According to the sermonizers and pamphleteers, the theatre offered unseemly mixtures not only of the social orders and the sexes but also of the ideas, faiths, and epistemologies of historical eras best kept separate.

Risks to women came not only from the public theatres but also from the ill-managed home: danger lay even in the private activities of reading and daydreaming.[11] Thomas Salter, for example, thought no woman should be allowed to read the 'Lascivious bookes of *Ouide*' and the other erotic elegists such as Catullus, Propertius, and Tibullus. Even the moral aims of classical books were ruined for women's uses, since all such books contain allusions to the stories of 'the filthie love (if I maie terme it love) of the Goddes themselves, and of thir wicked adulteries and abhominable fornications' to be found in Greco-Roman myth.[12] Because Virgil's *Aeneid* dwells on the affair of Dido and Aeneas, it is unsuitable for women. It does not matter that the epic presents the liaison between the Carthaginian queen and the founder of the Roman empire as a threat to both of their states: the episode may still prompt women's minds to wander into wanton territory. Salter's radical conclusion was that women should not be taught to read. Yet even the advocates of female education had reservations about the good fit of reading and chaste discipline. We consequently find Juan Luis Vives recommending a generous selection of religious texts for women but adding a warning to fathers and husbands: 'let her have no bookes of Poetry'.[13]

Back talk

The anti-classical prejudice had the unintended result of encouraging parody, satire, and further experimentation with 'idell pamphlets' and 'leud and wanton discourse of love'. A single example from the drama may illustrate the wit that zealous moralists inspired in the acting companies and, simultaneously, the lasting popularity of poems in the Ovidian style. In Thomas Middleton's comedy, *A Mad World, My Masters* (1608), a ludicrously jealous husband steps into the place of the careful householder, who is so often exhorted in sermons to keep his wife, daughter, and servants under watch. Middleton's aptly named Harebrain, suspicious of his young wife, gets himself into trouble by trying to control every aspect of her conduct, from her chastity to her reading habits and dreams. 'I have convey'd away all her wanton pamphlets, as *Hero and Leander, Venus and Adonis*; oh, two luscious mary-bone pies for a young married wife' (1.2.47), Harebrain confides to Gullman, the dubious stranger he hires to worm his way into his wife's confidences and induce her to read matter more suitable for 'a young married wife'.[14] Harebrain's choice is a handbook on repentance, written by the Jesuit Robert Parsons and popularly known as the *Resolutions*. With this book, Gullman is to accost Harebrain's wife and 'Terrify her, terrify her; go, read to her the horrible punishments for itching wantonness, the pains allotted for adultery; tell her her thoughts, her very dreams are answerable' (1.2).[15]

Working on the theory that erotic poetry is a bad thing for marriage, Middleton's Harebrain steals Shakespeare's and Marlowe's poems from his wife; meanwhile, a different type of fool in another play keeps his copy of *Venus and Adonis* under his pillow. Gullio of the second *Parnassus* play has heard that an ancient king kept Homer's *Iliad* under his pillow for inspiration, and he apparently hopes that Shakespeare's sexy poem will help him make 'long Iliads' in the war between the sexes, as the Roman elegist Propertius did with his mistress.[16] Although the impressionable Gullio and tyrannical Harebrain represent opposing attitudes towards Shakespeare's narrative poem, neither thinks of the one sensible thing to do with it, which is, of course, to read and re-read it.

Harebrain is correct on one point: Shakespeare's *Venus and Adonis* belongs in the company of Marlowe's audacious *Hero and Leander*, which interprets classical poetry as an unabashed invitation to sensual pleasure. In this poem, Marlowe amplifies the seduction of his short lyric, 'The Passionate Shepherd to his Love', again at the expense of its moral use. Horace had presented the duties of poetry to instruct and delight as coequal, but profit had gradually won out over pleasure during the centuries of poetic theory that separated the Elizabethans from the ancient Romans. Marlowe reverses the trend: why should he instruct, Shakespeare's bold contemporary implicitly asks, when he can tease, delight, and dominate his readers with the impunity of a pagan god? Marlowe consequently chose an explicitly erotic theme from classical myth, varied it to titillate and outrage readers, and broke off his poem just after his bold Leander and blushing Hero consummate their mutual passions. Marlowe offers no account of the mythic lovers' tragic deaths and shows no interest in the moral consequences of erotic and rhetorical forms of dalliance (lovemaking and sweet talk). Even his digressions elaborate those features of classical mythology that the moralists detested: his description of the temple of Venus, for instance, presents the fully *un*reformed pagan 'gods in sundry shapes, / Committing heady riots, incest, rapes'.[17]

It is into this heated scene of representation and debate that Shakespeare stepped. The incentives to take up classical materials were strong and

Shakespeare rose to the challenges posed by his contemporaries. Yet his distinctive contribution to the emerging poetic agenda was to foreground the challenge of the past over the present. As Shakespeare casts the scene of imitation, the modern poet who takes up classical themes discovers a double injunction. On the one hand, he must preserve the past through painstaking *imitation*: he must make it 'live in ... memory', to quote Shakespeare's Hamlet (2.2.406), by etching its words on the tablet of his mind. On the other hand, he faces an equally insistent demand to sustain the life of the classical past through *invention*, reviving the old by making it new. Shakespeare derives his sense of the ancients' absolute claim on poetic memory from the kind of imitation associated with Rome's greatest epic poet, Virgil, and uses it chiefly in *The Rape of Lucrece*. He associates his sense of a challenge to 'invent' with freer hand from Rome's greatest love poet, Ovid, and uses this mode in *Venus and Adonis* and other poems.

The classic boast

Shakespeare words his dedication of *Venus and Adonis* to Henry Wriothesley, earl of Southampton, with conventional modesty. His epigraph, by contrast, issues an extravagant boast, grandly printed in Latin as the language of the elite:

> Vilia miretur vulgus: mihi flavus Apollo
> Pocula Castalia plena ministret aqua.
> ('Let what is cheap excite the marvel of the crowd;
> for me may golden Apollo minister full
> cups from the Castalian fount.')[18]

According to this large boast, Shakespeare gets his poetic inspiration from the highest source, and, moreover, the cupbearer who brings him the waters of the Castalian fount (sacred to the muses) is the god of poetry, Apollo. It is no slight to the scale of his ambition to note that the boast derives from Ovid's first book of love elegies, the *Amores*. Shakespeare is asserting his ambitions as an Ovidian poet, after all, and so it is fitting for him to choose words from an Ovidian text for the epigraph to his poem. His boldness lies in taking over the words with which Ovid first asserted his claim to poetic immortality. By choosing Ovid's boast as his own, Shakespeare both confirms and rivals Ovid's poetic status, just as Ovid swapped places with Apollo as his source of inspiration.

The poetic commodity Ovid has to offer is his reputation for poetic genius that transcends his erotic subjects and slender genres. The demonstration of 'talent to burn' was the hallmark of Ovid's career, and he lavished his gifts on disreputable aspects of urban life (i.e., sex in the city). Shakespeare had reason to hope that Ovidian insouciance about erotic themes and established authorities (for example, Apollo and Augustus) would appeal to the earl of Southampton, who had taken his own bold steps in resisting his social superiors in matters of sex, love, and marriage.[19] No classical precedent was more congenial to the purpose of evading the state's reach into private affairs. From the beginning of his career, Ovid refused to compose poetry of state and instead created a market for poetic genres he passed off as 'games', 'trifles', and 'toys'.

Ovid began the *Amores* with the claim that he tried and failed to dedicate his Muse to the public genres of Augustan Rome. By his own admission, he was trying to put together an epic poem and was throwing around heavy metres and warlike themes when the god of love, Cupid, laughingly stole a foot from his epic metre and reduced the poet's genre to erotic elegy. In the remainder of his first book, Ovid lives down to his light genre by dedicating elegies to such domestic tragedies as daybreak (unwelcome to a lover in bed), the closed and guarded door to his girlfriend's bedroom, her alarming request for cash, and her hair loss due to a bad chemical treatment. It is not obvious that the poet will conclude such a book of elegies by claiming a place among the Greek and Latin poets who created or redefined entire genres. On what grounds, his readers must ask, does the poet assume his status as the peer of Homer, Sophocles, Aratus, and Menander as well as Lucretius, Virgil, and the earlier Latin elegists? Ovid's toying poems do not obviously lead to a claim of their power to endure through time alongside of the *Iliad*, *Odyssey*, and *Aeneid*.

Ovid's bravura performance in trifling verse illustrates his view that the immortal part of poets rests in the non-conformist elements of their poetry and not the decorum that moulds poetic expression to state interests. In the elegy from which Shakespeare quotes, *Amores* 1.15, Ovid articulates the political view that no citizen should be obligated to 'prostitute' his voice in the 'ungrateful forum' (6), whether the speech for hire belongs to statesmen, lawyers, or poets. Ovid starkly contrasts his goals with those of soldiers, politicians, and lawyers, who have chosen the approved careers for men in Rome.[20] By the poem's end, he calls on 'kings and king's triumphs' to 'yield' to the songs of poets (33). Ovid's trifling elegies, in short, formulate a high-minded view of poetry and a polemic about the liberties of subjects.[21] Shakespeare chose a potent Ovidian epigram to serve as a programme statement for *Venus and Adonis*.

Difficult loves from *Venus and Adonis* to 'The Phoenix and Turtle'

In *Venus and Adonis*, Shakespeare taps a story from *Metamorphoses* 10 to serve as the template for an ambitious project of Ovidian revision and modernization. Into this single tale, he interpolates several other tales from the *Metamorphoses* to create a critical anthology of tales about illicit and doomed love. The myths of Narcissus, Salmacis and Hermaphroditus, Pygmalion, and Myrrha illustrate the myriad forms of Ovidian change, brought on either by 'the fantastic possibility of endlessly satisfied desires', as one critic puts it, or by their frustration.[22] Shakespeare, who stresses internal sources of prohibition, dwells on the difficulty of achieving physical and emotional union with another when the desiring subject itself is not unified. Equally vexing for his Venus and Adonis are the changes time has wrought in the shape and texture of desires. In Shakespeare's poem, the ancient and modern worlds fail to speak to each other as often as they succeed.

Shakespeare's master change to his source is the frustration of the mutual affections enjoyed by Ovid's mythological couple. His Adonis wants nothing to do with Venus: 'Hunting he loved, but love he laughed to scorn' (4). Shakespeare's goddess is consequently thrown off her game and spends half of the narrative begging a kiss before she gets to her main talking points in Ovid, which concern the dangers of hunting the boar (it is best, she says, to stick to harmless creatures such as rabbits). The scandal of Shakespeare's poem is that there is no end of lust but no reciprocity, the foundation of sexual pleasure in the *Art of Love*, in which Ovid counselled, 'let both man and woman feel what delights them equally. / I hate embraces which leave not each outworn'.[23] By the poem's end, moreover, it appears that there never will be satisfaction for mortal lovers: when the lovely boy dies on the tusks of the boar and transforms into the anemone, Venus prophecies eternal erotic misery for human beings. Shakespeare's aetiological tale, critics agree, is not the story of how the anemone came to be (neither was Ovid's): it recounts how mutual pleasure in sexual relations came to be a dream set in the mythic past.

There are overwhelming differences between the amorous Venus and the 'unripe' Adonis. Already separated by libido and age, they discover a further gulf of temporalities. Adonis is something of a Renaissance moralist, while Venus, every inch a pagan goddess, is a glorious anachronism, puzzled by the failure of her erotic sway.[24] As the 'bold suitor' (6) in a gender-bending poem, she speaks with the urgency and lament of passionate shepherds from Theocritus and Virgil to Marlowe. Out of the rose-lipped mouth of the delectable Adonis, incongruously, comes the voice of renunciation familiar from the hard pastoral of Mantuan and the anti-classicism of the Elizabethan moralists.

Always speaking at cross-purposes, the pair divides even the moral and sensual uses of poetry. Venus issues pure sensual invitation, from one unforgettable proposal for role-playing ('you be the deer, I'll be the park') to another:

> 'Bid me discourse, I will enchant thine ear,
> Or like a fairy, trip upon the green,
> Or like a nymph with long dishevelled hair
> Dance on the sands, and yet no footing seen.'   (145–8)

Shakespeare's Venus jubilantly offers erotic advice in the tradition of Longus' *Daphnis and Chloe* and Ovid's *Art of Love*. She has, however, woefully miscalculated her audience: this Adonis is not the type to enjoy Dionysian release.

Their differences are reinforced by their incompatible readings of myth. Venus uses the tale of Ovid's Narcissus, for example, to reprimand her recalcitrant pupil:

> 'Is thine own heart to thine own face affected?
> Can thy right hand seize love upon thy left?
> Then woo thyself, be of thyself rejected;
> Steal thine own freedom, and complain on theft.
>   Narcissus so himself himself forsook,
>   And died to kiss his shadow in the brook.'   (157–62)

Venus's focus on sensual form leads Adonis to instruct her, in turn, in the moral significance of the tale she has twisted to her will:

> 'Fair queen', quoth he, 'if any love you owe me,
> Measure my strangeness with my unripe years.
> Before I know myself, seek not to know me.'   (523–5)

Adonis has no interest in fleshly readings. His passion is for the ethical prescription ('know thyself') touched on in Ovid's tale of the boy who would live long, according to prophecy, *unless* he came to know himself. Commentaries, annotations, and allegories move Adonis in a way that Ovid's sensually appealing fable cannot. Claiming the moral high ground, Adonis echoes Ovid's Elizabethan translator, Arthur Golding, who underscores the responsibility of 'readers [who] . . . earnestly admonisht are to be / Too seek a further meaning than the letter gives too see' (Epistle, 541–2). Adonis does not, however, gain interpretive mastery over Ovid's tale or Shakespeare's poem. The persuasions of Venus and Adonis alike are limited by their inability to conjoin the two poetic requirements: to instruct *and* delight.

Shakespeare further separates Ovid's lovers by reading their story in light of Ovid's story of the hermaphrodite. This bittersweet tale has at its core an image of union and healing, for it draws on the Platonic myth of the divided human subject: human beings once possessed both sexes in one body but were divided by an angry god, who left all humans in search of their other half through erotic union. Ovid's tale of Salmacis and Hermaphroditus, then, holds out the promise of integrating both the sexes and the fragmented human subject. Shakespeare touches on this ideal when Adonis at last offers a kiss to Venus and they seem to unite: 'Her arms do lend his neck a sweet embrace. / Incorporate then they seem; face grows to face' (539–40). Yet the union is a mirage. Adonis recoils from Venus' combustible sexuality, while Ovid's Hermaphroditus struggles against Salmacis and, when he succumbs to her ardour, curses the site of their unholy union. In Ovid's tale, union is worse than loneliness: there is no returning to the mythic time before the divisions of self and sex.

At one point in his career, Shakespeare imagines the hermaphroditic union of lovers, but not in the carnal *Venus and Adonis*. He reserves this vision for 'The Phoenix and Turtle', a metaphysical lyric he contributed to Robert Chester's anthology of allegorical poems about the perfect love of two birds. One is the phoenix, whose capacity to die and be reborn in flames suggests endless renewal in erotic passion, and the other is the turtle-dove, emblem of devotion. Chester's phoenix, disillusioned by a world in which envy overpowers love, finds her faith restored by the turtle's grief over his lost mate; the avian pair joins in death by fire, fully expecting to arise as one from their ashes. Shakespeare cancels Chester's hint of rebirth but permits the lovers an extraordinary union of body and spirit. The turtle finds solace in viewing himself as his lover's property and vice-versa: 'Either was the other's mine' (35) and they seem 'Neither two nor one' (40). The lovers thus recall and redeem Ovid's Salmacis and Hermaphroditus, whose bodies fused until they 'were not any lenger two but (as it were) a toy / Of double shape. Ye could not say it was a perfect boy, / Nor perfect wench: it seemed both and none of both to been' (*Metamorphoses* 4.468–70). Whereas Ovid's image hints at mutual deficiency, Shakespeare reveals perfection: 'Hearts remote, yet not asunder; / Distance, and no space was seen / 'Twixt this turtle and his queen' (29–30).

Unlike 'The Phoenix and Turtle', which presents spiritual union as a source of wonder, *Venus and Adonis* emphasizes the darker experiences of scepticism and doubt. Venus and Adonis are united chiefly in a struggle of will and, by the poem's end, this is the erotic condition imposed on the entire human race. In this poem, Shakespeare reconfigures Ovidian fables to tell a parable about the 'fall' of an erotic golden age into an iron age of sexual strife and betrayal, made yet more wretched by the 'remembrance' of a happier era. One cannot say that Shakespeare spoils Ovid's tale, however, since he goes out of his way to show that he uses Ovidian insights to improve on a relatively flat story. It is unclear why Ovid gave Venus and Adonis a purely external antagonist (the boar), but clear that Shakespeare saw the choice as a mistake. He consequently 'restores' erotic tensions and confusions, making the story both more Ovidian and modern in its scepticism about love. In this way, Shakespeare sustains the Ovidian art of transforming ancient and familiar myths into the new and strange.

The Rape of Lucrece

Shakespeare carries his project of renovating the classics into *The Rape of Lucrece*, which asks searching questions about the forms of agency and expression that the modern world inherits from the ancient one. Shakespeare's material, a tale of classical republicanism, announces a shift in focus from the sensual liberties of classical Rome to the political freedoms debated by Elizabethan intellectuals and parliamentarians. In general, Shakespeare follows the classical accounts of how the rape of Lucrece roused anti-tyrannical sentiment in Rome and led to the overthrow of the Tarquins and establishment of republican government. But he departs from them by limiting the overtly republican interests to the 'Argument' and conclusion. For reasons that bear scrutiny, he undoes the historically close fit between the rape and the republican plot.

At the poem's centre are concerns with the voice and agency of Lucrece, whose interests are not well served at the poem's end. Shakespeare's Lucrece is intensely aware of the political significance of her rape by Tarquin but nonetheless spends most of the poem in a struggle for words. Speech fails her in part because she can find no language to convey her trauma that does not distort it or begin to shape her actions: any verbal representation seems to be also a misrepresentation. Even the language of reason she must use to vindicate herself presents danger, for it implies emotional distance from the rape and thus insensitivity to it. Furthermore, Lucrece is unhappily conscious (as her orations on night, opportunity, and time show) that the blame for her rape does not fall exclusively on Tarquin. To a significant extent, all of Rome (including her spouse, father, and Junius Brutus) has let her down by failing to place constitutional bars between the tyrant's will and her chamber (302). With no political language at her disposal, Lucrece explores two poetic models for confronting grief. One is Ovidian lament, which ushers her towards decisive action; the other is Virgilian, which brings her face-to-face with despair and immobilizes her.

Lucrece begins with Ovidian complaint, appropriately for a heroine whose story Ovid told in his *Fasti*. Searching for precedents, she calls on Ovid's 'Philomel, that sing'st of ravishment' (1128) and revenge. Raped by her brother-in-law, Philomela denounces Tereus as a 'cruell Tyrant', who has violated her father's trust, her sister's marital rights, and her virginity, as well as 'the lawe' (*Metamorphoses* 6.677 and 680). When Tereus tears out her tongue to silence her, Philomela weaves her testimony into a tapestry and sends it to her sister, who helps her achieve revenge. Transformed into a nightingale, Philomela continues to sing her lament. When Lucrece calls Philomela to mind, she has not fully determined what she hopes to gain other than commiseration:

> 'As the dank earth weeps at thy languishment,
> So I at each sad strain will strain a tear,
> And with deep groans the diapason bear;
>   For burden-wise I'll hum on Tarquin still,
>   While thou on Tereus descants better skill.'   (1130–4)

The usefulness of myth lies in its very openness. For the interlude in which Lucrece meditates on her kinship with Philomela, she does not need to know whether she seeks consolation, revenge, or simply death. In the end, Philomela's grimly inspirational story helps Lucrece summon the words to write to her husband:

> First hovering o'er the paper with her quill.
> Conceit and grief an eager combat fight;
> What wit sets down is blotted straight with will;
> This is too curious-good, this blunt and ill.   (1297–1300)

While she collects her thoughts and commits them to paper, Lucrece is closest to being 'mistress of [her] fate' (1069): her prospects for delivering the speech that will take down the Tarquins and vindicate her seem strong.

In the incoherent speech Lucrece delivers, however, she fails even to name Tarquin as her assailant before killing herself. It seems hard to quarrel with Brutus's cold remark to Collatine, 'Thy wretched wife mistook the matter so, / To slay herself, that should have slain her foe' (1826–7). What happens to Lucrece between the moment of Ovidian self-authorship and the failure of words at her suicide? The answer to this question lies in Lucrece's reading of the 'skilful painting' (1367) representing scenes of Troy's fall. For Lucrece's rapt engagement with this painting, Shakespeare sets aside the classical texts that treat her story and reaches for Virgil. What mesmerizes Lucrece is the spectacle of woe: she hangs on the spectacle of Hecuba, in whose face 'all distress is stelled' (1444), and 'shapes her sorrow to the beldame's woes' (1458). Seeing that the painted Hecuba has 'much grief' yet 'not a tongue' (1463), Lucrece chooses to become the 'instrument' (1464) of long-dead woes: her sorrow is as mechanical as 'a heavy hanging bell,' which, 'Once set on ringing, with his own weight goes' (1493–4).

Shakespeare presents Lucrece as an erring reader when she 'feelingly ... weeps Troy's painted woes' (1492) but he does not, as Brutus does, dismiss her for 'mis[taking] the matter'. While Brutus is contemptuous of those who lose themselves in images of woe, Shakespeare represents such engrossment as a tragic error that dooms his heroic Lucrece. Counter to Philomela's tapestry, which prompted revolutionary action in Procne, the Virgilian painting takes the fire out of Shakespeare's Lucrece. It burdens her mind with the 'tears of things', in the phrase used by Virgil's Aeneas, when he gazed at the frieze of the Trojan War in Juno's temple.[25] As Virgil's epic successors knew, it is Aeneas' task to turn away from the past: instead of seeking out the traces of past woes, he learns to leave the dead behind and move purposefully towards his imperial goal.[26] Yet Shakespeare largely ignores Virgil's imperial plot and utilitarian lessons in the passions. In *The Rape of Lucrece*, he anthologizes the *Aeneid* as he previously anthologized Ovid's *Metamorphoses*. The parts of the *Aeneid* he brings together are tragic scenes that engross, distract, and puzzle the wills of its readers, rendering them incapable of decisive action. Shakespeare thus makes a strong claim about the source of Virgil's creative power: it is not his glorious vision of 'empire without end' (1.279) but his vision of a past whose haunting tragedies demand constant remembrance from the living.

A Lover's Complaint and the Sonnets

A Lover's Complaint presents a strong temptation to read both forwards and backwards in literary history. The poem has its clearest links with contemporary and medieval poetry in the complaint mode (Chaucer, Spenser, Churchyard, and Drayton offer compelling examples). Yet it subtly recasts the conventional representation of the desolate woman who condemns herself but remains the thrall of a powerful lover. The heroine of *A Lover's Complaint*, unlike Drayton's Rosamond or Churchyard's Jane Shore, is an anonymous and strong-minded maiden, whose rhetorical powers remind critics of the masculine lyric 'I' of the Sonnets rather than the standard acts of female impersonation or ventriloquism. Moreover, the emotional ties that the maiden has to her masculine seducer (himself a feminine youth) are complicated by her rivalrous ties to the apparently endless string of his

other conquests: each woman he has seduced is evidently capable of bestow-
ing rich jewels and composing 'deep-brained sonnets' which 'amplify / Each
stone's dear nature, worth and quality' (409–10). In the fiction of the poem,
women are on the move and their great ambition is to achieve the 'masculine'
capacity for wanton self-expression and bold action.

The chief classical source of *A Lover's Complaint* is once again Ovid.
The *Heroides* supplies the precedent for the maid's adventurous spirit and
close association with verse composition, while the tale of Pomona and
Vertumnus ('the Turner') in *Metamorphoses* 14 provides something of the
physical and dramatic context of the seduction. In Ovid's tale, the pastoral
Pomona tends to her walled orchard (an emblem of her own body) and
prohibits the efforts of young men to grow their 'plants in others' orchards'
(*ALC* 171). Pomona's desire for self-sovereignty matches that of the maid,
who relished her 'freedom': she was her 'own fee-simple' (143–4). Just as the
passionate youth of *A Lover's Complaint* uses theatrical craft to achieve his
will, Vertumnus adopts all manner of theatrical guises to get close to
Pomona.[27] Both use tales of other women's passions to spark the imagination in their new target. Vertumnus maintains a furious pace of narrative
persuasion until he at last discards disguise, reveals himself, and prepares to
rape Pomona. In Ovid's unsettling tale, Pomona contracts the same wound of
passion when she sees her lover in his own shape and gives herself to him: is it
rape or consent? *A Lover's Complaint* recalls this tale when the maid
discards her 'white stole of chastity' and, shaking off her 'sober guards and
civil fears' chooses to 'Appear to him as he to me appear[ed]' (297–9): is it
consent or fraud?

The classical source for the maiden's boldness with words is Ovid's
Heroides, verse epistles written (in the fiction) by the women whose
passion, ingenuity, and adventurousness enabled mythological heroes such
as Ulysses, Aeneas, Paris, and Theseus to achieve their heroic deeds. Like
Shakespeare's maid, Ovid's heroines remain unrepentant about their failed
experiments in love. While the decision to stand by a mistake may seem
merely obstinate, it is in fact not the error of giving their hearts and bodies
to the wrong man that they defend: it the right to err in ethical questions of
the greatest importance to their happiness and future. For the women of the
Heroides and *A Lover's Complaint* want, precisely, more control over the
disposition of their bodies and sexualities. Both poems test the grounds of
female virtue: is it verified by virginity and submission to the advice of
others? Or is it to be found in the bold exercise of choice? When the
anonymous maid asks, 'who ever shunned by precedent / The destined ill
she must herself assay?' (155–6), she anticipates Milton's Eve, who asks
the right question even if she makes the wrong decision when tempted with

the apple: 'And what is faith, love, virtue, unassay'd / Alone, and without exterior help sustain'd?'[28] *A Lover's Complaint* may not go quite as far as Milton, who asserted that he could not 'praise a fugitive and cloistered virtue', which he considered a 'blank virtue, not pure' (*Areopagitica*, p. 728), but the poem furnished material for Milton's bold revision of the story of the fall.

The Sonnets, which are linked to *A Lover's Complaint*, conduct even bolder experiments in classical imitation. In them, Shakespeare bypasses the usual means by which Elizabethan poets and humanists displayed their learning and ingenuity. Considering their well-established relationship to Ovid's *Metamorphoses*, the Sonnets reveal strikingly few traces of the mythological figures and tales that enjoyed enormous popularity in the poetry and fiction of Shakespeare's day. Adonis and Helen of Troy figure as paradigms of male and female beauty in one poem (53), while a nightingale affords the opportunity for a muted reference to Philomela in another sonnet (102), and Cupid makes a belated appearance in the last two poems of the sequence as it appeared in print (153 and 154). These mythological figures frankly contribute very little to the Sonnets, other than their status as classical references: they do not import or complicate meaning in the way that Ovidian allusions do in, for example, the great lyric sequence on which Elizabethans (including Shakespeare) draw most heavily, the *Rime Sparse* of the medieval Italian poet, Petrarch. Whereas he effectively rewrote episodes in the *Metamorphoses* as highlights in the story of the poet–lover's fall into a divided and metamorphic subjectivity, Shakespeare ignores the famous tales. His desultory classical allusions appear to be exceptions that prove the rule of his distinctive lyric aesthetic, one purged of ornamental allusions to classical myth.

How is it that Shakespeare imitates Ovid, if not through allusion to the dramatis personae and plots of particular tales, both of which are usually regarded as sure traces of a meaningful relationship between an ancient and a modern text? The Sonnets almost fully reject such forms of mediation: instead, Shakespeare takes up and transforms the overarching themes and artistic preoccupations most integral to the *Metamorphoses*. Notable examples include erotic possessions of will; the poem as an enduring memorial and monument; time as the devourer of human aspiration; and above all, change that subtly transforms the constitutions of bodies, minds, and emotions. These rank high among the themes Ovid used to weave together the varied tales that he found in ancient myth and with which he composed his *Metamorphoses* (the theme of changed bodies applies to his own habits of imitation as well as to his subject matter). It is through these overarching themes that Ovid weaves his varied and wandering tales into a coherent and artful form and, simultaneously, brings them from the oldest records of the written word to Ovid's own moment. In the Sonnets, these themes are as Shakespearean as they are Ovidian: by engaging the wit, poetic structure, and major themes of the *Metamorphoses*, while suppressing the urge to quote, Shakespeare (as reader and poet) breathes new life into Ovid's most influential poem and brings it up to his own day and moment of writing.

NOTES

1 The term, 'counter-classical', is that of W. R. Johnson, 'The Problem of Counter-Classical Sensibility and Its Critics', *California Studies in Classical Antiquity* 3 (1970), 123–51. On the formal innovation associated with the Elizabethan avant-garde, see Lorna Hutson, *Thomas Nashe in Context* (Oxford: Clarendon Press, 1989); and Georgia Brown, *Redefining Elizabethan Literature* (Cambridge University Press, 2004), especially pp. 36–52.

2 Stockwood, *A Sermon Preached at Paules Crosse on Barthelmew day, being the 24 of August. 1578*. Qtd in T. W. Baldwin, *William Shakspere's Small Latine & Lesse Greeke*, 2 vols. (Urbana: University of Illinois Press, 1944), I: 110.

3 Baldwin, *William Shakspere's Small Latine*, I: 111. The ban was unsuccessful and Ovid remained firmly ensconced in the school curriculum.

4 T. E. Hartley, *Proceedings in the Parliaments of Elizabeth I* (Leicester: Leicester University Press; Wilmington, DE: Michael Glazier, 1981–), 11: 40.

5 Golding, 'Preface too the Reader', lines 141 and 203, in Golding, *The XV. Bookes of P. Ouidius Naso, Entytled Metamorphosis*, ed. W. H. D. Rouse (Carbondale: Southern Illinois University Press, 1961).

6 Woodford, *Diary* (c. 1662). Osborn Shelves b. 41, Beinecke Library. Unpaginated.

7 Stubbes, *Anatomie of Abuses* (London, 1583), pp. 139–40.

8 See especially Jean E. Howard, *The Stage and Social Struggle in Early Modern England* (London: Routledge, 1994).

9 See Stephen Gosson, *Playes Confuted in fiue Actions* (London, 1582), sigs. G4^v–G5^r.

10 Stockwood, *A Sermon Preached at Paules Crosse*, pp. 135–6.

11 On issues of female literacy, see especially Margaret W. Ferguson, *Dido's Daughters: Literacy, Gender, and Empire in Early Modern England and France* (University of Chicago Press, 2003). For studies of the education and reading practices of women, see Caroline McManus, *Spenser's 'Faerie Queene' and the Reading of Women* (Newark: University of Delaware Press, 2002); and Sasha Roberts, *Reading Shakespeare's Poems in Early Modern England* (Basingstoke: Palgrave Macmillan, 2003).

12 Salter, *A Mirrhor mete for all Mothers, Matrones, and Maidens, intituled the Mirrhor of Modestie* (London, 1579), sig. D1^r.

13 Vives, *The office and duetie of an husband* (London, 1550), sig. P8^v.

14 Middleton, *A Mad World, My Masters*, ed. Standish Henning (London: E. Arnold, 1965).

15 The full title is *The first booke of the Christian exercise, appertaining to resolution* (Rouen, 1582).

16 See *The Returne from Parnassus, Part 1* 4.1 in *The Three Parnassus Plays*, ed. J. B. Leishman (London: Nicholson & Watson, 1949).

17 Marlowe, *Hero and Leander* 1.143–4, in *The Poems of Christopher Marlowe*, ed. Millar MacLure (London: Methuen, 1968).

18 Ovid, *Amores* 1.15.35–6, in *Heroides and Amores*, trans. Grant Showerman, rev. G. P. Goold, 2nd edn, Loeb Classical Library (Cambridge, MA: Harvard University Press; and London: Heinemann, 1977).

19 Southampton disappointed Lord Burleigh, his guardian and the queen's chief minister, when he refused to marry Burleigh's granddaughter, Lady Elizabeth Vere. Rather than comply, Southampton chose to pay a hefty fine of about £5,000.

20 For a discussion of the gender and sexual politics of elegy, see Paul Allen Miller, *Latin Erotic Elegy: An Anthology and Reader* (London: Routledge, 2002).

21 On Ovid's relationship to the conception of political liberties, see my 'Ovid and the Question of Politics in Early Modern England', *ELH* 70 (2003), 343–73.

22 Dennis Kay, *William Shakespeare: Sonnets and Poems* (New York: Twayne, 1998), p. 21.

23 *Ars amatoria* 2.682–3, in *The Art of Love and Other Poems*, trans. J. H. Mozley, rev. G. P. Goold, Loeb Classical Library (Cambridge, MA: Harvard University Press; and London: Heinemann, 1979).

24 Heather Dubrow emphasizes the generic differences between the pair: 'Venus and Adonis ... enact a tension in the generic potentials of Ovidian mythological poetry. Venus stands for the amoral eroticism so common in the mythological narratives of Ovid himself, while Adonis represents the pieties of *Ouide moralisé*' (*Captive Victors: Shakespeare's Narrative Poems* (Ithaca: Cornell University Press, 1987), p. 48).

25 Virgil, *Aeneid* 1.462, trans R. D. Williams (trans.), 2 vols. (New York: St Martin's Press, 1972).

26 On repetitions of the past in Virgil's *Aeneid*, see David Quint, *Epic and Empire* (Princeton University Press, 1993).

27 On the youth's theatricality, see Cheney, *Shakespeare, National Poet–Playwright*, esp. pp. 253–6.

28 Milton, *Paradise Lost* 9.335–6. All references to Milton are to *Milton's Poems and Major Prose*, ed. Merritt Y. Hughes (New York: Odyssey Press, 1957).

READING LIST

Barkan, Leonard. *The Gods Made Flesh: Metamorphosis and the Pursuit of Paganism*. New Haven: Yale University Press, 1986.

Bate, Jonathan. *Shakespeare and Ovid*. Oxford: Clarendon Press, 1993.

Callaghan, Dympna. 'Comedy and Epyllion in Post-Reformation England'. *Shakespeare Survey* 56 (2003), 27–38.

Cheney, Patrick. *Shakespeare, National Poet–Playwright*. Cambridge University Press, 2004.

Dubrow, Heather. *Captive Victors: Shakespeare's Narrative Poems*. Ithaca: Cornell University Press, 1987.

Enterline, Lynn. *The Rhetoric of the Body from Ovid to Shakespeare*. Cambridge University Press, 2000.

Greene, Thomas M. *The Light in Troy: Imitation and Discovery in Renaissance Poetry*. New Haven: Yale University Press, 1982.

Hulse, Clark. *Metamorphic Verse: The Elizabethan Minor Epic*. Princeton University Press, 1981.

Hyland, Peter. *An Introduction to Shakespeare's Poems*. New York: Palgrave Macmillan, 2003.

Kahn, Coppélia. *Man's Estate: Masculinity in Shakespeare*. Berkeley: University of California Press, 1981.

Keach, William. *Elizabethan Erotic Narratives: Irony and Pathos in the Ovidian Poetry of Shakespeare, Marlowe, and Their Contemporaries*. New Brunswick: Rutgers University Press, 1976.

12

PATRICK CHENEY

Poetry in Shakespeare's plays

> The truest poetry is the most feigning.
>
> *As You Like It*, 3.4.14[1]

In addition to writing such freestanding poems as *Venus and Adonis* or *A Lover's Complaint*, Shakespeare makes poetry an integral feature of his dramatic corpus. Most obviously, he writes much of this corpus in poetic verse, whether in blank verse or in rhyme (see Chapters 1 and 2 in this volume). But he also includes over 130 lyrics in his plays, as poems or songs, with over 100 of them original compositions.[2] Not simply, then, are his plays made largely of poetry but set-lyrics appear in them. Most often, Shakespeare clarifies the poet-figures who write, sing, or perform these lyrics, such as the courtier Orlando in *As You Like It*, who fondly hangs his love poems to Rosalind on trees in the Forest of Arden. In Shakespeare's plays, the performance of poetry becomes a recurrent stage action, and the presence of active poet-figures means that characters habitually carry on a conversation about poetry.

The epigraph to this chapter registers one such conversation, when the court clown Touchstone in *As You Like It*, also visiting the Forest of Arden, tries to woo the country girl Audrey:

TOUCHSTONE   Truly, I would the gods had made thee poetical.
AUDREY   I do not know what 'poetical' is. Is it honest in deed and in word? Is it a true thing?
TOUCHSTONE   No, truly; for the truest poetry is the most feigning.

(3.4.10–14)

If the tone of this conversation is playful, the terms are aesthetically serious, confirming that Shakespeare imagines poetry as both a language and an action ('deed and word'), and showing the author to enter a historical debate about the nature of poetry and the new medium it serves: theatre, as the climactic word 'feigning' perhaps hints. In Shakespearean drama, the conversation the audience hears turns out to exist in detailed, compelling form from the beginning of his dramatic career to the end – from *The Two Gentlemen of Verona* to *The Tempest* – and constitutes a sustained yet neglected fiction about the art of poetry within the plays.[3]

In this chapter, we shall look further into the presence of 'poetry' in Shakespeare's dramatic corpus. The topic is a vast one, so we shall need to confine the discussion to selected points and examples. The first section below details the general presence of poetry in the plays. The second section particularizes that presence through the genre of comedy in *As You Like It*, while the third examines a scene from tragedy recording Hamlet's dubious poem to Ophelia. The goal in all three sections will be to show Shakespeare's deep investment in poetry and its intimate connection with theatre. A concluding section addresses what is at stake when the world's most famous man of the theatre rehearses a detailed *poetic fiction* on the new London stage: a fresh, historically grounded portrait of Shakespeare as an early modern author.

Feigning poetry

To begin, we might recall Shakespeare's own vocabulary of poetry. For instance, as the dialogue from *As You Like It* indicates, he uses the word 'poetry' itself, along with the related terms 'poesy', 'poetical', 'poem', and 'poet' or 'poets' – a total of about fifty times.[4] Thus, in *Two Gentlemen* Proteus remarks to the Duke of Milan, 'Orpheus' lute was strung with poets' sinews' (*Riverside Shakespeare* 3.2.77) – Orpheus being a legendary founder of poetry in Greek and Roman mythology and understood in the Renaissance to be a figure for the civilizing power of the poet.[5] Similarly, Shakespeare uses 'rhyme' and its cognates, and 'verse' and its cognates (over 100 times); these are the more usual terms by which Shakespeare designates a poem or poetry. Thus, in *As You Like It* Orlando says, 'Hang there, my verse, in witness of my love' (3.2.1).[6]

Shakespeare often refers to the traditional sources of poetic inspiration, the Muse or Nine Muses, as when Iago, trying to invent a poem before Desdemona, remarks, 'my Muse labours, / And thus she is deliver'd' (2.1.126–7). As the earlier quotation on Orpheus indicates, Shakespeare links poets with such musical instruments as the lute or harp and the pastoral pipe. He does not often use generic terms for poetry, but he does occasionally use 'pastoral', 'sonnet', 'epitaph', 'satire', 'elegies', 'epigram', 'ballad', and (more often) 'song'. In *Love's Labour's Lost*, for instance, the country schoolmaster Holofernes asks Sir Nathaniel, the curate, 'will you hear an extemporal epitaph on the death of the deer' (*Riverside Shakespeare* 4.2.50–1), and produces a six-line memorial poem on said beast in a sixain stanza rhyming *ababcc* (56–61), beginning, 'The preyful Princess pierc'd and prick'd a pretty pleasing pricket' (56). The word 'ditty' recurs, as in *The Tempest* when Ferdinand says of the lyric song sung by Ariel, 'The ditty does remember my drowned father' (1.2.404). Sometimes, Shakespeare uses even more unfamiliar terms, as when Holofernes calls a poem 'a canzonet' (4.2.120), or Viola in *Twelfth Night* says she will 'write loyal cantons of contemned love' (1.5.225).

As mention of songs, pipes, lutes, and harps reveals, in Shakespearean drama as in Renaissance culture, the vocabulary of poetry is deeply connected to the vocabulary of music. Sometimes, Shakespeare means music (*Richard II* 5.5.41–3, *Winter's Tale* 5.3.98), but often he depends on the Elizabethan convention that metaphorizes music as poetry, song as lyric poetry, the musician as a poet. For the Elizabethans, Orpheus is more precisely the archetype of the singer–musician as civilizing poet, and Shakespeare's fellow writer Edmund Spenser had put this convention at the centre of his national art – his self-presentation as 'the Virgil of England'[7] – by depicting his Orphic persona, Colin Clout, as a musician–singer, in both his inaugural pastoral poem, *The Shepheardes Calender* (1579), and his national epic, *The Faerie Queene* (1596).[8] Shakespeare often follows suit, so that the original 100-plus dramatic lyrics firmly embed the figure of the poet, as well as the topic of poetry, in his plays, more so than perhaps has been realized. In *The Taming of the Shrew*, he reveals how closely he imagines the two arts, when the trickster Tranio says to Lucentio, 'Music and poetry use to quicken you' (1.1.36).

Moreover, Shakespeare mentions a whole host of mythological figures conventionally representative of poetry. In addition to Orpheus, whom he mentions a number of times and alludes to on several other occasions, he mentions Arion, another legendary founder of poetry, and alludes to him elsewhere; Pegasus, the flying horse who used his hoof to open the Muses' fountain on Mount Helicon; Actaeon, the voyeur of Diana who was turned into a stag and became for Shakespeare's favorite poet, Ovid, a figure for the author in political exile; and Prometheus, who stole fire from heaven and was punished for his crime, becoming a figure for the political danger of the poet's integrity. In *Two Gentlemen*, Shakespeare takes the shape-changing poet-figure Proteus from classical mythology (cf. *3 Henry VI* 3.2.192) and makes him a lead character in the plot. As Proteus' earlier reference to Orpheus indicates, this character takes a considerable interest in the art of poetry.

If we look into these mythological references, we discover a detailed network of discourse on the poet and his art. The network expands considerably when we consider Philomela, the Athenian princess raped by her brother-in-law Tereus and metamorphosed into the nightingale, the Western icon of the poet who produces powerful music out of tragic suffering – in Ovid and Virgil as in Spenser.[9] In two memorable moments of his career, one early and one late, Shakespeare brings the most important version of the Philomela myth on to the stage as a prop, through the 'book' of 'Ovid's Metamorphosis' (*Titus Andronicus* 4.1.41–2): in *Titus*, when Marcus says, 'This is the tragic tale of Philomel' (4.1.47); and in *Cymbeline*, when Iachimo discovers that Innogen (or Imogen) 'hath been reading late / The tale of Tereus; here the leaf's turned down / Where Philomel gave up' (2.2.44–6).[10]

Unlike his rival Ben Jonson, Shakespeare is notoriously reticent about naming historical figures other than those he fictionalizes in his English history plays or Roman tragedies, but as the case of *Titus* indicates he does occasionally name historical poets: in addition to Ovid, he mentions Horace, Juvenal, Petrarch, Mantuan, and Chaucer. In *Romeo and Juliet*, for instance, Mercutio says of Romeo, 'Now is he for the numbers that Petrarch flowed in' (2.4.34–5), while in *Shrew* Tranio tells Lucentio that they should not 'As Ovid be an outcast quite abjured' (1.1.33). Among Ovid's poems, Shakespeare certainly mentions his favourite book, the *Metamorphoses*, but also the *Ars Amatoria* (*Art of Love*) (*Shrew* 4.2.8) and the *Heroides* (*Heroical Epistles*), the latter quoted in Latin (*Shrew* 3.1.28–9; *3 Henry VI* 1.3.48).

In addition to classical and continental poets, Shakespeare brings English poets on to his stage. Most visibly, he presents John Gower, author of the medieval poem *Confessio Amantis*, as the Prologue and Chorus to *Pericles*, written probably in collaboration with George Wilkins: 'To sing a song that old was sung, / From ashes ancient Gower is come' (Prologue 1–2). Similarly, in *The Two Noble Kinsmen*, written late in collaboration with John Fletcher, the playwright(s) stage(s) Chaucer's 'The Knight's Tale', the opening chivalric poem of *The Canterbury Tales*, understood during the period (including by Spenser) as Chaucer's epic: 'A learned, and a poet never went / More famous yet 'twixt Po and Silver Trent. / Chaucer (of all admir'd) the story gives' (*Riverside Shakespeare*, Prologue 11–13).

Shakespeare can also use the stage to name even more contemporary English poets and books of poetry. In *The Merry Wives of Windsor*, for instance, Abraham Slender refers to his 'Book of Songs and Sonets' (1.1.158–9), also known as *Tottel's Miscellany* (1557), which first published poems by the Henrician court poets Sir Thomas Wyatt and Henry Howard, earl of Surrey. In *Twelfth Night*, the clown Feste sings a line from one of Wyatt's lyrics, 'Hey, Robin, jolly Robin' (4.2.58). In *Merry Wives* as well, Falstaff courts Mrs Ford by quoting a line from Sir Philip Sidney's *Astrophil and Stella*, 'Have I caught thee, my heavenly jewel' (3.3.43; *Astrophil and Stella* Second Song, line 1). While Shakespeare can certainly see poetry as a private, manuscript, or oral art, as his many references to 'ballads' and 'extempore' verse indicates, he tends to imagine poetry most often as a product of print culture (see Chapter 3 in this volume). In *Shrew*, for instance, Gremio tells Hortensio that he is enquiring after a schoolmaster for Bianca, one 'well read in poetry / And other books' (1.2.163–4). In *Love's Labour's Lost*, the fantastical Spaniard, Don Adriano de Armado, voices many of the contours we have mentioned, when he declaims, 'Assist me, some extemporal god of rhyme, for I am sure I shall turn sonnet. Devise, wit, write, pen, for I am for whole volumes in folio' (1.2.183–5).[11] Indeed, the intimate link between poetry and books runs throughout the Shakespearean dramatic corpus.

Although Shakespeare never names such important Greek, Roman, and English national poets as Homer, Virgil, and Spenser, he finds ways to get their massive poetic projects on to his stage: Homer, most directly in *Troilus and Cressida*, where we visit Troy; Virgil, throughout the dramatic canon, including numerous references to Aeneas and his tragic beloved, Dido, from the beginning (*2 Henry VI* 3.2.116–18, 5.2.62–4) to the end (*Tempest* 2.1.77–83); and Spenser, most visibly in two appearances by the Faerie Queene: Titania in *A Midsummer Night's Dream*; and Mistress Quickly, who performs the lead role in the playlet directed at Falstaff in the final scene of *Merry Wives* (5.5).[12] A vast amount of criticism exists on Shakespeare's engagement especially with Ovid and Virgil, to a lesser extent with Chaucer and Spenser, but most of it directs us to a salient point: this playwright uses the new theatre to engage the major Roman and English national poets and thus the art of the national poet himself.

Nor does Shakespeare name his most famous rival, Christopher Marlowe, but in *As You Like It* he alludes to Marlowe as 'the dead shepherd' (3.6.80), quotes a line from Marlowe's poem *Hero and Leander*, 'Who ever loved that loved not at first sight' (3.6.81; *Hero and Leander* 176), and perhaps alludes to Marlowe's death as 'a great reckoning in a little room' (3.4.10) – echoing Marlowe's much-quoted line from *The Jew of Malta*, 'infinite riches in a little room' (1.1.37).[13] Additionally, in *Merry Wives* the Welsh parson Sir Hugh Evans garbles Marlowe's great lyric, 'The Passionate Shepherd to His Love' (3.1.12–25); this play also refers to Marlowe's *Doctor Faustus* (4.5.54–5). Moreover, Shakespeare recurrently puts Marlovian super-heroes on to his stage, from York and Gloucester in the *Henry VI* plays, to Richard III in his historical tragedy and Hotspur in *1 Henry IV*, to Edmund in *King Lear* and *Coriolanus*.[14]

Shakespeare's dramatic and historical vocabulary for poetry is merely the tip of a theatrical iceberg. So many characters qualify as poet-figures that it would be hard to count them. In addition to such courtiers as Orlando, Shakespeare stages professional lyricists like the Fool in *King Lear*, who does not simply recite poems and sing songs to indict his sovereign for banishing

Cordelia and handing Britain over to Goneril and Regan, but, according to Lear himself, turns to lyric precisely because this occasion emerges. 'When were you wont to be so full of songs, sirrah?' Lear asks the Fool, who replies, 'I have used it, nuncle, e'er since thou mad'st thy daughters thy mothers' (1.4.132–4). We also meet tricksters like Autolycus in *The Winter's Tale*, who sings songs in the pastoral countryside of Bohemia, sometimes just for amusement, often his own: 'The lark that tirra-lyra chaunts, . . . / Are summer songs for me and my aunts, / While we lie tumbling in the hay' (4.3.8–12). Occasionally, Shakespeare uses lyric to invent the voice and inwardness of madness, as he does powerfully in the scattered rhymes of Ophelia: 'He is dead and gone, lady, / He is dead and gone' (*Hamlet* 4.5.29–30). At other times, he presents lyricists as supernatural songsters, like Puck in *A Midsummer Night's Dream*, the Witches in *Macbeth*, or Ariel in *The Tempest*, the last of whom voices some of the most profound lyrics in the English language: 'Full fathom five thy father lies, / Of his bones are coral made; / Those are pearls that were his eyes' (1.2.396–8).

Sometimes, too, we encounter professional poets, like Cinna in *Julius Caesar*, who does not recite any of his own verse but instead is killed by the angry Roman mob when it mistakes him for Cinna the conspirator: 'Tear him for his bad verses' (3.3.28). *Timon of Athens* opens with a figure named the Poet, and he turns out to be a print poet (1.1.27), complete with a voiced poetics, most of it contemptible, which we overhear him reciting: 'When we for recompense have prais'd the vild. / It strains the glory in that happy verse, / Which aptly sings the good' (15–17). Other professional singers like Balthasar in *Much Ado about Nothing* or Amiens in *As You Like It* do perform their lyric songs, and in the process produce some extraordinary lyrics that often get overlooked: Balthasar's 'Sigh no more, ladies' (2.3.53–68) or Amiens' 'Under the greenwood tree' (2.5.1–8, 30–7, 42–9). According to Hallett Smith, 'quite possibly the most resonant lyric lines Shakespeare ever composed' are sung not by a professional poet-figure at all but by the lost princes of Britain, Arviragus and Guiderius:[15]

> Fear no more the heat o' the sun,
>
> . . .
>
> Golden lads and girls all must,
> As chimney-sweepers, come to dust.　　　(4.2.257–62)

Unlike Spenser (or Jonson), Shakespeare does not clearly mark out figures in his dramatic works that 'shadoweth himself, as sometime Virgil under the name of Tityrus', to quote Spenser's glossarist, E. K., in *The Shepheardes Calender*.[16] Shakespeare's reticence in self-identification, like his habitual staging of such ill-kept author-figures as the Poet in *Timon*, goes some way toward explaining why we might have dismissed the topic of poetry in his plays.

If poet-figures produce lyrics, they do so in specific geographical locales, and Shakespeare tends to associate them with particular poetic genres: most memorably the countryside with pastoral, as in *As You Like It*; and the city with epic and romance, as in *Antony and Cleopatra*.[17] The country-court dynamic is arguably the most recognizable topography of Shakespearean drama; perhaps less often recognized, this topography has deep generic resonance, placing the major Virgilian and Spenserian forms of pastoral and epic right at the centre of Shakespeare's stage, from *Two Gentlemen* through *The Winter's Tale*. Shakespeare uses the stage to associate theatrical space with other poetic genres as well – the court or private chamber with lyric and sonnet.[18] Thus, in the final comedic scene from *Much Ado*, set in Leonato's house, Claudio pulls out of Benedick's 'pocket' a 'halting sonnet of his own pure brain, / Fashioned to Beatrice', and Hero pulls 'another' from the pocket of Beatrice, 'Containing her affection under Benedick' (5.4.87–90).[19]

Shakespeare imagines poetry as a playful art of entertainment, but he also understands the potency of poetry to perform cultural work, not always admirable. In *Two Gentlemen*, Proteus educates Thurio in the art of winning Silvia:

> You must lay lime to tangle her desires
> By wailful sonnets, whose composed rhymes
> Should be full-fraught with serviceable vows.   (3.2.68–70)

'Ay', the Duke replies, 'much is the force of heaven-bred poesy' (71), to which Proteus adds, 'Write till your ink be dry, ... / ... and frame some feeling line / That may discover such integrity; / For Orpheus' lute is strung with poets' sinews' (74–9). Just as Hamlet will use the play-within-the play, *The Mousetrap*, to 'catch the conscience of the king' (2.2.258), so Proteus advises Thurio to use the divine nature of poetry, with its Orphic power to affect an audience emotionally, to trap the desire of Silvia.

Sometimes, the conversation about poetry seems secreted in the dramatic discourse, as if we were hearing the voice of the author himself. In *Titus Andronicus*, when Marcus comes across the ravished Lavinia, he compares her, rather surprisingly, with Orpheus, and with Philomela: 'Fair Philomela, why, she but lost her tongue. ... / O had the monster [who raped you] seen those lily hands ... / He would have dropped his knife and fell asleep, / As Cerberus at the Thracian poet's feet' (2.4.38–51). Critics have long had difficulty comprehending the oddity of Marcus' long discourse, primarily because it seems to violate the psychological realism we expect of this author. Even though recent productions have demonstrated the stage worthiness of this speech, we cannot account for its weirdness until we recognize Shakespeare's concern to lay bare his own literariness, his intertextual authorship, especially with Ovid.[20] Marcus expresses horror at the tragedy he witnesses, while for his part Shakespeare reveals how he himself makes such tragedy.

In such intertextual moments, we become privy to something like the playwright's own poetic workshop. Thus, Shakespeare's conversation about poetry does not occur in a historical vacuum but responds to a larger conversation about poetry coming out of classical Greece and Rome, migrating to the Middle Ages, and entering Renaissance Europe and England. Some plays make this 'meta-poetics' (poetry about poetry) explicit (e.g., *Love's Labour's Lost* 4.2.99–102). In such a *meta-conversation*, we can witness Shakespeare entering into dialogue with the major canonical poets of Western literature, cut along generic lines.

To complement this more 'literary' use of poetry, Shakespeare includes a more formally theatrical one. For instance, he presents characters breaking out of their blank verse line into rhymed couplets in order to create a certain dramatic mood or effect. In the opening scene of *A Midsummer Night's Dream* Hermia engages in a detailed conversation with her lover Lysander in the blank verse used in earlier parts of the play, but then, inexplicably and amid speech, she moves into rhyme: 'By the simplicity of Venus' doves, / By that which knitteth souls and prospers loves' (171–2). Only when her friend Helena enters can we make some sense of the change, for Helena is the first character to speak fully in couplets. Thus, her first spoken line completes a couplet begun by Hermia in the preceding line:

HERMIA   God speed, fair Helena! Whither away?
HELENA   Call you me 'fair'? That fair again unsay.
            Demetrius loves your fair: O happy fair
            Your eyes are lodestars, and your tongue's sweet air
            More tunable than lark to shepherd's ear
            When wheat is green, when hawthorn buds appear.   (1.1.180–5)

In context, Helena's rhymed speech sounds stylized, at once artful and artificial, distinct yet perhaps comical. During the next fifty lines, she joins Hermia and even Lysander in maintaining the rhyme, but after these friends leave the stage, Helena delivers a twenty-six-line soliloquy in rhymed couplets, concluding, 'But herein mean I to enrich my pain, / To have his sight thither, and back again' (250–1). Such poetical dramaturgy opens up rather than closes down the actor's opportunities to reveal character and create dramatic effect – in the case of Helena, most likely a charming mockery of character.

One of the most striking instances of such dramaturgy concludes Act 3 of *Measure for Measure*, when Duke Vincentio concludes a long scene, the preceding 100 lines of which are significantly in prose, with a soliloquy in rhymed couplets. Here Shakespeare offsets the poetry of inwardness even more than in the case of Helena, because the Duke delivers his 22-line rhyme, not in iambic pentameter, but with a tetrameter line (eight rather than ten syllables) in mostly trochaic rather than iambic meter (the accent falling on the first rather than the second foot of each syllable):

> He who the sword of heaven will bear
> Should be as holy, as severe:
> Pattern in himself to know,
> Grace to stand, and virtue go.   (3.2.223–6)

The Duke does not read (or write) a poem, nor does he sing or recite a song; rather, he *performs a poem*. Shakespeare, rather than Vincentio, presents *character* through poetry. Why, we might ask, do so at this particular moment? Evidently, he wants to dramatize the stable ground of truth, important in a play that exhibits the Duke disguising himself as a friar in order to observe his hypocritical deputy, Angelo:

> Oh, what may man within him hide,
> Though angel on the outward side?
>
> . . .
>
> So disguise shall by th' disguised
> Pay with falsehood false exacting
> And perform an old contracting.   (3.2.233–4, 242–4)

In context, then, Shakespeare deploys a clearly marked form of poetry as a release from Venetian theatricality, even as the poetry gives voice to the Duke's plan to contend with the theatricality of Angelo.

We cannot fully measure the poetic dramaturgy here until we witness what happens next. For, once the Duke exits the stage, Act 4 opens with the dejected beloved of Angleo, Mariana, entering, accompanied by a '*Boy singing*' (stage direction) a song:

> Take, oh take those lips away,
>   That so sweetly were foresworn,
> And those eyes, the break of day,
>   Lights that do mislead the morn;
> But my kisses bring again, bring again,
> Seals of love, but sealed in vain, sealed in vain.   (4.1.1–6)

The fervent editorial dispute about whether Shakespeare wrote this song or not (strong arguments exist for both positions) may serve mainly as a distraction here, preventing us from fully appreciating the poetical dramaturgy, which participates in a remarkable theatrical movement, from the earlier prose dialogue, to the Duke's rhymed soliloquy, to the cloistered melancholy of lyric song.

When the disguised Duke re-enters, Mariana apologizes to 'the man of comfort' (8) for relying on 'music' to 'please' her 'woe' (11–13) – lend consolation to her sadness. But the Duke will have none of it, as if secretly coming out of his disguise to the audience:

> 'Tis good; though music oft hath such a charm
> To make bad good, and good provoke harm.   (4.1.14–15)

We need to see his rhymed rejoinder as more than simply a defense of music; self-consciously poetic, it is intrinsically a defence of poetry, as the presence of the song's lyrics anticipates and as the Duke's reference to the Orphic 'charm' of the art further clarifies. In theatrical disguise, the Duke emerges not simply as the speaker of his own rhyme but as a theorist of rhyme. In a play nominally about sexual justice, Shakespeare includes a conversation about poetry and theatre.

Of course, some plays seem more concerned with the art of poetry than others. The list includes *Two Gentlemen*, *Shrew*, *Love's Labour's Lost*, *Merry Wives*, *Much Ado*, *As You Like It*, *Twelfth Night*, *All's Well that End's Well*, *Cymbeline*, *The Winter's Tale*, and *The Tempest*. This list suggests that Shakespeare predominantly uses the genres of comedy and romance to transact his poetic fiction. Each of these plays could easily sustain an individual essay, and some, like *Love's Labour's Lost* and *As You Like It*, seem to be virtually about the relation between poetry and its twin Shakespearean art, theatre.

Yet several tragedies make important contributions to the conversation, especially *Titus*, *Romeo*, *Hamlet*, *Othello*, *Lear*, *Antony*, *Timon*, and (perhaps surprisingly) *Coriolanus*. The presence of Ovid's tale of Philomela in *Titus*; the renowned Petrarchan lyricism of *Romeo and Juliet*, which includes three and one-quarter sonnets (Prologue, 1.5.92–109, 2.Chorus); Iago's poem on Desdemona (2.1.128–57) and her own famed willow song (4.3.38–54); the haunting lyrics of the Fool (1.4, 2.4, 3.2) and of Edgar in disguise as Poor Tom (3.4, 3.6); and Coriolanus' difficulty in 'tun[ing]' his 'voice' to the applause of the people (2.3.76–7): these show the tragedian's all-abiding concern with the role of poetry on the new London stage. As Edgar powerfully puts it, 'The foul fiend haunts poor Tom in the voice / Of a nightingale' (*Riverside Shakespeare* 3.6.29–30).

Among the history plays, the first tetralogy is especially important, because it features Henry VI as a Spenserian author-figure, the shepherd-king: 'O god! methinks it were a happy life / To be no better than a homely swain; / To sit upon a hill, as I do now, / To carve out dials quaintly, point by point' (3 *Henry VI* 2.5.21–4).[21] But *Richard II* warrants close attention as well; the King's commitment to tragic lyricism is well known: 'Let's talk of graves, of worms and epitaphs, / Make dust our paper, and with rainy eyes / Write sorrow on the bosom of the earth' (3.2.145–7). Yet the archly theatrical Richard III's fear of poetry is often overlooked: 'A bard of Ireland told me once / I should not live long after I saw Richmond' (*Riverside Shakespeare* 4.2.98–9; see *Cambridge* 4.4.515, 5.3.305–8). In *1 Henry IV*, Shakespeare invents Hotspur's theatrical identity largely by making him a naturally poetic man who despises poetry:

> I had rather be a kitten and cry 'mew'
> Than one of these same metre ballad-mongers.
> . . .
> Nothing so [bad] as mincing poetry.
> 'Tis like the forced gait of a shuffling nag.
>
> (*1 Henry IV* 3.1.123–9)

The preceding inventory suggests how deep-seated the presence of poetry is in all four genres of Shakespeare's dramatic career, from its inception in the late 1580s till its close during the second decade of the seventeenth century. He puts on the stage a *vocabulary* of poetry, the *character* of the poet, the *prop* of the poem or poetic book, the *action* of poetry, the landscape or *scene* of poetry, the effect or *mood* of poetry, and both a *conversation* and a *fiction* about poetry.

Capricious poetry in *As You Like It*

The epigraph from *As You Like It* shows how deftly Shakespeare can use a comic conversation between characters to represent an engaging aesthetics of poetry pertaining to the interlock between poetry and theatre. When Touchstone tells Audrey that he wishes 'the gods had made [her] ... more poetical', he means 'Having the character of a poet' (*Oxford English Dictionary*, Definition 2.b, citing *As You Like It* 3.4.10–11). When viewed in context, this line, overheard by the melancholic courtier Jaques, identifies not simply the lustful wit of Touchstone but also the learned art of his author:

TOUCHSTONE   I am here with thee and thy goats as the most capricious poet
              honest Ovid was among the Goths.

JAQUES   O knowledge ill-inhabited, worse than Jove in a thatched house!

> TOUCHSTONE   When a man's verses cannot be understood, nor a man's good wit
> seconded with the forward child, understanding, it strikes a man
> more dead than a great reckoning in a little room. Truly, I would
> the gods had made thee more poetical.   (3.4.5–11)

In its historical context, 'poetical' means something like 'learned in the Elizabethan art of literary imitation' – that is, learned about Shakespeare's own rivalry with Ovid, but also both with the Elizabethan Ovidian poet par excellence, Marlowe, as the re-writing of the famous line from *The Jew of Malta* indicates, and with Jonson, whom Jaques embodies as Horatian satirist.[22]

In the first speech, Touchstone, marooned from court in the Forest of Arden, compares himself to Ovid, who was exiled from Rome by the Emperor Augustus because (Elizabethans believed) he was caught in a sexual embrace with Julia, the Emperor's daughter, and sent to Tomis, a barbaric land that Touchstone identifies with the Goths. The clown's wit naturally cascades, for he delights in his pun on 'goats' (beast of *lust*) and 'Goths' as a way to condemn the land he visits, and he wittily praises Ovid for being paradoxically 'capricious' and 'honest': the most honest poet is the most capricious – or inventive. Thus, Shakespeare suggests both a form of ethics and a mode of aesthetics, as he weaves language together to present Touchstone as an Ovidian poet of lustful desire who excels at verse because of his ingenious wit.

It is the scholarship underwriting this wit that Jaques maligns during his aside. His own wit cascading, he uses the image of the house to compare Touchstone's 'knowledge' with the 'thatch'd house' once visited by Jove. Here, Shakespeare combines two myths from Ovid's *Metamorphoses*: when Jove disguises himself as a shepherd before Mnemosyne, god of memory (6.114); and when Mercury and Bacchus disguise themselves as mortals in the pastoral cottage of Baucis and Philemon (8.611–724).[23] Jaques criticizes Touchstone's knowledge of Ovid, while Shakespeare alludes both to Marlowe's Ovidian scholarship and to Jonson's.

In his second speech, Touchstone nominally complains about Audrey's inability to understand his learned Ovidian art, equating such ignorant reception with death or oblivion, the loss of poetic fame. But Shakespeare's re-writing of Marlowe's line and evocation of his death in the small room in Deptford over who would pay the 'reckoning' or bill precisely *remembers* his dead colleague, contradicting Touchstone's point. As such, Shakespeare fictionalizes the loss of poetic fame in order to memorialize Marlowe's Ovidian renown, and to clear an original space for his own achievement.

Touchstone's complaint leads him to wish the gods had made Audrey more 'poetical'. When she expresses ignorance about the meaning of 'poetical', she raises a major question about the art of poetry, from Plato to Sidney: is poetry 'a true thing'? In the *Republic*, Plato had answered in the negative, and in *The Defence of Poesy* Sidney had rehearsed Plato's banishment of poets from his ideal state because they are liars – capricious or fanciful inventors – in order to defend them: poets are crucial to the ideal state because they invent fictions above nature and are thus able to deliver humankind into a 'golden' world.[24] For Sidney, poets can use delightful instruction to move readers to virtuous behaviour on behalf of the commonwealth. Wittily, Shakespeare shows the unlearned female able to articulate the question at the heart of classical, medieval, and Renaissance masculine poetics.

When Touchstone replies, 'No truly; for the truest poetry is the most feigning', his repetition of the concept of *truth* militates against his word 'feigning', producing around the concept of the 'poetical' a paradox necessary to unravel. The word 'feigning' can mean both *imaginative* and *deceptive*; Touchstone means the former, that the truest poetry is the most imaginative; but his author also evokes the latter.[25] Shakespeare does so not to agree with Plato, but to draw attention to the *theatricality* of poetry: the truest poetry is the most theatrical. In this way, Shakespeare acknowledges the theatricality of Ovid's poetry and of Marlowe's, even as he produces a statement defining the achievement of his own dramatic art. Significantly, this statement fuses the arts of poetry and theatre, suggesting not merely that poetry is theatrical but that theatre is made up of poetry, is substantively about poetry, and is often in service of poetry.

Dubious poetry in *Hamlet*

In *Hamlet*, Shakespeare widens the conversation about poetry from aesthetics to philosophy and science. Yet, according to most critics, he makes his Prince 'the English Renaissance's greatest tribute to the theatrical man'.[26] While this view has great appeal to those who restrict Shakespeare's authorship to plays in performance, it neglects Hamlet's own complementary interest in the art of poetry. In addition to his advice to the actors who visit Elsinore castle, Hamlet names, during these very scenes, two poetic genres – the 'chanson' or French chivalric song (2.2.383) and the 'epitaph' (482) – and repeatedly he breaks into song, most often about Jephthah's daughter before Polonius: ' "One fair daughter, and no more, / The which he loved passing well" ' (371–2). But Hamlet also presents himself as a student of the great national epic of Virgil, the *Aeneid*, including its reception and recent staging by Marlowe in his tragedy *Dido, Queene of Carthage*, when the Prince asks the lead actor to perform 'Aeneas' tale to Dido' (404–5).[27]

Right before the players enter the royal castle, Polonius reads to King Claudius and Queen Gertrude a love letter and a poem that the Prince has composed to Ophelia:

> [*Reads the letter*]
> POLONIUS   'To the celestial and my soul's idol, the most beautified Ophelia'–
>   That's an ill phrase, a vile phrase, 'beautified' is a vile phrase. But you
>   shall hear. Thus:
>   'In her excellent white bosom, these, *et cetera.*'
> QUEEN   Came this from Hamlet to her?
> POLONIUS   Good madam, stay awhile. I will be faithful.
>   'Doubt thou the stars are fire,
>   Doubt that the sun doth move,
>   Doubt truth to be a liar,
>   But never doubt I love.
>   'O dear Ophelia, I am ill at these numbers. I have not art to reckon my
>   groans; but that I love thee best, O most best, believe it. Adieu.
>   Thine evermore, most dear lady, whilst this machine is to him,
>   Hamlet.'   (2.2.109–22)

Hamlet is not the only one who is ill at these numbers; routinely, critics dismiss the poem as doggerel verse, without recognizing the dramatic utility of such a poetic rehearsal.

Philip Edwards, editor of the Cambridge edition, is genuinely perplexed: 'Hamlet's letter to Ophelia is a great puzzle; it is so affected, juvenile and graceless. We should be glad to take it as part of Hamlet's recent heartless treatment of Ophelia but it is very firmly said that Ophelia, in obedience to her father, has refused to receive his letters (2.1.106–7; 2.2.143–4). If this is one of Hamlet's real love-letters, why did Shakespeare make him write like Don Armado in *Love's Labour's Lost*' (p. 135). Such perplexing moments of poetic representation, however, afford a more productive site for analysis than such criticism allows.

In context, Polonius joins Claudius and Gertrude in using Hamlet's letter and poem to interpret the motives of his 'antic disposition' (1.5.172) – his supposed madness after his father's untimely death and his mother's hasty remarriage. In other words, Polonius produces the letter containing the poem to plumb Hamlet's interiority, to discover the motive for his histrionic conduct. As Polonius boasts, 'I will find / Where truth is hid, though it were hid indeed / Within the centre' (2.2.155–7). The truth Polonius later claims to discover is that of the young man's erotic melancholy, caused when his beloved, listening to the authority of her father, repels her lover's devotion (3.1.170–2).

Yet the audience becomes privy rather to Polonius' folly; in the artifact of Hamlet's poem, we discover a 'centre' that remains 'hid', a 'truth' that continues to be opaque: a work of art that puts the hunters off the scent. In this regard, the dramatic scene of poetry stages the central problem this play rehearses: in response to a ghostly call to revenge, Hamlet re-invents tragic inwardness, performing his famed consciousness.[28]

Consciousness is indeed the topic of Hamlet's letter and poem. In particular, the document identifies the prince as a Petrarchan lover and poet. (That Shakespeare thinks of Petrarchism here emerges when Hamlet uses the word 'numbers' to describe his verse – the very word Mercutio uses to describe Romeo's Petrarchism, quoted earlier.) The scraps of discourse Polonius teasingly reads from Hamlet's letter participate in the conventions of Elizabethan Petrarchism. Specifically, Hamlet addresses Ophelia in the language of Petrarchan idolatry, describing his beloved first as 'celestial' – a divine body gloriously above his own decaying 'machine' – and then as 'my soul's idol' – the object of his interior adoration. By evoking Petrarchism here, Shakespeare draws a historical genealogy for the invention of inwardness, with himself in the role of counter-Petrarchan heir. Equally Petrarchan is Hamlet's (or is it Polonius'?) singling out of a female body part: 'In her excellent white bosom, these, etc.' In the history of Petrarchism, it might be difficult to find not simply a briefer blazon but a more splendid representation of female interiority as physiological vacancy and absence – something truly interior. Gertrude finds this poetic conceit so repulsive she instinctively recoils ('Good madam, stay awhile').

For his part, Polonius recoils from another of Hamlet's words: 'beautified'. Critics have long observed that Hamlet attaches to Ophelia the word that fellow writer Robert Greene used when criticizing Shakespeare back in 1592 as an 'upstart crow, beautified with our feathers'.[29] We have here, then, a rather unusual historical moment. Shakespeare presents his Petrarchan prince being maligned in public for his erotic poetic diction, while the author himself airs his own public maligning by a colleague. If Shakespeare laughs at himself, and perhaps returns the laugh to the dead Greene as part of a public hearing, he therefore signs the scene with his own authorial stamp. Such a moment suggests some of the sophisticated art that Shakespeare uses to reckon the Petrarchan numbers he makes so patently ill.

Consciousness also lies at the heart of the four-line verse Hamlet composes to Ophelia, as the quadruple anaphora of 'Doubt' and the climactic word 'love' records. The contents again are formally Petrarchan; this Petrarchan lover attempts a Petrarchan poem. Yet rather than a sonnet, he pens a trimeter line in trochaic meter, rhyming *abab*. The concrete images of 'stars', 'fire', and 'sun' both brighten and heat up the erotic beat of the verse, but they also help set up a characteristic Shakespearean interlock between an exterior show and an interior truth. Belying the simplicity (and vacuity) of the verse is its deep philosophical, theological, and scientific resonance.

Long ago, Harry Levin placed Hamlet's poem in the dubitative tradition of Western philosophy – what he calls 'the philosophical outlook of skepticism'[30]. He quotes Sir Walter Ralegh, 'The Skeptick doth neither affirm, nor denie any Position; but doubteth it' (p. 54); and more famously John Donne: 'The new philosophy calls all in doubt' (p. 54). According to Walter N. King, who follows up on Levin, the decisive historical event underwriting Hamlet's poem is the 1543 publication of Copernicus' *De revolutionibus orbium coelestium*, which rejected the Ptolemaic theory of a geocentric universe to posit a heliocentric theory: 'The stars, Hamlet asserts, may not be igneous planetary bodies, as they appear to be to the naked eye. The earth may orbit about the sun. If so, the traditional moral and metaphysical truth regarding man's centrality in the universe may be a lie. Nevertheless, Hamlet's love need not be doubted.'[31]

While the sceptical problematic in Hamlet's Petarchan poem may, in Levin's words, 'mix … cosmology with intimacy' along the lines of 'the Metaphysical School' of Donne (p. 54), this approach does not account for Hamlet's Petrarchism, and especially his bad Petrarchism. Nor should we try simply to make sense of the poem as a puzzle in the Prince's personality; while reading it as a function of character leads to a dead-end, we may see the poem as an unusual register of the author's own counter-Petrarchism. Shakespeare's disproportionate loading of deep philosophy on to a 'juvenile' quatrain becomes a wry but patent sign of Shakespearean authorship. Often, this author inserts a *bad poem* in order to create *great drama*.

The central word in Hamlet's poem, 'Doubt', has in fact been seen to have at least three different meanings: '(1) to be skeptical (as about the ancient truths about the stars and the sun); (2) to suspect (that, e.g., truth might be a liar); (3) to disbelieve e.g., Hamlet's love'.[32] As David Leverentz puts it, Hamlet sends Ophelia 'an ambiguous poem, which can be read as "Never doubt that I love" or "Never suspect that I love" '.[33] However doggerel the verse may be, Shakespeare is careful to enclose in it Hamlet's famous penchant for word play and ambiguity.

As such, we cannot tell if Hamlet's poem is a verse testament to his faith to Ophelia – his spiritual care for her – or merely another form of antic disposition: 'Believe it'. The question over the Prince's motives lingers, and in so doing raises the dynamic central to the play as a whole: that between inner truth and outer appearance. To borrow Hamlet's own vocabulary, does the poem to Ophelia 'denote' him 'truly' or does it perform an 'action that a man might play'? Does it merely 'seem' or does it 'have that within which passes show' (1.2.83–5)? Hamlet's famed theatrical vocabulary during his first appearance leads us to a concluding observation: Shakespeare uses the poem to Ophelia to represent not merely the question of Hamlet's interiority, poised as it is on the threshold between medieval Christianity and modern philosophy, but also his own fundamental theatricality. *The truest poetry is the most feigning.*

Poet of the theatre

Shakespeare's engagement with the art of poetry in such plays as *Hamlet* and *As You Like It* suggests a new model of Shakespearean authorship. In particular, Shakespeare's sustained rehearsal of a fiction about the poet and the art of poetry, couched in dialogue with the major poets of the classical, medieval, continental, and English tradition – Virgil, Ovid, Chaucer, Petrarch, Spenser, Marlowe – calls into question the notion that Shakespeare is simply a 'man of the theatre': a playwright, actor, and shareholder in an acting company concerned with the business of his profession, and taking little interest in the 'literary' merit or afterlife of his plays. If, as Lukas Erne recently argues, Shakespeare wrote plays for both page and stage, as scripts to be performed and books to be read, and that, like Spenser and Jonson, he was concerned after all with his literary reputation,[34] we might conclude that the specifically *poetic* conversation rehearsed in his plays helps to re-classify him: he is at once a poet and a playwright, a new sixteenth-century author we might call a *literary* poet–playwright.

In this chapter, we have seen how often Shakespeare uses his new authorship to fuse the form of poetry with the form of theatre, making the art of the poet integral with the art of the playwright. Shakespeare is not simply the consummate man of the theatre but a theatrical man who wrote enduring poems, engaged vigorously with the Western poetic tradition, and made the art of the poet an abiding figure on the new London stage. In the end, he transformed both media in which he worked, poems as well as plays, and made this his principal legacy to future English and European authors. In all his works, the English poet–playwright succeeded in making the truest poetry the most theatrical, the truest theatre poetical.

NOTES

1 All quotations from Shakespeare's poems and plays will be from Cambridge editions, unless noted to come from *The Riverside Shakespeare*, ed. G. Blakemore Evans, et al. (Boston: Houghton, 1997).

2 See *Shakespeare's Songs and Poems*, ed. Edward Hubler (New York: McGraw Hill, 1959).

3 Most often, critics write about Shakespearean 'metadrama' – his theatre about theatre; see, e.g., Anne Righter (Barton), *Shakespeare and the Idea of the Play* (London: Chatto & Windus, 1964). On 'metapoetry', see Gary Schmidgall, *Shakespeare and the Poet's Life* (Lexington: University Press of Kentucky, 1990), pp. 123–60; Peter Hyland, *An Introduction to Shakespeare's Poems* (Basingstoke: Palgrave Macmillan, 2003), pp. 35–41; Ekbert Faas, *Shakespeare's Poetics* (Cambridge University Press, 1996).

4 Marvin Spevack, *A Complete and Systematic Concordance to the Works of Shakespeare*, 6 vols. (Hildesheim: Georg Olms Verlagsbuchhandlung, 1968–70).

5 See Thomas H. Cain, 'Spenser and the Renaissance Orpheus', *University of Toronto Quarterly* 41 (1971), 24–47; David Armitage, 'The Dismemberment of Orpheus: Mythic Elements in Shakespeare's Romances', *Shakespeare Survey* 39 (1986), 123–33.

6 By 'poet', Shakespeare sometimes means 'playwright' (*Ham* 2.2.328); and when he uses the word 'poem' he means 'play' (*Ham* 2.2.366).

7 Thomas Nashe, *Pierce Pennilesse*, in *The Works of Thomas Nashe*, ed. Ronald B. McKerrow; rev. F. P. Wilson, 5 vols. (Oxford: Blackwell, 1958), I: 299.

8 Patrick Cheney, *Spenser's Famous Flight: A Renaissance Idea of a Literary Career* (University of Toronto Press, 1993).

9 See Cheney, *Spenser's Famous Flight*, pp. 81–6; and *Shakespeare, National Poet–Playwright* (Cambridge University Press, 2004), pp. 130–4, 234–6.

10 See Ann Thompson, 'Philomel in *Titus Andronicus* and *Cymbeline*', *Shakespeare Survey* 31 (1978), 23–32.

11 See Wendy Wall, 'Turning Sonnet', in *Imprint of Gender: Authorship and Publication in the English Renaissance* (Ithaca: Cornell University Press, 1993), pp. 23–109.

12 For Homer, translated by George Chapman starting in 1598, see Reuben A. Brower, *Hero and Saint: Shakespeare and the Graeco-Roman Tradition* (Oxford University Press, 1971), pp. 78, 80, 274–5. For Virgil (and Ovid), see Heather James, *Shakespeare's Troy: Drama, Politics, and the Translation of Empire* (Cambridge University Press, 1997). For Spenser, see Patrick Cheney, 'Shakespeare's Sonnet 106, Spenser's National Epic, and Counter-Petrarchism', *English Literary Renaissance* 31 (2001), 331–64.

13 *Christopher Marlowe: The Complete Plays*, ed. Mark Thornton Burnett, Everyman Library (London: Dent; Rutland, VT: Tuttle, 1999); *The Collected Poems of Christopher Marlowe*, ed. Patrick Cheney and Brian J. Striar (Oxford University Press, 2006).

14 On Marlowe in Shakespeare, see Thomas Cartelli, *Marlowe, Shakespeare, and the Economy of Theatrical Experience* (Philadelphia: University of Pennsylvania Press, 1991); James Shapiro, *Rival Playwrights: Marlowe, Jonson, Shakespeare* (New York: Columbia University Press, 1991).

15 Smith, introduction to *Cymbeline*, *Riverside Shakespeare*, p. 1,568.

16 *The Poetical Works of Edmund Spenser*, ed. J. C. Smith and Ernest de Selincourt, 3 vols. (Oxford: Clarendon, 1909–10), vol. I.

17 On pastoral in *As You Like It*, see Paul Alpers, *What is Pastoral?* (University of Chicago Press, 1996), pp. 71–8, 123–34, 197–203. On romance and epic in *Antony and Cleopatra*, see Garrett A. Sullivan, Jr, 'Sleep, Epic, and Romance in

Antony and Cleopatra', in *Antony and Cleopatra: New Critical Essays*, ed. Sara Munson Deats (London: Routledge, 2005), pp. 259–73.

18 The locus classicus is John Donne's 'The Canonization': 'We'll build in sonnets pretty rooms' (32) (in *John Donne's Poetry*, ed. Arthur L. Clements, 2nd edn (New York: Norton, 1992)).

19 See Patrick Cheney, 'Halting Sonnets: Poetry and Theatre in *Much Ado about Nothing*', in *A Companion to Shakespeare's Sonnets*, ed. Michael Schoenfeldt (Oxford: Blackwell, 2006).

20 See Jonathan Bate, *Shakespeare and Ovid* (Oxford: Clarendon, 1993).

21 On the Spenserian shepherd-king, see Cheney, *Shakespeare, National Poet–Playwright*, pp. 43, 63, 77, 245, 272.

22 James P. Bednarz, *Shakespeare & the Poets' War* (New York: Columbia University Press, 2001), pp. 108–11.

23 Shakespeare also probably glances at Marlowe, *1 Tamburlaine* 1.2.198 and 5.1.184–7; see Cheney, *Shakespeare, National Poet–Playwright*, p. 146.

24 Plato, *Republic*, Book 10, in *The Collected Dialogues of Plato*, ed. Edith Hamilton and Huntington Cairns (Princeton University Press, 1961); Sidney, *Defence of Poesy*, in *Sir Philip Sidney: Selected Prose and Poetry*, ed. Robert Kimbrough, 2nd edn (Madison: University of Wisconsin Press, 1983), p. 108.

25 The *Oxford English Dictionary* cites this line under Definition 1, 'Given to inventing; imaginative', but goes on to cite *A Midsummer Night's Dream* 1.1.31 under Definition 2, 'Dissembling, deceitful'.

26 Richard Helgerson, *Self-Crowned Laureates: Spenser, Jonson, Milton, and the Literary System* (Berkeley: University of California Press, 1983), p. 159.

27 See, e.g., Philip Edwards (ed.), *Hamlet, Prince of Denmark* (Cambridge University Press, 2003), p. 149.

28 See Harold Bloom, *'Hamlet': Poem Unlimited* (New York: Riverhead, 2003); Stephen Greenblatt, *Will in the World: How Shakespeare Became Shakespeare* (New York: Norton, 2004), esp. 298–303.

29 See Harry Levin, *The Question of Hamlet* (New York: Viking, 1959), pp. 63–4; Greenblatt, *Will in the World*, p. 215.

30 Levin, *Question*, p. 54.

31 King, *Hamlet's Search for Meaning* (Athens: University of Georgia Press, 1982), p. 52.

32 *Hamlet*, ed. Barbara A. Mowat and Paul Werstine, Folger Shakespeare Library (Washington DC: Folger, 2005), p. 88.

33 Leverentz, 'The Woman in Hamlet', in *Representing Shakespeare: New Psychoanalytic Essays*, ed. Murray M. Schwartz and Coppélia Kahn (Baltimore: Johns Hopkins University Press, 1980), p. 119.

34 Lukas Erne, *Shakespeare as Literary Dramatist* (Cambridge University Press, 2003).

READING LIST

Bate, Jonathan. *The Genius of Shakespeare*. London: Macmillan-Picador, 1997.

Cheney, Patrick. *Shakespeare, National Poet–Playwright*. Cambridge University Press, 2004.

Duncan-Jones, Katherine. *Ungentle Shakespeare: Scenes from His Life*. Arden Shakespeare. 3rd series. London: Thomson Learning, 2001.

Erne, Lukas. *Shakespeare as Literary Dramatist*. Cambridge University Press, 2003.

Faas, Ekbert. *Shakespeare's Poetics*. Cambridge University Press, 1996.

Greenblatt, Stephen. *Will in the World: How Shakespeare Became Shakespeare*. New York: Norton, 2004.

Helgerson, Richard. *Self-Crowned Laureates: Spenser, Jonson, Milton, and the Literary System*. Berkeley: University of California Press, 1983.

Hyland, Peter. *An Introduction to Shakespeare's Poems*. Basingstoke: Palgrave Macmillan, 2003.

Schalkwyk, David. *Speech and Performance in Shakespeare's Sonnets and Plays*. Cambridge University Press, 2002.

Schmidgall, Gary. *Shakespeare and the Poet's Life*. Lexington: University Press of Kentucky, 1990.

13

DAVID SCHALKWYK

Poetry and performance

Performance is central to Shakespeare's poems, not merely because the world's most famous man of the theatre was a major poet, but also because, by illuminating the vexed but neglected question of agency, it elucidates the ethical as well as the political dimensions of these poems. In the twentieth century, attention to the theatrical context of Shakespeare's poetry waxed and waned. Critics who emphasized the dramatic nature of the Sonnets especially in the middle part of the century[1] were overtaken by those who insisted on reading the poetry *against performance*: for their wordplay;[2] their exploration of the consciousness of private experience;[3] the invention of a modern, *poetic* subjectivity;[4] or the dynamics of a voice internalized by the solitary reader.[5] More recently, however, commentators have restored both the theatrical and linguistic aspects of performance to the poems.[6] The lyrical or narrative modes of a long poem or a sonnet may be performative in three different senses: (1) 'dramatic', if it uses the representative modes of drama, conveying the embodiment, enactment or expression of events, attitudes, or feelings, rather than merely describing them; (2) 'rhetorical', if it uses rhetorical devices to evoke emotions or attitudes or even prompt particular forms of action or behaviour;[7] and (3) 'transformative', if it mobilizes the performative force of speech acts to act upon or change the world.[8]

The first two are well known. The third, in which language is used to transform the world, needs some explanation. Transformative speech acts are neither true nor false, but rather effective or ineffective in accordance with pre-existing conventions.[9] The force that they put into effect is often ethical or political. When I use a performative speech act like a promise, I am committing myself to a future act. And I commit myself in the act, *in* saying the words, 'I promise . . .' This act itself is public rather than private. It does not matter what I feel or even what I intend *inwardly* for me to be bound by the *public act* of my promise. Even if I make a promise with the inward intention of breaking it, I am still bound by my undertaking. The words I use transform my relationship to someone else in the world. They place an ethical burden upon me, which holds even if I break the promise. Such speech acts gain their transformative *force* from a combination of relationships, rules, and conditions in which language and social institutions interact. As speech acts they bring together personal intention, linguistic convention, and forms of social power. Promises and oaths play a pivotal role in both Shakespeare's Sonnets and narrative poems.

Transformative performatives should be differentiated from rhetorical acts. Shakespeare's poetry is informed by linguistic devices or tropes which, according to classical rhetoric, produce emotional effects in the reader (see Chapter 8 in this volume). If a particular use of language is meant to produce an effect on its audience – to change the way they feel, think, or act – then it is also a performative speech act. But how is a speech act that makes me feel sadness, pity, or anger different from a promise, verdict, or commitment? The effect of a transformative speech act is carried out *in* its utterance, provided that all the required social conditions and linguistic conventions are met. I say 'I do' in appropriate circumstances, and I am now married; a judge says 'Guilty!', and the accused *is* guilty; a linesperson saying 'Out!' *makes* the tennis-player's serve invalid. There is no such direct, logical relationship between the utterance and its effect in rhetorical speech acts,[10] where the outcome of the aim to move, persuade, excite, or instruct is finally unpredictable. My attempt to make someone take pity on me by declaring how intensely I burn for them, or how exquisitely beautiful they are, may or may not have its intended effect. There is no way of telling exactly what it will do. *Rhetorical* speech acts are calculated to have a force on a listener or reader, but that force is incalculable and unpredictable. *Transformative* speech acts, on the other hand, have an immediate effect the moment they are uttered, often against the intentions of their speakers or audience. Often they cannot be retracted. They may be more powerful than merely rhetorical performatives, since they carry the force of a whole linguistic, cultural, or ethical system. In the Sonnets and narrative poems, Shakespeare explores agency through the ways in which such supra-personal force may either shape and transform individuals or else be appropriated by the embodied agency that such people possess by being members of a linguistic community.

Venus and Adonis and *The Rape of Lucrece*

It is striking that rather than celebrating the rhetorical power of language in his two major narrative poems, Shakespeare dwells on its impotence.[11] In *Venus and Adonis* and *The Rape of Lucrece*, characters use language to persuade an unwilling person to perform, or submit to, undesired sexual intercourse. Each poem offers a mirror image of the power relations of the other. Venus may be stronger than the desired boy, subjecting him to the comic indignity of being carried away tucked under her arm, but no matter how often she manoeuvres herself into positions in which physical consummation may be possible – either lying on top of him, or pulling him on top of her – his refusal to participate, to *perform*, leaves her exasperated. Even her name as the goddess of love, and her usual capacity to engender desire, are undermined by the counter-effective force of her rhetoric: 'I hate not love', Adonis retorts, 'but your device in love, / That lends embracements unto every stranger' (789–90). Both aspects of Venus's performance – her physical 'embracements' and her rhetorical 'device' – thus thwart the consummation of her desire. She cannot force herself upon her unwilling lover, and her rhetorical performance *exacerbates* his indifference, turning it into contemptuous rejection. Faced with the failure of rhetoric (recall that its effects are contingent and uncertain), Venus has no performative speech acts, which effect their action *in* their utterance, in her armoury. She tries to promise him things that she hopes he will find attractive (229–44). But a promise works only when the promisee desires what is promised; otherwise it is a threat.[12]

The performative shift from promise to threat points to the 'tender and aggressive aspects' of sexuality[13] embodied in the vignette of Adonis's stallion:

> What recketh he his rider's angry stir.
> His flattering 'Holla' or his 'Stand, I say'?
> What cares he now for curb or pricking spur,
> For rich caparisons or trappings gay?
> He sees his love, and nothing else he sees,
> For nothing else with his proud sight agrees. (283–8)

The lack of authority in Venus's speech acts, either to flatter or command, is comically transferred to Adonis, who finds himself powerless to control his animal because of the intensity of the horse's arousal. The performative force of both Adonis's entreaty and command are overwhelmed by single-minded desire, which places the animal beyond the human world. It no longer pays any attention to the anthropomorphizing attractions of human value, freeing itself from its usual role as a theatrical vehicle of its rider's show: 'He sees his love, and nothing else he sees, / For nothing else with his proud sight agrees' (287–8). This is an apt description of Tarquin's state of mind before he rapes Lucrece. Of course, Adonis's horse does not rape his fancied mare. And that is precisely the point. The concept of rape does not apply to animals, no matter how much we may be tempted to see in their behaviour a mirror of our own. The compelling single-mindedness of the animal is transformed into something much darker when we consider its applicability to all-consuming human – especially male – desire in *The Rape of Lucrece*.

Both poems rest on the crucial conceptual distinction between physical action and performative transformation. For although it is a physical, non-linguistic, act, sexual intercourse is as much a performative act as a promise, threat, or verdict. Much of the comic lightness of *Venus and Adonis* is made possible by our sense that there is not much at stake in the sexual contest between Venus's desire and Adonis's reluctance. It would merely be one more adulterous affair notched up by the goddess of love, and the poem's pastoral and classical setting works against a moral or Christian sense that Adonis would be damaged or compromised by allowing himself to be seduced. The tragic aspect of the poem lies in Adonis's wilful determination to engage in the manly pursuit of the boar rather than allowing himself to become the effeminized object of female desire.

Despite the fact that the later poem echoes its predecessor's concern with the powerless nature of particular kinds of rhetoric, the transformative nature of sexual intercourse as a performative act is central to *The Rape of Lucrece*, and it is surrounded by other powerful performatives. The first of these is Collatine's theatrical display of his wife's beauty and chastity:[14]

> ... Collatine unwisely did not let
> To praise the clear unmatchèd red and white
> Which triumphed in the sky of his delight,
> ...
> For he the night before, in Tarquin's tent,
> Unlocked the treasure of his happy state:
> What priceless wealth the heavens to him had lent
> In the possession of his beauteous mate.   (18–25)

What appears to be a mere description is a series of performative boasts and challenges, staged through the female body.[15] Furthermore, the narrator shifts between endorsing the view of women as a precious object possessed by men and warning against the moral and practical dangers of doing so: 'why is Collatine the publisher / Of that rich jewel he should keep unknown / From thievish ears, because it is his own?' (33–5).[16] These shifts arise from the presented uncertainty between reported and direct speech. Does the narrator or Collatine conceive of Lucrece as an 'unlocked ... treasure'? And to whom do we attribute the fatal tension between such 'wealth' merely 'lent' by 'the heavens' or held as a 'possession'? Does Collatine qualify the beauty of Lucrece's eyes ('Where mortal stars, as bright as heaven's beauties, / With pure aspects did him peculiar duties') through the self-centred reminder of her marital obedience (including, presumably, sexual compliance), or is this added, speculatively, by the narrator? Such ambiguity between different voices is one of the advantages of narrative over theatrical dialogue, in which the mixing of different perspectives and values is more difficult to sustain.[17] Nor is Collatine's the only voice that is literally confused with that of the narrator. 'Honour and beauty, in the owner's arms, / Are weakly fortressed from a world of harms' (27–8) is clearly a commentary in the narrative voice, but it introduces a military image of Lucrece as an object embattled and besieged – like Ardèa itself – that is central to Tarquin's later conception of the rape. Who is the 'owner' of the 'honour' in line 27? Does Lucrece personify such 'honour'? In which case, does it belong to her or to Collatine? Or is she merely the vehicle of Collatine's 'honour', which he possesses only for as long as she remains within the compass of his 'arms', in all senses of the word? These questions are central to the way in which we read the act of penetration that constitutes Lucrece's rape. Answering them one way or another determines the performative nature of the physical act of succumbing to another's 'arms'.

Once Tarquin has persuaded himself that 'nothing else with his proud sight agrees', he allows no consideration of honour, friendship, or pity to overrule his desire, which appears, like the stallion, to be sexual or instinctual. But Tarquin's determination to rape his cousin's wife is both a response to the performative aspects of Collatine's utterances (boastful, provocative) and a counter-performative (retaliatory, self-assertive): it is a transformative act that annuls his cousin's claim to absolute possession of a wife. Such possession allows him to 'scorn to change [his] state with kings' (Sonnet 29).

The narrator's claim that Tarquin's 'neglect' of 'his honour, his affairs, his friends, his state' is physiological, stemming from 'the coal which in his liver glows' (45–7), squares with Tarquin's own rationalization of his act. But such rationalization cannot take into account the performative force of rape. It is less physiological (although we should not underrate the force of physical violation) than social and cultural; it arises from the very considerations that Tarquin 'neglects' in his headlong pursuit. He is, however, not unaware of these pressures, since on his way to Lucrece's chamber he rehearses both the unsatisfying, ephemeral nature of sexual satisfaction and the social shamefulness of its achievement (203–14). Contrary to Tarquin's conviction that he is commanded by an *instinctive* nature over which he has no control, the narrator re-deploys Tarquin's metaphor of martial adventure (278–9) to highlight the primarily non-sexual nature of his pursuit:

> Her breasts like ivory globes circled with blue,
> A pair of maiden worlds unconquerèd,
> Save of their lord no bearing yoke they knew,

And him by oath they truly honourèd.
These worlds in Tarquin new ambition bred,
    Who like a foul usurper went about
    From his fair throne to heave the owner out.   (407–13)

At the centre of this curiously unerotic *description* of Lucrece's nakedness and the moment of intensified determination that sets her rapist's course of action lies a crucial speech act: the 'oath' that ties Lucrece to her husband. The mainspring of Tarquin's desire is less her beauty than her oath of fidelity to her husband which, driven by homosocial and rank-inflected rivalry, he wishes to annul, negating its binding and consolidating force. If Lucrece is the place where Collatine's honour is located, then that is where it must be destroyed. As a performative, this is a political act; and it will have dire but unforeseen political consequences.

Characteristically, Tarquin never considers the consequences of the rape for Lucrece. If Adonis's horse saw nothing but his 'love', it is not clear, despite the lengthy descriptions by the narrator of Lucrece's dazzling beauty, that Tarquin sees her at all. She is a mere instrument of a purpose far darker than the lusty sexuality of Venus or the stallion. He is well aware that his action will carry more weight for Lucrece than a physical violation, horrible as that would be. She is to him as Desdemona is to Othello – a blank sheet 'made to write whore upon' (*Othello* 4.2.74) – the vehicle of a performative act, the force of which is directed primarily at the man whose 'yoke' she bears, whose 'honour' she carries, and who has boasted of his peerless 'ownership' of her. Tarquin's threat is therefore less physical than horribly symbolic. He threatens not merely to kill her, but also to use her as a silenced prop in the dumb show of her own dishonour and shame. Lucrece is caught between the prospect of her dead body being used to proclaim a slanderous performative force and being the living stage of Tarquin's homosocial revenge upon her husband. She has little power to resist the transformative force of the rape, but by choosing to stay alive she retains a degree of agency, which allows her to remobilize her body for counter-performative acts of her own.

The consequences of the rape are immediately predictable, but ultimately also unforeseeable. Tarquin underestimates his own transformation by the act, possibly because he had convinced himself that it was driven by mere lust. In an echo of Shakespeare's Sonnet 129, Lucrece and Tarquin are equally, but very differently, transfigured by its action:

He like a thievish dog creeps sadly thence;
She like a wearied lamb lies panting there.
He scowls, and hates himself for his offence;
She, desperate, with her nails her flesh doth tear.

He faintly flies, sweating with guilty fear;
   She stays, exclaiming on the direful night;
   He runs, and chides his vanished loathed delight.   (736–42)

Many commentators dwell upon the 'Augustinian' problem of Lucrece's suicidal response to her transfiguration. Augustine argues that if Lucrece did not consent to the rape, she is innocent, and therefore she damns herself by committing suicide.[18] Her body may have been violated, but provided that she was coerced, her mind or soul remains unstained. But whatever Lucrece's intentions may have been, they are not the place where the performative effects of the rape are staged. The public nature of speech acts helps us to see this: provided the conditions of performance are met, a speech act takes effect publicly, irrespective of the interior state of mind of its agent. My promise remains a promise, no matter that I had no intention of fulfilling it; I am married the moment the priest or secular official makes the conventional pronouncement, whatever reservations I may have in my heart.

A particularly horrible and violent form of speech act, Lucrece's rape carries forces and effects that lie beyond the volition of either party.[19] They depend entirely upon cultural conventions, values, and modes of power. She is violated not merely by the single act of rape, but also by the public, patriarchal values that determine the meaning of the rape, of which her family are as much part as her rapist. The most intense of Lucrece's anguish arises from her sense of the inevitable, public shame that derives from the nature of her 'oath' to her husband, and which is intrinsic to her place at the intersection of the private and public orders. The undecidable place between private and public domains that Lucrece occupies after her rape is encapsulated by the paradox of her desperate apostrophe: 'O unfelt sore, crest-wounding private scar' (812). Anticipating Mary Wroth's anguished representation of the tortured theatrical display of the female lover's body,[20] Lucrece is intensely sensitive, like Cleopatra, of the display of her 'private scar' in the public arenas of poetry, song, and folk wisdom.[21] The rape also destroys her sense of self, which is almost wholly informed by the conviction, internalized from the public arena, that as the vehicle of Collatine's honour she has been irreparably damaged: 'My honey lost, and I a drone-like bee, / Have no perfection of my summer left, / But robbed and ransacked by injurious theft' (836–8).

Lucrece responds to the irresistible transformations of her rape by first turning to mere rhetoric, in a series of impotent laments and curses that have as little effect as Venus's attempts to persuade Adonis to love her in return, or her own earlier efforts to deflect Tarquin from his purpose. Some have felt that the length and the intensity of Lucrece's rhetoric after the rape is a tedious distraction. But it serves two crucial purposes. For the first time it reveals her subjectivity: it expresses the tortured interiority of a person who has up to now been seen in instrumental terms, as an object of desire, ownership, or spectacle.[22] It also underlines the contingent effects of rhetoric as opposed to the transformative force of performative acts, like the rape itself or Lucrece's marriage oath. Lucrece succumbs to Tarquin's threat, not because she fears death, but rather because her dead body would have falsely shamed her, and by extension, publicly staged her husband's dishonour. By the same token, though, she believes that her raped body, though alive, will have been transformed into the living sign of her eternal stain. Both silenced and violently appropriated to the point of self-alienation, she therefore transforms the powerlessness of mere rhetoric (her fruitless pleas before the rape, and her vain lamentation and curses after it) into both a counter-performance and counter-performative, using her violated body as their stage or vehicle. Paradoxically, this entails staging her death, for only such a decisive display of her *own* agency has the power to proclaim her innocence and shame her rapist:

> ... Collatine may know
> Her grief, but not her grief's true quality.
> She dares not thereof make discovery,
>   Lest he should hold it her own gross abuse,
>   Ere she with blood had stained her stained excuse
> ...
> To shun this blot she would not blot the letter
> With words, till action might become them better.   (1312–23)

She stages her suicide as a meticulously calculated, theatrical performance which is simultaneously a performative act of considerable power. In order to ensure that her suicide has the effects she desires, she exacts from her husband and his companions an oath – matching her own marriage vows – to revenge her violation.[23] Lucrece thus reclaims possession of her body: her suicide is simultaneously a declaration of innocence and an accusation of the guilty party. But in reclaiming herself through the performative agency of suicide she also releases herself to be re-appropriated in further performative and theatrical acts.[24] This new appropriation is staged chiefly by Lucius Brutus – another consummate actor – who uses the potency of her performative act as an occasion for casting off his own 'antic disposition' (*Hamlet* 1.5.172) and pursuing the political aim of ending the Tarquins' despotic rule:

> When they had sworn to this advisèd doom,
> They did conclude to bear dead Lucrece thence,
> To show her bleeding body thorough Rome,

> And so to publish Tarquin's foul offence;
> Which being done with speedy diligence,
> The Romans plausibly did give consent
> To Tarquin's everlasting banishment.   (1849–55)

Cheney draws our attention to the theatrical discourse employed in this concluding stanza, especially in the concerted display of Lucrece's theatrically 'bleeding body' in the public arenas of the city, and the theatrical applause of the citizens ('plausibly').[25] The poem registers, he suggests, a 'cultural shift from poetry to theatre, print publication to staged show'. Whether or not it can sustain such a large claim, *The Rape of Lucrece* does explore the ethical dimensions of action and passivity within the political sphere through the union, in poetry, of performance and performative actions. Between the first mode in which Lucrece is 'published' and the second, she finds a space for agency (however circumscribed) through the transformative force of performative actions, through which she displaces the deadly weight of her husband's praise with her own fatal accusation of her violator. That she continues to blame herself even as she tries to restore her husband's honour and accuse her rapist is a sign of the double aspect of performative actions with regard to agency. They are fundamentally enabling, because they allow individual subjects to appropriate the transformative powers of language as a whole; but they also necessarily limit such agency, since language does not belong to individuals but in part shapes them in the image of the society as a whole. Lucrece and Tarquin are both 'captive victors' of the performative powers of speech acts (including such actions as rape and suicide), able to appropriate available modes of agency, but incapable of controlling or predicting their consequences.

Shake-speares Sonnets

Shakespeare's Sonnets are centrally concerned with the performative transformation of the poetics of praise into the poetics of blame. This transformation (or, more accurately, the undecidable shuttling between praise and blame) arises from the ethical dimensions of transformative speech acts, which complicate the ways in which the Petrarchan tradition from which Shakespeare draws usually represents the relations of power and emotion between the poet, the figure addressed in the poem, and its broader audience or readers.

Performance informs the Sonnets in two related ways. First, the profession of their poet as a 'common player' – whose 'public means' and 'public manners' 'subdues' his 'nature' 'to what it works in, like the dyer's hand'

(Sonnet 11) – imbues the poems with an acute self-consciousness of their author's place as a man of the theatre. The poems are aware of their poet's theatrical context both as a form of social stigma and as a place of presentation or show.[26] Secondly, Shakespeare employs performative speech acts, often in distinctly theatrical ways, to invoke an ethics of reciprocity that seeks to 'leave out difference' (Sonnet 105). Such speech acts attempt to relinquish the sociological burden of the profession of theatrical performance.

Sonnet 23 is one of most obviously 'theatrical' of the poems:

As an unperfect actor on the stage,
Who with his fear is put besides his part,
Or some fierce thing replete with too much rage,
Whose strength's abundance weakens his own heart;
So I, for fear of trust, forget to say
The perfect ceremony of love's rite,
And in mine own love's strength seem to decay,
O'ercharged with burden of mine own love's might:
O let my [b]ooks[27] be then the eloquence
And dumb presagers of my speaking breast,
Who plead for love, and look for recompense,
More than that tongue that more hath more expressed.
   O learn to read what silent love hath writ:
   To hear with eyes belongs to love's fine wit.

The dramatic quality of the sonnet stems not only from its theatrical opening simile, but also from its implicit dialogical form: it is a response to an accusation (by its addressee) that the poet has in some way failed in his performance of an expected 'ceremony'. The player–poet acknowledges the charge, but he deflects it by attributing his own 'unperfect' behaviour to problems inherent in the fact that he is expected to *stage* 'love's rite' publicly. The player–poet thus tries to evade blame by invoking an ethics of performance that is paradoxically anti-theatrical.

He is an 'unperfect actor' because he is overcome by stage fright. But why can't he live up to the demands of his profession, in all senses of the word? His stammering delivery is not caused by a merely personal inadequacy, but rather from the public situation over which he has little control. He is overwhelmed by the social stigma of being a common player required to perform in a *different* kind of theatre: the courtly stage of proffered love and flattery. He is also overwhelmed by the very feelings he is expected to express: the public space in which they must be declared produces a gap between their felt intensity and conventional expectation, rendering what he wants to say socially inappropriate or improper. The public performance of love required by the courtly theatre of patronage and compliment paradoxically over-whelms the poet precisely *because* he is a man of the theatre. He therefore pleads with the powerful beloved to shift the relationship from the public arena to the private space of the page, where it would be possible to invite an ethics of free, reciprocated, or mutually shared love, uncomplicated by the politics and economy of public competition and display. The key to the ethics sought by the poem lies equally in its plea for 'recompense' and its ambiguous 'fear of trust'. The vulnerability that it simultaneously exposes and attempts to hide arises from the difficulty of forging the intimacies of loving trust in a public arena, in which the familiarity or intimacy that it seeks is impossible to sustain. 'Books' in this context (for which we might read 'poetry') become the place where the socially debilitating 'public manners' and 'habits' (both as regular modes of behaviour and clothing) might be effaced or elided. In the written word theatrical performance might be replaced by the more private, intimate arena of reading.

Sonnet 23 presents a paradox: a theatrical performance represented in poetry, it eschews the stage in favour of the page. Based on a plea to the beloved to abandon his own theatrical expectations for the *poetic* address of sonnets like this one, the poem invokes performance, but it does not manage to mobilize the transforming power of performative speech acts. The plea in Sonnet 23 is purely rhetorical. It is as susceptible to uncertainty and impotence as similarly rhetorical pleas in *Venus and Adonis* and *The Rape of Lucrece*.

Sonnet 125, the penultimate sonnet to the young friend, is a recapitulation of Sonnet 23, but in a different key. Its opening lines invoke the performative dimensions of public ceremony, followed by a plea for a more intimate form of reciprocity, in a further complication of the incompatible ethical dimensions of public performance and love.

> Were 't aught to me I bore the canopy,
> With my extern the outward honouring,
> Or laid great bases for eternity,
> Which proves more short than waste or ruining?
> Have I not seen dwellers on form and favour
> Lose all and more, by paying too much rent,
> For compound sweet forgoing simple savour,
> Pitiful thrivers, in their gazing spent?
> No, let me be obsequious in thy heart,
> And take thou my oblation, poor but free,
> Which is not mixed with seconds, knows no art
> But mutual render, only me for thee.
>   Hence, thou suborned informer! A true soul
>   When most impeached stands least in thy control.

Like 23, this Sonnet negotiates the passage between private feeling and public display via a theatrical mode in which the question of audience is crucial. It also opens with an exculpatory invocation of public 'rite' or 'ceremony'. To the implicit charge that he has not engaged in the expected public forms of display and allegiance, the servant–poet asks a hypothetical question: 'What would I have lost if I'd followed your expectation by building a dependable foundation for our relationship on a public display of honour and affection?' The second quatrain turns the implicit accusation into a subtle counter-charge, carefully attenuated by its being put as a question. Those who have indeed engaged in the public rites of display have turned out to be mere 'pitiful thrivers' (another version of 'captive victors'): poor fools who have wasted their material and emotional resources in the expectation of profit that has never accrued to them. Furthermore, the young friend who demands such show from his lover should bear part of the blame for this deceptive economy: he is as much a 'dweller on form and favour' as his false admirers.

The third quatrain rejects the economy of the theatre of courtly devotion. It recapitulates Sonnet 23's plea for a withdrawal into an intimate or private space of mutual trust where free poverty is preferable to the enslaved expenditure of public show. The crux of the poem, where power and ethics collide, is line 10, where the speech act, 'take thou my oblation', hovers undecidedly between a plea and a command. Despite its echo of the plaintive weakness of Sonnet 23, Sonnet 125 attempts to transform both the politics and the ethics of the relationship through performatives. The paradoxical anti-theatricality of the earlier poem stems from the vulnerability of the 'unperfect' actor upon a public stage. It is the place where he should be in his element, but for that very reason it exposes the impropriety of his feelings to a wider, disapproving, and competitive audience. The theatricality decried in the two sonnets is a courtly theatre – it lies between completely public show and private intimacy – where men are expected to stage their devotion in the pitiful hope of 'recompense' (Sonnet 23.11). Paradoxically, though, instead of gaining from their performance they spend *themselves* in mere 'gazing'. If Shakespeare's servant-poet yearns to transcend the stigma of the public theatre, he also rejects the stage of courtly display, arguing that both its questionable ethics and debilitating economy destroy true friendship or love.

Like Sonnet 23, 125 attempts to forge a private, unobserved space in which a free, trusting exchange of hearts would be possible. It offers a freely given, 'mutual render' while also attempting to shame the recipient into a reciprocating gift of himself. But like its predecessor, it remains caught up in a situation of unequal power. Just as the promise of a thing not desired turns out to be a threat, so an oblation has to be accepted by the recipient to be a gift. The friend is urged to 'let' his poet be 'obsequious in [his] heart' rather than in the public arena of the 'dwellers on form and favour'. If the event of 'mutual render, only me for thee' is a kind of theatre, it is theatre pared down to the most fundamental kind of performative act: the free exchange of selves, untouched by the publicity of audience or gallery. Such an exchange is a performative act, just like the rape and suicide in *The Rape of Lucrece*, albeit with a different effect: it is an exercise of love rather than power and shame.

The most dramatic turn comes in the couplet's startling shift in the direction of address and reception. The addressee of the sonnet appears to be the well-born friend. But now a different audience is revealed. The interruption of the 'suborned informer' destroys the dream of a space removed from the public gaze.[28] By transforming its most intimate performative act of solicited love into the self-affirming speech acts of angry dismissal and moral independence, Sonnet 125 performs the paradox at the heart of the Sonnets' relation to performance. There can be no withdrawal from the public stage to private page in the player–poet's relationship with the young aristocrat. All the player–poet can finally muster are the performative acts of shaming the beloved into reciprocal action or a declaration of personal independence from the questionable stage on which he expected to perform.

The rejection of the courtly theatre of questionable devotion performed in Sonnet 125, and the increasing acceptance of the social and personal stigma of making oneself a 'motley to the view' in Sonnets like 124 (especially in the affirmative, 'No, I am that I am' of Sonnet 121), suggest that Shakespeare finally affirms the independent integrity of his professional theatre, through which he gained both wealth and social standing as a gentleman. The antitheatricality of some of the Sonnets is therefore aimed at a particular form of theatre, not theatre as such.

'The Phoenix and Turtle'

'The Phoenix and Turtle' is a short, strongly emblematic poem in which the theatre appears at first sight to play little part. Performance is, however, concentrated in both its theatrical occasion and its performative modes of speech. A strongly directive or imperative voice controls the poem from its opening alternation between invitation and proscription to its closing invitation to communal prayer. The 'bird of loudest lay' (1) is called upon to play the part of the 'herald sad and trumpet' (3) to the 'chorus of [the] tragic scene' (52), while figures less appropriate are excluded through re-iterated prohibition: 'But thou . . . / To this troop come thou not near' (8).

Those who wish to identify the unspecified bird of the opening stanza overlook the fact that the poem creates a community of affect or emotion, which embraces or marginalizes readers according to their capacity to share in its combined sense of wonder and loss. Some will identify themselves with the chorus; others, like the 'suborned informer' of Sonnet 125, will remain eavesdroppers, excluded, like the 'shrieking harbinger' (5) and 'fowl of tyrant wing' (10), from the poem's invitation to prayer. The birds invoked or indicted will thus recognize themselves.

The event equally celebrated and lamented by 'The Phoenix and Turtle' is the passing of the kind of love that the Sonnets seek through their gift of 'mutual render' (125) and their desire to 'leave out difference' (105):

> Phoenix and the turtle fled
> In a mutual flame from hence.
>
> So they loved, as love in twain
> Had in essence but in one. (23–6)

Although the 'theme' at its centre is made up of descriptive utterances, their effects are performative. In so far as the poem's paradoxical object defies logical description, the speech acts that convey its wonder simultaneously bring it into being. Phoenix and turtle constitute the impossible unity in separation of a peculiar ideal of love, but the poem underlines the fact that this unique combination of truth, beauty, and love has not merely died, but has actively 'fled / In a mutual flame' (23–4) from an inhospitable world. Forced to cry out in amazement at the already immolated wonder, Reason itself assumes the unusual role of chorus to the now tragic scene. It appropriates the opening, directive voice of the narrator, and closes, as the poem begins, with an invitation directed at a self-identifying community of those 'either true or fair' to 'sigh a prayer' for 'these dead birds' (66–7). Reason thus transforms itself from detached arbiter of logic and fact into a constituent of a community that paradoxically enacts 'truth and beauty' by simultaneously celebrating and mourning its emblematic passing (64).

Using the occasion of the theatre and the performative power of the *directive* voice, the poem constitutes a community of anyone able to align themselves with its impossible ideal of totally reciprocal love, unimpeded by the 'differences' that constitute the theatre, and by extension, the world itself.

A Lover's Complaint

Cheney argues that the trajectory of the relationship between poetry and theatre should not be traced as the subsumption of one by the other, but rather as the fusion of the two genres in the peculiar career that Shakespeare fashioned for himself as a national poet–playwright. Part of his evidence is provided by *A Lover's Complaint*, printed with the Sonnets in the 1609 Quarto, in which, as he puts it, we find 'the direct representation of poetry and theatre' (p. 239). *A Lover's Complaint* rehearses the theatrical discovery of the eavesdropper in Sonnet 125 and its public exposure of private feeling. The narrator overhears the complaint narrated by the fallen young woman to the 'reverend man' (57), who, chancing upon her private display of grief, provides a sympathetic audience. The poem strikingly represents the young man's seduction as a form of theatre or performance,[29] focusing especially on the young woman's consciousness of its performative quality. His 'craft of will' combines the accomplished craftiness of young man's desire with Shakespeare's own name and the artful fictions of the theatre itself:

> 'To make the weeper laugh, the laugher weep,
> He had the dialect and different skill,
> Catching all passions in his craft of will.'   (124–6)

The young woman deliberately depicts the seducer as an extraordinarily accomplished *actor*, able to transform the emotional states of a wide-ranging audience. The poem makes much of the promiscuity of his performative reach: his wide-ranging desire is matched by readiness of his multiple audiences to find pleasure in his 'subduing tongue' (120). In his androgynous beauty, his extraordinary power over his admirers, and his amoral incapacity for trust, he is like the young man of the Sonnets. But he also encapsulates the combination of poetry and performance that constitute both the Sonnets' mode and the object of their aversion: he turns the sonnet into a vehicle of promiscuous circulation rather than 'mutual render'. By re-deploying the sonnets written by his previous lovers against the complaining woman – using the former's voice to his own persuasive purposes – he echoes the way in which Shakespeare represents the sonnet's multiple situations of address in his plays.[30] All these voices are in turn refracted through the voice, first, of the young woman of the complaint, and then the poem's anonymous, eaves-dropping narrator.

This multiple layering of voices produces a theatrical effect that is para-doxically impossible – or very difficult to achieve – on stage. The theatre can draw attention to its own modes of theatricality, but it can do so only through a disjunctive 'baring of the device' – the breaking of theatrical illusion to reveal the actor rather than the character s/he is playing.[31] *A Lover's Complaint* uses the 'discourse of the theatre' not merely to highlight theatrical aspects of the behaviour of characters (such as the histrionic mode of the young man's seduction), but also to represent and enact the seductive pleasures of theatre itself. Its central narrative and theatrical device is the young woman's use of the direct speech of her lover to tell her story. The poem thus embodies a theatrical or performative mode of address in the young woman, who is also, unexpectedly, its most accomplished actor. She embodies the voice of the person who is 'other' to her, telling us not merely *that* he said something, but making what he said *her own*. This is remarkable considering her alienation from the man who induced her to believe his vows, gained her trust, used her, and then abandoned her. When we first encounter her on the bank of the river, she is tearfully eradicating the signs of his histrionic success: tearing up his sonnets and casting his tokens of love into the river. Although she begins conventionally enough, with a *blazon* of the young man's physical attractiveness, her narrative representation of his theatrical qualities is soon transformed into a theatrical embodiment of the voice that seduced her:

> 'For further I could say this man's untrue,
> And knew the patterns of his foul beguiling,'
> . . .
> 'And long upon these terms I held my city,
> Till thus he 'gan besiege me: "Gentle maid,
> Have of my suffering youth some feeling pity,
> And be not of my holy vows afraid." '   (169–79)

The use of the modal form verb 'I could say . . .' indicates a split between the person who knows what she *should* think of the transparent fictionality of the young man's 'show' and the subjectivity that had always already succumbed to the charms of that performance, as much through her own will as any craft(iness) of his. The statement of what ought to have been (and in fact was) apparent – note the verbs 'say . . . knew . . . heard . . . saw . . . knew . . . thought' – is undercut when she moves from indirect to direct voice. She becomes an actor, making the seducer's charmed performance her own.

Through that transferred role the reader now occupies the role of the young woman, hearing the young seducer's performance with her ears, seeing it through her eyes. Despite the moral loading of the narrative once the young woman resumes her own voice, we are thus directly exposed to the seductive histrionics of her lover. This reiteration of the seduction is more complex and interesting than the first. We are not merely seeing and hearing the young man's performance; we witness the performance of the young woman playing the role of the young man, so that the tears she sheds become the tears he shed in proof of the sincerity of his feelings and the truthfulness of his vows. As in all acting, she transforms herself into him: his words become her own; his prevarications are compellingly transformed into her fictions;

his androgynous body becomes hers. These are the transformations of the theatre itself: its falsity and seductiveness are as complicit in its pleasurable effects as the young man's show.[32]

Despite her full knowledge of the duplicity of the young man's performance, the seduced woman confesses that she would do it again:

> 'O, that infected moisture of his eye,
> O, that false fire which in his cheek so glowed,
> O, that forced thunder from his heart did fly,
> O, that sad breath his spongy lungs bestowed,
> O, all that borrowed motion seeming owed,
> Would yet again betray the fore-betrayed,
> And new pervert a reconcilèd maid.'   (323–9)

Her vocatives invoke the qualities of the actor: the 'infected' tear, 'false' complexion, 'forced' passion, 'sad' rhetoric, and the 'borrowed motion' of simulated action. They are precisely the qualities that she has herself displayed in the performance of her tale. We know that actors are false, yet we take repeated pleasure in their 'borrowed motions'. The young woman knows this too. Whatever moral or merely psychological lesson we may take from A Lover's Complaint about the vagaries of the will in the sexual encounters between men and women, at a *performative* level the poem enacts the entrancing, pleasurable, but also perilous, seductions of the theatre itself.

NOTES

1 Robert Benckelman, 'The Drama in Shakespeare's Sonnets', *College English* 10 (1948), 138–44; G. K. Hunter, 'The Dramatic Technique of Shakespeare's Sonnets', *Essays in Criticism* 3 (1953), 152–64; and Georgio Melchiori, *Shakespeare's Dramatic Meditations: An Experiment in Criticism* (Oxford University Press, 1976).

2 Stephen Booth, *An Essay on Shakespeare's Sonnets* (New Haven: Yale University Press, 1969) and *Shakespeare's Sonnets* (New Haven: Yale University Press, 1977).

3 Heather Dubrow, *Captive Victors: Shakespeare's Narrative Poems and Sonnets* (Ithaca: Cornell University Press, 1987), p. 150.

4 Joel Fineman, *Shakespeare's Perjured Eye: The Invention of Poetic Subjectivity in the Sonnets* (Berkeley: University of California Press, 1986).

5 Helen Vendler, *The Art of Shakespeare's Sonnets* (Cambridge, MA: Harvard University Press, 1997).

6 See David Schalkwyk, *Speech and Performance in Shakespeare's Sonnets and Plays* (Cambridge University Press, 2002); Lynne Magnusson, *Shakespeare and Social Dialogue: Dramatic Language and Elizabethan Letters* (Cambridge University Press, 1999); and Patrick Cheney, *Shakespeare, National Poet–Playwright* (Cambridge University Press, 2004).

7 Philip Sidney, *The Defence of Poesy*, in *Sir Philip Sidney: A Critical Edition of the Major Works*, ed. Katherine Duncan-Jones (Oxford University Press, 1989), pp. 212–51.

8 See J. L. Austin, *How To Do Things With Words* (Oxford University Press, 1975); and John R Searle, *Speech Acts: An Essay in the Philosophy of Language* (Cambridge University Press, 1969).

9 'Illocutionary' acts in Austin, *How To Do Things With Words*, pp. 98ff.

10 'Perlocutionary' acts in Austin, *How To Do Things With Words*, pp. 99 and 121.

11 Cf. Dubrow, *Captive Victors*, p. 19.

12 See Dubrow, *Captive Victors*, pp. 36ff.

13 John Roe (ed.), *Poems* (Cambridge University Press, 1992), line 267n.

14 Peter Hyland, *An Introduction to Shakespeare's Poems* (London: Palgrave Macmillan, 2003), pp. 109ff; Coppélia Kahn, 'The Rape in Shakespeare's *Lucrece*', *Shakespeare Studies* 9 (1976), 45–72; Berry, 'Woman, Language and History in *The Rape of Lucrece*', in *The Cambridge Shakespeare Library, Volume II: Shakespeare Criticism*, ed. Catherine M. S. Alexander (Cambridge University Press, 2003); and Katharine Eisaman Maus, 'Taking Tropes Seriously: Language and Violence in Shakespeare's *Rape of Lucrece*', *Shakespeare Quarterly* 37 (1986), 66–82.

15 See Arthur F. Marotti's ' "Love is not love": Elizabethan Sonnet Sequences and the Social Order', *ELH* 49 (1982), 396–428.

16 See *Much Ado About Nothing* 1.1.168–72.

17 M. M. Bakhtin calls this mixing of voices or 'heterogossia'. See *The Dialogic Imagination*, ed. Michael Holquist, trans. Caryl Emerson and Michael Holquist (Austin: University of Texas Press, 1981); and V. N. Voloshinov, *Marxism and the Philosophy of Language*, trans. Ladislav Matejka and I. R. Titunik (Cambridge, MA: Harvard University Press, 1986).

18 See John Roe (ed.), *Poems*, pp. 23ff; and Colin Burrow (ed.), *Complete Sonnets and Poems* (Oxford University Press, 2002), pp. 66ff.

19 See Burrow (ed.), *Complete Sonnets and Poems*, pp. 72–3.

20 See Mary Wroth, *Pamphilia to Amphilantus*, in *The Poems of Lady Mary Wroth*, ed. Josephine A. Roberts (Baton Rouge: Louisiana University Press, 1983), Sonnet 42.

21 *Antony and Cleopatra* 5.2.215–17.

22 See Hyland, *Introduction*, pp. 120ff.

23 See David Schalkwyk, *Speech and Performance in Shakespeare's Sonnets and Plays*, p. 53.

24 See Philippa Berry, 'Woman, Language and History in *The Rape of Lucrece*', in *The Cambridge Shakespeare Library, Volume II: Shakespeare Criticism*, ed. Catherine M. S. Alexander (Cambridge University Press, 2003), pp. 458–64: p. 463.

25 *Shakespeare, Poet–Playwright*, pp. 142–3; see also Heather Dubrow, *Shakespeare and Domestic Loss* (Cambridge University Press, 1999), p. 59.

26 See Heather Dubrow, ' "Incertainties now crown themselves assur'd": The Politics of Plotting Shakespeare's Sonnets', *Shakespeare Quarterly* 47 (1996), 291–305.

27 The 1609 quarto reads 'books'.

28 This is a recapitulation of the world of *Hamlet*, which renders every private moment relentlessly public. See Schalkwyk, *Speech and Performance*, ch. 3.

29 Cheney, *Shakespeare, Poet–Playright*, pp. 239–66.

30 See Schalkwyk, *Speech and Performance* for an extended discussion of the Sonnets' relation to performance.

31 See V. Shklovsky, 'Art as Technique', in *Russian Formalist Criticism: Four Essays*, trans. Lee T. Lemon and Marion J. Reis (Lincoln: University of Nebraska Press, 1965), pp. 3–24.
32 See Tanya Pollard, *Shakespeare's Theatre: A Sourcebook* (Oxford: Blackwell, 2004), for the castigation of the theatre for its corrupting pleasures.

READING LIST

Austin, J. L. *How To Do Things With Words*. Oxford University Press, 1975.

Berry, Philippa. 'Woman, Language, and History in *The Rape of Lucrece*'. In *The Cambridge Shakespeare Library, Volume II: Shakespeare Criticism*. Ed. Catherine M. S. Alexander. Cambridge University Press, 2003, pp. 458–64.

Dubrow, Heather. *Captive Victors: Shakespeare's Narrative Poems and Sonnets*. Ithaca: Cornell University Press, 1987.

Hunter, G. K. 'The Dramatic Technique of Shakespeare's Sonnets'. *Essays in Criticism* 3 (1953), 152–64.

Hyland, Peter. *An Introduction to Shakespeare's Poems*. London: Palgrave Macmillan, 2003.

Magnusson, Lynne. *Shakespeare and Social Dialogue: Dramatic Language and Elizabethan Letters*. Cambridge University Press, 1999.

Maus, Katharine Eisaman. 'Taking Tropes Seriously: Language and Violence in Shakespeare's *Rape of Lucrece*'. In *Shakespeare: The Critical Complex: Shakespeare's Poems*. Ed. Stephen Orgel and Sean Keilen. New York: Garland, 1999, pp. 296–82.

Melchiori, Georgio. *Shakespeare's Dramatic Meditations: An Experiment in Criticism*. Oxford University Press, 1976.

Parker, David. 'Verbal Moods in Shakespeare's Sonnets'. *Modern Language Quarterly* 30 (1969), 331–9.

Schalkwyk, David. *Speech and Performance in Shakespeare's Sonnets and Plays*. Cambridge University Press, 2002.

Vendler, Helen. *The Art of Shakespeare's Sonnets*. Cambridge, MA: Harvard University Press, 1997.

14

SASHA ROBERTS

Reception and influence

The reception history of Shakespeare's poems is important not only for charting changing attitudes towards literary expression that, in turn, have shaped the discipline of literary studies; or, indeed, for reaching a better understanding of how Shakespeare's poetry works. It matters because it prompts us to take a step back: to think again about what it is we (and others) value most about poetry; why we are drawn to poetry in the first place, and why we continue to read, sometimes to labour over it. Reception history, in other words, is not just about history. It is about what makes literature special.

Because Shakespeare's canonical status has long been assured, his poetry is now assumed to be especially rewarding, beautiful, skilful, profound. But it was not always so. In Shakespeare's lifetime the Sonnets slipped into obscurity while the narrative poems brought him an ambivalent reputation as both a marvellously skilled poet and a purveyor of popular, wanton literature. The popularity of *Venus and Adonis* in the period is undisputed: it was not only Shakespeare's most frequently reprinted work before the Restoration but one of his most frequently transcribed works in manuscript in the seventeenth century – outstripping the plays from *Hamlet* to *Lear*, *1 Henry IV* to *Richard II*, *Love's Labour's Lost* to *Twelfth Night*, and exceeded only by the songs from *The Tempest* and Sonnet 2. But by the eighteenth century much had changed. Not only had the narrative poems fallen to the periphery of the Shakespearean canon, but the Sonnets had become something of an aesthetic and sexual embarrassment. How could the nation's Bard write such passionate love poems to another man? What went wrong?

The ensuing controversy over Shakespeare's Sonnets takes us on a journey through cultural histories of taste (both literary and sexual) to vital debates about poetry itself: its purpose, its origins, its rewards. Above all, the incorporation of the Sonnets within a Romantic poetic agenda by Coleridge, the deployment of the Sonnets by Oscar Wilde at the close of the nineteenth century in defence of art and passionate expression, and the use of the narrative poems by Coleridge and Ted Hughes to develop theses of poetic truth, speak to changing views on the place and promise of poetry. But poetic form is itself protean, changing in unexpected ways. The appropriation of some of Shakespeare's most haunting lines from *The Tempest* by a seventeenth-century miscellany, a songbook, and by T. S. Eliot prompt the question of what it means to approach dramatic verse as poetry, as song, and as lyric – and of where we draw the fragile lines between poetic genres. More widely, to engage with the reception of Shakespeare's poems is to confront the categories of critical analysis that we use to approach literature; the terms by which we read. The truism still holds true: what we see is what we look for. The question remains: is this restricting or enabling?

The Sonnets and narrative poems in early modern England

It doesn't all reduce to sex, but gender and desire nonetheless play a significant part in the reception history of Shakespeare's poems before the Restoration. The story begins not with the Sonnets but with *Venus and Adonis*, swiftly praised for its Ovidian wit and sweet verse and, more widely, placed alongside the plays as testament to Shakespeare's deft handling of the theme of love. In this respect, as Patrick Cheney argues, Shakespeare's career was conceived not as that of a playwright forced to turn to poetry during the plague years but as a *poet–playwright*, a 'new writing institution combining poems and plays in a single career'.[1] John Weever's tribute to Shakespeare in 1595, for instance, praised 'thy children' (Shakespeare's characters) that 'burn in love': 'Rose-checkt *Adonis* with his amber tresses / Faire fire-hot *Venus* charming him to love her / Chaste *Lucretia*', 'lust-stung *Tarquine*', and '*Romea-Richard*'.[2] Similarly, Francis Meres's often-cited praise for Shakespeare in 1598 – 'the sweete wittie soule of *Ouid* lives in mellifluous & honey-tongued *Shakespeare*, witnes his *Venus* and *Adonis*, his *Lucrece*, his *sugred* Sonnets among his private friends, &c'. – appears in the wider context of his argument that, like Ovid for 'the Latines', Shakespeare is 'the most passionate among us to bewaile and bemoane the perplexities of Love'.[3]

But by the turn of the seventeenth century this attention to Love, and to *Venus and Adonis* in particular, had become something of a critical liability. Gabriel Harvey's well-known note in the margins of his copy of Speght's *Chaucer* trivializing *Venus and Adonis* as the reading matter of immature readers anticipates this trend: 'the younger sort takes much delight in Shakespeare's Venus and Adonis; but his Lucrece, and his tragedy of Hamlet, Prince of Denmarke, have it in them to please the wiser sort'.[4] Similarly, the *Parnassus* plays performed at Cambridge University (c.1599–1602) launched an extended satire upon *Venus and Adonis*: as the shrewd press-corrector Judicio remarks of Shakespeare, 'His sweeter verse contaynes hart throbbing line/Could but a graver subject him content, / Without love's foolish lazy languishment'.[5]

The perceived problem with *Venus and Adonis* was primarily one of readership (Roberts, pp. 13–14). While the most obvious readership of Elizabethan erotic narrative poems were the classically educated young gentlemen of the Universities and the Inns of Court, the very fact that they were written in English made them – and by extension a corpus of Ovidian erotic mythology – available to a wider reading public of less educated readers, both male and female. *Venus and Adonis*, with its intimate portrayal of a woman lusting after a young man, soon became fashioned as the light literature of lightweight readers who read merely for pleasure and titillation; hence the most often-cited lines from the poem were precisely its bawdy set-piece, Venus's erotic blazon of her body ('I'll be a park'), inviting Adonis to 'graze' on her 'lips', 'hillocks' and 'fountains' (229–40). Accordingly, in the *Parnassus* plays the poem is a favourite of the dim-witted Gullio – 'Let this duncified world esteeme of Spe[n]cer and Chaucer, Ile worshipp sweet Mr. Shakespeare, and to honoure him will lay his *Venus and Adonis* vnder my pillowe' – while in Heywood's *The Fair Maide of the Exchange* (1607) Bowdler ridiculously attempts to seduce a wench by citing verbatim Venus' blazon, 'Ile be a parke'.[6]

While male readers of *Venus and Adonis* were lampooned for their intellectual weakness (hence Gullio's inability to appreciate Spenser), women readers of the poem were fashioned as especially vulnerable to the erotic temptations presented by the poem: in this respect the reception history of *Venus and Adonis* reveals how discourses of reading were gendered in the period. Indeed, the extensive allusions to women reading *Venus and Adonis* – more than for any other Shakespearean work before the 1640s – constitute a *trope* of the eroticized woman reader of Shakespeare that assumes women's independence as readers in early modern literary culture.[7] For instance, in *The Scourge of Folly. Consisting of satyricall Epigramms* (c.1611), John Davies of Hereford laments that Shakespeare's 'lewd *Venus*', like Ovid's 'Art of Loue', teaches women 'loues designes':

> Fine wit is shewn therein: but finer 'twere
> If not attired in such bawdy Geare,
> But be it as it will: the coyest Dames,
> In priuate reade it for their Closset-games.[8]

Worse still, 'the Lines so draw them on, / To the venerian speculation' – to erotic fantasy – that 'they will think of it sith *Loose* Thought is free' (p. 232).

Davies' conflation of textual and sexual experience in the body of the woman reader of *Venus and Adonis* is repeated in other allusions to women's venerian reading of Shakespeare in the period: Richard Brathwaite's attack upon gentlewomen 'carrying' *Venus and Adonis* 'even in their naked Bosomes' (1630), Thomas Cranley's account of a prostitute's bedchamber with a copy of *Venus and Adonis* 'lying upon a shelf close underneath' (1635), and John Johnson's remarkable vision of Shakespeare creeping 'into the womens closets about bedtime' (1641).[9] Although these allusions perform different generic and rhetorical functions, like Davies's poem they often slide between condemnation and titillation, vehemence and voyeurism. Fissured with ironies, they are not to be taken at face value.

Indeed, contemporary allusions to both men and women reading *Venus and Adonis* reveal little about historical practices of reading. Rather, what they fundamentally address are the economics of the evolving early modern literary industry: the cultivation of new markets of readers; the cultural impact of populist literature; the uncontrolled dissemination of literature in print; the independence of readers in the literary marketplace. More widely, the discourse of contemporary commentary on *Venus and Adonis* is resolutely focused upon love and lust: other issues explored by the poem, such as metamorphosis, nature, death, or discipline, receive no attention. Contemporary commentary on the poem is thus strikingly reductive; far more than commentary on Shakespeare's plays in the period, which, with the prefatory matter of the First Folio, addressed a wider range of topics (characterization, nature, language, style, and dramaturgy, for instance).

A more complex picture emerges by turning to the fragmented archival record of early modern readers of *Venus and Adonis*. The example of two gentlewomen readers of the poem suggests how women in the period might – in different ways – assume authority for themselves over their reading matter. Thus, Anne, Lady Southwell (1573–1636) undertook a defence of 'devine Poesy' against the 'disgrace' of 'some wanton Venus or Adonis', while Frances Wolfreston (1607–77) was unashamed to autograph her copy of the poem, making it available to her children as part of her library, and apparently marking its most notorious passage, Venus's bawdy blazon.[10] But more far-reaching in its critical implications is the commonplacing (excerpting) of *Venus and Adonis*. While our modern critical practice is to seek an overall explication of a literary work – privileging the larger narrative, the big ideas – early modern readers sought out *sententiae* from literature: pithy maxims, often with a moralizing or exemplary message, that could be applied to all manner of topics and circumstances. In so doing they transformed the meanings, contexts, and indeed the texts of literary works. Thus, while some readers drew from the racy passages of *Venus and*

Adonis (for instance, Daniel Leare's verse miscellany from the 1630s incorporates Venus' blazon into a 'Song' on kissing), others plucked lines from the poem into pockets of surprising wisdom. In the printed commonplace book *England's Parnassus* (1600), Venus's exhortation to Adonis to use his body sexually – 'Foul cank'ring rust the hidden treasure frets, / But gold that's put to use more gold begets' (767–8) – is extracted under the general heading of 'Use': removed from the seduction narrative, the couplet loses all trace of irony to acquire a new tone of gravity and common sense.[11] With a keener awareness of the sententious use of literature in early modern England, we may arrive at a more nuanced understanding of its multiple and malleable meanings.

Lucrece reiterates this point. Unlike *Venus and Adonis*, *Lucrece* maintained a reputation as a serious piece of work enabling the likes of Harvey to class it as 'wiser' reading alongside *Hamlet*. This was not simply a function of subject matter: the chaste over the erotic; the birth of Republican Rome over Ovidian metamorphosis. Since St Augustine, Lucrece's suicide had been a topic of ethical debate in humanist circles and beyond; hence the extended deliberation on suicide in Shakespeare's poem. It is this debate that frames the marginal and chapter headings inserted in reprints of *Lucrece* from Quarto 6 (1616), and that was developed by Francis Quarles in his poem appended to Q9 of *Lucrece* (1655; see Roberts, pp. 102–29). But this debate is also ignored in the sententious use of the poem. Not only were extracts from the poem incorporated into a generalizing rubric and rhetoric with no reference to the Lucrece legend – as in John Abbott's c.1670s miscellany that, under the heading 'On Time', extracted the couplet 'It cheares ye plowman [with] increasefull crops, / And wasts huge stones w[i]th little water-drops' (958–9) – the 'chaste' poem was also plucked for its vision of eroticized female beauty, naked and supine, 'like a vertuous monument she lyes' (386–412). In one seventeenth-century miscellany, for instance, the passage is extracted and pronouns altered to create the impression of a shared erotic scene of a woman in bed with a man: 'Her lilly hand *his* rosy cheekes lyes under / Cooseninge ye pillow of a lawfull kisse' (my italics). Situated among other amorous verses in the miscellany (such as 'A louers mind', 'Beauty', and 'Praise of a uirgin'), the *Lucrece* extract reads like a Caroline poem on fulfilled desire.[12]

A similar transformation takes place with the Sonnets (Roberts, pp. 153–79). For Katherine Duncan-Jones, the silence that apparently greeted the publication of the 1609 Sonnets indicates that early readers 'may have found the collection disconcerting, disappointing or even shocking', particularly in their portrayal of same-sex passion.[13] Individual sonnets transmitted in manuscript sometimes appear with titles and textual variants that construct conventionally heterosexual love poems; isolated from the latent narrative of homoerotic desire of the 1609 sonnet sequence they are relocated among Caroline amatory verse. For instance, in his 1630 manuscript miscellany Robert Bishop included a version of Shakespeare's Sonnet 106 ('When in the chronicle of wasted time') – headed 'On his M[ist]ris Beauty' and conflated with an eighteen-line poem by William Herbert on his mistress's picture – amid amorous and anti-feminist verse on 'Women'.[14] Similarly, John Benson's edition of *Shakespeare's Poems* (1640) is argued to excise same-sex passion by altering the pronouns and order of the Sonnets; thus for Bruce Smith 'Benson's edition of 1640 is a sign that the cultural moment of Shakespeare's sonnets had passed' with its poetic possibilities for 'ambivalent alliances between male bonding and sexual desire'.[15]

But this is a misleading impression for in fact Benson's edition launches straight into some of the most amorous of the 'fair youth' sonnets with no embarrassment at their provocative pronouns. Indeed, the more significant alteration made by Benson to the Sonnets was to tone down the vitriol of the 'dark lady' sonnets and present them precisely as 'Immoderate' (as in his titles for Sonnet 129, 'The expense of spirit in a waste of shame', and Sonnet 147, 'My love is as a fever') – rather as Daniel, revising his sonnets (appended to the unauthorized *Astrophil and Stella* (1591), STC 22536) into the sequence *Delia* (1592), excised the bitterest sonnets against his mistress' venomous desire. As Margreta de Grazia has argued, the real scandal of Shakespeare's Sonnets was not their portrayal of same-sex passion but their depiction of a sordid, adulterous liaison with a promiscuous woman.[16] This may explain the absence of the dark lady sonnets in the manuscript tradition and the coincidence of two seventeenth-century annotations to surviving copies of the 1609 Sonnets that appear amid the pages of the dark lady subsequence and signal dissatisfaction: one annotator to the Steevens-Huntington copy entirely crossed out Sonnet 129, 'The expense of spirit in a waste of shame', while another remarked after Sonnet 154, 'What a heap of wretched Infidel Stuff'.[17]

The wider significance of Benson's edition of the *Poems* lies not, however, in the field of sexual politics but of literary canonization. Benson's promotion of the *Poems* as 'Seren, cleere, and eligantly plaine, such gentle straines as shall recreate and not perplexe your braine, no intricate or cloudy stuffe to puzzell intellect, but perfect eloquence, such as will raise your admiration to his praise' has been dismissed as wishful thinking – and his edition lambasted for the revisions made to the poems.[18] But not only was Benson following the creative habits of readers in manuscript; in the same year he issued two volumes of Jonson's poems (*Execration against Vulcan. With divers Epigrams ... Neuer Published before* and *Horatius Flaccus. His Art of*

Poetry. Englished by Ben Jonson. With other Workes of the Author . . . never Printed before), and thus he brought to prominence the lyric poetry of the country's two leading (dead) poet–playwrights. Quarles's 1655 edition of *Lucrece* continues the work of canonization, with a frontispiece portrait and celebration of Shakespeare on the titlepage as 'the incomparable Master of our English poetry'; 'poetry', that is, both lyric and dramatic. Understanding Shakespeare as poet–playwright – as a manipulator of voice and character – makes clearer sense of the *Poems* as published by Benson: as verse spoken by different personae in different situations, like characters in a play, not as a continuous outpouring from a single, coherent poetic self. Indeed, it was this latter understanding of the Sonnets that was precisely to prove so perplexing and puzzling to later readers.

The Sonnets in the eighteenth and nineteenth centuries

By the mid-eighteenth century, the era of Shakespeare as poet–playwright had passed: 'his disposition was more inclined to the drama than to the other kinds of poetry', argued Edmond Malone, even as he edited the poems in 1780. Thus, Shakespeare's poems were pushed to the margins of the Shakespearean canon; above all, the sonnet form with its tight compression and 'forced conceit' had fallen out of favour. As editor George Steevens put it, 'what has truth or nature to do with Sonnets?' Such 'laboured perplexities of language, and such studied deformities of style, prevail throughout these Sonnets', leaving the reader in a 'fog'.[19] It is the enduring nature of such critical dissatisfaction that remains surprising: although Shakespeare's Sonnets were championed by the likes of Tennyson, Rossetti, and Elizabeth Barrett Browning ('bless them as short sighs from [Shakespeare's] large poetic heart', 1842), they continued to be condemned as obscure and 'excessive' (Henry Hallam, 1839), 'dull and unintelligible' (Hazlitt, 1902), marred by 'arrogance and ignorance' (Peter Alexander, 1929; all cited in Rollins, *Sonnets*, I: 360–5).

But of course what made Shakespeare's Sonnets so much more controversial was their subject matter: passion between men (although the assumed integrity of the first subsequence which gives rise to this impression has recently been questioned).[20] Bad enough that Shakespeare should be writing sonnets; worse still that he should infuse them with the sordid suggestion of sodomy. Sonnet 20, in particular, exercised Steevens' sense of sexual propriety: 'It is impossible to read this fulsome panegyrick, addressed to a male object, without an equal mixture of disgust and indignation' (Vickers (ed.), VI: 288). Edmond Malone, defending his decision to reprint the Sonnets in 1780, acknowledged that Shakespeare was 'injudicious in the choice of his subject' but sought to recuperate Sonnet 20 within the discourse of custom: the 'indignation' it provoked 'might perhaps have been abated if it had been considered that such addresses to men, however indelicate, were customary in our authour's time, and neither imported criminality, nor were esteemed indecorous' (Vickers (ed.), VI: 296 and 551).

However, the threat of indignation lasted well into the nineteenth century; in 1840, for instance, D. L. Richardson described Sonnet 20 as 'one of the most painful and perplexing [poems] I ever read ... I could heartily wish that Shakespeare had never written it' (cited in Rollins, *Sonnets*, I: 55). This threat was not simply bound up in attitudes towards homosexuality, but towards poetry itself. In his drama, of course, Shakespeare depicted a slew of dubious characters – not least adulterers, murderers, and tyrants – but no-one accused him of writing from experience. In the wake of Romanticism, poetry was habitually regarded as a highly personal mode of expression signifying experience, emotion, authenticity, and originality. As Frank Erik Pointner suggests, 'Romantics used to read Elizabethan sonnets as if they were Romantic poems in which author and speaker are not to be distinguished, a misapprehension which ironically led to the [biographic] interest in Shakespeare's *Sonnets* in the nineteenth and far into the twentieth century' (Pointner, pp. 118–19). Thus, in 1796 Schlegel argued that Shakespeare's Sonnets 'paint most unequivocally the actual situation and sentiments of the poet; they make us acquainted with the passions of the man; they even contain remarkable confessions of his youthful errors', while Wordsworth responded to them as 'poems in which Shakespeare expresses his own feelings in his own Person': 'Scorn not the Sonnet; Critic ... with this key / Shakespeare unlocked his heart' (cited in Pointner, pp. 119–20, and Rollins, *Sonnets*, I: 134).

But this *confessional* mode of reading and writing poetry – a mode that was so much at odds with early modern poetic culture – proved to be a troublesome lock to pick, as the convoluted arguments of Coleridge on Sonnet 20 illustrate. Commending the Sonnets to his son in his *Marginalia* – 'read with a deep Interest. ... [T]hey will help to explain the mind of Shakespeare' – Coleridge remarked that 'if thou would'st understand these Sonnets, thou must read the Chapter in Potter's Antiquities on the Greek Lovers', which argued that 'nothing unseemly' occured between male 'Lovers' in ancient Greece.[21] 'This pure Love Shakespere appears to have felt – to have been no way ashamed of it. ... Yet at the same time he knew that so strong a Love' risked giving way to physical 'Desire':

in this feeling he must have written the 20th Sonnet, but its possibility seems never to have entered even his Imagination. It is noticeable, that not even an

Allusion to that very worst of all possible Vices (for it is wise to think of the Disposition [towards sodomy], as a vice, not of the absurd & despicable Act, as a crime) not even any allusion to it in all his numerous Plays.[22]

Coleridge's strained efforts to deny the dangerous 'Disposition' in Sonnet 20, or indeed the Shakespearean canon, continued in *Table Talk*: 'It seems to me that the Sonnets could only have come from a man deeply in love with a woman – and there is one Sonnet, which from its incongruity of tone I take to be a purposed blind', a deception; probably Sonnet 20, given his attention to the poem in *Marginalia*.[23] For a twenty-first-century reader, the slippage between Coleridge's layers of denial is almost palpable.

And yet the dark lady sonnets (127–52), with all their vitriol, cynicism, and downright bawdy, arguably presented even more of a challenge. Thus, in a volume of the Sonnets later owned by Coleridge, Wordsworth wrote:

These sonnets ^beginning at 127^ to his Mistress, are worse than a game at a puzzle-peg. They ^are^ abominably harsh, obscure & worthless. The others are for the most part much better, and have many fine lines & passages. They are also in many places warm with passion. Their chief faults, and heavy ones they are, are sameness, tediousness, ~~laboriousness~~, quaintness, & elaborate obscurity.

(Wordsworth's excisions)

In response, Coleridge wrote, 'With the exception of the *Sonnets* to his Mistress (& even of these the expressions are unjustly harsh) I can by no means subscribe to the above pencil mark of W. Wordsworth': although taking issue with Wordsworth's private assessment of the Sonnets' 'faults', he makes a qualified 'exception' in the case of the dark lady sonnets.[24]

More readily incorporated into a Romantic poetic agenda was the portrayal of poetic immortality in the Sonnets (Coleridge cited Sonnet 81 as 'proof' of Shakespeare's awareness 'of his own comparative greatness'; cited in Pointner, p. 123) and the exercise of imagination. Thus, in his Fourth Lecture on Shakespeare in 1811–12, Coleridge argued that 'one of the greatest criterions of a true poet' was the 'blending of thoughts into each other' and cited as examples Sonnet 33 ('Full many a glorious morning have I seen') and Sonnet 113 ('Since I left you, mine eye is in my mind'). Such a 'union of thoughts', a 'bringing all into one', serves to make even the reader 'an active creative being'.[25] Similarly, Keats admired the apt and unexpected in Shakespeare's imagery and his apparently effortless turn of phrase, citing Sonnet 12 ('When lofty trees I see barren of leaves ... / And Summer's green all girded up in sheaves') as an example: 'I never found so many beauties in the sonnets – they seem to be full of fine things said unintentionally – in the intensity of working out conceits'. Responding to Shakespeare's reflexive provocation – 'he overwhelms a genuine Lover of Poesy with all manner of abuse, talking about – "a poets rage" ... [and] "Time's antique pen" ' – Keats called Shakespeare 'the Whim King!', who let his thoughts follow conceits wherever they will.[26]

But how far could the Sonnets' 'confession' of 'youthful errors' be excused by whimsy? By the later-nineteenth century, the battle intensified against the confessional school of sonnet reading: 'the Sonnets are dramatic – otherwise their author would be "a sycophant, a flatter, a breaker of marriage vows, a whining and inconstant person"' (Ebenezer Forsyth, 1867); 'the writers who treat the sonnets as biographic materials ... cast aspersions on the moral character of our admired poet' (Bolton Corney, 1862).[27] Of course, reclaiming the Sonnets as dramatic was not the only way to divest them of their dubious morality; the more radical route was to confront the moral context in which Shakespeare's Sonnets had come to be viewed. In his novella *The Portrait of Mr. W. H.* (1889), which first appeared in the widely read *Blackwood's Edinburgh Magazine*, Oscar Wilde did both, writing a provocative account of passion between men and a burlesque upon autobiographical modes of reading Shakespeare that, in turn, questions the extraordinary lengths to which literary theories can be taken. As the *Tablet* of 1889 remarked: 'the question remains – is Mr. Wilde joking?'.[28]

In brief, *The Portrait of Mr W. H.* turns upon the 'Willie Hughes theory of Shakespeare's Sonnets' developed by the fictional Cyril Graham: that Shakespeare's Sonnets were written to a beautiful young boy actor, Willie Hughes (the W. H. of the title-page).[29] Cyril produces a forged portrait of Willie Hughes as proof of the theory; challenged by his friend Erskine, he then commits suicide 'in order to show how firm and flawless his faith in the whole thing was' (p. 166). In turn, the narrator becomes convinced of the theory – 'I felt as if I had been initiated into the secret of that passionate friendship' (p. 210) – and after extensive research seeks to persuade Erskine of its validity. But the tables are strangely turned: as soon as the narrator writes up his findings, he no longer believes in them, while Erskine becomes so convinced he intends to commit suicide in defence of the theory. As the narrator brilliantly puts it, 'no man dies for what he knows to be true. Men die for what they want to be true' (p. 219). In fact Erskine dies of consumption, not suicide, but the narrator is nonetheless heartbroken over the loss of his friend.

Richard Halpern argues that *The Portrait of Mr W. H.* 'gave rise to public doubt about [Wilde's] sexual orientation' and at the later trials he 'would have to answer for the suspicions the *Portrait* created', while Kate Chedgzoy points out that the *Portrait* reconstructs the Sonnets 'in the image of the homosexual coterie publications with which Wilde was himself involved'.[30]

In this way the reception history of the Sonnets becomes woven into the history of the articulation and defence not merely of same-sex passion, but of an emergent homosexual identity at the turn of the twentieth century. But the *Portrait* also takes a swipe at the Bacon–Shakespeare authorship controversy recently stoked by the American Ignatius Donelly, who argued that Francis Bacon wrote Shakespeare's plays: as the *Court Circular* of 6 July 1889 remarked, the Willie Hughes theory 'is ingeniously worked out, but, of course, no more to be taken seriously than Mr. Donnelly's Shakespearean craze'.[31] More widely, *Portrait* develops Wilde's thinking on the extraordinary, even mysterious, power of words that he was later to develop in 'The Critic as Artist'. Shakespeare 'forges false words of love' yet, writes the narrator:

> Words have their mystical power over the soul, and form can create the feeling from which it should have sprung. Sincerity itself, the ardent, momentary sincerity of the artist, is often the unconscious result of style [and] the use of certain phrases and modes of expression can stir the very pulse of passion.
>
> (p. 199)

In this respect we might read the reception history of the Sonnets in the context of conflicting notions of the relationship between form and content. It was not that the Romantics were uninterested in form – they were so intensely – but form was a vehicle to the main purpose of literary endeavour, the imaginative expression of emotion. For Wilde, form itself 'can create' feeling almost unwittingly; thus art becomes the creator and locus of experience: 'it is Art and Art only, that reveals us to ourselves. ... Art, as often happens, had taken the place of personal experience'. In turn, Wilde's *Portrait* and Shakespeare's punning on 'Will in over-plus' in the Sonnets (135.2) was to become a departure point for Joyce's challenge to formal convention – and the literary canon – in *Ulysses*.[32]

The narrative poems and the working poet: Coleridge and Hughes

Coleridge's deliberations on the Sonnets were piecemeal and, to an extent, private; by contrast, in his Fourth Lecture of 1811–12 and lecture notes he turned to *Venus and Adonis* 'to illustrate the principles of poetry' (Coleridge, *Shakespearean Criticism*, II: 62). Bypassing 'the unpleasing nature of the subject' of *Venus and Adonis*, Coleridge used the poem to develop his thesis of the chief 'requisites of a poet – namely, deep feeling and exquisite sense of beauty', combined with 'imagination, or the power by which one image or feeling is made to modify many others and by a sort of *fusion to force many into one*' (Coleridge, I: 193 and 187–8).

To illustrate this very particular understanding of imagination as modification and fusion, Coleridge cited Adonis's flight from Venus at dusk: 'Look! how a bright star shooteth from the sky, / So glides he in the night from Venus' eye' (*Venus and Adonis* 815–16). 'How many images and feelings are here brought together without effort and without discord', enthuses Coleridge: 'the beauty of Adonis – the rapidity of his flight – the yearning yet hopelessness of the enamoured gazer – and a shadowy ideal character thrown over the whole'. That 'shadowy ideal' character is the humane voice of the narrator, conflated by Coleridge to Shakespeare and 'impressing the stamp of humanity, of human feeling' over inanimate objects and animals: 'Lo, here the gentle lark, [weary of rest, / From his moist cabinet mounts up on high. ...]' (*Venus and Adonis* 853–8; Coleridge, I: 187–9). Similarly, Shakespeare's description of 'the purblind hare' (*Venus and Adonis* 679–708) demonstrates his 'love of natural objects' – a love, of course, that was at the heart of so much Romantic poetry (Coleridge, I: 190). Thus, Coleridge casts *Venus and Adonis* as a prototype Romantic poem – a poem immersed in nature, beauty, imagery, and imagination – and Shakespeare as a prototype Romantic poet, responding so instinctively to the topics that 'possessed' him as if he was 'under the agency of some superior spirit' (Coleridge, I: 64). It was something of a controversial stand: in the eighteenth century, even when defending the narrative poems, Edmond Malone complained of their 'wearisome circumlocution' (1780), while through the nineteenth century many were to agree with William Hazlitt that the poems were mere 'ice-houses ... as hard, as glittering, and as cold' (1817) – standing at odds against the riches of his plays.[33]

By contrast, Coleridge argued that the narrative poems exist on a continuum with Shakespeare's plays. In *Venus and Adonis* and *Lucrece*, 'even then, the impulse to the drama was secretly working in him'. This 'impulse' was manifested both in terms of characterization – '*Venus and Adonis* seemed at once the characters themselves, but more, the representations of those characters by the most consummate actors' – and imagery. 'The scenes of unbroken images, unbroken, and therefore minute and as picturesque as language was capable of' in the narrative poems was, for Coleridge, characteristic of Shakespeare's mature plays (indeed, M. M. Badawi argues that Coleridge was 'the first English critic to see the dramatic value of Shakespeare's imagery').[34]

Nearly 200 years later, Ted Hughes took up the challenge of the continuum between Shakespeare's poems and plays. In his controversial *Shakespeare and the Goddess of Complete Being* (1992), Hughes argues that the poems are foundational for Shakespeare's plays, artistically, philosophically, and psychologically. Shakespeare's *oeuvre* develops out of two archetypal myths – 'The Tragic Equation' – first addressed in *Venus and Adonis* and *Lucrece*: the rejection of female sexuality (the Goddess Venus) by male rationality (Adonis) with tragic consequences, and her revenge ('the charge of the Boar'); the overpowering of male rationality by raging iconoclasm ('the Tarquin moment') in the tragic violation of female chastity (Lucrece) – a violation that brings down the surrounding world. This 'Tragic Equation', fissured with the struggle between Puritanism and Catholicism, drives the cycle of Shakespeare's works from the narrative poems and Sonnets to the late plays, where, as Anthony Paul explains, the assaulted and rejected female is restored as the Goddess of Complete Being – the wholeness of nature, 'a dream of an unattainable unfallen state of integrated human identity'.[35]

For Hughes, the purpose of art is to put us back in touch with 'the mythic plane'; thus Shakespeare, in unfolding the archetypal myths of Complete Being, is a 'shaman': a foreseer and healer through and in art. And for Tom Paulin, *Goddess* works as a piece of 'mythic criticism'. But *Goddess* was also met with critical hostility: 'the only psyche this book seems to illuminate is Hughes's own', complained Lachlan Mackinnon in *The Independent*, while Terry Eagleton argued in *The Guardian* that Hughes used his book on Shakespeare to describe himself, 'a poet of primitive violence [and] incessant sexual strife'.[36] As such, Hughes was working in analogous ways to Coleridge: both used the narrative poems to develop a thesis of poetry that describes their own work as much as it illuminates Shakespeare's. More widely, the reception of *Goddess* is a pertinent reminder of the subtle work of generic categories in literary analysis. In large part, what drives the perplexity and discomfort with Hughes's *Goddess* is its refusal to conform – to behave as a disciplined critical work (running to over 500 pages with hardly any notes, acknowledgement of critical literature, or a bibliography), or remain within the realm of creative writing. But generic indiscipline has, of course, a rich literary history.

Song and the porous poetic genre

Turning, albeit too briefly, to the shorter poems in the Shakespearean canon (*A Lover's Complaint*, *The Passionate Pilgrim*, 'The Phoenix and Turtle') is to confront the ways in which poetry embedded among other poetic genres and voices has had a troubled critical history. *A Lover's Complaint*, with its moving lament of the seduction and betrayal of a fallen woman, has only recently been reconsidered as a companion-piece to the Sonnets, with which it was originally printed in 1609 (see Roberts, pp. 146–53; Burrow (ed.), pp. 140–3; Duncan-Jones (ed.), p. 91). *The Passionate Pilgrim*, which includes five Shakespearean sonnets and lyrics amid a cluster of poems on passion, has largely interested critics in terms of the dissemination of Shakespeare's Sonnets and the cachet of his name by 1599 – not as a dialogic volume that works through intertextuality (see Burrow (ed.), p. 81). The relationship of 'The Phoenix and Turtle' to the 'diverse Poeticall Essaies' on 'the *Turtle* and *Phoenix. Done by the best and chiefest of our moderne writers*' appended to Robert Chester's *Love's Martyr* (1601) continues to elude critics: the intertextual readings of G. Wilson Knight's *The Mutual Flame* (1955) moved away from the literalism of earlier critical approaches that sought to identify the poem as a political or personal allegory, but his attempt to explicate 'the meaning' of the poem in an unstated 'biographical ... experience [that] may lie behind the poem' remains problematic (*The Mutual Flame*, pp. 145, 148). More widely, the shifts of voice and register (grave and light, theological and logical, poem and 'Threnos') *within* 'The Phoenix and Turtle' have rendered the poem a critical enigma; 'the reader halts, never quite sure what it is, to *read* this poem'.[37] Among other things (not least length), the unstated critical preference for consistency – of genre, of voice, of text – that has characterized the reception history of Shakespeare's poems has unwittingly privileged the single-authored, single-genre work (the narrative poems and Sonnets) above the polylogic lyric poem.

Of course, Shakespeare's lyrics are also to be found in his plays – and the porous nature of poetic genre in the early modern period is no better illustrated than by the fate of Ariel's magical song from *The Tempest*, 'Full fathom five' (1.2.400–9). Singing 'invisible', Ariel creates a mystical atmosphere that allays both fury and passion, and Ferdinand cannot help but follow the 'music' (1.2.374–92):

> Full fathom five thy father lies,
> Of his bones are coral made;
> Those are pearls that were his eyes;
> Nothing of him that doth fade,
> But doth suffer a sea-change
> Into something rich and strange.
> Sea-nymphs hourly ring his knell:
> Hark, now I hear them, ding dong bell.
> [*Spirits dispersedly echo the burden 'ding dong bell'*]
> (*The Tempest* 1.2.396–403)

'The ditty does remember my drown'd father', responds Ferdinand, immediately integrating Ariel's 'Song' into the dramatic narrative. This may seem to take us far from poetry *per se*, and particularly from the scene of reading.

To be sure, on stage Ariel's Song, like the many other songs that punctuate the plays of Shakespeare, are performance pieces: remarkable opportunities to underline, interrupt, or create an atmosphere; to compound or rupture a dramatic narrative. Indeed, the songs of Shakespearean drama are not only dependent for their interpretation upon the specific context of their utterance within plays, but upon specific *productions* of the play in performance. But, as R. S. White argues, the idea of inserting a song into a dramatic piece has non-dramatic origins in the use of songs in Elizabethan prose romance (such as George Gascoigne's *The Adventures of Master F. J.*) and subsequently in sonnet cycles (such as Sidney's *Astrophil and Stella*). The 'inserted aesthetic piece' of the song thus traverses romance, sonnet sequence, and drama: an indication of the *porous* nature of these generic categories as they were emerging and converging at the cusp of the seventeenth century.[38]

More than this, however, the *inserted* Song was also readily *excerpted* by early modern readers of poetry. Indeed, in the transmission of Shakespeare's plays in seventeenth-century manuscripts the songs often dominate over other excerpts: the most frequently cited lines from *The Winter's Tale*, for example, are Autolycus's song ('Lawn as white as driven snow', 4.4.218–30), appearing in four miscellanies. And precisely because *The Tempest* furnished early modern readers (listeners?) with two popular songs – Ariel's 'Where the bee sucks' (5.1.88–94) in no less than six miscellanies and 'Full fathom five' (1.2.396–403) in five miscellanies – it constitutes Shakespeare's most frequently transmitted play in manuscript before 1700. In Francis Norreys's and Henry Balle's mid-seventeenth-century verse miscellany, for instance, 'Full fa[th]om [five] Thy father lies' appears as the first of five 'Songs [out of] Shakespeare', all drawn from *The Tempest* and with only minor textual variants from the First Folio in which the play was first published. Norreys' and Balle's miscellany is unusual in indicating not only the author of the 'Songs' (authorship was often left unregistered in manuscript miscellanies) but their speaker: 'Ariel' appears as a marginal left heading.[39] Nonetheless, divorced from the play and situated among amatory, bawdy, satirical, religious, and occasional verse (they are followed, for instance, by an epigram 'on a welchman' and Carew's erotic poem, 'A Rapture'), the 'Songs' look less like dramatic interludes than lyric poetry. This is another pertinent reminder of how user-inflected, and hence variable, the disciplines of dramatic poetry and lyric poetry were in the period: in the field of reception, generic divisions begin to break down.

But the song does not end here, for in 1659 appeared Robert Johnson's musical setting of 'Full fathom five' in the printed songbook *Cheerfull Ayres or Ballads. First composed for one single Voice and since set for three Voices.*

By John Wilson Dr in Musick (Oxford, 1659), followed by 'Where the bee sucks' (pp. 6–9). Indeed, many verses which we now read resolutely as lyric poems were categorized and arguably performed as songs in the period, not least John Donne's *Songs and Sonnets*. What difference does a musical setting make? What does it mean to *hear* lyric poetry as *lyric*; as words set to music? In the key of G major, Ariel's mystical 'ditty' on death is transposed to a 'cheerfull ayre'; the tempo may be slow but the major key is never in doubt (by contrast, minor keys typically sound more mournful); particular words are arguably given extra emphasis through a long-held note (minims and dotted minims) at the beginning or end of a musical phrase – 'Full', 'pearles', 'eyes', 'fade', 'change', 'strange', and 'knell' – while the 'ding dong bell' sequence evokes the cascade of a (slow) peal of bells. Further, the context of the verse has shifted from dramatic and lyric poetry to the musical songbook, and its production from the stage to the page of personal reading and recollection (the manuscript miscellany) to performance – whether privately with 'one single Voice' or socially among 'three Voices'. (More widely, the song's allusion to death and sea-change might have had powerful resonance in the aftermath of the civil wars and at the cusp of the Restoration.) But the best-known manipulation of Ariel's 'Song' could hardly be described as cheerful. T. S. Eliot's mournful Modernist lament, *The Waste Land* (1922), famously cites the lines 'Those were pearls that were his eyes' and Ferdinand's 'this music crept by me upon the waters' (*Tempest* 1.2.391; *The Waste Land* 1.48, 2.125, and 3.257). The effect is haunting: for a fleeting moment, the mundanity, isolation, and waste of modern life – a life fragmented; hence the fragmented form and voices of Eliot's poem – is punctuated by the lyrical beauty of Shakespeare's lines.

And yet only the elite may be haunted: that is, those fully conversant with Shakespeare's plays in the 1920s and able to recognize Eliot's allusion (not least *The Waste Land's* dedicatee, Ezra Pound). By contrast, disseminated as a 'cheerfull ayre' in Restoration England, Ariel's 'Song' may have reached a more socially diverse audience. As such, Ariel's 'Song' is a pertinent reminder of the demographics – and democratics – of the reception of Shakespeare's poetry. For generic categories are also, to an extent, socially coded: drama, lyric poetry, and popular song may reach different audiences. Even more intriguing, then, is the slippage between those generic categories.

The reception history of Shakespeare's poems is a history of the changing conceptual categories we use to approach literature: wit, rhetoric, imitation (early modern); argument, expression, morality (Augustan); imagery, imagination, feeling (Romantic); form, authorship, art (Wilde). The twentieth century, perhaps more than any other, has seen a proliferation in categories of critical analysis. This has generally served Shakespeare's poems well.

Renewed attention to literary and rhetorical tradition – mythological, Ovidian, sonnet, and lyric – has enabled the re-evaluation of the narrative poems and helped to break the deadlock of autobiographical approaches to the Sonnets. Similarly, the resurgence of formalist analysis in the mid twentieth century produced close readings of the Sonnets that refused to be bogged down by the troubled search for authenticity and identity. New Bibliography, with its characteristic commitment to textual authority, both instigated research into the production of Shakespeare's poems and led to dismissal of their early printed texts, while the more recent history of the book is challenging and expanding our understanding of the transmission and reception of the poems across manuscript and print. New Historicism and Cultural Materialism have stimulated interest in the social dimensions of the poems, above all in terms of how they are shaped by (and shape) culture, history, and politics. But, arguably, the critical categories that have made the most significant impact upon the poems' reception at university level since the late twentieth century have been feminist criticism and queer studies – enabling not only new readings of gender, sexuality, rhetoric, and desire in the poems, but new connections to be drawn between the poems and plays.

For the future, we might do well to rethink the place of aesthetics. Beauty, so variable, value-laden, and therefore perilous, is often overshadowed by other concerns in modern criticism of Shakespeare's poems. Indeed, beauty has become the modern critical embarrassment. But Shakespeare's remarkable poetry is, so very often, beautiful to its readers that we should find ways of contemplating, a little better, just how this should be so.

NOTES

1 Cheney, *Shakespeare, National Poet–Playwright* (Cambridge University Press, 2004), p. 63.
2 Weever, 'Ad Gulielmum Shakespeare', *Epigrammes in the Oldest Cut* (1595), sig. E6; cited in *Shakspere Allusion-Book: A Collection of Allusions from 1591 to 1700*, ed. C. M. Ingleby, L. Toulmin-Smith, and F. J. Furnival, 2 vols. (London: Oxford University Press, 1932), I: 24.
3 Francis Meres, *Palladis Tamia. Wits Treasury* (1598), pp. 279 and 284; also cited in *Shakspere Allusion-Book*, I: 46–8.
4 Harvey cited in *Shakspere Allusion-Book*, I: 56.
5 *The Second Part of the Returne from Parnassus*, later published as *The Retourne from Parnassus Or The Scourge of Simony* (1606), rpt in J. B. Leishman (ed.), *The Three Parnassus Plays* (London: Nicholson and Watson, 1949), lines 301–4.
6 *The First Part of the Returne from Parnassus* in *The Three Parnassus Plays*, lines 1200–5; Karl Snyder (ed.), *A Critical Edition of the Fair Maide of the Exchange by Thomas Heywood* (London: Garland, 1980) 3.3.80–96.

7 I develop these arguments further in 'Ladies "never look / But in a Poem or in a Play-book": Women's Recreational Reading of Shakespeare in Early Modern England', in *The Engendering of the Female Reader in England and America, 1500–1800*, ed. Heidi Brayman Hackel (Philadelphia: University of Pennsylvania Press, forthcoming).

8 John Davies of Hereford, 'Papers Complaint, compild in ruthfull Rimes Against the Paper-spoylers of these Times', *The Scourge of Folly. Consisting of satyricall Epigramms* (c.1611), pp. 231–2.

9 Richard Brathwaite, *The English Gentleman* (1630) p. 28; Thomas Cranley, *Amanda or The Reformed Whore* (1635), p. 32; John Johnson, *The Academy of Love describing ye folly of younge men and ye fallacy of women* (1641), p. 99.

10 Anne, Lady Southwell, Commonplace Book c.1630s, Folger Shakespeare Library MS: V.b.198, fol. 3; for a transcript of the complete miscellany, see *The Southwell-Sibthorpe Commonplace Book. Folger Ms. V.b.198*, ed. Jean Klene (Tempe, AZ.: Medieval & Renaissance Texts & Studies, 1997). For Frances Wolfreston, see Sasha Roberts, *Reading Shakespeare's Poems in Early Modern England* (Basingstoke: Palgrave Macmillan, 2003), 45–7, 50–3; and Paul Morgan, 'Frances Wolfreston and "Hor Bouks"', *The Library*, 6th series, 11 (1989), 197–219.

11 Daniel Leare, verse miscellany (c.1630s), British Library Add MS 30982, fol. 22; *England's Parnassus* (1600), p. 297.

12 John Abbot, verse miscellany (c.1670s), Bodleian Rawl. poet. D. 954, fol. 41; British Library Add. MS 27406, fols. 74–78ᵛ.

13 Katherine Duncan-Jones (ed.), *The Sonnets and 'A Lover's Complaint'*, Arden 3rd series (London: Thomas Nelson, 1999), pp. 69 and 72.

14 Robert Bishop, verse miscellany (1630), Rosenbach Foundation, MS 1083/16, fols. 256ᵛ–7. For a transcript of the sonnet with collations (but not the additional eighteen lines by Herbert), see H. E. Rollins (ed.), *A New Variorum Edition of Shakespeare. The Sonnets*, 2 vols. (Philadelphia: J. B. Lippincott, 1944), p. 260; on the manuscript transmission of the Sonnets, see Roberts, *Reading Shakespeare's Poems*, pp. 172–83; and Arthur Marotti, 'Shakespeare's Sonnets as Literary Property', in *Soliciting Interpretation: Literary Theory and Seventeenth-Century English Poetry*, ed. Elizabeth D. Harvey and Katharine Eisaman Maus (University of Chicago Press, 1990), pp. 143–73.

15 Bruce Smith, *Homosexual Desire in Shakespeare's England: A Cultural Poetics* (Ithaca: Cornell University Press, 1991), p. 270.

16 Margreta de Grazia, 'The Scandal of Shakespeare's Sonnets', *Shakespeare Survey* 47 (1994), 35–49. For Daniel, see Roberts, *Reading Shakespeare's Poems*, pp. 164–5; and Ilona Bell, *Elizabethan Women and the Poetry of Courtship* (Cambridge University Press, 1992), p. 143.

17 See Duncan-Jones (ed.), *Sonnets*, pp. 69–70.

18 Benson, 'To the Reader', *Poems* (1640), sigs. 2–2ᵛ. Intriguingly, this eulogy is repeated word for word in the 1640 edition of Carew's *Poems*; see Roberts, *Reading Shakespeare's Poems*, p. 160; and Mary Hobbs, *Early Seventeenth-Century Verse Miscellany Manuscripts* (Aldershot: Scolar Press, 1992), p. 98.

19 Malone, *Supplement to the Edition of Shakespeare's Plays* (1780); Steevens, *Supplement to the Edition of Shakespeare's Plays* (1780); both cited in Brian Vickers (ed.), *Shakespeare: The Critical Heritage*, VI: 287, 40, and 289, respectively.

20 See Sasha Roberts, 'Shakespeare's *Sonnets* and English Sonnet Sequences', in *Early Modern English Poetry: A Critical Companion*, ed. Patrick Cheney, Andrew Hadfield, and Garrett Sullivan (Oxford University Press, 2007), pp. 172–83; and Heather Dubrow, ' "Incertainties now crown themselves assur'd": The Politics of Plotting Shakespeare's *Sonnets*', *Shakespeare Quarterly* 47 (1996), 291–305.

21 Coleridge, *The Collected Works*, ed. Lewis Patton and Peter Mann, 16 vols. (Princeton University Press, 1971), XII: 1. *Marginalia*, p. 41, cited in Frank Erik Pointner, 'Bardolatry and Biography: Romantic Readings of Shakespeare's *Sonnets*', in *British Romantics as Readers: Intertextualities, Maps of Misreading, Reinterpretations*, ed. Michael Gassenmeier et al. (Heidelberg: Universitatsverlag C. Winter, 1998), p. 127; J. Potter, *Archaeologica Graeca 1: I* (1808), pp. 239 ff., cited in Pointner, 'Bardolatry and Biography', p. 128.

22 *Collected Works* XII: 1. *Marginalia*, ed. George Whalley (London: Routledge & Kegan Paul, 1984), p. 42, cited in Pointner, 'Bardolatry and Biography', p. 127.

23 *Collected Works*, XIV: 1. *Table Talk*, ed. Carl Woodring (London: Routledge, 1990), 18 May 1833, p. 378.

24 *Complete Works*, XII: 1. *Marginalia*, p. 41, cited in Pointner, 'Bardolatry and Biography', pp. 126–7.

25 Coleridge, *Shakespearean Criticism*, ed. Thomas Middleton Raysor, 2 vols. (1960; London: Everyman's Library, 1974) II: 65. The Fourth Lecture was noted by one J. Tomalin.

26 Keats cited in R. S. White, *Keats as a Reader of Shakespeare* (London: Athlone Press, 1987), pp. 222–3. On Keats' use of the narrative poems, see John Kerrigan, 'Keats and *Lucrece*', *Shakespeare Survey* 41 (1988), 103–18; and Billy T. Boyar, 'Keats's "Isabella": Shakespeare's *Venus and Adonis* and the Venus–Adonis Myth', *Keats–Shelley Journal* 21 (1972–3), 160–9.

27 Forsyth, *Shakspere: Some Notes on His Character and Writings* (Edinburgh, 1867), p. 22; Corney, *The Sonnets of William Shakespeare* (London, 1862), p. 11; both cited in Rollins (ed.), 140.

28 See Horst Schroeder, *Oscar Wilde, The Portrait of Mr W. H.: Its Composition, Publication and Reception* (Braunschweig: Technische Universitat Carolo-Wilhelmina zu Braunschweig, 1984), p. 15.

29 Oscar Wilde, *The Portrait of Mr. W. H.* (first pub. 1892; rpt in *The Artist as Critic: Critical Writings of Oscar Wilde*, ed. Richard Ellman (University of Chicago Press, 1968)), p. 212.

30 Richard Halpern, *Shakespeare's Perfume: Sodomy and Sublimity in the Sonnets, Wilde, Freud, and Lacan* (Philadelphia: University of Pennsylvania Press, 2002), p. 36; and Kate Chedgzoy, *Shakespeare's Queer Children: Sexual Politics and Contemporary Culture* (Manchester University Press, 1995), p. 144.

31 Cited in Schroeder, *Oscar Wilde, The Portrait of Mr W. H.*, p. 19; see also Halpern, *Shakespeare's Perfume*, pp. 43–4.

32 On the deployment of Shakespeare's Sonnets by Joyce and Ezra Pound, see Kathryne V. Lindberg, 'A Battle of Puns and the Extra Pound: Joyce and Pound

over Shakespeare's Authorizing "Will" ', *Boundary* 2 18 (1991), 157–73. Wilde, *Portrait of Mr W. H.*, cited by Lindberg, p. 165.

33 Malone, cited in Vickers (ed.), *Critical Heritage*, VI: 287–8; Hazlitt, *Characters of Shakespeare's Plays* (1817), cited in H. E. Rollins (ed.), *A New Variorum Edition of Shakespeare. The Poems* (Philadelphia: J. B. Lippincott, 1938), p. 466.

34 Coleridge, *Shakespearean Criticism*, II: 64; M. M. Badawi, *Coleridge: Critic of Shakespeare* (Cambridge University Press, 1973), p. 167.

35 Anthony Paul, 'The Poet Laureate's National Poet', in *Reclamations of Shakespeare*, ed. A. J. Hoenselaars (Amsterdam, GA: Rodopi, 1994), pp. 159–72: p. 160. See also Neil Rhodes, 'Bridegrooms to the Goddess: Hughes, Heaney and the Elizabethans', in *Shakespeare and Ireland: History, Politics, Culture*, ed. Mark Thornton Burnett and Ramona Wray (Houndmills: Macmillan, 1997), pp. 152–72.

36 Heaney, Paulin, Mackinnon, and Eagleton, cited by Paul, 'The Poet Laureate's National Poet', pp. 160–2.

37 Barbara Everett, 'Sit Upon a Golden Bough to Sing: Shakespeare's Debt to Sidney in "The Phoenix and Turtle" ', *Times Literary Supplement*, 16 February 2001, 13–15; see also Burrow (ed.), *Complete Sonnets and Poems*, pp. 87–8. Rollins' *Poems* provides a useful overview of the earlier reception history of the shorter poems, esp. pp. 564–83 and 585–603.

38 R. S. White, 'Functions of Poems and Songs in Elizabethan Romance and Romantic Comedy', *English Studies* 68 (1987), 392–405: p. 392.

39 Verse miscellany owned by Norreys, Balle (mid-seventeenth century), British Library Egerton MS 2421, fol. 6ᵛ. 'Full fa[th]oms [five]' appears without punctuation and with only minor textual variants (spellings and contractions) to the First Folio text. For a transcript of 'Full fathom five', see *The Tempest*, ed. David Lindley (Cambridge University Press, 2002), pp. 252–3.

READING LIST

Burrow, Colin (ed.). *Complete Sonnets and Poems*. Oxford University Press, 2002.

Coleridge, Samuel Taylor. *Shakespearean Criticism*. 2 vols. Ed. Thomas Middleton Raysor. 1960; London: Everyman's Library, 1974.

Duncan-Jones, Katherine (ed.), *The Sonnets and 'A Lover's Complaint*, Arden 3rd series (London: Thomas Nelson, 1999).

Marotti, Arthur. 'Shakespeare's Sonnets as Literary Property'. In *Soliciting Interpretation: Literary Theory and Seventeenth-Century English Poetry*. Ed. Elizabeth D. Harvey and Katharine Eisaman Maus. University of Chicago Press, 1990, pp. 143–73.

Pointner, Frank Erik. 'Bardolatry and Biography: Romantic Readings of Shakespeare's *Sonnets*'. In *British Romantics as Readers: Intertextualities, Maps of Misreading, Reinterpretations*. Ed. Michael Gassenmeier et al. Heidelberg: Universitatsverlag C. Winter, 1998, pp. 117–36.

Roberts, Sasha. *Reading Shakespeare's Poems in Early Modern England*. Basingstoke: Palgrave Macmillan, 2003.

Rollins, Hyder Edward (ed.). *A New Variorum Edition of Shakespeare. The Sonnets*. 2 vols. Philadelphia: J. B. Lippincott, 1944.

A New Variorum Edition of Shakespeare. The Poems. Philadelphia: J. B. Lippincott, 1938.

Schiffer, James, 'Reading New Life into Shakespeare's Sonnets: A Survey of Criticism'. In *Shakespeare's Sonnets: Critical Essays.* Ed. James Schiffer. New York: Garland, 1999, pp. 3–71.

Shakspere Allusion-Book: A Collection of Allusions from 1591 to 1700. Ed. C. M. Ingleby, L. Toulmin Smith, and F. J. Furnival. 2 vols. London: Oxford University Press, 1932.

Vickers, Brian (ed.). *Shakespeare: The Critical Heritage.* 6 vols. London: Routledge & Kegan Paul, 1981.

REFERENCE WORKS ON SHAKESPEARE'S POETRY

For criticism and scholarship on individual poems and major topics, see the Reading lists at the end of each chapter. The following information can also be supplemented with Dieter Mehl, 'Shakespeare Reference Books', in *The Cambridge Companion to Shakespeare*, ed. Margreta de Grazia and Stanley Wells (Cambridge University Press, 2001), pp. 297–313.

Biographies

A full, factual, and reliable biography remains Park Honan's *Shakespeare: A Life* (1998; Oxford University Press, 2000). Stephen Greenblatt's *Will in the World: How Shakespeare Became Shakespeare* (New York: Norton, 2004) was a finalist for the National Book Award in the United States, while James Shapiro's *A Year in the Life of William Shakespeare: 1599* (New York: Harper Collins, 2005) deserves mention, particularly as the first biographical study to devote attention to Edmund Spenser, England's national poet during Shakespeare's professional career.

See also Stanley Wells, *Shakespeare: A Dramatic Life* (London: Sinclair-Stevenson, 1994), paperback title: *Shakespeare: The Poet and his Plays* (London: Methuen, 1997); Dennis Kay, *Shakespeare: His Life, Work, and Era* (New York: William Morrow, 1992); Richard Dutton, *William Shakespeare: A Literary Life* (Basingstoke: Macmillan, 1988); E. A. J. Honigmann, *Shakespeare: The 'Lost Years'* (Manchester University Press, 1985); Samuel Schoenbaum, *William Shakespeare: Records and Images* (New York: Oxford University Press, 1981) and *William Shakespeare: A Documentary Life* (Oxford University Press, 1975), the narrative and documents of which are included in *William Shakespeare: A Compact Documentary Life* (Oxford University Press, 1977; paperback edition 1978).

Editions

For the first modern edition to print all of Shakespeare's non-dramatic poetry (and in inexpensive paperback), see *The Complete Sonnets and Poems*, edited by Colin Burrow for Oxford World's Classics (Oxford University Press, 2002).

Other modern editions print Shakespeare's Sonnets separately from his other poems. For the Sonnets and in most cases *A Lover's Complaint*, see the Folger Shakespeare Library's reissue edition of *Shakespeare's Sonnets*, ed. Barbara A. Mowat and Paul Werstine (New York: Washington Square Press, 2004); Stephen

Orgel, *Sonnets* (New York: Penguin, 2001); Helen Vendler, *The Art of Shakespeare's Sonnets* (Cambridge, MA: Harvard University Press–Belknap, 1997); Katherine Duncan-Jones (ed.), *Shakespeare's Sonnets*, Arden 3rd series (London: Thomas Nelson, 1997); G. Blakemore Evans (ed.), *Sonnets* (Cambridge University Press, 1996); John Kerrigan (ed.), *'The Sonnets' and 'A Lover's Complaint'* (1986, Harmondsworth: Penguin Books, 1995); and Stephen Booth (ed.), *Shakespeare's Sonnets* (New Haven: Yale University Press, 1977).

For the other poems, see Jonathan Crewe (ed.), *Narrative Poems* (New York: Penguin, 1999); John Roe (ed.), *Poems* (Cambridge University Press, 1992); and F. T. Prince (ed.), *Poems*, Arden 2nd series (London: Methuen, 1960).

Still invaluable are the two volumes in the Variorum Shakespeare edited by Hyder Edward Rollins: *A New Variorum Edition of Shakespeare: The Sonnets*, 2 vols. (Philadelphia: J. B. Lippincott, 1944); and *A New Variorum Shakespeare: The Poems* (Philadelphia: J. B. Lippincott, 1938).

For editions of Robert Chester's *Love's Martyr*, which first publishes 'The Phoenix and Turtle', see Carleton Brown (ed.), *Poems by Sir John Salusbury and Robert Chester*, Early English Text Society (London: K. Paul, Trench, Trübner, 1914); and Alexander B. Grosart (ed.), *Robert Chester's Love's Martyr*, New Shakespeare Society (London, 1878).

For editions of *The Passionate Pilgrim*, see Hyder Edward Rollins (ed.), *The Passionate Pilgrim* (New York: Scribner's, 1940); and Joseph Quincy Adams (ed.), *The Passionate Pilgrim* (New York: Scribner's, 1939).

Forthcoming editions include a second edition of Roe (ed.), *The Poems* (Cambridge University Press, 2006); a second edition of Evans (ed.), *Sonnets*, with an introduction by Stephen Orgel (Cambridge University Press, 2006); Katherine Duncan-Jones and Henry Woudhuysen (eds.), *Poems*, Arden 3rd series (London: Thomson Learning, 2006); and Raphael Lyne and Cathy Shrank (eds.), *Poems* (London: Longman, 2010).

Bibliographies

The most comprehensive and easily accessible bibliography is the *World Shakespeare Bibliography Online*. This database catalogues annotated entries for all books, articles, book reviews, dissertations, theatrical productions, reviews of productions, audiovisual materials, electronic media, etc., concerning Shakespeare and published or produced between 1964 and 2006.

A complete, up-to-date, and briefly annotated bibliography is available in *Shakespeare Quarterly* (available on CD-ROM).

Concordances

The standard concordance is Marvin Spevack, *The Harvard Concordance to Shakespeare*, 8 vols. (Cambridge, MA: Harvard University Press, 1973), which is based on the computerized *A Complete and Systematic Concordance to the Works of Shakespeare* (Hildesheim: Georg Olms, 1968–70) by the same editor. Both concordances are keyed to the *Riverside Shakespeare*. See below under 'Shakespeare on the Internet' (p. 286) for concordance work that can be done on a personal computer.

Periodicals/Magazines

There are several well-established journals dedicated solely to Shakespeare studies. The oldest periodical is *Shakespeare Jahrbuch*, which features, in German and English, scholarly articles, book reviews, and reports on Shakespeare productions in the German-speaking world. *Shakespeare Quarterly* was founded in 1950 by the Shakespeare Association of America, and includes critical essays, book reviews, and reviews of theatrical and cinematic productions from around the world. Established in 1948, *Shakespeare Survey* devotes each annual volume to a theme, one play, or group of plays, and features reviews of the previous year's textual and critical studies and of major British performances. *Shakespeare Studies*, founded in 1965, similarly includes essays and reviews on a yearly basis.

Shakespearean Research and Opportunities, also established in 1965, reports on the Modern Language Association annual conference and features reviews and selected papers as well as a section entitled 'Research in Progress'. *The Shakespeare Newsletter* began publication in 1951, and offers news, reviews of books and performances, abstracts, and brief critical articles. *The Upstart Crow: A Shakespeare Journal*, founded in 1980, contains essays, notes, poems, and ideas concerning Shakespeare's works.

Monographs

A number of important monographs on Shakespeare's poems have been published, especially during the past few years. A few of the monographs look at the canon of Shakespeare's poems more broadly, while some look at individual poems, especially the Sonnets.

Shakespeare's poems and poetry

For monographs on the Sonnets, narrative poems, and sometimes the other poetry, see Patrick Cheney, *Shakespeare, National Poet–Playwright* (Cambridge University Press, 2004); Sasha Roberts, *Reading Shakespeare's Poems in Early Modern England* (Basingstoke: Palgrave Macmillan, 2003); Peter Hyland, *An Introduction to Shakespeare's Poems* (Basingstoke: Palgrave Macmillan, 2003); A. D. Cousins, *Shakespeare's Sonnets and Narrative Poems* (Harlow: Longman, 2000); Dennis Kay, *William Shakespeare: Sonnets and Poems* (New York: Twayne, 1998); Heather Dubrow, *Captive Victors: Shakespeare's Narrative Poems and Sonnets* (Ithaca: Cornell University Press, 1987); and G. Wilson Knight, *The Mutual Flame: On Shakespeare's 'Sonnets' and 'The Phoenix and the Turtle'* (London: Methuen, 1962).

Forthcoming is Michael Schoenfeldt's *Cambridge Introduction to Shakespeare's Poetry* in the Cambridge Introductions to Literature series (2009).

On Shakespeare's poetics, see also David Willbern, *Poetic Will: Shakespeare and the Play of Language* (Philadelphia: University of Pennsylvania Press, 1997); Eckbert Faas, *Shakespeare's Poetics* (Cambridge University Press, 1996); and George T. Wright, *Shakespeare's Metrical Art* (Berkeley: University of California Press, 1988).

The Sonnets

Copious monographs devoted to the Sonnets alone have been published over the years. See Paul Edmundson and Stanley Wells, *Oxford Shakespeare Topics: Shakespeare's Sonnets* (Oxford University Press, 2004); David Schalkwyk, *Speech and Performance in Shakespeare's Sonnets and Plays* (Cambridge University Press, 2002); Lisa Freinkel, *Reading Shakespeare's Will: The Theology of Figure from Augustine to the Sonnets* (New York: Columbia University Press, 2002); Helen Vendler, *Ways into Shakespeare's Sonnets* (London: University of London, 1990); David K. Weiser, *Mind in Character: A Reading of Shakespeare's Sonnets* (Columbia: University of Missouri Press, 1987).

Two of the most influential books have been Joel Fineman, *Shakespeare's Perjured Eye: The Invention of Poetic Subjectivity in the Sonnets* (Berkeley: University of California Press, 1986); and Joseph Pequigney, *Such Is My Love: A Study of Shakespeare's Sonnets* (University of Chicago Press, 1985).

See also Gerald Hammond, *The Reader and Shakespeare's Young Man Sonnets* (London: Macmillan; and Totowa, NJ: Barnes and Noble, 1981); Hallett Smith, *The Tension of the Lyre: Poetry in Shakespeare's Sonnets* (San Marino: Huntington Library, 1981); Kenneth Muir, *Shakespeare's Sonnets* (London: Allen & Unwin, 1979); Paul Ramsey, *The Fickle Glass: A Study of Shakespeare's Sonnets* (New York: AMS Press, 1979); Katherine M. Wilson, *Shakespeare's Sugared Sonnets* (London: Allen and Unwin; and New York: Barnes and Noble, 1974); Philip Martin, *Shakespeare's Sonnets: Self, Love, and Art* (Cambridge University Press, 1972); Stephen Booth, *An Essay on Shakespeare's Sonnets* (New Haven: Yale University Press, 1969); James Winny, *The Master-Mistress: A Study of Shakespeare's Sonnets* (London: Chatto and Windus; New York: Barnes and Noble, 1968); Hilton Landry, *Interpretations in Shakespeare's Sonnets: The Art of Mutual Render* (Berkeley: University of California Press, 1963); Edward Hubler, *The Sense of Shakespeare's Sonnets* (New York: Hill and Wang, 1962); and J. B. Leishman, *Themes and Variations in Shakespeare's Sonnets* (1961; New York: Harper and Row, 1963).

The narrative poems

Though limited in number, a few monographs do examine the narrative poems. On *Venus and Adonis*, see Anthony Mortimer, *Variable Passions: A Reading of Shakespeare's 'Venus and Adonis'* (New York: AMS Press, 2000); and Yves Peyré and François Laroque, *William Shakespeare: Venus and Adonis* (Paris: Didier Erudition and CNED, 1998).

On *The Rape of Lucrece*, see Thomas R. Simone, *Shakespeare and Lucrece: A Study of the Poem and Its Relation to the Plays* (Salzburg: Institut für Englische Sprache und Literatur, Universität Salzburg, 1974). See also Ian Donaldson, *The Rapes of Lucretia: A Myth and Its Transformations* (Oxford: Clarendon Press, 1982); and Stephanie H. Jed, *Chaste Thinking: The Rape of Lucretia and the Birth of Humanism* (Bloomington: Indiana University Press, 1989).

On *A Lover's Complaint*, see especially John Kerrigan, *Motives of Woe: Shakespeare and 'Female Complaint': A Critical Anthology* (Oxford University Press, 1991). See also Richard Allan Underwood, *Shakespeare on Love: The Poems and the Plays.*

Prolegomena to a Variorum Edition of 'A Lover's Complaint' (Salzburg: Institut für Anglistik und Amerikanistik Universität Salzburg, 1985); and Mac D. P. Jackson, *Shakespeare's 'A Lover's Complaint': Its Date and Authenticity*, University of Auckland Bulletin 72 English Series 13 (Auckland: University of Auckland Press, 1965).

For important books on English Renaissance narrative poetry in general, with valuable studies of Shakespeare's narrative poems, see Georgia Brown, *Redefining Elizabethan Literature* (Cambridge University Press, 2004); Clark Hulse, *Metamorphic Verse: The Elizabethan Minor Epic* (Princeton University Press, 1981); and William Keach, *Elizabethan Erotic Narratives: Irony and Pathos in the Ovidian Poetry of Shakespeare, Marlowe and Their Contemporaries* (New Brunswick: Rutgers University Press, 1977).

'The Phoenix and Turtle'

On Shakespeare's great philosophical lyric, see especially William H. Matchett, *'The Phoenix and the Turtle': Shakespeare's Poem and Chester's 'Loues Martyr'* (London: Mouton, 1965); and G. Wilson Knight, *The Mutual Flame* (listed above). See also William Plumer Fowler, *Shake-speare's Phoenix and Turtle: An Interpretation* (Portsmouth, NH: Peter E. Randall, 1986); Richard Allen Underwood, *Shakespeare's "The Phoenix and Turtle": A Survey of Scholarship* (Salzburg: Institut für Engl. Sprache u. Literatur, Universität Salzburg, 1974). Also important to consult is Marie Axton, *The Queen's Two Bodies: Drama and the Elizabethan Succession* (London: Royal Historical Society, 1977).

Collections of essays

For recent collections of essays on Shakespeare's poems, see Stephen Orgel and Sean Keilen (eds.), *Shakespeare's Poems* (New York: Garland, 1999), which reprints seminal essays.

See also Philip C. Kolin (ed.), *'Venus and Adonis': Critical Essays* (New York: Garland, 1997), which includes nineteen reprinted essays from the eighteenth to the late twentieth centuries, and seven original essays by leading scholars; and James Schiffer (ed.), *Shakespeare's Sonnets: Critical Essays* (New York: Garland, 1999), which similarly features three reprinted essays and sixteen new essays.

Forthcoming essay collections include Michael Schoenfeldt (ed.), *A Companion to Shakespeare's Sonnets* (Oxford: Blackwell, 2006); Patrick Cheney, Andrew Hadfield, and Garrett Sullivan (eds.), *Early Modern English Poetry: A Critical Companion* (New York: Oxford University Press, 2007), which includes individual essays on the narrative poems, the Sonnets, and 'The Phoenix and Turtle'; and Shirley Zisser, *'A Lover's Complaint': Critical Essays* (Aldershot, Hants: Ashgate Press, 2006).

Other research tools

Other invaluable tools for research on Shakespeare's poetry include Brian Vickers (ed.), *Shakespeare: The Critical Heritage*, 6 vols. (London: Routledge & Kegal Paul, 1974–1981), which collects commentary on Shakespeare from 1623 to 1801; and *The Shakspere Allusion-Book: A Collection of Allusions to Shakspere from 1591 to 1700*, ed. C. M. Ingleby, L. Toulmin Smith, and F. J. Furnivall, rev. John Munro, preface by Edmund Chambers, 2 vols. (1909; Freeport, NY: Books for Libraries Press, 1970), which collects commentary on Shakespeare from the title dates.

Shakespeare on the Internet

For the homepage of the Shakespeare Association of America, log on at: http://www.shakespeareassociation.org/main/main.asp. Includes SAA Bulletin Archive (available from 2000 to the present) and information on the annual SAA conference.

To purchase 'The Shakespeare Collection' from Thomson Gale, log on at: http://www.gale.com/shakespeare/. Includes a comprehensive online resource for Shakespeare studies, using the Arden edition, along with full-text criticism, journals, and primary source material.

For other sites, see the following:

The complete non-dramatic works of Shakespeare: http://www.shakespeare-online.com/sonnets/

Shakespeare Concordance: http://www.it.usyd.edu.au/~matty/Shakespeare/. A concordance for both the poems and the plays.

Shakespearean Poetry Search: http://quarles.unbc.ca/shakescan/. Includes concordance-like abilities and hyper-text capabilities for all of Shakespeare's non-dramatic works.

An annotated guide to Shakespeare resources on the Internet: http://shakespeare.palomar.edu/. Organized by Terry Gray at Palomar College in California.

INDEX

Cambridge Companions to ...

AUTHORS

TOPICS